HURON COUNTY PUBLIC LIBRARY

P9-AQB-849

008 239657 1

HURON COUNTY LIBRARY

BEYOND SHELTER

A Study of NHA Financed

Housing for the Elderly

Copyright 1973 by the Canadian Council on Social Development

Published in July 1973 by the Canadian Council on Social Development
55 Parkdale, Box 3505, Postal Station C, Ottawa K1Y 4G1

ISBN 0-88810-182-1
Library of Congress Catalog Card Number: 73-85952

Price: $6.00

BEYOND SHELTER

A STUDY OF NATIONAL HOUSING ACT

FINANCED HOUSING FOR THE ELDERLY

Michael J. Audain
Study Director

Elizabeth Huttman
Chief Investigator

Judith Duchemin
Douglas Halverson
Senior Research Assistants

147060

The Canadian Council on Social Development

MAY 1 1974

MAY 1 1974

STUDY ADVISORY COMMITTEE

Dr. J.A. MacDonell (Chairman)   Faculty of Medicine, University
                                   of Manitoba, Winnipeg

Mr. Luc Durand   Architect, Montreal

Mrs. Margaret Gallilee   Former President, Vancouver
                                   Housing Association

Mrs. Sylvia Goldblatt   Social Development Officer, Central
                                   Mortgage and Housing Corporation,
                                   Ottawa

Mr. Thomas Knighton   Former President, Ottawa Senior
                                   Citizens Council

Dr. Marvin Lipman   Director, Social Development Opera-
                                   tions, Central Mortgage and Housing
                                   Corporation, Ottawa

Mrs. Frances McHale   Board of Directors, Ontario Housing
                                   Corporation, London

Mr. Maurice Miron   Program Director, The Canadian Council
                                   on Social Development, Ottawa

Mr. Gordon Priest   Family and Housing Section, Census
                                   Division, Statistics Canada, Ottawa

Mr. Edward Roach   Executive Director, Halifax Senior
                                   Citizens Housing Corporation

Dr. Cope Schwenger   School of Hygiene, University of
                                   Toronto

Dr. Nicolas Zay   Director, School of Social Work,
                                   Laval University, Quebec

CONTENTS

PREFACE

In a country whose social institutions are as diverse as Canada, a national study of a question that has great local variation is an ambitious enter- prise. Some might even consider it foolhardy! Nevertheless, broad brush reviews have their place in the paraphernalia of social research strategies.

This study, like most, ran into its share of difficulties and delays; that these were overcome is a tribute to the generous help extended by many organizations and people.

On behalf of The Canadian Council on Social Development, I would particularly like to thank the Central Mortgage and Housing Corporation for the financial support that they extended to the study and the cooperation that their head office and regional staff provided throughout its duration.

Among the many groups across Canada that helped us were provincial housing corporations and commissions that distributed management survey question- naires to their public housing authorities, the hundreds of housing managers who took the trouble to complete and return questionnaires (often accompanied by long letters), the staff and residents of the 19 developments selected for case studies, and many persons employed in public and voluntary social agencies.

The project Advisory Committee reviewed the design of the study and, in addition to providing encouragement throughout, considered the study's findings and framed recommendations.

Dr. Elizabeth Huttman, of the Sociology Department, California State College at Hayward (formerly with the University of British Columbia School of Social Work), worked on the study design and served as a valuable consultant. She prepared the instruments for the user and management surveys and supervised the data processing and analysis as well as undertaking some field work in British Columbia.

Among the many other staff who worked on the project were the senior research assistant, Douglas Halverson, who spent over a year organizing statistics, planning surveys, carrying out field work, and writing preliminary reports; Joyce Rigby and Marie Seto, who conducted case studies and user interviews; Merideth Morris, the principal coder; Judith Duchemin, another senior research assistant, who, with Janet Lee worked on the survey analysis and report writing; and William L. Nicholls II of the Berkeley Survey Research Center, who devised the sampling process for the management survey. Susan Becker of the Council's Publications and Information Division, provided editorial help. Finally, Céline Clearwater somehow managed all the typing as well as field work in the province of Quebec.

Michael J. Audain
Study Director

9

PART I

GENERAL INTRODUCTION

GENERAL INTRODUCTION

The decision to launch this study stemmed from two important areas of
concern in The Canadian Council on Social Development's work of
researching and promoting sound social policies for Canada. Throughout the Council's more than half century of existence, it had been
interested in the problems of old people, a concern that was brought to
a head by the sponsorship of the Canadian Conference on Aging in 1966.
The work of Council board members and staff continues in the field of
aging. On the other hand, the assignment of a special priority to
housing was only consumated with sponsorship of the Canadian Conference
on Housing in 1968. Since then a number of studies and conferences in
the housing field have gone forward under the auspices of the Council's
citizen-oriented Housing Committee. It was not unnatural that at some
point the concerns about housing and aging should become blended in the
form of a project that deals with both fields.

More precisely, the decision to commence a study of the housing that
had been specially designed for the elderly arose from fears expressed
in the late 1960s by people and organizations associated with the Council
(including those in positions of responsibility in government) that this
sort of accommodation might not be adequately meeting the needs of senior
citizens that lie beyond the simple provision of shelter. A good deal
had been learned about requirements for important design details such as
non-slip floors and bathroom handrails; but not much was known about the
lifestyle of residents and whether the housing suited their needs, the
perceptions of those who built and operated the accommodation, and
particularly about the availability and use of social facilities and
services.

The building of specialized accommodation for senior citizens who are
neither paupers nor seriously physically incapacitated is a fairly recent
phenomenon in Canada. Whereas prior to World War II housing developments
of this type were very rare, now practically every urban centre in Canada
can boast of at least one. Developments range in size from less than 10
dwelling units in small villages to more than 400 in metropolitan areas
(one of over 600 units is currently under construction).

The explanation for this trend has to do with the growth of greater
acceptance of community responsibility for the welfare of the aged; it
is also connected with changing demographic patterns, lifestyles, and
social legislation. Elderly persons now represent a considerably larger
proportion of a more urban-based population, while at the same time
opportunities for living with grown-up children have diminished with
increasing geographic mobility and the shrinkage of cheap housing stock
in downtown areas of large cities. Also, the provision of special housing

for the elderly is recognized as one way of compensating for income deficiencies suffered by this group in comparison to the whole population. At the same time, higher pensions have made it more possible for elderly people to consider maintaining independent residences as opposed to living with children, in boarding houses, or in municipal "homes for the aged."

In a period in which the democratic ethos encourages the individual's capacity to determine his own life directions - whether this be for young people, the poor, native people, or women - it was natural that much of the motivation for this inquiry should have had to do with questions pertaining to maintaining independence for old people as late in life as possible. Existing research, such as one of Zay's Montreal studies,[1] indicated that, given a choice, elderly people prefer independent living arrangements to institutional care. Indeed, a U.S. Department of Housing and Urban Development document stresses, "From the standpoint of the welfare and happiness of the elderly residents themselves, as well as the standpoint of benefit to the community, the success of housing for the elderly can be measured largely by the extent to which it helps residents to maintain their independence."[2]

The debilitating effects of living in highly institutionalized settings are known to the elderly as well as to many experts who believe that more independent living arrangements should be substituted. In a seminal study of institutional accommodation for the elderly in England, Townsend called for more independent housing arrangements with special services attached to them, declaring that "in the long run such housing should largely replace institutional homes as understood and administered today."[3] Adequate alternative accommodation for senior citizens also has financial implications; Zay found in Montreal that almost half of the old people in expensive institutional care could have led independent lives.[4] They were not in institutions because they needed special care but because of socio-psychological factors such as isolation, feelings of insecurity and fear of the future and, in a number of cases, the lack of readily available alternatives. Townsend found much the same in England, where principal reasons for admission to homes for the aged included homelessness and financial insecurity.[5]

---

1 Nicolas Zay, Personnes âgées en Hébergement collectif, Institut de Gérontologie, Université de Montréal, février 1965.

2 U.S. Department of Housing and Urban Development, Low-Rent Housing Handbook, Washington, 1968, Ch. 3, Section 3, p. 1.

3 Peter Townsend, The Last Refuge: A Survey of Residential Institutions and Homes for the Aged in England and Wales, London, Routledge and Kegan Paul, 1962.

4 Nicolas Zay, L'Entrée des Personnes âgées en Hébergement collectif, Institut de Gérontologie, Université de Montréal, 1966.

5 Townsend, op. cit.

But as Beyer and Nierstrasz have emphasized, "The goal of maintaining a high proportion of the aged in their own homes can only be satisfactorily achieved if communities embark on extensive programs of domiciliary care and community services."[6] And this applies even to any purpose-designed housing for old people. Because the elderly spend most of their day at home, the authors of this study realized that close-at-hand social, health and recreation facilities were a major need. Also, because old people are more susceptible to illness than the general population, it was obvious that a range of supportive social services needed to exist, whether supplied by the development or the community. Thus, it was decided that a major part of this inquiry would have to focus on the availability of social services and facilities and how they are related to the housing users.

It was also felt that there was a particular need to focus on another aspect of the elderly's residential environment: management. Schwenger's study of two subsidized housing projects for the elderly in Metropolitan Toronto had raised questions about the responsibility of management in relation to the provision of health services,[7] while preliminary correspondence with social service agencies across Canada raised questions about the sophistication of managers in using community resources and obtaining social services for residents. At the same time, it was evident that a good deal of frustration was being encountered by managers who believed it was not their duty to provide social services but who, on the other hand, found community agencies reluctant to do so.

Thus, it was decided that the main areas for investigation would involve social services and facilities in housing for the elderly, the characteristics and preferences of users, and the management function - all within a general objective of simply learning more about that housing that had been built for Canadian senior citizens in the last two decades.

One additional thing should be said; in opting for a study of housing developments for the elderly as opposed to studying their living arrangements in a number of environments (e.g. with children, in private apartment buildings, houses that they own, or nursing homes) there was no intention to necessarily favor one arrangement over others; rather, it was recognized that there had been a number of community studies of the aged at the local level in Canada and that it was now appropriate to review the situation of those living in specially designed housing. Indeed, the study's Advisory Committee and staff are firmly committed to widening the variety of housing opportunities for the elderly in society so that they can exercise more choice.

---

6 Glenn Beyer and R. Nierstrasz, Housing the Aged in Western Countries, Amsterdam, Elsevier, 1967.

7 C.W. Schwenger and L.A. Sayers, "The Role of the Public Health Nurse in the Integration of Community Services to the Aged," a paper presented to the International Congress of Gerontology, Washington, D.C., August 28, 1969.

Scope of the Study

For the purpose of defining the national scope of the study it was
decided to confine it to housing financed by the Central Mortgage and
Housing Corporation under provisions of the National Housing Act.
This had the effect of excluding accommodation built by private entrepreneurs or public agencies that had not made use of NHA assistance;
but at the same time it served to provide a common denominator among
the great variety of developments stutied. Within this accommodation
there are two main divisions: housing built by, or operated and built by
public housing agencies; and housing built and operated by what are
generally termed non-profit housing corporations. The other principal
breakdown is between self-contained and hostel accommodation.[8] It is
estimated that the universe of 746 housing developments studied accounted
for approximately 90 per cent of accommodation for the elderly of this
type built and occupied in the period 1946-70.

Excluded from the study's universe was housing occupied after December
31, 1970 and developments that described themselves as nursing homes.
The December 1970 occupancy date was selected for convenience, although
it eliminated from the scope of the study a great deal of accommodation
that was either being built or occupied at that date; nursing homes were
excluded because it was felt that they present quite different problems
and issues from those that preoccupied this study. However, it should
be noted that a number of the developments included in the study had
nursing floors or wings attached to them, although they primarily offered
self-contained or hostel accommodation to the ambulatory elderly.

What about specific objectives? To summarize, the study at its outset
sought to reveal information about housing for the elderly in Canada in
relation to the following questions:

1) How much accommodation for the elderly, and of what type, has been
built under NHA in various regions of the country?

2) What legislation and assistance programs financed building housing
for the elderly?

3) What are the characteristics, lifestyles, preferences, and concerns
of residents in housing for the elderly?

4) Who manages the housing and what are the attitudes of these people
about their task?

5) What is the availability of social, health and recreation facilities
and services?

---

8 These terms are defined later in Part I.

6) To what extent do location factors affect user satisfaction?

7) To what extent do residents of housing for the elderly engage in community activities and to what extent are community organizations and agencies involved in the accommodation?

8) What is the nature of social interaction among residents in the developments?

9) What are the cost differentials between different types of accommodation and social facility and service arrangements?

It will be seen that the study's findings (Part VI) address themselves to most of the above questions with the exception of the one dealing with costs. For various reasons, it proved impossible to collect and analyze sufficient data to allow statements on this subject.

Related Literature

No study should be done in isolation from previous research. The field of geriatrics has a wealth of publications and an extensive literature from which the study team benefited; however, because an excellent bibliography of Canadian sources in the field of aging has recently been published, it was decided to forego the customary practice of appending a bibliography. Instead, readers are urged to consult The Seventh Age: A Bibliography of Canadian Sources in Gerontology and Geriatrics.[9] This work is valuable for its numerous references to the shelter aspects of the aging field as well as the entire subject.

Readers who are keen to broaden their background knowledge of policy issues surrounding the aging process in Canada are advised to consult the report of the Senate Committee on Aging,[10] as well as the background papers and proceedings of the Canadian Conference on Aging.[11] These contain many papers on all aspects of growing old in Canada as well as recommendations directed to government decision-makers and others. Several sound reviews of social services available for senior citizens at the regional and local levels in various parts of Canada are also available. Among them are the

---

9   Environics Research Group Limited, The Seventh Age: A Bibliography of Canadian Sources in Gerontology and Geriatrics, 1964-1972, Central Mortgage and Housing Corporation, 1973.

10 The Senate of Canada, Final Report of the Special Committee of the Senate on Aging, Ottawa, Queen's Printer, 1966.

11 Canadian Conference on Aging, Background Papers, Ottawa, Canadian Welfare Council, 1966; and Canadian Conference on Aging, Proceedings, Ottawa, Canadian Welfare Council, 1966.

Social Planning and Review Council of British Columbia's recent
A Study of Community Care for Seniors;[12] also from British Columbia,
Retirement in the Capital Region of B.C.[13] which reviews the implica-
tions for physical, economic, and social development of the elderly
in Victoria; and the Social Planning Council of Metropolitan Toronto's
The Aging - Trends, Problems and Prospects[14] - another recent review
of the status of the elderly in a large Canadian city. Examples of
similar broad studies carried out in smaller communities are the
Family and Children Services of Hants County, Nova Scotia, Community
Care of the Elderly;[15] and Stevens, The Aging Population of Wellington
County.[16] Important for its review of the health aspects of aging is
Schwenger and Sayers, Socio-Medical Study of the Aged.[17]

Moving to the housing aspect of community supports for the elderly,
the only existing Canadian study with national pretentions is At Home
After 65,[18] published by our Council in 1964. This study was a modest
descriptive review based largely on impressions gathered from a cross-
country tour and regional consultations. There have, however, been a
number of interesting local studies of an exploratory nature, perhaps
the most recent being The Elderly and Their Environment,[19], a Toronto
pilot study published in 1971 which reports on group discussions held
with residents of senior citizens homes, private apartments, and roomers.

---

12   Social Planning and Review Council of British Columbia, A Study of
     Community Care for Seniors, Vancouver, 1972.

13   Capital Region Planning Board of British Columbia, Retirement in the
     Capital Region of B.C., Victoria, December 1969.

14   Social Planning Council of Metropolitan Toronto, The Aging - Trends,
     Problems, and Prospects, Toronto, March 1973.

15   Family and Children's Services of Hants County, Community Care of
     the Elderly: A Study of the Elderly Population of Hants County, N.S.,
     Windsor, Nova Scotia, 1969.

16   V.S. Stevens, The Aging Population of Wellington County, Guelph,
     Ontario Agricultural College, 1959.

17   C.W. Schwenger and L.A. Sayers, A Socio-Medical Study of the Aged
     1965-66, Ottawa, Department of National Health and Welfare, 1967.

18   At Home After 65, Housing and Related Services for the Aging, Ottawa,
     Canadian Welfare Council, 1964.

19   The Elderly and Their Environment, Toronto, Environics Research Group
     Limited, 1971.

Zay's Personnes âgées en Hébergement collectif[20] carried out in Montreal
is probably the most in-depth study of residents in specialized accommodation for the elderly. That work, together with his L'Entrée des Personnes
âgées en Hébergement collectif,[21] is interesting for its advanced typology
of stages of physical incapacity as well as for its findings on the effect
of an institutional environment on the lives of old people. On an international comparative basis, Beyer and Nierstrasz, Housing the Aged in
Western Countries,[22] is probably the best work. It is also important for
its discussion of the costs of institutionalization as opposed to sub-
sidizing services for the elderly living in the community. Another broad
overview study of interest is Retirement Housing in California.[23]
Hamovitch[24] has also discussed the housing needs of the elderly in a U.S.
context.

Back in Canada, there have been a number of studies of particular housing
developments, among the most interesting of which is the Conseil des
Oeuvres de Montréal, Evaluation de Deux Projets de Logements à Loyer Modique
pour Personnes âgées;[25] and the Conseil des Oeuvres et du Bien-être de Québec's
study of 68 institutions for the elderly published under the title Etude
des Foyers d'hébergement pour personnes âgées dans le diocèse de Québec;[26]
among many university theses in the field there is Priest's An Investigation
of the Elderly in the Urban Environment with Special Reference to their
Housing,[27] which particularly focuses on location factors. Of course, some
of the best user studies have been carried out in the United Kingdom, of
which Grouped Flatlets for Old People[28] is one example and New Housing for
the Elderly[29] another.

20 Zay, op. cit.

21 Zay, op. cit.

22 Beyer and Nierstrasz, op. cit.

23 Rosabelle Price Walkley, Wiley P. Mangam, Susan Roth Sherman, Suzanne
   Dodds, and Daniel M. Wilner, Retirement Housing in California, Berkeley,
   Diablo Press, 1966.

24 See for example, M.B. Hamovitch, J.A. Peterson, A.E. Larson, Perceptions
   and Fulfillment of Housing Needs of an Aging Population, Los Angeles,
   University of Southern California Gerontology Center, 1969.

25 Evaluation de Deux Projets de Logements à Loyer Modique pour Personnes
   âgées, Conseil des Oeuvres de Montréal, 1959.

26 Conseil des Oeuvres et du Bien-être de Québec, Etude des Foyers d'hébergement pour personnes âgées dans le diocèse de Québec, Québec, février
   1968.

27 Gordon Edward Priest, An Investigation of the Elderly in the Urban Environment with Special Reference to their Housing, unpublished M.A. thesis,
   Simon Fraser University, 1970.

28 Ministry of Housing and Local Government, Grouped Flatlets for Old People -
   A Sociological Study, London, H.M.S.O., 1968.

29 Dilys Page and Tom Muir, New Housing for the Elderly - A Study of Housing
   Schemes for the Elderly Provided by the Hanover Housing Association,
   London, Bedford Square Press, 1971.

The housing needs of senior citizens have also been the focus of a number of community studies carried out by voluntary organizations, such as Housing Needs of Winnipeg Senior Citizens,[30] and a report prepared by the Social Planning Council of Greater Niagara.[31]

There is also a small body of literature that addresses itself to the design and management of housing environments for the elderly. Much of Marie McGuire's work in the United States has dealt with this subject[32] and in Canada CMHC recently published a revised edition of Housing the Elderly.[33] The latter contains many valuable hints on building and design questions. Another recent work that contains papers of interest to management staff (although more directed to institutional settings) is our Council's Administration of Homes for the Aged.[34] Also of special interest for its description of the British warden scheme is Age Concern's Role of the Warden in Grouped Housing.[35] Two American publications of special interest to managers are Westmayer's Management of Public Housing for the Elderly,[36] and also a recent U.S. federal government guide.[37]

---

30 Age and Opportunity Bureau, Housing Needs of Winnipeg's Senior Citizens, Winnipeg, 1959.

31 A Study of the Type of Development that Applicants for Senior Citizen and Geared-to-Income Housing Would Like to Live in and Where they Would Like to See it Located in Niagara Falls, Social Planning Council of Greater Niagara, February 1970.

32 For example, Marie McGuire, Design of Housing for the Elderly: A Checklist, Washington, National Association of Housing and Redevelopment Officials, 1972.

33 Housing the Elderly, Ottawa, Central Mortgage and Housing Corporation, July 1972.

34 Administration of Homes for the Aged, a Workbook on the Human Aspects of Administration of Homes for the Aged, Based on Presentations Given at the National Seminar for Administrators of Homes for the Aged in Canada, Ottawa, The Canadian Council on Social Development, March 1971.

35 Age Concern, Role of the Warden in Grouped Housing, London, National Old People's Welfare Council, 1972.

36 Troy Westmayer, Management of Public Housing for the Elderly, New York, New York University Graduate School of Public Administration, 1963.

37 U.S. Department of Housing and Urban Development, Management of Housing for the Elderly: A HUD Guide, Washington, 1972.

Research Plan

In carrying out the study, it was decided to use the survey method supplemented by case studies and a review of legislation and statistics. The surveys attempt to obtain as objective as possible a picture of the characteristics of housing developments, their residents, and managers. And to supplement this fairly hard type of data, the case studies provide in-depth pictures of particular housing developments.

The legislative and statistical profiles (Part II) include a review of national and provincial legislation affecting the financial aspects of constructing and operating self-contained and hostel accommodation for the elderly. This part of the study also provides national and provincial breakdowns of the characteristics of the 746 different housing developments that had been built under the National Housing Act for senior citizens and were occupied on December 31, 1970. These developments contained a total of 23,979 self-contained dwelling units and 7,908 hostel beds. While these statistics are interesting in their own right, the task of compiling them was necessary in order to construct a sampling frame for the manager survey.

The purpose of the manager survey was to obtain as accurate as possible a picture of the nature of NHA financed housing for the elderly from the point of view of the sponsoring organization. The mail survey is based on a representative sample of 294 developments across Canada. The survey report (Part III) provides information about the characteristics of residents, the existence of facilities and services, staffing arrangements, social participation both inside of and external to the development, as well as the characteristics of managers. It concludes with a special section dealing with the financial aspects of non-profit developments. An explanation of methodology employed in the manager survey is contained in Appendix 1 and the questionnaire itself is reproduced in Appendix 2.

To overcome rigidities inherent in the social survey approach, 19 case studies of individual housing developments were undertaken with the objective of exploring the environmental dynamics of senior citizens' housing and obtaining a better understanding of the factors that determine resident satisfaction, social interaction, and community integration. The case studies have value both for their illustration of interesting types of design and service arrangements as well as for their portrayal of various situations (often unforeseen) that can arise in housing old people.

The criteria for the selection of the case studies is reviewed in chapter 1, Part IV, so it suffices here to say that an attempt was made to obtain as many variations in development type as possible while consciously erring on the side of focusing attention on developments that were highly recommended as attractive places for old people to live in. In writing accounts of the case studies, we made an attempt to relate each of them to a theme illustrating a particular approach to accommodating the elderly - each theme being made explicit in the case study's title.

Field workers spent approximately one week on each case study, fewer days in small developments and somewhat longer in large ones. They conducted interviews with housing managers and other development staff, officials of the sponsoring organizations, representatives of local social service and health agencies, and other relevant people in the community. As well as engaging in general on-site observation, the field workers also interviewed a random sample of residents; the results of these interviews were written-up separately in the user survey.

The user survey represents the study's attempt to solicit the consumer's view about life in housing developments for the elderly. The survey was conducted on a random basis in the 19 developments selected for case study and, as the user survey methodology (Appendix 3) indicates, while not strictly representing a nationally valid sample of persons who live in NHA housing for the elderly, the demographic characteristics of the residents interviewed and the types of developments they inhabited corresponded sufficiently closely with those reported in the scientific-ally structured management survey to merit serious attention and inclusion in this report.

As well as presenting data about the demographic characteristics of residents of NHA housing developments for the elderly, the user survey contains interesting information about the past housing experience of residents, their access to services and location, and patterns of social participation. The survey report also reviews residents' use of social services and recreation facilities and makes some assessment of their general level of satisfaction with the accommodation. Besides documenting what many practitioners in the field of housing the elderly and geriatrics already suspect about the users of senior citizens housing, the user study indicates one or two preferences that may challenge the popular wisdom. Readers of this part of the report will find the user survey interview schedule contained in Appendix 4 helpful.

Some Definitions

Many of the principal terms employed in this study vary in their usage in housing and social service circles across Canada; it was therefore necessary to select a series of terms for operational purposes and adhere to them consistently. The choice of the terms was arbitrary in part, but an effort was made to adopt the most popular yet least controversial usage.

Short definitions of some of the study's most strategic terms follow:

Accommodation type: The type of living quarters contained within a housing development for the elderly. Basically, developments were grouped by accommodation type as being self-contained, hostel, or mixed.

CMHC: The Central Mortgage and Housing Corporation, the federal govern-ment's housing agency that is charged with administration of the National Housing Act.

Community facilities: Social and community premises such as halls and libraries that were situated beyond the site of the housing development.

The elderly: The older part of the Canadian population, usually those in advanced life aged over 60 or 65 years. Other terms used interchangeably in the study are "old people," "the aged," and "senior citizens."

High-rise: In the context of this study, apartment or hostel buildings that contain three or more floors.

Hostel accommodation: Accommodation in a housing development for the elderly that offers the residents a single or double bed/sitting room and meals in a central dining room or cafeteria. Hostels do not necessarily offer a more intensive level of care, although usually more on-site services and facilities are available.

Housing development: Grouped accommodation for senior citizens that is operated by a single sponsor and built contiguously on the same site. Synonyms employed across the country include "project," "home for the aged," "lodge," "foyer," and "residence."

Infirmary: A facility for temporary nursing care (one month or less) located in the housing development for the elderly.

Manager: The officials responsible for the operation of a housing development for the elderly. In some parts of the country he or she may be referred to as the administrator, executive director, or superintendent. In the manager survey questionnaire this official was defined as "the management person who has the most direct contact with the residents and is closest to supervising the over-all operation of this particular housing development." As many non-profit sponsors lacked paid officials, they commonly designated one of the members of their board (such as the secretary-treasurer) to take on such day-to-day responsibilities.

Mixed accommodation: Accommodation which contains a mixture of self-contained dwelling units and hostel rooms in the same development.

NHA: The abbreviation used throughout the study for the National Housing Act, the Canadian federal government's principal legislative instrument for the implementation of housing policy. All the accommodation for senior citizens within the purview of this study was built with capital funds supplied under the NHA.

Non-profit housing: Accommodation built with NHA loans (and sometimes provincial and municipal government assistance) under what, at the time of the study, were sections 16 and 16A and is currently section 15. At the time of the study, rents of residents of non-profit housing were not subsidized under the National Housing Act, although there have lately been one or two precedents in which NHA section 44 subsidies became applicable to residents in certain non-profit developments. Non-profit housing has been built by corporations established by municipal or provincial governments, churches, service clubs, ethnic groups, and other voluntary associations.

Nursing home: Offers medically supervised care to residents who are no longer generally ambulatory and need continuous care. Nursing homes for the elderly were beyond the purview of this study.

Physical capacity: The term used to describe the capacity of residents to undertake activities and care for themselves. The levels of physical capacity employed were "no incapacity," "slightly limited ability," "moderately limited ability," and "seriously limited ability." Each of these terms are defined in the manager survey questionnaire and the user survey interview schedule as well as in the two survey reports.

Public housing: Housing built under the public housing sections of the NHA (sections 35A and 35D at the time of the study but currently sections 40 and 43). In public housing, residents' rents are subsidized according to a geared-to-income rent scale, with federal, provincial (and sometimes municipal) government cost-sharing in the subsidies.

Self-contained accommodation: Accommodation in a housing development for the elderly that offers residents dwelling units which have their own entrance and contain a kitchen and bathroom; self-contained developments may be built as detached houses, row houses, or apartment buildings.

Social animator: The term of choice used in the study's recommendations (Part VII) to denote a paid worker responsible for assisting residents to plan social and recreation activities and encouraging other sorts of participation in the housing environment. The terms used to describe this function in the management survey were "group leadership service" and "group worker."

Sponsor Group: The particular form of organization that undertakes the sponsorship of either a public or non-profit housing development. Sponsor groups include: churches, provincial and municipal governments, service clubs, and ethnic groups.

Sponsor type: The agency or organization responsible for building and managing a housing development for the elderly. Basically, there are two major types of sponsors: public housing agencies and non-profit housing corporations.

User: In the context of this study, residents of NHA financed housing for the elderly.

Findings

From the various parts of the study, data was consolidated and inter-
preted in a general statement of findings (Part VI). These findings
attempt to summarize some of the study's more salient lessons, but
they by no means do complete justice to the difficult issues on which
generalizations are made; therefore for more in-depth consideration
the reader is advised to directly examine the data reported in the
relevant part of this volume.

One word of warning - because of the paucity of existing research on
housing for the elderly in Canada, there is a tendency to expect much
from studies such as this. However, it is regretful that the study
will not in itself answer or speak to all the diverse concerns of the
resident, the manager, the sociologist, the economist, or the architect -
although we hope it will be of some interest to all the foregoing.
Actually, the work substantiates the need for more research on the
accommodation and residential environment needs of the elderly;[38] and
since further studies should probably be done at the local level where
it is easier to apply controls and more strategically possible to obtain
sound data, it is hoped that this work will perhaps provide a reference
against which the findings of local studies can be considered.

Recommendations

Part VII of the study contains a series of recommendations based on the
study's findings. These recommendations were drawn up by the study
Advisory Committee on the basis of the statement of findings and a review
of the other material that makes up the study. These recommendations will
likely be of interest to all levels of government, the design, health,
and social service professions, as well as voluntary organizations.

---

38   See recommendation in Part VII concerning further research.

PART II

LEGISLATIVE AND STATISTICAL PROFILES

CONTENTS

CHAPTER 1

INTRODUCTION

This part of the study seeks to make available some basic background
information about legislation on housing for the elderly as well as a
comprehensive set of statistics indicating the variety of housing for
old people financed under the National Housing Act (NHA) that had been
occupied by the end of 1970. A legislative review is probably not very
new; nevertheless, it is believed that the readers of this study, many of
whom may be unfamiliar with the financial and administrative aspects of
housing for the aged in Canada, will find it useful. The statistical
material, not available elsewhere, had to be produced in order to provide
a correct universe from which a sample could be selected for the mail
survey of housing sponsors and managers. As the focus of this study is
primarily directed toward understanding some of the environmental needs
of old people, less time than would have been liked was spent on the
analysis of the legislative instruments and statistics. The data in this
part was, however, extremely useful in developing our general statement of
findings, and it is hoped that it will prove of interest to researchers
who have a special concern with institutional problems and questions of
resource allocation.

Exploring the Legislation

Few difficulties were encountered in collecting information about
national and provincial legislation pertaining to housing the elderly
and its administration. Primarily, correspondence was relied on, followed
in some instances by telephone calls and visits to provincial capitals.
Memorandum papers prepared for the CMHC Low Income Housing Study Group
were also helpful.

Generation of Statistics

In this study, staff did not expect to face difficulties in gathering
statistical data about housing developments for the elderly financed
under the National Housing Act. However, it was soon found that the
tabular material CMHC had available was insufficient; thus, reference had
to be made directly to mortgage loan and grant approvals. As this data
was not available in a conveniently retrievable form, it was necessary
for study staff to consult all the mortgage and grant files in the CMHC
head office relating to housing for the elderly.

Since the procedures followed may be of interest to other researchers,
it might be worth briefly recounting them. Once the mortgage and grant
files had been thoroughly examined, we were obliged to consolidate them
since in many cases two or more agreements existed between CMHC and a
sponsor relating to a single development. For instance, by the end of
1970, CMHC had made 1,014 loans under NHA sections 16 and 35D to provide
accommodation for the elderly (Canadian Housing Statistics, 1970, Table
50). Besides these, the corporation had made 73 contributions under NHA
section 35A to public housing developments containing accommodation either
built specifically for senior citizens or suitable for them.

When this consolidation was completed. 871 housing developments were identified, resulting from 1,087 separate agreements between CMHC and housing sponsors. However, the process by which these figures were developed did not guarantee complete accuracy, as the files represented developments in varying stages of completeness. Fortunately, sometimes letters or memos from CMHC branch offices were found that indicated whether a loan represented a new development or merely an addition to an existing one. In other cases, the files did not contain this information. Other loan approval files related to developments on which construction had not started or been completed. Problems of this sort were later rectified by correspondence with CMHC regional offices and provincial housing corporations.

In considering CMHC contributions and loans for public housing projects, we were faced with the problem of deciding whether developments which were occupied by both senior citizens and families should be included in the universe. We found that one-bedroom and bachelor units in public housing were either designated "suitable for senior citizens" or "specifically approved for senior citizens" although, in many cases, units occupied by senior citizens only constituted a small portion of the total development - a tenth to a quarter or less. After considering this question, the study staff decided to include developments with units "specifically approved for senior citizens" in the universe and discard those that were only designated "suitable." This removed 24 developments from the preliminary universe.

In dealing with housing for the elderly in the province of Quebec, study staff were confronted with problems resulting from a special arrangement the province had worked out with the federal government relating to social housing. Canadian Housing Statistics, 1970, Table 50, suggested that from 1946 to 1970, the federal government had contributed funds toward the production of 2,881 dwelling units and 10,912 hostel beds in Quebec under NHA sections 16 or 35D. Actually, loans under the non-profit NHA section 16 to individual developers in Quebec had not been made since 1968, prior to which 1,042 self-contained units and 1,542 hostel beds were built. The remaining self-contained units and hostel beds had been financed directly by the Quebec government, although it in turn received an annual allocation of funds for this purpose from CMHC.

In 1968, the first year in which the Quebec Housing Corporation ran its own program for elderly people, loans for 4,000 hostel beds were approved. In 1969, Quebec Housing Corporation loan approvals covered an additional 6,000 hostel beds and by April, 1971, the corporation had approved loans for a total of 12,000 hostel beds. At the time of our study, however, the vast majority of this accommodation had not been constructed. With the help of Quebec Housing Corporation officials, it was determined that only 557 dwelling units and 4,034 hostel beds had been completed and occupied by the end of 1970. This accommodation has been included in the non-profit sector of the universe since CMHC appears to compile housing built by the Quebec Housing Corporation with its NHA section 16 figures. The developments are also managed by non-profit groups rather than offices municipaux (the Quebec equivalent of public housing authorities).

In addition to the province of Quebec, the provinces of Manitoba and Saskatchewan supplied us with comprehensive lists of housing developments that had received NHA assistance. Although unit and bed figures supplied by these provinces tended to vary slightly from those supplied by CMHC, we adhered to the latter. In many cases, the discrepancies may have arisen from non NHA financed accommodation in some developments in these provinces.

After adjustments of the type outlined above to our preliminary universe of 871 housing developments for the elderly, as well as corrections resulting from a variety of other checks, we ended up with a universe of 746 developments containing 23,979 dwelling units and 7,908 hostel beds. This figure represents NHA financed housing specifically designated for senior citizens, occupied on December 31, 1970.

CHAPTER 2

CANADA

National Housing Act

The government of Canada, through the National Housing Act, assists the
building of housing for the elderly by providing mortgage loans and grants
to both public and non-profit sponsors. All aspects of the federal government's NHA programs are administered by its Crown agency, the Central
Mortgage and Housing Corporation.

CMHC usually does not directly initiate housing accommodation for the aged.
Instead, it responds to applications by provincial, municipal, and private
bodies wishing to do so. NHA social housing programs have traditionally
tended to be of two types: assistance to the non-profit sector and assistance
to public housing agencies. The division of NHA financed housing into non-
profit and public housing sectors is a useful one for analytical purposes
since it defines two fairly distinctive types of housing sponsors; however,
it also has a degree of legislative sanction because of the fact that the
two sectors have generally made recourse to different NHA sections.

Non-profit sponsors have generally obtained NHA assistance under section
16 of the act.[1] Under this section, CMHC may lend a sponsor up to 95 per
cent of the lending value of a low rental housing project. The mortgage
loan is repayable over a 50-year period at a preferential interest rate
(usually approximately $1\frac{1}{2}$ per cent below the current NHA rate for home
ownership). For the first 15 years of the loan, CMHC retains control of
the rents. In the period 1946-70, approximately 40 per cent of the funds
advanced under this NHA section were for housing for the elderly. Loans
are available for both self-contained dwelling units and hostel bed
accommodation; however, there is nothing now in the legislation to prevent
loans from being made for nursing or convalescent care homes. Although
loans for the construction of family accommodation have frequently been
made to private entrepreneurs, by the end of 1970 there had only been one
case where a loan for housing for the elderly was made to other than a
public agency or a non-profit corporation. (It was made to a private
nursing home operator). Loans made under this section generally carried
no subsidy other than the below-market rate of interest.

Assistance for the construction of public housing is provided under sections
35A[2] and 35D[3] of the National Housing Act. Both sections support the
construction of self-contained and hostel accommodation for senior citizens,
although neither are specifically designated for the elderly. Section 35A

---

1 Section 16 was renumbered in 1969 and entitled "Loans for Low Rental
   Projects." From 1964 to 1969, the section was numbered 16A and referred
   to as the "non-profit" section. From 1946 to 1964, the relevant section
   was number 16, but referred to as the "limited dividend" section. In
   1971, the National Housing Act was renumbered with this section becoming
   section 15.

2 In 1971 renumbered section 40.

3 In 1971 renumbered section 43.

enables the federal government to make grants up to 75 per cent of the capital costs of new public housing projects undertaken jointly with provincial governments and also enables the federal government to bear 75 per cent of the operating losses of such housing. The legislation enables CMHC, in conjunction with its provincial partner, to determine: 1) the type and cost of land; 2) the type, number, cost and rents of the housing units; 3) the rates of interest and amortization that may be charged against the capital costs; and 4) the conditions under which the accommodation may be disposed. Prior to the 1964 NHA amendments, a federal-provincial partnership arrangement under section 35A was the only way in which rent subsidies could become available for housing built and managed by public housing authorities.

Section 35D, inserted into the National Housing Act in 1964, allows the federal government to "make a loan to a province, municipality, or public housing agency for the construction or acquisition of a public housing project." Such a loan cannot exceed 90 per cent of the capital cost as determined by CMHC and must be for a term not exceeding 50 years from the date of completion or acquisition of a project. Once the federal loan is repaid, the housing project becomes the property of the public housing agency which applied for it.

Under NHA section 35E[1], CMHC is permitted to enter into agreements with public housing agencies to contribute 50 per cent of the annual losses for units let to low income households at rents that do not meet the cost of amortizing and operating the public housing project. This section is generally used in combination with section 35D, but has, in a few cases, been used to subsidize housing financed under section 16 when a provincial housing corporation has taken over projects originally built by non-profit sponsors.

Other Federal Legislation

In addition to programs operating under the National Housing Act, senior citizens in Canada benefit from other legislation which, although not strictly related to housing, exercizes a significant impact on the well-being of the elderly. This legislation consists of the Canada Pension Plan, the Canada Assistance Plan, and the provisions for old age security (including the guaranteed income supplement).

The basic old age pension, provided under the Old Age Security Act to all Canadians aged 65 and over, was $82.88 a month in late 1972. This pension is administered by the Department of National Health and Welfare through regional offices across the country. Since 1966, a guaranteed annual income supplement has been available to persons receiving the old age security pension but with limited other income. In late 1972, the benefits

---

1 In 1971 renumbered section 44.

under this program brought the total old age pension and supplement for a single person to $150 a month and $285 for a couple. The amount of supplement is determined in relation to a sliding scale. To establish eligibility for any supplement, a single person must not have a yearly income in excess of $1,632 over the old age pension; a couple must not have a yearly income in excess of $2,880 over the old age pension.

The Canada and Quebec pension plans, enacted in 1965, commenced retirement pensions in 1967. A retirement pension under the Canada or Quebec pension plans is payable to persons aged 65 to 70 years old, providing the person has made contributions to the plan and is retired from active employment. All contributors, on reaching age 70, receive the full pension whether they retire or not. In 1972, the highest monthly pension paid under the Canada Pension Plan was $77.81. The maximum benefit possible, $110, will be payable in 1973. To receive such a sum, a beneficiary would have had to have made contributions to the plan since its inception in 1966.

The Canada Assistance Plan, enacted in 1966, provides for federal cost sharing of provincial and municipal welfare assistance payments and social services. Generally speaking, it permits the federal government to reimburse provinces and municipalities for 50 per cent of the cost of selected welfare services initiated by provincial and municipal governments. Such services may include rehabilitation, case work, community development, and homemaker and day care services to persons who qualify under a needs test. The plan also provides for 50 per cent cost sharing by the federal government of the costs of residential institutions, including homes for the aged and nursing homes.

Distribution of the Elderly

At the time of the 1971 census, 1,744,400 Canadians or 8 per cent of the total population were aged 65 years and over. As one might expect, the two Canadian provinces with the highest populations, Ontario and Quebec, had the largest number of old people in the country. Table 1 indicates that 36.9 per cent of the population aged 65 years and over lived in Ontario and 23.7 per cent lived in Quebec. British Columbia had 11.8 per cent of the elderly population, followed by Alberta, Manitoba, Saskatchewan, Nova Scotia, New Brunswick, Newfoundland, and Prince Edward Island. The Yukon and Northwest Territories had the lowest number of elderly people.

In terms of proportion of provincial population aged 65 and over, Table 1 indicates that Prince Edward Island led the country with 11.1 per cent. It was followed by Saskatchewan (10.2 per cent), Manitoba (9.7 per cent), British Columbia (9.4 per cent), Nova Scotia (9.2 per cent), New Brunswick (8.6 per cent), Ontario (8.4 per cent), Alberta (7.3 per cent), Quebec (6.9 per cent). Newfoundland, with only 6.1 per cent of its population aged 65 and over, had the lowest proportion of elderly people for any province, although the Yukon had only 2.8 per cent and the Northwest Territories, 2.2 per cent.

TABLE 1

POPULATION, AND POPULATION 65 YEARS OF AGE AND OVER, BY PROVINCE (JUNE 1971)

PROVINCE	POPULATION (THOUSANDS)	PROPORTION CANADIAN POPULATION	POPULATION 65 YEARS & OVER (THOUSANDS)	PROPORTION OF CANADIAN POPULATION 65 & OVER	PROPORTION OF PROVINCIAL POPULATION 65 AND OVER
Nfld.	522.1	2.4%	32.1	1.8%	6.1%
P.E.I.	111.6	.5%	12.3	.7%	11.1%
N.S.	789	3.7%	72.5	4.2%	9.2%
N.B.	634.6	2.9%	54.7	3.1%	8.6%
Quebec	6,027.8	27.9%	413.0	23.7%	6.9%
Ontario	7,703.1	35.7%	644.4	36.9%	8.4%
Manitoba	988.2	4.6%	95.6	5.5%	9.7%
Sask.	926.2	4.3%	94.8	5.4%	10.2%
Alberta	1,627.9	7.5%	118.8	6.8%	7.3%
B.C.	2,184.6	10.1%	205.0	11.8%	9.4%
Yukon	18.4	.1%	.5	*	2.8%
N.W.T.	34.8	.2%	.8	*	2.2%
CANADA	21,568.3	100%	1,744.4	100%	8.1%

* Less than .1 per cent.

Source: Canada, Statistics Canada, 1971 Census of Canada, Special Bulletin, Population, Specified Age Groups and Sex, Census Divisions and Subdivisions.

Accommodation Distribution in Relation to Elderly Population

Table 2, which integrates the 1971 census figures with NHA financed housing for the elderly occupied at the end of December 1970, indicates that there were 13.7 dwelling units and 4.5 hostel beds per thousand elderly persons in Canada as a whole. By province, in terms of the number of self-contained dwelling units per thousand persons aged 65 and over, British Columbia led the country with 23.2 units, followed by Manitoba (22.5), Ontario (22.3), Prince Edward Island (18.4), Nova Scotia (8.9), Saskatchewan (7.2), New Brunswick (4.0), Newfoundland (2.7), Quebec (1.7), and Alberta (.9). The Northwest Territories had the highest dwelling unit count in the country: 33.1 dwelling units per thousand aged persons.

TABLE 2

OCCUPIED NHA FINANCED DWELLING UNITS AND HOSTEL BEDS FOR THE ELDERLY
(DECEMBER 1970) PER THOUSAND POPULATION OVER AGE 65 (JUNE 1971)

PROVINCE	POPULATION 65 AND OVER (THOUSANDS)	OCCUPIED DWELLING UNITS	OCCUPIED DWELLING UNITS PER THOUSAND POPULATION 65 AND OVER	OCCUPIED HOSTEL BEDS	HOSTEL BEDS PER THOUSAND POPULATION OVER 65
Nfld.	32.1	86	2.7	122	3.8
P.E.I.	12.3	227	18.4	62	5.0
N.S.	72.5	642	8.9	372	5.1
N.B.	54.7	221	4.0	616	11.3
Quebec	413.0	710	1.7	1,160	2.8
Ontario	644.4	14,374	22.3	1,653	2.6
Manitoba	95.6	2,151	22.5	1,640	17.2
Sask.	94.8	678	7.2	991	10.5
Alberta	118.8	104	.9	82	.7
B.C.	205.0	4,761	23.2	1,210	5.9
N.W.T.	.8	25	33.1	0	0
CANADA	1,744.4	23,979	13.7	7,908	4.5

These figures do not necessarily indicate the priority that has been placed on building self-contained accommodation specifically designated for the elderly in the various provinces. For example, although the table indicates that Alberta had the lowest proportion of NHA financed housing, Alberta for many years sponsored its own housing program for the elderly which proceeded without NHA assistance. Also, while figures indicate that Quebec made few claims on NHA money for housing its old people, until recently the care and accommodation of old people in the province of Quebec was largely considered solely the prerogative and responsibility of charitable institutions.

In terms of providing hostel beds financed by NHA funds, Table 2 indicates a different pattern emerged. Manitoba led the way with 17.2 beds per thousand population aged 65 years and over, followed by New Brunswick (11.3), Saskatchewan (10.5), British Columbia (5.9), Nova Scotia (5.1), Prince Edward Island (5.0), Newfoundland (3.8), Quebec (2.8), and Ontario (2.6). Alberta had the lowest count: .7 hostel beds per thousand elderly population. Again, Alberta's extraordinarily low proportion can be accounted for by its own provincial program that proceeded for years without federal assistance.

By the end of 1970, strictly in per capita terms of NHA program utiliza-
tion to accommodate the elderly, Manitoba led the way, followed by British
Columbia and Ontario. Alberta, Quebec, and Newfoundland had made the
least claims on NHA resources to accommodate their senior citizens.

Sponsorship and Accommodation Types

Table 3 shows that of the 746 housing developments built for the elderly
and occupied at the end of 1970, 530 (71 per cent) had been built by the
non-profit sector and 216 (29 per cent) by public housing agencies. Non-
profit sponsors accounted for 12,820 (53 per cent) of the total 23,979
dwelling units and 7,669 (97 per cent) of all hostel beds. Public housing
agencies were responsible for 11,159 (47 per cent) of all dwelling units,
and 239 (3 per cent) of all hostel beds.

A further glance at Table 3 indicates that for non-profit and public
housing combined, Ontario built the most dwelling units, followed by
British Columbia and Manitoba. Ontario had also built the most hostel
beds, followed closely by Manitoba, British Columbia, and Quebec.

TABLE 3

NHA FINANCED DEVELOPMENTS FOR THE ELDERLY BY SPONSOR AND ACCOMMODATION TYPES

PROVINCE	NON-PROFIT HOUSING			PUBLIC HOUSING			TOTAL		
	Develop-ments	Dwelling Units	Hostel Beds	Develop-ments	Dwelling Units	Hostel Beds	Develop-ments	Dwelling Units	Hostel Beds
Nfld.	4	70	122	1	16	0	5	86	122
P.E.I.	22	227	62	0	0	0	22	227	62
N.S.	9	86	372	13	556	0	22	642	372
N.B.	13	64	616	13	157	0	26	221	616
Quebec	99	710	1,160	0	0	0	99	710	1,160
Ontario	95	5,382	1,414	161	8,992	239	256	14,374	1,653
Manitoba	87	1,898	1,640	6	253	0	93	2,151	1,640
Sask.	78	419	991	11	259	0	89	678	991
Alberta	4	104	82	0	0	0	4	104	82
B.C.	119	3,860	1,210	9	901	0	128	4,761	1,210
N.W.T.	0	0	0	2	25	0	2	25	0
CANADA	530	12,820	7,669	216	11,159	239	746	23,979	7,908

When public housing is considered alone, Ontario built by far the most
dwelling units, followed at a very great distance by British Columbia
and Nova Scotia. By the end of 1970, neither Quebec, Prince Edward Island
nor Alberta had built any accommodation for the elderly as part of their
regular public housing programs.

Table 4 details national and provincial figures for housing developments
built at the end of 1970, by development and sponsor type. The figures
for the whole of Canada reveal that almost 99 per cent of the 216 public
housing developments consisted solely of self-contained accommodation,
only three developments containing a mix of self-contained and hostel or
nursing beds. In the non-profit sector, 301 developments or 57 per cent
were solely self-contained, 109 or over 20 per cent contained hostel
accommodation, and 120 or 23 per cent were mixed.

Also according to Table 4, in the public housing sector, Ontario had the
most developments solely consisting of dwelling units, followed by Nova
Scotia and New Brunswick. The only three mixed public housing developments
were in Ontario. In the non-profit sector, British Columbia had the most
developments solely consisting of self-contained dwelling units, followed
by Ontario and Manitoba. As far as non-profit hostels were concerned,
Quebec had the most, followed by British Columbia and Saskatchewan. In
terms of non-profit mixed developments, Quebec had by far the most, followed
by Saskatchewan and a long way behind by Manitoba.

Table 5 shows the sponsorship of non-profit developments examined by variety
of sponsor types. We were unable to determine sponsor type for 199 developments or 38 per cent of the total of 530 non-profit developments. But of
the remaining 331 developments, 103 or 31 per cent were sponsored by
municipalities, 99 or 30 per cent by service clubs, 44 or 13 per cent by
churches and religious orders, 42 or 13 per cent by provincial governments,
26 or 8 per cent by ethnic groups, and 17 or 5 per cent by other types of
bodies, including private entrepreneurs, mixtures of other groups, and special
community corporations.

Most of the developments sponsored by service clubs were in British Columbia,
Manitoba and Ontario, while the majority of municipally sponsored developments tended to be mainly in Saskatchewan and Ontario. The province with
the most developments sponsored by ethnic groups was Manitoba. All the
developments sponsored directly by provincial governments were in Prince
Edward Island and Ontario.

TABLE 4

PROVINCIAL BREAKDOWN OF NHA FINANCED DEVELOPMENTS FOR THE ELDERLY BY ACCOMMODATION AND SPONSOR TYPES

	SELF-CONTAINED	HOSTEL	MIXED*	TOTAL
Newfoundland				
Public	1	0	0	1
Non-Profit	1	2	1	4
P.E.I.				
Public	0	0	0	0
Non-Profit	19	3	0	22
Nova Scotia				
Public	13	0	0	13
Non-Profit	3	4	2	9
New Brunswick				
Public	13	0	0	13
Non-Profit	4	8	1	13
Quebec				
Public	0	0	0	0
Non-Profit	7	22	70	99
Ontario				
Public	158	0	3	161
Non-Profit	80	13	2	95
Manitoba				
Public	6	0	0	6
Non-Profit	62	17	8	87
Saskatchewan				
Public	11	0	0	11
Non-Profit	26	19	33	78
Alberta				
Public	0	0	0	0
Non-Profit	2	2	0	4
British Columbia				
Public	9	0	0	9
Non-Profit	97	19	3	119
N.W.T.				
Public	2	0	0	2
Non-Profit	0	0	0	0
CANADA				
Public	213	0	3	216
Non-Profit	301	109	120	530

* Contains a combination of mixed self-contained and hostel or nursing accommodation.

TABLE 5

NHA FINANCED NON-PROFIT DEVELOPMENTS FOR THE ELDERLY BY SPONSOR TYPE

PROVINCE	ETHNIC GROUPS[1]	SERVICE CLUBS	CHURCHES	MUNICI-PALITIES	PROVINCIAL GOVERNMENTS	OTHERS[2]	NO INFOR-MATION	TOTAL
Nfld.	0	0	2	0	0	0	2	4
P.E.I.	0	0	0	0	22	0	0	22
N.S.	0	0	1	2	0	1	5	9
N.B.	0	5	1	1	0	1	5	13
Quebec	1	1	1	0	0	5	91	99
Ontario	2	18	4	38	20	0	13	95
Manitoba	15	27	13	3	0	2	27	87
Sask.	0	8	12	55	0	3	0	78
Alberta	1	1	1	0	0	0	1	4
B.C.	7	39	9	4	0	5	55	119
TOTAL	26	99	44	103	42	17	199	530

1 Includes religious-ethnic groups (e.g. Mennonites).

2 Includes private entrepreneurs, mixtures of other groups and special community corporations.

Size and Location

Table 6 indicates the location of NHA financed housing for the elderly by accommodation type and size. When the universe of 746 developments is considered, the table reveals that 244 developments or 33 per cent had 20 or less dwelling units and/or hostel beds, 153 developments or 20 per cent had 21-40 units and/or hostel beds, 199 developments or 27 per cent had 41-80 units and/or hostel beds, 95 developments or 13 per cent had 81-149 units and/or hostel beds, and 55 developments or 7 per cent had 150 or more units and/or hostel beds.

Of the universe of 746 developments, 240 (32 per cent) were located in metropolitan areas, 52 (7 per cent) were situated in major urban areas, and 454 (61 per cent) were in small towns.

Of the 514 strictly self-contained developments, 240 (47 per cent) consisted of 20 or less units, 105 (20 per cent) had 21-40 units, 87 (17 per cent) had 41-80 units, 53 (10 per cent) had 81-149 units, and 29 (6 per cent) had 150 or more units.

44

```
                              TABLE 6

        NHA FINANCED DEVELOPMENTS FOR THE ELDERLY, LOCATION
                 BY ACCOMMODATION TYPE AND SIZE
```

	SIZE[1]	METROPOLITAN AREAS[2]	MAJOR URBAN AREAS[2]	SMALL TOWNS[2]	TOTAL
Self-Contained	1	30	10	200	240
Developments	2	39	11	55	105
	3	49	18	20	87
	4	42	3	8	53
	5	28	1	0	29
Hostel	1	2	0	2	4
Developments	2	4	0	23	27
	3	4	2	35	41
	4	14	2	9	25
	5	8	0	4	12
Mixed	1	0	0	0	0
Developments	2	1	0	20	21
	3	3	3	65	71
	4	4	2	11	17
	5	12	0	2	14
ALL DEVELOPMENTS	1	32	10	202	244
	2	44	11	98	153
	3	56	23	120	199
	4	60	7	28	95
	5	48	1	6	55

1 Size categories: (1) 20 or less (2) 21-40 (3) 41-80 (4) 81-149 (5) 150+

2 Statistics Canada census categories

Note that the count was only for units in self-contained developments, beds in hostel developments, units and beds combined in the mixed developments and "all developments" column.

Of the 109 strictly hostel developments, four developments or just over 4 per cent consisted of 20 beds or less, 27 (24 per cent) had 21-40 beds, 41 (38 per cent) had 41-80 beds, 25 (23 per cent) had 81-149 beds, and 12 (11 per cent) had 150 beds or more.

Of the 123 mixed developments, all contained more than 20 beds and/or units - 21 developments or 17 per cent had 21-40 beds and/or units, 71 developments or 58 per cent had 41-80 beds and/or units, 17 developments or 14 per cent had 80-149 beds and/or units, and 14 developments or 11 per cent had 150 or more beds and/or units.

As one might expect, the size of the developments varied in relation to
the size of the community. Generally speaking, the larger developments
were found in communities with higher populations. Of all the developments
of 20 units and/or beds or less, an analysis of the figures in Table 6
indicates that 13 per cent were located in metropolitan areas, 4 per cent
in major urban areas, and 83 per cent in small towns. Of the developments
with 21-40 units and/or beds, 29 per cent were in metropolitan areas, 7
per cent in major urban areas, and 64 per cent in small towns. Of the
developments with 41-80 units and/or beds, 28 per cent were in metropolitan
areas, 12 per cent in major urban areas, and 60 per cent in small towns.
For the developments with 81-149 units and/or beds, 63 per cent were in
metropolitan areas, 7 per cent in major urban areas, and 30 per cent in
small towns. When it came to the largest developments, those with 150 or
more units and/or beds, 87 per cent were located in metropolitan areas,
2 per cent in major urban areas, and 11 per cent in small towns.

When only the 530 non-profit developments were considered (Table 7), 149
developments or 28 per cent consisted of 20 or less units and/or beds;
103 developments or 19 per cent had 21-40 units and/or beds; 169 developments or 32 per cent had 41-80 units and/or beds; 75 developments or 14
per cent had 81-149 units and/or beds; and 34 developments or 6 per cent
had 150 or more units and/or beds.

Table 7 also indicates that 177 non-profit developments (33 per cent) were
located in metropolitan areas, 22 developments (4 per cent) were in major
urban areas, and 331 developments (63 per cent) were in small towns.

When 216 developments in the public housing sector are considered (only
three of which are strictly self-contained accommodation), Table 8 indicates
that 95 developments (44 per cent) consisted of 20 or less units, 50
developments (23 per cent) had 21-40 units, 30 developments (14 per cent)
had 41-80 units, 20 developments (9 per cent) had 81-149 units, and 21
developments (10 per cent) had 150 or more units and/or beds.

In the total public housing sector, 63 developments or 29 per cent were
located in major metropolitan areas, 30 developments or 14 per cent in
major urban areas, and 123 developments or 57 per cent in small towns.

Table 9 provides a breakdown of non-profit housing developments for the
elderly by accommodation type, size, and province. Generally, it might
be noted that hostel and mixed developments tended to be larger than self-
contained developments. In Canada as a whole, there were only four hostel
developments and no mixed developments with 20 beds or less, whereas 145
self-contained developments were in this category. Of the large developments in excess of 150 dwelling units and/or beds, 11 were self-contained
developments, 12 were hostel developments, and 11 were mixed developments.
Fifteen of the 34 largest developments were in Ontario.

TABLE 7

LOCATION OF NHA FINANCED NON-PROFIT DEVELOPMENTS FOR THE ELDERLY BY ACCOMMODATION TYPE AND SIZE

	SIZE[1]	METROPOLITAN AREAS[2]	MAJOR URBAN AREAS[2]	SMALL TOWNS[2]	TOTAL
Self-Contained	1	20	6	119	145
Developments	2	28	2	25	55
	3	39	5	13	57
	4	30	0	3	33
	5	11	0	0	11
Hostel	1	2	0	2	4
Developments	2	4	0	23	27
	3	4	2	35	41
	4	14	2	9	25
	5	8	0	4	12
Mixed	1	0	0	0	0
Developments	2	1	0	20	21
	3	3	3	65	71
	4	4	2	11	17
	5	9	0	2	11
ALL DEVELOPMENTS	1	22	6	121	149
	2	33	2	68	103
	3	46	10	113	169
	4	48	4	23	75
	5	28	0	6	34

1 Size categories: (1) 20 or less (2) 21-40 (3) 41-80 (4) 81-149
                     (5) 150+

2 Statistics Canada census categories.

Note that the count was only for units in self-contained developments, beds in hostel developments, units and beds combined in the mixed developments and "all developments" columns.

47

TABLE 8

NHA FINANCED PUBLIC HOUSING DEVELOPMENTS FOR THE ELDERLY, LOCATION BY ACCOMMODATION TYPE AND SIZE

	SIZE[1]	METROPOLITAN AREAS[2]	MAJOR URBAN AREAS[2]	SMALL TOWNS[2]	TOTAL
Self-Contained	1	10	4	81	95
Developments	2	11	9	30	50
	3	10	13	7	30
	4	12	3	5	20
	5	17	1	0	18
Hostel	1	0	0	0	0
Developments	2	0	0	0	0
	3	0	0	0	0
	4	0	0	0	0
	5	0	0	0	0
Mixed	1	0	0	0	0
Developments	2	0	0	0	0
	3	0	0	0	0
	4	0	0	0	0
	5	3	0	0	3
ALL DEVELOPMENTS	1	10	4	81	95
	2	11	9	30	50
	3	10	13	7	30
	4	12	3	5	20
	5	20	1	0	21

1 Size categories: (1) 20 or less (2) 21-40 (3) 41-80 (4) 81-149 (5) 150+

2 Statistics Canada census categories.

Note that the count was only for units in self-contained developments, beds in hostel developments, units and beds combined in the mixed developments and "all developments" columns.

TABLE 9

CANADA, NON-PROFIT HOUSING DEVELOPMENTS BY ACCOMMODATION TYPE AND SIZE

PROVINCE	SIZE*:	SELF-CONTAINED					HOSTEL					MIXED					TOTAL				
		1	2	3	4	5	1	2	3	4	5	1	2	3	4	5	1	2	3	4	5
Nfld.		0	0	1	0	0	0	1	0	1	0	0	0	0	1	0	0	1	1	2	0
P.E.I.		16	1	2	0	0	0	0	2	1	0	0	0	0	0	0	16	1	4	1	0
N.S.		1	1	1	0	0	0	0	2	2	0	0	0	0	1	1	1	1	3	3	1
N.B.		4	0	0	0	0	0	2	5	0	1	0	0	1	0	0	4	2	6	0	1
Quebec		0	1	1	5	0	0	10	9	3	0	0	11	48	8	3	0	22	58	16	3
Ontario		35	10	16	9	10	0	0	5	4	4	0	1	0	0	1	35	11	21	13	15
Manitoba		34	14	9	5	0	0	1	5	7	4	0	1	2	3	2	34	16	16	15	6
Sask.		23	2	1	0	0	0	8	9	2	0	0	8	18	4	3	23	18	28	6	3
Alberta		0	0	2	0	0	1	0	1	0	0	0	0	0	0	0	1	0	3	0	0
B.C.		32	26	24	14	1	3	5	3	5	3	0	0	2	0	1	35	31	29	19	5
N.W.T.		0	0	0	0	0	0	0	0	0	0	0	0	0	0	0	0	0	0	0	0
CANADA		145	55	57	33	11	4	27	41	25	12	0	21	71	17	11	149	103	169	75	34

* Size categories: (1) 20 or less (2) 21-40 (3) 41-80 (4) 81-149 (5) 150+

Note that the count was only for units in self-contained developments, beds in hostel developments, units and beds combined in the mixed developments and "all developments" columns.

Table 10 provides a similar breakdown for the public housing sector; 95 (44 per cent) of the developments had 20 units or less, and 17 of the 21 developments in the largest size category of 150 units and/or beds or more were located in Ontario.

TABLE 10

CANADA, PUBLIC HOUSING DEVELOPMENTS BY ACCOMMODATION TYPE AND SIZE

PROVINCE SIZE[1]:	SELF-CONTAINED					MIXED					TOTAL				
	1	2	3	4	5	1	2	3	4	5	1	2	3	4	5
Nfld.	1	0	0	0	0	0	0	0	0	0	1	0	0	0	0
P.E.I.	0	0	0	0	0	0	0	0	0	0	0	0	0	0	0
N.S.	8	4	0	0	1	0	0	0	0	0	8	4	0	0	1
N.B.	12	1	0	0	0	0	0	0	0	0	12	1	0	0	0
Quebec	0	0	0	0	0	0	0	0	0	0	0	0	0	0	0
Ontario	60	41	27	16	14	0	0	0	0	3	60	41	27	16	17
Manitoba	3	0	2	1	0	0	0	0	0	0	3	0	2	1	0
Sask.	8	2	0	1	0	0	0	0	0	0	8	2	0	1	0
Alberta	0	0	0	0	0	0	0	0	0	0	0	0	0	0	0
B.C.	1	2	1	2	3	0	0	0	0	0	1	2	1	2	3
N.W.T.	2	0	0	0	0	0	0	0	0	0	2	0	0	0	0
CANADA	95	50	30	20	18	0	0	0	0	3	95	50	30	20	21

1 Size categories: (1) 20 or less (2) 21-40 (3) 41-80
(4) 81-149 (5) 150

Note that there were no public housing hostel developments.

Ratio of Hostel Beds to Dwelling Units

The ratios of hostel beds to dwelling units in NHA financed housing for the elderly are shown in Table 11. There were .3 hostel beds per dwelling unit in Canada as a whole at the end of 1970. New Brunswick had the highest ratio (2.8), followed by Quebec (1.6), Saskatchewan (1.5), Newfoundland (1.4), Alberta (.8), Manitoba (.8), Nova Scotia (.6), and British Columbia and Prince Edward Island (.3). Ontario had the lowest ratio of hostel beds to dwelling units, with only .1 hostel beds per dwelling unit.

As there were only 239 hostel beds built by public housing agencies as part of three mixed Ontario developments, there was an insignificant ratio of hostel beds to dwelling units in the public housing sector. However, when the non-profit sector is considered by itself, the country as a whole had .6 hostel beds per dwelling unit with the provinces arranged in the following order: New Brunswick 9.6; Nova Scotia 4.3; Saskatchewan 2.4; Newfoundland 1.7; Quebec 1.6; Manitoba .9; Alberta .8; Ontario, British Columbia and Prince Edward Island .3.

TABLE 11

RATIO OF NHA FINANCED HOSTEL BEDS TO DWELLING UNITS BY PROVINCE AND SPONSOR TYPE

	DWELLING UNITS	HOSTEL BEDS	RATIO OF HOSTEL BEDS TO DWELLING UNITS
Newfoundland			
Public	16	0	0
Non-Profit	70	122	1.7
TOTAL	86	122	1.4
Prince Edward Island			
Public	0	0	0
Non-Profit	227	62	.3
TOTAL	227	62	.3
Nova Scotia			
Public	556	0	0
Non-Profit	86	372	4.3
TOTAL	642	372	.6
New Brunswick			
Public	157	0	0
Non-Profit	64	616	9.6
TOTAL	221	616	2.8
Quebec			
Public	0	0	0
Non-Profit	710	1,160	1.6
TOTAL	710	1,160	1.6
Ontario			
Public	8,992	239	*
Non-Profit	5,382	1,414	.3
TOTAL	14,374	1,653	.1
Manitoba			
Public	253	0	0
Non-Profit	1,898	1,640	.9
TOTAL	2,151	1,640	.8
Saskatchewan			
Public	259	0	0
Non-Profit	419	991	2.4
TOTAL	678	991	1.5
Alberta			
Public	0	0	0
Non-Profit	104	82	.8
TOTAL	104	82	.8
British Columbia			
Public	901	0	0
Non-Profit	3,860	1,210	.3
TOTAL	4,761	1,210	.3
Northwest Territories			
Public	25	0	0
Non-Profit	0	0	0
TOTAL	25	0	0
CANADA			
Public	11,159	239	*
Non-Profit	12,820	7,669	.6
TOTAL	23,979	7,908	.3

* Less than .1

CHAPTER 3

NEWFOUNDLAND

The 32,100 persons aged 65 and over in Newfoundland at the time of the 1971 census had available 86 dwelling units and 122 hostel beds, financed under provisions of the National Housing Act by the end of 1970. This provided the province with 2.7 dwelling units per thousand elderly people, compared with 13.7 in Canada as a whole, and 3.8 hostel beds per thousand elderly persons, compared with 4.5 in Canada as a whole.

Public Housing Legislation

The Newfoundland and Labrador Housing Corporation was responsible, under terms of An Act to Incorporate the Newfoundland and Labrador Housing Corporation passed in 1967, for the development and management of public housing in the province. In 1970, the corporation reported to the Minister Responsible for Fisheries, Community and Social Development and Housing. Until the end of 1970, the corporation concentrated on building family accommodation, although 16 units specifically designated for senior citizens were built in two public housing developments mainly occupied by families.

Non-Profit Housing

Under terms of the Senior Citizens Housing Act, the provincial government was authorized to guarantee the repayment of loans made to non-profit groups under terms of NHA Section 16. The province could also make direct loans to housing associations developing and managing accommodation under terms of the Housing Association Loans Act. Under the Local Government Act, properties owned and used by charitable institutions (including non-profit housing associations) are exempt from municipal taxes.

Supplementary Programs

In 1970 the Department of Public Welfare accommodated 301 persons in 21 supervised boarding homes run by private operators. The department licensed and supervised the accommodation and, under terms of the Social Assistance Act, provided a boarding home allowance not exceeding $75 for an ambulatory elderly person and $100 a month for a bedridden one.

The provincial government also maintained an institution for the aged and infirm known as Hoyle's Home. This was administered under the Homes for the Aged and Infirm Act and accommodated 221 persons. In addition, the Newfoundland government had from time to time made special grants available toward the provision of accommodation for the elderly. For example, in 1956, the Department of Finance started making annual capital grants of $30,000 a year (to continue over a 10-year period) toward the construction of St. Patrick's Nursing Home operated by the Roman Catholic Episcopal Corporation. The government also announced that it would make other grants amounting to 20 per cent of construction costs for other such special care accommodation.

Statistics

By the end of 1970, public housing agencies in Newfoundland had built 16 housing units for senior citizens. These units were financed under the National Housing Act. During the same period of time the non-profit sector had built 70 units and 122 hostel beds. Table 12 indicates the sponsorship of developments in Newfoundland by type of accommodation.

TABLE 12

NEWFOUNDLAND DEVELOPMENTS BY SPONSOR AND ACCOMMODATION TYPES

	PUBLIC HOUSING	NON-PROFIT	TOTAL
Self-Contained	1	1	2
Hostel	0	2	2
Mixed	0	1	1
TOTAL	1	4	5

In Table 13, it is apparent that two of the three developments for which sponsorship information was available had been built by church groups.

TABLE 13

NEWFOUNDLAND DEVELOPMENTS, ACCOMMODATION TYPE BY SPONSOR GROUPS

	SELF-CONTAINED	HOSTEL	MIXED	TOTAL
Church	0	1	1	2
Province*	1	0	0	1
No information	1	1	0	2
TOTAL	2	2	1	5

* Public housing.

53

The size range of developments in Newfoundland can be seen in Table 14.
It seems that none of the five developments in the province had more than
150 units or beds.

TABLE 14

NEWFOUNDLAND DEVELOPMENTS BY SPONSOR TYPE, ACCOMMODATION TYPE AND SIZE

SIZE*	PUBLIC HOUSING			NON-PROFIT			TOTAL
	SELF-CONTAINED	HOSTEL	MIXED	SELF-CONTAINED	HOSTEL	MIXED	
1-20	1	0	0	0	0	0	1
21-40	0	0	0	0	1	0	1
41-80	0	0	0	1	0	0	1
81-149	0	0	0	0	1	1	2
150 +	0	0	0	0	0	0	0
TOTAL	1	0	0	1	2	1	5

* Note that the count was for only units in self-contained developments,
beds in hostel developments, units and beds combined in mixed
developments and the total column.

Table 15, which indicates the location of Newfoundland developments, shows
that four of the five developments were located in St. John's, the largest
proportion located in a metropolitan census area in any province.

TABLE 15

NEWFOUNDLAND DEVELOPMENTS, LOCATION BY SPONSOR TYPE

	PUBLIC HOUSING	NON-PROFIT	TOTAL
Metropolitan Areas	0	4	4
Major Urban Areas	0	0	0
Small Towns	1	0	1
TOTAL	1	4	5

CHAPTER 4

PRINCE EDWARD ISLAND

The 12,300 persons aged 65 and over in Prince Edward Island at the time of the 1971 census had available 227 dwelling units and 62 hostel beds financed under provisions of the National Housing Act by the end of 1970. This provided the province with 18.4 dwelling units per thousand elderly people, compared with 13.7 in Canada as a whole, and 5.0 hostel beds per thousand elderly persons, the Canadian norm being 4.5.

Public Housing Legislation

Prince Edward Island Housing Authority, established in 1966, was responsible for public housing. In 1969 it took over the responsibilities of the Senior Citizens Housing Corporation and the Prince Edward Island Housing Commission for building accommodation for senior citizens. The Prince Edward Island Housing Authority was empowered to enter into agreements with the federal government under the NHA public housing sections; however, by 1970, it had only done so in respect to family accommodation.

The Prince Edward Island Housing Authority had chosen to build housing for the elderly in the province by borrowing funds under NHA section 16, as if the housing authority were a non-profit corporation. Housing built by this agency for old people has therefore been classified in the non-profit sector, even though in most respects it conforms to accommodation built by provincial housing corporations in other provinces.

Non-Profit Housing

Prince Edward Island had no specific legislation to provide grants or rent subsidies to non-profit community groups for building housing for the elderly. However, as outlined above, the Prince Edward Island Housing Authority (the provincial government's housing agency) had chosen to build housing accommodation for the elderly throughout the Island by using the NHA section 16.

Supplementary Programs

A number of "special care homes" had been built in addition to self-contained developments for senior citizens. Although the construction of this accommodation was carried out by the Prince Edward Island Housing Authority, the management and administration was the responsibility of the Department of Health and Welfare.

Under terms of the Welfare Assistance Act, maintenance allowances could be paid for residents of licensed nursing homes and homes for the aged, hostels for transients, and other institutions offering residential or rehabilitative accommodation.

Statistics

All the 227 dwelling units and 62 hostel beds in Prince Edward Island
were financed under NHA non-profit arrangements although, as noted above,
the Prince Edward Island Housing Authority (the government's housing
agency) actually built most of them. This accommodation was grouped
in 22 developments, as indicated in Table 16. Three of the developments
contained strictly hostel accommodation and the remainder were self-
contained. Table 17 indicates that again all the senior citizens
developments in the province were built under provincial government
sponsorship.

TABLE 16

PRINCE EDWARD ISLAND DEVELOPMENTS BY SPONSOR AND
ACCOMMODATION TYPES

	PUBLIC HOUSING	NON-PROFIT	TOTAL
Self-Contained	0	19	19
Hostel	0	3	3
Mixed	0	0	0
TOTAL	0	22	22

TABLE 17

PRINCE EDWARD ISLAND DEVELOPMENTS, ACCOMMODATION TYPE BY
SPONSOR GROUPS

	SELF-CONTAINED	HOSTEL	MIXED	TOTAL
Provincial	19	3	0	22
Other	0	0	0	0
TOTAL	19	3	0	22

The size range of developments in Prince Edward Island can be seen in
Table 18. A strong bias toward self-contained developments with 20 units
or less will be noticed in Table 19, with 16 of the Island's 22 developments in this category. Table 19 shows that all 22 were located in
small communities, there being no census metropolitan or major urban
areas in the province.

TABLE 18

PRINCE EDWARD ISLAND DEVELOPMENTS, BY SPONSOR TYPE, ACCOMMODATION TYPE AND SIZE

SIZE*	PUBLIC HOUSING			NON-PROFIT			TOTAL
	SELF-CONTAINED	HOSTEL	MIXED	SELF-CONTAINED	HOSTEL	MIXED	
1-20	0	0	0	16	0	0	16
21-40	0	0	0	1	0	0	1
41-80	0	0	0	2	2	0	4
81-149	0	0	0	0	1	0	1
150+	0	0	0	0	0	0	0
TOTAL	0	0	0	19	3	0	22

* Note that the count was only for units in self-contained developments, beds
  in hostel developments, units and beds combined in mixed developments, and
  the total column.

TABLE 19

PRINCE EDWARD ISLAND DEVELOPMENTS, LOCATION BY SPONSOR

	PUBLIC HOUSING	NON-PROFIT	TOTAL
Metropolitan Areas	0	0	0
Major Urban Areas	0	0	0
Small Towns	0	22	22
TOTAL	0	22	22

CHAPTER 5

NOVA SCOTIA

The 72,500 persons aged 65 and over in Nova Scotia at the time of the 1971 census had available 642 dwelling units and 372 hostel beds financed under provisions of the National Housing Act by the end of 1970. This provided the province with 8.9 dwelling units per thousand elderly people, compared with 13.7 in Canada as a whole, and 5.1 hostel beds per thousand elderly people, compared with the Canadian norm of 4.5.

Public Housing Legislation

Under terms of the Housing Development Act, the Nova Scotia Housing Commission had been given over-all responsibility for the development and management of public housing in the province. It was empowered to enter into agreements with the federal government to obtain funds under either NHA section 35A or 35D but, prior to 1970, the development of public housing under the federal-provincial NHA section 35A partnership appeared to be the preferred arrangement.

The Nova Scotia Housing Commission is responsible to the member of the Executive Council who is charged with the administration of the Housing Development Act by the Governor-in-Council. Housing projects were managed on a day-to-day basis by local or regional housing authorities.

Non-Profit Housing

The Nova Scotia Housing Commission may advance or lend moneys, or guarantee moneys loaned to persons, companies, corporations or groups for the purpose of constructing housing accommodation of all types including cooperative multiple housing, or acquiring and rehabilitating housing units.

Supplementary Programs

The Department of Public Health could make grants of up to $3,000 per bed for one-third of the beds constructed in custodial or nursing care homes. In addition, the Department of Public Welfare could pay two-thirds of the maintenance costs of persons placed in such accommodation by a welfare official.

Municipal homes for the aged could be established with the approval of the Minister of Public Welfare. In 1970, there were 13 municipal homes operating in Nova Scotia, with a total bed capacity of 600 persons.

Statistics

By the end of 1970, public housing agencies had built 556 units of NHA financed housing for the elderly in Nova Scotia and the non-profit sector had built 86 dwelling units and 372 hostel beds. This accommodation was situated in 22 developments divided by sponsor and accommodation type, as indicated in Table 20. As in practically all other provinces, public housing agencies had only built self-contained developments, while the non-profit groups built a range of developments of different types of accommodation.

TABLE 20

NOVA SCOTIA DEVELOPMENTS, BY SPONSOR AND ACCOMMODATION TYPES

	PUBLIC HOUSING	NON-PROFIT	TOTAL
Self-Contained	13	3	16
Hostel	0	4	4
Mixed	0	2	2
TOTAL	13	9	22

Table 21 details the activities of individual sponsor groups in Nova Scotia. As information was lacking about the sponsorship of five of the nine developments in the non-profit sector, little can be validly said about the sponsorship pattern, except perhaps to note that we were unable to identify any developments in the province that had been sponsored by service clubs.

TABLE 21

NOVA SCOTIA DEVELOPMENTS, ACCOMMODATION TYPE BY SPONSOR GROUPS

	SELF-CONTAINED	HOSTEL	MIXED	TOTAL
Churches	0	1	0	1
Municipalities	0	1	1	2
Province[1]	13	0	0	13
Other[2]	0	0	1	1
No Information	3	2	0	5
TOTAL	16	4	2	22

1 Public housing.

2 Includes private entrepreneurs, mixture of other groups and special corporations.

The size range of developments in Nova Scotia is shown in Table 22. It will be noticed that there was good representation in all five size categories.

TABLE 22

NOVA SCOTIA DEVELOPMENTS, BY SPONSOR, ACCOMMODATION TYPE AND SIZE

SIZE*	PUBLIC HOUSING			NON-PROFIT			TOTAL
	SELF-CONTAINED	HOSTEL	MIXED	SELF-CONTAINED	HOSTEL	MIXED	
1-20	8	0	0	1	0	0	9
21-40	4	0	0	1	0	0	5
41-80	0	0	0	1	2	0	3
81-149	0	0	0	0	2	1	3
150+	1	0	0	0	0	1	2
TOTAL	13	0	0	3	4	2	22

* Note that the count was only for units in self-contained developments, beds in hostel developments, units and beds combined in mixed developments, and the total column.

Table 23, which indicates the location of Nova Scotia developments, shows the concentration of effort in housing the elderly to have been in small communities - 14 of the 22 developments having been built in small towns. Surprisingly, only two of the total had been built in Halifax, the largest city in the Atlantic Provinces.

TABLE 23

NOVA SCOTIA DEVELOPMENTS, LOCATION BY SPONSOR TYPE

	PUBLIC HOUSING	NON-PROFIT	TOTAL
Metropolitan Areas	1	1	2
Major Urban Areas	4	2	6
Small Towns	8	6	14
TOTAL	13	9	22

CHAPTER 6

NEW BRUNSWICK

The 54,700 persons aged 65 and over in New Brunswick at the time of the 1971
census had available 221 dwelling units and 616 hostel beds financed under
provisions of the National Housing Act by the end of 1970. This provided the
province with 4.0 dwelling units per thousand elderly people, compared with
13.7 in Canada as a whole, and 11.3 hostel beds per thousand elderly people -
the Canadian norm being 4.5.

Public Housing Legislation

Public housing in New Brunswick was developed by the New Brunswick Housing
Corporation, under terms of the New Brunswick Housing Act. The legislation
permitted the provincial government to enter into agreements with CMHC and
municipalities for both family and senior citizens housing. Although public
housing was previously built jointly with the federal government under NHA
section 35A, by 1970, the province had switched to use of section 35D in
order to lessen the amount of initial provincial investment. The province
itself provides the 10 per cent equity needed to match the 90 per cent
federal loan and pays 45 per cent of the operating deficits of public
housing, except in "designated growth areas" where the province pays 50
per cent.

By 1970, the New Brunswick Housing Corporation was attempting to coordinate
public housing with regional development plans and economic growth programs.
For instance, according to provincial criteria, public housing for senior
citizens may only be built in municipalities with hospitals and "auxiliary
homes."

Public housing was managed on behalf of the New Brunswick Housing Corporation by a full- or part-time manager (frequently the official who acted
as the provincial government's agent in the district) with only tenant
selection and evictions devolved to local housing authorities.

Non-Profit Housing

The Senior Citizens Housing Act, administered by the Minister of Health
and Welfare, enabled the provincial government to make grants (to non-
profit corporations for the construction of self-contained dwelling units)
of up to $500 a dwelling or 50 per cent of the capital costs of the project,
whichever was less (exclusive of the CMHC loan).

Under terms of the Auxiliary Home Act, administered by the Minister of
Finance and Industry, the provincial government could make grants in the
amount of $2,000 a bed or 50 per cent of the equity required to non-profit
sponsors for "auxiliary homes." (Auxiliary homes include nursing homes
and residences for disabled, infirm and aged persons).

Supplementary Programs

Tax relief was available to non-profit housing corporations through two statutes. The Social Service and Education Act permitted the provincial secretary to rebate the sales tax on goods used in the construction of housing for the elderly and an exemption from municipal taxation was possible under the Municipal Tax Act.

Non-profit homes for the elderly might also be paid allowances for the maintenance costs of residents under the Social Allowances Act. In addition, a system of municipal homes for the infirm and elderly existed under the supervision of the Department of Welfare.

Statistics

At the end of 1970, 157 dwelling units had been built by New Brunswick public housing sponsors and 64 dwelling units and 616 hostel beds by the non-profit sector. This accommodation was situated in 26 developments, divided by sponsor and accommodation type, as indicated in Table 24. As in practically all other provinces, public housing agencies built exclusively self-contained accommodation while non-profit groups built self-contained, hostel and mixed developments.

TABLE 24

NEW BRUNSWICK DEVELOPMENTS BY SPONSOR AND
ACCOMMODATION TYPE

	PUBLIC HOUSING	NON-PROFIT	TOTAL
Self-Contained	13	4	17
Hostel	0	8	8
Mixed	0	1	1
TOTAL	13	13	26

Table 25 details the activities of the individual sponsor groups in New Brunswick. Disregarding developments for which information was not available and the 13 public housing developments, it will be noticed that the service clubs had been particularly active in the non-profit sector: they sponsored five of the remaining eight developments.

TABLE 25

NEW BRUNSWICK DEVELOPMENTS, ACCOMMODATION TYPE BY
SPONSOR GROUPS

	SELF-CONTAINED	HOSTEL	MIXED	TOTAL
Service Clubs	4	1	0	5
Churches	0	1	0	1
Municipalities	0	1	0	1
Province[1]	13	0	0	13
Other[2]	0	1	0	1
No Information	0	4	1	5
TOTAL	17	8	1	26

1 Public housing.

2 Includes private entrepreneurs, mixture of other
   groups and special corporations.

The size range of developments in New Brunswick can be seen in Table 26.
It will be noticed that practically all the public housing developments
contained 20 units or less. It is also interesting to note that of the
26 total developments in the province, only one contained over 80 units
or beds.

TABLE 26

NEW BRUNSWICK DEVELOPMENTS, BY SPONSOR TYPE, ACCOMMODATION TYPE AND SIZE

SIZE*	PUBLIC HOUSING			NON-PROFIT			TOTAL
	SELF-CONTAINED	HOSTEL	MIXED	SELF-CONTAINED	HOSTEL	MIXED	
1-20	12	0	0	4	0	0	16
21-40	1	0	0	0	2	0	3
41-80	0	0	0	0	5	1	6
81-149	0	0	0	0	0	0	0
150+	0	0	0	0	1	0	1
TOTAL	13	0	0	4	8	1	26

* Note that the count was only for units in self-contained developments,
   beds in hostel developments, units and beds combined in mixed developments
   and the total column.

Table 27, which indicates the location of New Brunswick developments, shows the strong bias toward small communities; 21 of the 26 developments in the province were located in small towns. Saint John, the only metropolitan area in the province, had three developments.

TABLE 27

NEW BRUNSWICK DEVELOPMENTS, LOCATION BY SPONSOR TYPE

	PUBLIC HOUSING	NON-PROFIT	TOTAL
Metropolitan Areas	1	2	3
Major Urban Areas	1	1	2
Small Towns	11	10	21
TOTAL	13	13	26

CHAPTER 7

QUEBEC

The 413,000 persons aged 65 and over in Quebec at the time of the 1971 census had available 710 dwelling units and 1,160 hostel beds financed under provisions of the National Housing Act by the end of 1970. This provided the province with 1.7 dwelling units per thousand elderly people, compared with 13.7 in Canada as a whole, and 2.8 hostel beds per thousand elderly people, compared with 4.5 for Canada as a whole.

Public and Non-Profit Housing

In the province of Quebec, a unique combination of public housing and non-profit sponsorship exists. Prior to the creation of the Quebec Housing Corporation in 1967, a number of non-profit developments were built with loans under NHA section 16, but without provincial government financial support. In 1970, CMHC started making an annual allocation of funds to the Quebec Housing Corporation for building accommodation for families and senior citizens. In the case of family housing, the Quebec Housing Corporation finances developments proposed by local offices municipaux, bodies that serve as housing authorities. However, by the end of 1970, accommodation for the elderly had not been built by offices municipaux; instead, non-profit corporations sponsored by religious orders, municipalities and service clubs carried out this work. They would submit applications to the QHC to obtain 100 per cent capital financing.

Rent subsidies for QHC financed developments for the elderly are available from the Department of Social Affairs. In 1971, the rent scales established by the department assured that every resident had, after payment of his rent, a minimum of $31 a month for personal expenses. Residents were required to pay 50 per cent of their income above the old age security pension and guaranteed income supplement for rent. In addition, the Department of Social Affairs reimbursed the sponsors of any senior citizens developments for any deficits that still existed after rents had been paid according to this formula.

The QHC, the provincial public housing agency, played a very active role in providing accommodation for the elderly. However, since the funds for its activities were made available through NHA section 16 and the managing groups are other than those that managed family public housing, the statistical section of this profile includes QHC accommodation for the aged in the non-profit sector.

An important piece of legislation that will ultimately effect new citizens housing developments in Quebec is Bill 65, An Act Respecting Health and Social Services, passed by the National Assembly in 1971. The legislation provides for the establishment of regional health and social service councils throughout the province charged with the responsibility of encouraging the

community to define its social and health needs, coordinating and
establishing priorities and planning. The councils will regulate and
supervise charitable institutions within their territory, presumably
including non-profit housing sponsors. The legislation provides that
the board of directors for a "reception centre" (such as a non-profit
housing development) shall consist of two residents, two government-
appointed members representative of local social and economic groups,
one member elected by non-professionals in the centre, one member
jointly appointed by the hospitals in the area, and one member elected
by local social service agencies. When the "reception centre" is
maintained by a non-profit corporation, two additional directors may
be elected from the corporation. This legislation obviously has
implications for the future of non-profit developments and is illus-
trative of the Quebec government's interest in diminishing the barriers
between public and voluntary agencies in the social service and health
fields.

Statistics

By the end of 1970, 710 dwelling units and 1,160 hostel beds had been
built in Quebec. This accommodation was situated in 99 developments as
indicated in Table 28. As mentioned earlier in this profile, all the
developments built with Quebec Housing Corporation assistance have been
categorized in the non-profit sector since CMHC has not compiled these
developments in their own public housing statistics and they are, in
fact, administered by non-profit groups.

An interesting factor in Table 28, however, is the predominance of mixed
developments: the 70 mixed developments out of a total of 99 constituted
by far the highest proportion for any province. However, many of the
developments in the mixed category consist largely of hostel accommodation with usually four or five self-contained units. In some cases,
these units actually have been occupied by staff.

TABLE 28

QUEBEC DEVELOPMENTS BY SPONSOR AND ACCOMMODATION TYPE

	PUBLIC HOUSING	NON-PROFIT	TOTAL
Self-Contained	0	7	7
Hostel	0	22	22
Mixed	0	70	70
TOTAL	0	99	99

CHAPTER 8

ONTARIO

The 644,400 persons aged 65 and over in Ontario at the time of the 1971 census had available 14,374 dwelling units and 1,653 hostel beds financed under provisions of the National Housing Act by the end of 1970. This provided the province with 22.3 dwelling units per thousand elderly people, compared with 13.7 in Canada as a whole, and 2.6 hostel beds per thousand elderly people, compared with 4.5 for Canada as a whole.

Public Housing Legislation

The Ontario Housing Development Act enabled the provincial government and municipalities to enter into agreements with the Central Mortgage and Housing Corporation to use NHA sections 35A and 35D. By 1970, however, the Ontario Housing Corporation used only the section 35D loan arrangement. Under this arrangement it provided the full 10 per cent non-federal equity and bore $42\frac{1}{2}$ per cent of the operating deficits. The federal government (under NHA section 35E) bore 50 per cent of the operating deficits and the municipality, the remaining $7\frac{1}{2}$ per cent. This has been the formula for family public housing but in the case of senior citizens units, the province gave municipalities an option: either OHC would pay the entire 50 per cent non-federal share of the operating subsidy (with the municipality claiming taxes not in excess of $25 a unit), or the province could use the formula for family accommodation.

When this study was done, the Ontario Housing Corporation had only built developments specifically designated for senior citizens outside Metropolitan Toronto. These developments are managed either directly by the corporation or by one of Ontario's approximately 40 local housing authorities. In Metro Toronto, the Metropolitan Toronto Housing Company, a non-profit corporation, had been building housing for the elderly under NHA section 16 for a number of years. In 1966 it started using the NHA section 35D public housing arrangement, but it bore the full 10 per cent non-federal capital cost and the entire 50 per cent non-federal operating subsidy. The only provincial government assistance it received was a $500 capital grant per unit. The Metropolitan Toronto Housing Company was directed by the commissioner of the Housing Department of Metropolitan Toronto, who was also responsible for a housing registry and the operation of homes for the aged.

In February 1973, the Oakville Senior Citizens' Residence was opened - a joint project of the Ontario Housing Corporation and the Ontario Ministry of Community and Social Services. This 164 dwelling unit and 173 hostel room complex was built by the OHC and managed under the direction of a board of directors, three of whom were appointed by the Minister Responsible for OHC, three by the Minister of Community and Social Services, and the seventh being the chairman of a county home for the aged. This development, which included an infirmary, might be the predecessor of a new form of accommodation for the elderly in the public housing sector.

Non-Profit Housing

Under terms of the Elderly Persons Housing Aid Act, the provincial government may make grants of $500 a unit for the capital cost of non-profit
housing projects for the elderly as long as these projects are financed
with NHA section 16 loans. The Elderly Persons Housing Aid Act, originally
administered by the Homes for the Aged Branch of the Department of Welfare,
recently came under the Ontario Housing Corporation.

Supplementary Programs

The Homes for the Aged Act requires every municipality to provide care for
infirm or old people in a proper home. Homes for the aged have been built
throughout Ontario with the assistance of grants from the Department of
Social and Family Services. These grants do not exceed 50 per cent of
the capital cost.

The Charitable Institutions Act provides that capital grants of $2,500 per
bed or 50 per cent of the construction cost, whichever is less, may be
made by the provincial Department of Social and Family Services to homes
for the aged operated by voluntary bodies. NHA section 16 loans may meet
as much of the remaining costs as the federal government will allow. In
addition, maintenance grants are also available from the provincial government.

Statistics

The 8,992 dwelling units and 239 hostel beds built by public housing agencies
in Ontario and the 5,382 dwelling units and 1,414 hostel beds built by
non-profit groups were situated in 256 developments, as outlined in Table
32. Perhaps the most surprising aspect of the NHA financed housing for the
elderly in Ontario was the overwhelming predominance of self-contained
developments, both in public and non-profit housing. The table indicates
that 238 (or 93 per cent) of the developments provided only self-contained
dwelling units. Other provinces generally had a broader mix of accommodation.

TABLE 32

ONTARIO DEVELOPMENTS, BY SPONSOR AND ACCOMMODATION TYPE

	PUBLIC HOUSING	NON-PROFIT	TOTAL
Self-Contained	158	80	238
Hostel	0	13	13
Mixed	3	2	5
TOTAL	161	95	256

Table 33 details the activities of individual sponsor groups in Ontario. The provincial government is obviously the greatest sponsor, with 172 separate developments. These are built and managed mainly by the Ontario Housing Corporation. The provincial government is followed by municipalities with 47 developments and service clubs with 18. Approximately 32 of the municipally sponsored developments were in Toronto, a result of the Metropolitan Toronto Housing Company's activities.

TABLE 33

ONTARIO DEVELOPMENTS, ACCOMMODATION TYPE BY SPONSOR GROUPS

	SELF-CONTAINED	HOSTEL	MIXED	TOTAL
Ethnic Groups	0	2	0	2
Service Clubs	17	1	0	18
Churches	3	1	0	4
Municipalities*	43	1	3	47
Province*	171	0	1	172
No Information	4	8	1	13
TOTAL	238	13	5	256

* Includes public housing.

The size range of developments in Ontario may be seen in Table 34. It will be noticed that all size categories are well represented and that while developments with 20 units or less accounted for 95 or 37 per cent of the total, the size category with 150 and over units and beds accounted for 32 developments or 13 per cent of the total. There did not appear to be a significant difference between the size range of public housing and non-profit developments.

Table 35 reveals that even in a province as highly urbanized as Ontario, 114 (45 per cent) of all developments were situated in small towns.

TABLE 34

ONTARIO DEVELOPMENTS, BY SPONSOR TYPE, ACCOMMODATION TYPE AND SIZE

SIZE*	PUBLIC HOUSING			NON-PROFIT			TOTAL
	SELF-CONTAINED	HOSTEL	MIXED	SELF-CONTAINED	HOSTEL	MIXED	
1-20	60	0	0	35	0	0	95
21-40	41	0	0	10	0	1	52
41-80	27	0	0	16	5	0	48
81-149	16	0	0	9	4	0	29
150+	14	0	3	10	4	1	32
TOTAL	158	0	3	80	13	2	256

* Note that the count was only for units in self-contained developments, beds in hostel developments, units and beds combined in mixed developments, and the total column.

TABLE 35

ONTARIO DEVELOPMENTS, LOCATION BY SPONSOR TYPE

	PUBLIC HOUSING	NON-PROFIT	TOTAL
Metropolitan Areas	49	51	100
Major Urban Areas	30	12	42
Small Towns	82	32	114
TOTAL	161	95	256

CHAPTER 9

MANITOBA

The 95,600 persons aged 65 years and over in Manitoba at the time of the
1971 census had available 2,151 dwelling units and 1,640 hostel beds
financed under provisions of the National Housing Act by the end of 1970.
This provided the province with 22.5 dwelling units per thousand elderly
people, compared with 13.7 in Canada as a whole, and 17.2 hostel beds per
thousand elderly people, compared with the Canadian norm of 4.5.

Public Housing Legislation

Public housing in Manitoba was built under terms of the Manitoba Housing
and Renewal Corporation Act administered by the Manitoba Housing Corporation. This legislation provided for the development of public housing
either through joint action with the federal government (under NHA section
35A), or by means of loans under NHA section 35D. The practice of the
Manitoba Housing Corporation had been to require 50 per cent municipal
cost-sharing of capital costs and annual subsidies for public housing.
In 1970, however, the legislation was amended so that there would be no
municipal contribution.

Public housing was managed by local housing authorities, with rents set
according to the CMHC geared-to-income scale. Until 1970, the legislation
was administered by the Manitoba Department of Health and Social Services.
In 1970, it was transferred to the Manitoba Housing Corporation, which in
turn is responsible to the minister of Municipal Affairs.

Non-Profit Housing

Senior citizens housing sponsored by non-profit groups in Manitoba was
assisted by the provincial government, under terms of the Elderly and
Infirm Persons Act, administered in 1970 by the Department of Health and
Social Development. For housing developments initiated by non-profit
sponsors such as service clubs and municipalities, the province offered a
grant of up to one-third the capital cost or $1,700 a unit for self-contained
bachelor accommodation, and of up to one-third the capital cost or $2,150
a unit for self-contained one-bedroom apartments. Up to one-third the
capital cost or $700 a bed was available for hostel accommodation and
$2,000 a bed could be obtained for "special care accommodation." The
sponsoring organization was required to raise 20 per cent of the capital
cost without incurring debt, or at least 10 per cent of the cost in
addition to a suitable serviced site. The remainder of the capital funds
was generally borrowed under NHA section 16.

Supplementary Programs

Under the Social Allowances Act, the provincial government bears the
entire cost of expenses for those who, because of age, physical or mental
health, or physical or mental incapacity, require care for more than 90
days in a private or non-profit home for the aged and infirm. The province
reclaims 50 per cent of these payments under the Canada Assistance Plan.

Statistics

By the end of 1970, 253 public housing units had been built in Manitoba
for the elderly under the NHA, while non-profit sponsors had built 1,898
dwelling units and provided 1,640 hostel beds. This accommodation was
situated in 93 developments as shown in Table 36. As with all provinces
except Ontario, public housing agencies concentrated on providing self-
contained accommodation, while non-profit sponsors built a reasonable mix
of developments.

TABLE 36

MANITOBA DEVELOPMENTS BY SPONSOR AND ACCOMMODATION TYPES

	PUBLIC HOUSING	NON-PROFIT	TOTAL
Self-Contained	6	62	68
Hostel	0	17	17
Mixed	0	8	8
TOTAL	6	87	93

Table 37 details the activities of individual sponsor groups in Manitoba.
Disregarding the six public housing developments and the 27 developments
for which sponsorship information was not available, the strong activities
of service clubs in this province can be seen. These organizations
sponsored 27 different developments, while ethnic groups sponsored 15
developments and churches, 13.

Table 38 gives the size range of developments in Manitoba. There was a
good representation of all size categories although the smallest (20
units or less) accounted for 37 (or 40 per cent) of all developments.

TABLE 37

MANITOBA DEVELOPMENTS, ACCOMMODATION TYPE BY SPONSOR GROUPS

	SELF-CONTAINED	HOSTEL	MIXED	TOTAL
Ethnic Groups	9	5	1	15
Service Clubs	23	1	3	27
Churches	5	6	2	13
Municipalities	1	2	0	3
Province[1]	6	0	0	6
Other[2]	2	0	0	2
No Information	22	3	2	27
TOTAL	68	17	8	93

1 Public housing.

2 Includes private entrepreneurs, mixture of other groups and special corporations.

TABLE 38

MANITOBA DEVELOPMENTS, BY SPONSOR TYPE, ACCOMMODATION TYPE AND SIZE

SIZE*	PUBLIC HOUSING			NON-PROFIT			TOTAL
	SELF-CONTAINED	HOSTEL	MIXED	SELF-CONTAINED	HOSTEL	MIXED	
1-20	3	0	0	34	0	0	37
21-40	0	0	0	14	1	1	16
41-80	2	0	0	9	5	2	18
81-149	1	0	0	5	7	3	16
150+	0	0	0	0	4	2	6
TOTAL	6	0	0	62	17	8	93

* Note that the count was only for units in self-contained developments, beds in hostel developments, units and beds combined in mixed developments, and the total column.

Table 39, which indicates the location of Manitoba developments, clearly
illustrates the predominance of Winnipeg, the province's only census
metropolitan area. The table indicates that 35 (38 per cent) of the
province's developments were situated in the Winnipeg area, the other 58
being in small towns.

TABLE 39

MANITOBA DEVELOPMENTS, LOCATION BY SPONSOR TYPE

	PUBLIC HOUSING	NON-PROFIT	TOTAL
Metropolitan Areas	3	32	35
Major Urban Areas	0	0	0
Small Towns	3	55	58
TOTAL	6	87	93

CHAPTER 10

SASKATCHEWAN

The 94,800 persons aged 65 and over in Saskatchewan at the time of the
1971 census had available 678 dwelling units and 991 hostel beds financed
under provisions of the National Housing Act by the end of 1970. This
provided the province with 7.2 dwelling units per thousand elderly people,
compared with 13.7 in Canada as a whole, and 10.5 hostel beds per thousand
elderly people, compared with 4.5 for all Canada.

Public Housing Legislation

Until 1970, public housing in Saskatchewan was built jointly by the
federal and provincial governments under terms of NHA section 35E.
Under terms of the Housing and Urban Renewal Act, the provincial government shared 20 per cent of the capital cost and operating losses of public
housing projects, with municipalities paying the remaining 5 per cent.
The province exercized its authority through the director of housing and
urban renewal, an official of the Department of Municipal Affairs, since
Saskatchewan did not have a public housing corporation.

By the end of 1970, public housing legislation had only been used to
build self-contained accommodation for the elderly; the province's main
programs for old people came under another statute. Rents for public
housing units were set according to the CMHC scale, except that minimum
rents were established to prevent the rents of non-profit developments
in the same community from being undercut.

Non-Profit Housing

Under the Housing and Special Care Homes Act, the minister of welfare
could make grants of up to 80 per cent of the capital cost of approved
non-profit housing developments for the elderly. He could also make loans
of up to 60 per cent of the funds a municipal housing corporation had to
raise over and above loans available under NHA section 16. In addition,
the legislation provided that the province could make annual grants of up
to $60 per bed for hostel accommodation and up to $40 per unit in self-
contained developments. The program was administered by the provincial
Department of Welfare, through its Community Special Care Services Branch.

Supplementary Programs

The Saskatchewan non-profit legislation was somewhat unique in that it also
provided for provincial financing of geriatric centres in various localities
for aged persons requiring a level of care over and above that provided in
self-contained and hostel type developments. The Department of Welfare
developed an integrated and comprehensive approach to the provision of
accommodation for all people. There were five distinctive care levels –
ranging from supervisory care to limited personal care.

Under the Saskatchewan Assistance Act, the provincial government may make
monthly maintenance payments to residents of nursing and special care
homes to ensure their adequate care. The rate for persons requiring
supervisory and personal care in 1970 was $210 a month and the rate for
patients requiring extensive personal and nursing care was $310 per month.

Statistics

By the end of 1970, public housing agencies had built 259 dwelling units
for the elderly, while non-profit sponsors had built 419 dwelling units
and 991 hostel beds. This accommodation was situated in 89 developments
as indicated in Table 40. Public housing agencies had only built self-
contained accommodation, while non-profit sponsors had built a broad range
of self-contained, hostel, and mixed developments.

TABLE 40

SASKATCHEWAN DEVELOPMENTS BY SPONSOR AND ACCOMMODATION TYPES

	PUBLIC HOUSING	NON-PROFIT	TOTAL
Self-Contained	11	26	37
Hostel	0	19	19
Mixed	0	33	33
TOTAL	11	78	89

Table 41 shows individual sponsor groups in Saskatchewan. The preponderance
of municipal sponsors is evident: 66 of the 89 developments were built by
local governments.

The size range of developments in Saskatchewan can be seen in Table 42.
A total of 79 (or 89 per cent) of the developments contained 80 beds and
units or less and all but two of the self-contained developments had 40
units or less.

Table 43, which indicates the location of Saskatchewan developments, reveals
that the elderly are concentrated in small communities, 78 of the 89 develop-
ments·being in small towns and the remaining 11 situated in the province's
two metropolitan areas: Regina and Saskatoon.

TABLE 41

SASKATCHEWAN DEVELOPMENTS, ACCOMMODATION TYPE BY SPONSOR GROUPS

	SELF-CONTAINED	HOSTEL	MIXED	TOTAL
Service Clubs	8	0	0	8
Churches	3	6	3	12
Municipalities[1]	25	13	28	66
Other[2]	1	0	2	3
TOTAL	37	19	33	89

1 Includes public housing developments.

2 Includes private entrepreneurs, mixture of other groups and special corporations.

TABLE 42

SASKATCHEWAN DEVELOPMENTS, BY SPONSOR, ACCOMMODATION TYPE AND SIZE

SIZE*	PUBLIC HOUSING			NON-PROFIT			TOTAL
	SELF-CONTAINED	HOSTEL	MIXED	SELF-CONTAINED	HOSTEL	MIXED	
1-20	8	0	0	23	0	0	31
21-40	2	0	0	2	8	8	20
41-80	0	0	0	1	9	18	28
81-149	1	0	0	0	2	4	7
150+	0	0	0	0	0	3	3
TOTAL	11	0	0	26	19	33	89

* Note that the count was only for units in self-contained developments, beds in hostel developments, units and beds combined in mixed developments, and the total column.

TABLE 43

SASKATCHEWAN DEVELOPMENTS, LOCATION BY SPONSOR TYPE

	PUBLIC HOUSING	NON-PROFIT	TOTAL
Metropolitan Areas	2	9	11
Major Urban Areas	0	0	0
Small Towns	9	69	78
TOTAL	11	78	89

CHAPTER 11

ALBERTA

The 118,800 persons aged 65 and over in Alberta at the time of the 1971 census had available 104 dwelling units and 82 hostel beds financed under provisions of the National Housing Act by the end of 1970. This provided the province with .9 dwelling units per thousand elderly people, compared with 13.7 in Canada as a whole, and .7 hostel beds per thousand elderly people, while the Canadian norm was 4.5.

Public Housing Legislation

The Alberta Housing Act, which provided for provincial participation in cost sharing in National Housing Act public housing programs, was passed in 1952. No public housing was actually built for either families or senior citizens, however, until after the act was rewritten in 1965. At that time the legislation was amended to provide for provincial participation in both NHA sections 35A and 35D (public housing arrangements).

In 1969, the Alberta government, in conjunction with municipalities, decided to start building public housing under NHA section 35D. Provincial legislation provided that the province should bear 40 per cent of the capital costs (over and above the CMHC loans) and operating losses, with the municipalities contributing 10 per cent of the latter.

The Alberta Housing and Urban Renewal Corporation, established by an amendment of the Alberta Housing Act in 1967, was responsible for the development of public housing in the province. The management of developments usually devolved on local housing authorities. The corporation was responsible to the Minister of Municipal Affairs.

For many years, Alberta concentrated on developing housing for the elderly through its own foundation program rather than NHA funding. Only in 1970 was a special section on senior citizens housing projects inserted in the Alberta Housing Act. In the same year the Alberta Housing Corporation, acting under the provisions of public housing legislation, started constructing two high-rise apartments for the elderly. However, since these were not completed and occupied by the end of 1970, they were not included in the statistical summary.

Non-Profit Housing Legislation

The Alberta government, through the Alberta Housing and Urban Renewal Corporation and under the terms of the Alberta Housing Act, could make a grant of up to one-third of the capital costs of self-contained accommodation, or of up to 50 per cent of the cost of lodge (hostel) accommodation to non-profit sponsors interested in building senior citizens housing.

This legislation was designed to complement NHA section 16 loans and the non-profit sponsor was required to enter into an agreement with the Alberta Housing and Urban Renewal Corporation respecting management, rents, and disposition of the dwelling, etc. The provincial Department of Social Development also had to be consulted about the need for senior citizens housing in the community.

The non-profit sponsor for self-contained accommodation had to pay any deficits that might be incurred. However, the sponsor for hostel accommodation could be required to enter into an agreement with a local senior citizens foundation under which the foundation might (under the Homes for the Aged Act) provide subsidy payments. In 1970, the Alberta Housing and Urban Renewal Corporation set maximum rents in senior citizens accommodation at $80 per month for one person in a single dwelling unit, or $55 per person in a double unit. The hostel accommodation rate was $90 per person in a single room and $80 per person in a double room.

Alberta Housing Foundations

The distinctive feature about legislation affecting housing for the elderly in Alberta was that for over a decade the province operated a program of its own. This program, which had no relation to the National Housing Act, was launched by Premier Ernest Manning in 1958. The object was to construct a province-wide network of senior citizens homes, mainly hostel accommodation which the government called "lodges."

Under the Homes for the Aged Act, the province was divided into 50 foundation areas, within which one or more municipalities might establish a housing foundation to provide accommodation for the aged. The idea was basically that the municipalities would make available serviced land, the province would build the housing, and the local foundation pay any operating deficits. Such accommodation was exempt from municipal taxes.

The program was popular and by the end of 1970, the number of foundations had grown to 55. These bodies built 69 lodges, each of which accommodated 50 people. Self-contained units in Edmonton and Calgary were also built to accommodate 736 people. Altogether, 4,186 senior citizens were housed. Since financial burdens grew too heavy for the provincial government to bear on its own, however, it began in 1970 to take advantage of NHA funds.

Supplementary Programs

Besides the Homes for the Aged Act, under which the provincial government could construct lodges sponsored by local housing foundations, two provincial hostels for single men - one in Calgary and one in Edmonton - were built under terms of the Welfare Homes Act. While these institutions are not specifically for the elderly most residents were elderly men unable to care for themselves. They received meals, sleeping accommodation, medical attention, and clothing.

Statistics

The 104 self-contained dwellings and 82 hostel beds built in Alberta with
NHA financing by the end of 1970 were arranged in developments as indicated
in Table 44. Since the province had begun to use NHA financing for senior
citizens housing, the four developments that had been built were under non-
profit sponsorship: two were self-contained developments and the other two
contained exclusively hostel accommodation.

TABLE 44

ALBERTA DEVELOPMENTS, BY SPONSOR AND ACCOMMODATION TYPES

	PUBLIC HOUSING	NON-PROFIT	TOTAL
Self-Contained	0	2	2
Hostel	0	2	2
Mixed	0	0	0
TOTAL	0	4	4

Table 45 shows that an ethnic group, a service club, and a church organization each built one of the three developments for which we have information.

TABLE 45

ALBERTA DEVELOPMENTS, ACCOMMODATION TYPE BY SPONSOR GROUPS

	SELF-CONTAINED	HOSTEL	MIXED	TOTAL
Ethnic Groups	0	1	0	1
Service Clubs	1	0	0	1
Churches	0	1	0	1
No Information	1	0	0	1
TOTAL	2	2	0	4

Table 46 shows the size of Alberta developments. Three of the four developments were medium and the other was small.

TABLE 46

ALBERTA DEVELOPMENTS, BY SPONSOR TYPE, ACCOMMODATION TYPE AND SIZE

SIZE*	PUBLIC HOUSING			NON-PROFIT			TOTAL
	SELF-CONTAINED	HOSTEL	MIXED	SELF-CONTAINED	HOSTEL	MIXED	
1-20	0	0	0	0	1	0	1
41-80	0	0	0	2	1	0	3
TOTAL	0	0	0	2	2	0	4

* Note that the count was only for units in self-contained developments, beds in hostel developments, units and beds combined in mixed developments, and the total column.

Table 47 shows that the four Alberta developments were evenly split between metropolitan areas and small towns.

TABLE 47

ALBERTA DEVELOPMENTS, LOCATION BY SPONSOR TYPE

	PUBLIC HOUSING	NON-PROFIT	TOTAL
Metropolitan Areas	0	2	2
Major Urban Areas	0	0	0
Small Towns	0	2	2
TOTAL	0	4	4

CHAPTER 12

BRITISH COLUMBIA

The 205,000 persons aged 65 and over in British Columbia at the time of the 1971 census had available 4,761 dwelling units and 1,210 hostel beds financed under provisions of the National Housing Act by the end of 1970. This provided the province with 23.2 dwelling units per thousand elderly people, compared with 13.7 in Canada as a whole, and 5.9 hostel beds per thousand elderly people, compared with 4.5 for all Canada.

Public Housing Legislation

All public housing in British Columbia was built jointly by the federal and provincial governments under section 35A of the National Housing Act. Section 35D, or the loan arrangement, was not used because there was no provincial housing corporation. (There were also no local housing authorities). Under section 35A the federal government, through CMHC, advanced 75 per cent of the capital cost of a housing project as well as 75 per cent of the operating losses. The province bore the remaining 25 per cent of the capital costs and $12\frac{1}{2}$ per cent of the operating losses. Under the British Columbia Housing Act, municipalities had to pay $12\frac{1}{2}$ per cent of the operating losses for public housing projects in their community.

Public housing in British Columbia, including that for senior citizens, was managed by the B.C. Housing Management Commission. The commission was created in 1967 under the British Columbia Housing Act. It brought together civil servants from the three levels of government involved in public housing: two from the province, two from the federal CMHC, and one from the municipality. Although the commission was charged with managing public housing and recommending additional housing needs, the provincial Department of Municipal Affairs was responsible for housing policy.

Early in 1971, public housing rents for senior citizens varied from $34 to $58 for single occupancy (median about $48) and from $45 to $70 for double occupancy (median about $60).

Non-Profit Housing

The provincial government assisted non-profit housing in British Columbia under the terms of the Elderly Citizens Housing Aid Act, a statute administered by the provincial secretary. This legislation enabled the provincial government to make grants to municipalities and non-profit corporations to provide self-contained accommodation for the elderly. The provincial grants covered one-third of the construction cost of self-contained accommodation or 35 per cent of the cost for boarding (hostel) accommodation. The definition of cost took into account the cost of land, architect's fees, landscaping and heating, cooking and lighting fixtures. The sponsoring municipality or non-profit

group was required to make a cash contribution of at least 10 per cent of
the cost of self-contained housing and 15 per cent of the cost of boarding
home accommodation. The remaining construction costs were usually met with
a federal loan under section 16 of the National Housing Act. Provincial
legislation did not provide operating subsidies for non-profit groups but
the developments were generally exempt from municipal property taxes.
Occupants of developments built with provincial grants had to be ambulatory
and not in need of medical attention other than that which a visiting
doctor could provide. Besides this, their total fixed income could not
exceed the equivalent of 140 per cent of the federal old age security pension
and guaranteed income supplement.

Supplementary Programs

A home for the elderly in Kamloops was operated under terms of the Homes
for the Aged and Infirm Act. This home, established in 1893, accommodated
approximately 150 men in private rooms. There was also a communal recreation
room. The home was authorized to care for destitute men who had not
established themselves in any municipality and were unable to maintain
themselves because of chronic illness or other continuing inabilities.

The Municipal Act, 1957, permitted cities, towns, or district municipalities
to establish homes for the aged, infirm or disabled. A municipality could
purchase or lease property for this purpose and construct and maintain the
necessary buildings. The municipality set the conditions under which the
accommodation was made available. Ten such municipal homes, with a total
capacity of about 300 beds, were operating in the province in 1970.

Other provincial legislation that to some degree affected the elderly
included the Welfare Institution Licensing Act, which provided for provincial
licensing and supervision of welfare institutions and private boarding homes
for children and aged persons, and the Health Act, under which private
boarding and lodging houses were regulated.

In 1972, the provincial government instituted a special $50 annual grant
for homeowners and tenants aged 65 years and over, presumably to reduce
the cost of municipal taxes for the elderly.

Statistics

The 4,761 dwelling units and 1,210 hostel beds built with National Housing
Act assistance in British Columbia by the end of 1970 were in 128 developments, as indicated in Table 48. The table shows that non-profit sponsors
have made a much greater contribution to housing elderly people than the
public housing sector. Also, non-profit sponsors built self-contained,
hostel and mixed developments, whereas public housing agencies confined
themselves to self-contained developments. Public housing agencies produced
901 self-contained units, while non-profit sponsors built 3,860 dwelling
units and 1,210 hostel beds (see Table 3).

```
                        TABLE 48

       BRITISH COLUMBIA DEVELOPMENTS, BY SPONSOR AND
                    ACCOMMODATION TYPES

                   PUBLIC HOUSING   NON-PROFIT   TOTAL

Self-Contained           9              97        106

Hostel                   0              19         19

Mixed                    0               3          3

TOTAL                    0             119        128
```

Table 49 shows the activities of individual sponsor groups in British Columbia. Disregarding the nine public housing developments as well as developments for which information was unavailable, we see the strong activity of service clubs in this province. These organizations built 39 developments, whereas churches built nine and ethnic groups, seven.

TABLE 49

BRITISH COLUMBIA DEVELOPMENTS, ACCOMMODATION TYPE BY SPONSOR GROUPS

	SELF-CONTAINED	HOSTEL	MIXED	TOTAL
Ethnic Groups	5	2	0	7
Service Clubs	37	2	0	39
Churches	4	3	2	9
Municipalities	3	1	0	4
Province[1]	9	0	0	9
Other[2]	4	1	0	5
No Information	44	10	1	55
TOTAL	106	19	3	128

1 Public housing.

2 Includes private entrepreneurs, mixture of other groups and special corporations.

The size of developments in British Columbia is shown in Table 50. There was good representation of all sizes except for the largest. Both public housing agencies and non-profit groups built developments of all sizes, although the non-profit groups tended to build by far more small developments on the whole than did public housing sponsors.

TABLE 50

BRITISH COLUMBIA DEVELOPMENTS, BY SPONSOR, ACCOMMODATION TYPE AND SIZE

SIZE*	PUBLIC HOUSING			NON-PROFIT			TOTAL
	SELF-CONTAINED	HOSTEL	MIXED	SELF-CONTAINED	HOSTEL	MIXED	
1-20	1	0	0	32	3	0	36
21-40	2	0	0	26	5	0	33
41-80	1	0	0	24	3	2	30
81-149	2	0	0	14	5	0	21
150+	3	0	0	1	3	1	8
TOTAL	9	0	0	97	19	3	128

* Note that the count was only for units in self-contained developments, beds in hostel developments, units and beds combined in mixed developments, and the total column.

Table 51, which indicates the location of British Columbia developments, points to the fact that non-profit developments for the elderly have been fairly evenly distributed between metropolitan areas and small towns (Vancouver and Victoria being the only two census metropolitan areas in the province), whereas public housing developments have been built almost exclusively in metropolitan areas.

TABLE 51

BRITISH COLUMBIA DEVELOPMENTS, LOCATION BY SPONSOR TYPE

	PUBLIC HOUSING	NON-PROFIT	TOTAL
Metropolitan Areas	8	67	75
Major Urban Areas	0	0	0
Small Towns	1	52	53
TOTAL	9	119	128

PART III

MANAGER SURVEY

CONTENTS

CHAPTER 1

INTRODUCTION

This part of the study presents the results of a national mail survey
of 294 managers and sponsors of NHA financed housing for the elderly.
Basic information about the distribution of housing developments for
the elderly in Canada was presented in Part II; this survey represented
an attempt to get beyond the basic statistics to gain a better understanding of the nature of senior citizens housing developments, the
characteristics of residents, the services and facilities available
and, most important, to shed some light on the perceptions that managers
and sponsors have about their role in housing old people.

Methodology

The survey was based on a nationally stratified probability sample
selected from the universe of all CMHC financed developments for the
elderly built between 1946 and 1970 (excluding nursing homes and mixed
housing developments for families and elderly persons). The sample
included 294 developments and may be regarded as highly representative
of the universe. Details concerning sample construction are contained
in Appendix 1.

The questionnaire (see Appendix 2), which had been pretested in the
Ottawa area, was mailed to the manager or sponsor of each development
selected. The term "manager/sponsor" was used because many small non-
profit developments lack a paid manager. It was requested that the
questionnaire be completed "by the management person who has the most
direct contact with the residents and is closest to supervision of the
operation of this particular housing development" in order to solicit
response by the staff member functionally responsible for overall
management and administration. It was also suggested that the respondent
might want to consult with others involved in the development - including
residents - in completing the questionnaire.

As a result of three mailings and follow-up, there was a 94 per cent
response rate: 88 per cent in public housing and 97 per cent in non-
profit developments. Altogether, the 294 questionnaires returned and
processed represented 39 per cent of the universe of 746 developments.

The accuracy of the data presented here is, of course, dependent on the
managers' knowledge and veracity. Information on some matters, such as
the facilities available, may be more accurate than others, e.g. user
characteristics.

In examining tables, it should be borne in mind that percentages are re-
corded for the number of developments which answered a particular question,
not the total sample. Where it is considered that a significant number
of no answers have the effect of skewing the response, this is alluded
to in the text's interpretation.

CHAPTER 2

DEVELOPMENT CHARACTERISTICS

This chapter may be regarded as a supplement to the information obtained
in the Legislative and Statistical Profiles (Part II). Much of the data
collected in this survey pertaining to basic development characteristics
was already available for the universe, but it was useful for the sample
validity analysis presented in Appendix 3. What is contained in this
chapter is therefore essentially what was unavailable on a national
basis for Part II.

Development Size by Resident Population

Classifying the size of a development by the number of residents is more
precise than simply aggregating dwelling units and hostel rooms (as in
Part II), for it enables one to take into account single or double
occupancy of units and rooms.

Defining size in terms of the number of residents, Table 1 reveals some
interesting regional variations. Most of the developments were small to
medium-sized ones: 79 per cent housed up to 80 residents and 21 per cent
accommodated more than 80 residents. Except in Quebec and British Columbia,
more developments were in the smallest category of 20 or fewer residents
than in any of the other four size categories, and in these regions nearly
all developments contained under 80 persons. In Quebec, 87 per cent of
the developments were in the medium-sized range of 21-80 persons. In
British Columbia, 29 per cent of the developments were in the larger 81-
149 resident category.

In the 20 residents and under category, the Atlantic Provinces were by
far the most heavily represented and Quebec the least heavily represented.
In the 21-40 and 41-80 categories, Quebec was the most heavily represented;
in the 81-149 category, British Columbia was the most heavily represented;
and in the 150 and over category, Ontario was the most heavily represented.

Table 2 reveals the relationship between number of residents and accommodation type. It is clear that most of the self-contained developments were
fairly small - up to 40 residents - and that the hostel and mixed developments had a much larger proportion of developments in the 41-80 resident
category.

97

TABLE 1

DEVELOPMENTS, NUMBER OF RESIDENTS BY REGION

	SMALL	MEDIUM		LARGE		N
	20 Residents And Under	21-40 Residents	41-80 Residents	81-149 Residents	150 Residents Or Over	
Atlantic Provinces	29	19	10	3	3	64
	45.3%	29.7%	15.6%	4.7%	4.7%	100%
Quebec	1	10	17	1	2	31
	3.2%	32.3%	54.8%	3.2%	6.5%	100%
Ontario	25	21	20	13	10	89
	28.1%	23.6%	22.5%	14.6%	11.2%	100%
Prairies	17	9	14	9	4	53
	32.1%	17.0%	26.4%	17.0%	7.5%	100%
British Columbia	9	8	17	10	4	48
	18.8%	16.7%	35.4%	20.8%	8.3%	100%
TOTAL	81	67	78	36	23	285
	28.4%	23.5%	27.4%	12.6%	8.1%	100%

TABLE 2

DEVELOPMENTS, NUMBER OF RESIDENTS BY ACCOMMODATION TYPE

	SMALL	MEDIUM		LARGE		N
	20 Residents And Under	21-40 Residents	41-80 Residents	81-149 Residents	150 Residents And Over	
Self-Contained	79	49	45	22	18	213
	37.1%	23.0%	21.1%	10.3%	8.5%	100%
Hostel	2	11	18	8	2	41
	4.9%	26.8%	32.9%	19.5%	4.9%	100%
Mixed	0	7	15	6	3	31
	0%	22.6%	48.4%	19.4%	9.7%	100%
TOTAL	81	67	78	36	23	285
	28.4%	23.5%	27.4%	12.6%	8.1%	100%

Table 3 indicates the relationship between number of residents and
sponsor type. Both public and non-profit housing were mainly concentrated in small and medium sized developments (under 81 residents).
However, public housing was much more heavily represented than non-
profit housing in the smallest size category. In the medium and large
size categories, non-profit housing was more heavily represented, e.g.
non-profit housing was twice as likely as public housing to be found
in the 81-149 size category.

TABLE 3

DEVELOPMENTS, NUMBER OF RESIDENTS BY SPONSOR TYPE

	SMALL	MEDIUM		LARGE		N
	20 Residents And Under	21-40 Residents	41-80 Residents	81-149 Residents	150 Residents And Over	
Non-Profit	48 23.5%	48 23.5%	61 29.9%	30 14.7%	17 8.3%	204 100%
Public Housing	33 40.7%	19 23.5%	17 21.0%	6 7.4%	6 7.4%	81 100%
TOTAL	81 28.4%	67 23.5%	78 27.4%	36 12.6%	23 8.1%	285 100%

Type of Building

Table 4 shows that 46 per cent of the developments had fewer than three
floors, 17 per cent were high-rise buildings of three or more floors,
24 per cent were row housing, and 9 per cent were detached or semi-
detached bungalows. Only about 24 per cent of the developments contained
elevators - no doubt in all the high-rise buildings, as well as some of
the two-storey developments. But this still leaves about three-quarters
of the under-three-storey buildings without elevator service, although
it is likely that a portion of them were two-storey buildings.

A small development usually consisted of an apartment building of less
than three floors, row housing, or bungalows. However, among larger
developments housing over 40 residents there were more high-rises and
the proportion increased greatly with size - from 23 per cent of the
developments with 41-80 residents to 57 per cent of those with 150 or
more residents.

Public housing developments were more likely than non-profit ones
to be apartment buildings, but not more likely to be high-rises.

TABLE 4

DEVELOPMENTS, TYPE OF BUILDING BY NUMBER OF RESIDENTS

	APARTMENT BUILDING LESS THAN 3 FLOORS	APARTMENT BUILDING, 3 OR MORE FLOORS	ROW HOUSING	BUNGALOWS	MIXED	N
20 Residents Or Under	35 44.3%	2 2.5%	36 45.6%	6 7.6%	0 0%	79 100%
21-40 Residents	30 44.8%	4 6.0%	22 32.8%	10 14.9%	1 1.5%	67 100%
41-80 Residents	48 61.5%	18 23.1%	7 9.0%	5 6.4%	0 0%	78 100%
81-149 Residents	11 30.6%	12 33.3%	2 5.6%	3 8.3%	8 22.2%	36 100%
150 Residents Or More	5 21.7%	13 56.5%	1 4.3%	1 4.3%	3 13.0%	23 100%
TOTAL	129 45.6%	49 17.3%	68 24.0%	25 8.8%	12 4.2%	283 100%

Type of Unit

Most of the 251 self-contained or mixed developments had both one-
bedroom and bachelor apartments; however, 15 developments (6 per cent)
contained bachelor units only - presumably therefore excluding married
couples. Altogether, 169 developments had at least some bachelor units.
Of the 74 hostel and mixed developments, 91 per cent had some double
rooms and many had more doubles than singles.

Sharing

As Table 5 indicates, a considerable proportion of the hostel and mixed
developments - 70 per cent - had at least some residents sharing baths
or toilets, and 42 per cent had residents sharing both. The highest
rate of sharing was in Ontario and the Prairies, where all hostel or
mixed developments had at least some sharing; the lowest was in Quebec
where only 34 per cent of these developments had some sharing.

TABLE 5

HOSTEL AND MIXED DEVELOPMENTS, RESIDENTS SHARING
BATHS OR TOILETS, BY REGION

	SHARING BATH ONLY	SHARING TOILET ONLY	SHARING BATH AND TOILET	SHARING NEITHER	N
Atlantic Provinces	2 12.5%	0 0%	12 75.0%	2 12.5%	16 100%
Quebec	7 24.1%	3 10.3%	0 0%	19 65.5%	29 100%
Ontario	0 0%	0 0%	2 100%	0 0%	2 100%
Prairies	1 5.9%	3 17.6%	13 76.5%	0 0%	17 100%
British Columbia	5 50.0%	0 0%	4 40.0%	1 10.0%	10 100%
TOTAL	15 20.3%	6 8.1%	31 41.9%	22 29.7%	74 100%

Neighborhood Type

Table 6 shows the distribution of developments by neighborhood type and region. Thirty-eight per cent of the sample were in older residential areas, 32 per cent in the suburbs, 24 per cent downtown, and only 6 per cent in rural settings. In the Atlantic Provinces, developments were most likely to be in older residential areas and only very few were in rural areas. In Quebec, developments were most likely to be in downtown areas (71 per cent). In Ontario, the Prairies, and British Columbia, they were most likely to be in suburban and older residential neighborhoods.

As Table 7 indicates, in metropolitan areas the suburbs had the highest proportion of developments, followed by older residential neighborhoods. In major urban areas, downtown and older residential neighborhoods had the highest proportion; while in small towns, older residential neighborhoods had the highest proportion, followed by downtown and suburban neighborhoods.

TABLE 6

DEVELOPMENTS, NEIGHBORHOOD TYPE BY REGION

	DOWNTOWN	OLDER RESIDENTIAL	SUBURBAN	RURAL	N
Atlantic Provinces	12 22.2%	27 50.0%	12 22.2%	3 5.6%	54 100%
Quebec	22 71.0%	2 6.5%	4 12.9%	3 9.7%	31 100%
Ontario	18 19.8%	35 38.5%	38 41.8%	0 0%	91 100%
Prairies	7 13.7%	20 39.2%	19 37.3%	5 9.8%	51 100%
British Columbia	7 14.9%	21 44.7%	15 31.9%	4 8.5%	47 100%
TOTAL	66 24.1%	105 38.3%	88 32.1%	15 5.5%	274 100%

TABLE 7

DEVELOPMENTS, NEIGHBORHOOD TYPE BY COMMUNITY SIZE[1]

	DOWNTOWN	OLDER RESIDENTIAL	SUBURBAN	RURAL	N
Metropolitan Areas	14 13.9%	39 38.6%	44 43.6%	4 4.0%	101 100%
Major Urban Areas	8 38.1%	8 38.1%	5 23.8%	0 0%	21 100%
Small Towns	44 28.9%	58 38.2%	39 25.7%	11 7.2%	152 100%
TOTAL	66 24.1%	105 38.3%	88 32.1%	15 5.5%	274 100%

1 Census classifications.

Table 8 indicates the relationship between neighborhood type and number
of residents. The small and medium-sized developments with up to 80
residents were most likely to be in older residential neighborhoods or
the suburbs, followed by downtown and rural neighborhoods. The larger
developments of 81-149 residents were concentrated in older residential
neighborhoods and the largest developments of 150 or more residents
were mainly situated in the suburbs.

In downtown neighborhoods, medium-sized developments of 41-80 residents
were the ones most heavily represented; in the older residential areas
developments in the 81-149 resident category were the most heavily
represented; in the suburbs the largest developments were the ones most
heavily represented; and in rural areas developments housing 41-80
residents were most heavily represented.

TABLE 8

DEVELOPMENTS, NEIGHBORHOOD TYPE BY NUMBER OF RESIDENTS

	DOWNTOWN	OLDER RESIDENTIAL	SUBURBAN	RURAL	N
20 Residents And Under	18 24.3%	33 44.6%	18 24.3%	5 6.8%	74 100%
21-40 Residents	12 19.0%	22 34.9%	26 41.3%	3 4.8%	63 100%
41-80 Residents	22 29.7%	24 32.4%	21 28.4%	7 9.5%	74 100%
81-149 Residents	5 15.6%	18 56.3%	9 28.1%	0 0%	32 100%
150 Residents And Over	4 17.4%	6 26.1%	13 56.5%	0 0%	23 100%
TOTAL	61 22.9%	103 38.7%	87 32.7%	15 5.6%	266 100%

Table 9 shows the distribution of developments by neighborhood and accommodation type. Of the accommodation types, mixed developments were the ones most heavily represented in downtown neighborhoods and self-contained the least. Self-contained developments were the ones most heavily represented in older residential neighborhoods and mixed developments the least. Self-contained developments were the ones most heavily represented in suburban neighborhoods and hostels the least. Hostels were the ones most heavily represented in rural areas and self-contained developments the least.

TABLE 9

DEVELOPMENTS, NEIGHBORHOOD TYPE BY ACCOMMODATION TYPE

	DOWNTOWN	OLDER RESIDENTIAL	SUBURBAN	RURAL	N
Self-Contained	39 19.1%	88 43.1%	70 34.3%	7 3.4%	204 100%
Hostel	14 34.1%	12 29.3%	9 22.0%	6 14.6%	41 100%
Mixed	13 44.8%	5 17.2%	9 31.0%	2 6.9%	29 100%
TOTAL	66 24.1%	105 38.3%	88 32.1%	15 5.5%	274 100%

Table 10 shows the relationship between neighborhood type and sponsor type. Each of the two sponsor types were about equally represented in different types of neighborhoods, except in the case of suburban and rural ones. In the suburbs, public housing was very slightly more heavily represented and in rural areas non-profit housing was considerably more heavily represented.

TABLE 10

DEVELOPMENTS, NEIGHBORHOOD TYPE BY SPONSOR TYPE

	DOWNTOWN	OLDER RESIDENTIAL	SUBURBAN	RURAL	N
Non-Profit	47 24.2%	73 37.6%	60 30.9%	14 7.2%	194 100%
Public	19 23.8%	32 40.0%	28 35.0%	1 1.3%	80 100%
TOTAL	66 24.1%	105 38.3%	88 32.1%	15 5.5%	274 100%

Types of Households Nearby

Table 11 indicates the types of households nearby developments in relation to neighborhood type. Twenty-one per cent of all developments were in neighborhoods populated with mostly other elderly people, 75 per cent were in areas that had mostly families with children, 3 per cent were in areas where young adults and childless households were predominant, and 1 per cent were in areas occupied by transients.

TABLE 11

DEVELOPMENTS, TYPES OF HOUSEHOLDS NEARBY BY NEIGHBORHOOD TYPE

	MOSTLY ELDERLY	MOSTLY FAMILIES WITH CHILDREN	MOSTLY CHILDLESS HOUSEHOLDS AND SINGLES	MOSTLY TRANSIENTS	N
Downtown	20 37.0%	36 18.3%	4 44.4%	1 50.0%	61 23.3%
Older Residential	19 35.2%	77 39.1%	3 33.3%	0 0%	99 37.8%
Suburban	13 24.1%	71 36.0%	2 22.2%	1 50.0%	87 33.2%
Rural	2 3.7%	13 6.6%	0 0%	0 0%	15 5.7%
TOTAL	54 100%	197 100%	9 100%	2 100%	262 100%

Not surprisingly, developments with mostly elderly people nearby were more likely to be in downtown and older residential neighborhoods than in the suburbs or rural areas. Developments surrounded by families with children were most likely to be in older residential neighborhoods, followed closely by suburban areas. Developments with mainly single persons and childless households were most likely to be located in downtown and older residential neighborhoods.

To look at it another way, residents of downtown developments were much more likely to be surrounded by elderly neighbors than were those living in other areas – but even so, only 33 per cent of the downtown developments were actually in neighborhoods occupied mainly by old people.

Table 12 shows that non-profit housing developments were more likely than public housing developments to be in neighborhoods occupied by mostly elderly people and, conversely, less likely to be surrounded with families and children. Self-contained, hostel and mixed accommodation types were about equally represented in the different "types of households nearby" categories, although mixed developments were slightly more likely to be in areas with mostly elderly and slightly less likely to be in areas with mostly families and children.

TABLE 12

DEVELOPMENTS, TYPES OF HOUSEHOLDS NEARBY BY SPONSOR TYPE

	MOSTLY ELDERLY	MOSTLY FAMILIES WITH CHILDREN	MOSTLY CHILDLESS HOUSEHOLDS AND SINGLES	MOSTLY TRANSIENTS	N
Non-Profit	46 23.1%	145 72.9%	6 3.0%	2 1.0%	199 100%
Public Housing	13 16.3%	64 80.0%	3 3.8%	0 0%	80 100%
TOTAL	59 21.1%	209 74.9%	9 3.2%	2 .7%	279 100%

CHAPTER 3

RESIDENT CHARACTERISTICS

This chapter supplements data about resident characteristics found in
the user survey (Part V). The validity of the data reported here depends
on the accuracy of managers' estimates, this being probably not as good
as information provided directly by residents; but on the other hand
the sample is more representative than the one selected for the user
survey.

Sex

Table 13 indicates the proportion of males in developments. In 57 per
cent of the developments for which we obtained responses, less than a
quarter of the residents were male; in 34 per cent of the developments
one-quarter to one-half of the residents were male; and in only 6 per
cent were over half of the residents male. Hostels had a higher
proportion of male residents than self-contained or mixed developments.

TABLE 13

DEVELOPMENTS, PROPORTION OF MALE RESIDENTS BY ACCOMMODATION TYPE

	$\frac{1}{4}$ OR LESS MALE	$\frac{1}{4}$ TO $\frac{1}{2}$ MALE	$\frac{1}{2}$ AND MORE MALE	N
Self-Contained	127 60.2%	64 30.3%	20 9.5%	211 100%
Hostel	18 42.9%	17 40.5%	7 16.7%	42 100%
Mixed	18 58.1%	11 35.5%	2 6.5%	31 100%
TOTAL	163 57.4%	92 32.4%	29 10.2%	284 100%

Age

Table 14 indicates that 56 per cent of developments reported that the
majority of all their residents were under 75 years of age, 35 per
cent reported that the majority of residents were 75 years and older,
and 9 per cent reported that residents were about evenly split between
the two age groups. Residents in self-contained accommodation tended

to be younger than hostel residents: 65 per cent of developments
reported that the majority of self-contained residents were under 75
years, but only 31 per cent reported that the majority of hostel
residents were. Conversely, only 26 per cent of developments reported
that the majority of self-contained residents were 75 and over, whereas
64 per cent reported that the majority of hostel residents were. Two
per cent of developments reported that the majority of their residents
in self-contained accommodation were under 65, whereas no developments
reported that the majority of their hostel residents were.

TABLE 14

DEVELOPMENTS, AGE BY ACCOMMODATION TYPE

	MAJORITY UNDER 75 YEARS	MAJORITY 75 YEARS AND OVER	HALF UNDER 75 YEARS AND HALF ABOVE 75 YEARS	N
Residents in Self-Contained Units	170 65.1%	69 26.4%	22 8.4%	261[1] 100%
Residents in Hostel Rooms	19 31.1%	39 63.9%	3 4.9%	61 100%
ALL RESIDENTS[2]	161 55.9%	100 34.7%	27 9.4%	288 100%

1 N is greater than 220 as some developments contained both self-contained and hostel accommodation.

2 These figures are for all residents - whether in self-contained or in hostel units. They are not therefore the sum of the figures above.

Health

Health was investigated by asking managers to check a series of statements related to residents' physical capacities. Table 15 shows that in
61 per cent of the developments managers reported that over three-quarters
of the residents had no physical incapacities; in 12 per cent about one-
half to three-quarters had no physical incapacities; in 7 per cent one-
quarter to one-half had no physical incapacities; in 16 per cent one-
quarter or less had no physical incapacities; and in 5 per cent all the
residents were said to have some degree of physical incapacity. These
estimates suggest that a large proportion of the population of NHA
financed housing developments for the elderly lack the sorts of disabilities
commonly associated with old age. This was substantiated by the findings
of the user study (see Part V).

Table 15 also reveals differences between accommodation types. Seventy-four per cent of the self-contained developments reported that over three-quarters of their residents had no incapacities, compared with 26 per cent of mixed developments and only 15 per cent of hostel developments. On the other hand, only 1 per cent of self-contained developments reported that all residents had some degree of physical incapacity, compared with 15 per cent of hostel developments and 19 per cent of mixed developments.

TABLE 15

DEVELOPMENTS, PROPORTION OF RESIDENTS WITH NO PHYSICAL INCAPACITIES
BY ACCOMMODATION TYPE

	ALL RESIDENTS WITH SOME PHYSICAL INCAPACITY	$\frac{1}{4}$ OF RESIDENTS OR LESS WITH NO PHYSICAL INCAPACITY	$\frac{1}{4}$ TO $\frac{1}{2}$ OF RESIDENTS WITH NO PHYSICAL INCAPACITY	$\frac{1}{2}$ TO $\frac{3}{4}$ OF RESIDENTS WITH NO PHYSICAL INCAPACITY	$\frac{3}{4}$ OR OVER OF RESIDENTS WITH NO PHYSICAL INCAPACITY	N
Self-Contained	3 1.4%	16 7.6%	14 6.6%	21 10.0%	157 74.4%	211 100%
Hostel	6 15.0%	20 50.0%	2 5.0%	6 15.0%	6 15.0%	40 100%
Mixed	6 19.4%	8 25.8%	3 9.7%	6 19.4%	8 25.8%	31 100%
TOTAL	15 5.3%	44 15.6%	19 6.7%	33 11.7%	171 60.6%	282 100%

As Table 16 indicates, public housing residents had a considerably lower rate of physical incapacity than non-profit housing residents: 76 per cent of public housing developments reported that over three-quarters of their residents had no physical incapacity - compared with 55 per cent of non-profit developments. Of course, this difference can be accounted for by the large proportion of hostel accommodation (with its older residents) in the non-profit sector.

Table 17 shows that there was not a great deal of regional variation in residents' health - except in Quebec. There, only 9 per cent of developments reported that over three-quarters of their residents had no physical incapacities - compared with 61 per cent for the national sample. Also, 25 per cent of all Quebec developments claimed that all residents had some physical incapacity - compared with only 5 per cent for the national sample. The latter situation can again be accounted for by the predominance of hostel accommodation in Quebec.

When it came to neighborhood type, those developments in which in excess of three-quarters of all residents had some physical incapacities tended to be more heavily represented in downtown and rural neighborhoods than in older residential or suburban ones. In comparison, developments with less disabled residents were more heavily represented in older residential and suburban neighborhoods than in downtown and rural ones.

TABLE 16

DEVELOPMENTS, PROPORTION OF RESIDENTS WITH NO PHYSICAL INCAPACITIES BY SPONSOR TYPE

	ALL RESIDENTS WITH SOME PHYSICAL INCAPACITY	$\frac{1}{4}$ OF RESIDENTS OR LESS WITH NO PHYSICAL INCAPACITY	$\frac{1}{4}$ TO $\frac{1}{2}$ OF RESIDENTS WITH NO PHYSICAL INCAPACITY	$\frac{1}{2}$ TO $\frac{3}{4}$ OF RESIDENTS WITH NO PHYSICAL INCAPACITY	$\frac{3}{4}$ OR OVER OF RESIDENTS WITH NO PHYSICAL INCAPACITY	N
Non-Profit	12 6.0%	41 20.5%	13 6.5%	25 12.5%	109 54.5%	200 100%
Public Housing	3 3.7%	3 3.7%	6 7.3%	8 9.8%	62 75.6%	82 100%
TOTAL	15 5.3%	44 15.6%	19 6.7%	33 11.7%	171 60.6%	282 100%

TABLE 17

DEVELOPMENTS, PROPORTION OF RESIDENTS WITH NO PHYSICAL INCAPACITIES BY REGION

	ALL RESIDENTS WITH SOME PHYSICAL INCAPACITY	$\frac{1}{4}$ OF RESIDENTS OR LESS WITH NO PHYSICAL INCAPACITY	$\frac{1}{4}$ TO $\frac{1}{2}$ OF RESIDENTS WITH NO PHYSICAL INCAPACITY	$\frac{1}{2}$ TO $\frac{3}{4}$ OF RESIDENTS WITH NO PHYSICAL INCAPACITY	$\frac{3}{4}$ OR OVER OF RESIDENTS WITH NO PHYSICAL INCAPACITY	N
Atlantic Provinces	1 1.6%	13 21.3%	0 0%	3 4.9%	44 72.1%	61 100%
Quebec	8 25.0%	14 43.8%	3 9.4%	4 12.5%	3 9.4%	32 100%
Ontario	2 2.2%	4 4.3%	14 15.2%	12 13.0%	60 65.2%	92 100%
Prairies	2 3.8%	8 15.1%	1 1.9%	7 13.2%	35 66.0%	53 100%
British Columbia	2 4.5%	5 11.4%	1 2.3%	7 15.9%	29 65.9%	44 100%
TOTAL	15 5.3%	44 15.6%	19 6.7%	33 11.7%	171 60.6%	282 100%

111

Table 18 focuses on the incidence of residents with seriously limited
ability (unable to accomplish many daily tasks such as walking, washing,
keeping house, talking, seeing, or hearing). Sixty-four per cent of
developments reported having no residents in this category, 29 per cent
had a quarter or less, 4 per cent had one-quarter to one-half, and only
3 per cent had over half. As one would expect, self-contained developments
had fewer persons with seriously limited physical ability: 75 per cent
of the self-contained developments had no residents with seriously limited
ability – compared with 43 per cent of the mixed developments and 25 per
cent of the hostels. Also, no self-contained developments reported that
one-quarter of their residents had seriously limited physical abilities,
although 20 per cent of the mixed developments and 33 per cent of hostels
did.

It should not be assumed, however, that all the residents of self-contained
developments were healthy enough to completely fend for themselves, or
that all the residents of hostel developments required some form of special
care. In fact, as Table 18 shows, 25 per cent of the self-contained developments indicated that up to one-quarter of their residents had seriously
limited ability. Furthermore, as Table 19 shows, 31 per cent indicated
that up to a quarter of their residents had moderately limited physical
ability (noticeable handicaps in one activity or faculty needing limited
or continuous aid) and 3 per cent indicated that one-quarter to one-half
of their residents were in this category. Nine per cent of the self-
contained developments indicated that a simple majority of their residents
had slightly limited ability (some minor difficulty either in moving about,
communicating, and/or keeping house) and 2 per cent even indicated that
the majority of their residents had moderately limited abilities.

TABLE 18

DEVELOPMENTS, PROPORTION OF RESIDENTS WITH SERIOUSLY LIMITED PHYSICAL ABILITY BY ACCOMMODATION TYPE

	NONE	$\frac{1}{4}$ OR LESS	$\frac{1}{4}$ TO $\frac{1}{2}$	$\frac{1}{2}$ AND OVER	N
Self-Contained	150	49	0	0	199
	75.4%	24.6%	0%	0%	100%
Hostel	10	17	7	6	40
	25.0%	42.5%	17.5%	15.0%	100%
Mixed	13	11	3	3	30
	43.4%	36.7%	10.0%	10.0%	100%
TOTAL	173	77	10	9	269
	64.3%	28.6%	3.7%	3.3%	100%

Table 19 shows that of the total sample, 54 per cent of developments had
no residents with moderately limited ability, 37 per cent of developments
had one-quarter or less with moderately limited physical ability, 6 per
cent had one-quarter to one-half, and 4 per cent had over half in this
category.

112

TABLE 19

DEVELOPMENTS, PROPORTION OF RESIDENTS WITH MODERATELY LIMITED PHYSICAL ABILITY BY ACCOMMODATION TYPE

	NONE	¼ OR LESS	¼ TO ½	½ AND OVER	N
Self-Contained	132	63	6	1	202
	65.3%	31.2%	3.0%	.5%	100%
Hostel	7	20	9	6	42
	16.7%	47.6%	21.4%	14.3%	100%
Mixed	8	18	1	4	31
	25.8%	58.1%	3.2%	12.9%	100%
TOTAL	147	101	16	11	275
	53.5%	36.7%	5.8%	4.0%	100%

Another matter connected with health concerns the extent to which housing for the elderly serves as the final habitation in their life cycle. Table 20 indicates that there was a fair degree of variation in death rates between different developments. But in 28 per cent of the developments, no resident had died in the past year; in 34 per cent of the self-contained developments, and 13 per cent of the hostels, no residents had died in the past year. In only 8 per cent of the developments - 3 per cent of self-contained and 23 per cent of hostel and mixed developments - had 10 or more residents died during the past year. Of course, factors that would influence these figures would be the size of the development, the age range of residents, and the length of time it had been operating. Also, it should be borne in mind that the actual death rate of residents is considerably higher than the figures indicate since it is likely that many residents were moved first to a hospital or chronic care facility before they died.

TABLE 20

DEVELOPMENTS, NUMBER OF RESIDENTS WHO DIED IN PAST YEAR BY ACCOMMODATION TYPE

	NONE DIED	1-2 DIED	3-5 DIED	6-9 DIED	10 OR OVER DIED	N
Self-Contained	70	88	29	11	6	204
	34.3%	43.1%	14.2%	5.4%	3.0%	100%
Hostel	5	7	12	6	9	39
	12.8%	17.9%	30.8%	15.4%	23.1%	100%
Mixed	0	9	11	3	6	29
	0%	31.0%	38.0%	10.3%	20.7%	100%
TOTAL	75	104	52	20	21	272
	27.6%	38.2%	19.1%	7.4%	7.7%	100%

Income Source

Table 21 shows that in 70 per cent of developments managers reported that the majority of residents' income came solely from the old age security pension and the guaranteed income supplement. In 28 per cent of developments, most residents had some savings or other income in addition to their pension; in only 3 per cent of developments did the majority of residents have substantial savings or other income. The residents of non-profit housing developments tended to be considerably better off than those in public housing: in 84 per cent of the public housing the majority of residents' income was solely the old age security pension - compared with 64 per cent in non-profit developments.

TABLE 21

DEVELOPMENTS, PREDOMINANT INCOME SOURCE OF SIMPLE MAJORITY OF
RESIDENTS BY SPONSOR TYPE

	DEPENDENT SOLELY ON OLD AGE SECURITY PENSION (OAS) AND GUARANTEED INCOME SUPPLEMENT	DEPENDENT ON OAS PENSION, SOME SAVINGS OR OTHER INCOME	DEPENDENT ON OAS PENSION AND SUBSTANTIAL SAVINGS OR OTHER INCOME	N
Non-Profit	131 63.9%	65 31.7%	9 4.4%	205 100%
Public Housing	66 83.5%	13 16.5%	0 0%	79 100%
TOTAL	197 69.4%	78 27.5%	9 3.2%	284 100%

Table 22 shows income source by region. Perhaps the most noticeable figures in the table are those for the Prairies. Here, in 50 per cent of the developments the majority of residents had some savings in addition to their pension - compared with 28 per cent for the national sample. In 6 per cent of developments residents had substantial savings - compared with 3 per cent for the national sample. The very low incomes of residents in Quebec also stands out: in 97 per cent of the Quebec developments the majority of residents depended solely on the old age pension and guaranteed income supplement - compared with 70 per cent for the national sample.

114

TABLE 22

DEVELOPMENTS, INCOME SOURCE OF SIMPLE MAJORITY OF RESIDENTS BY REGION

	DEPENDENT SOLELY ON OLD AGE SECURITY PENSION (OAS) AND GUARANTEED INCOME SUPPLEMENT	DEPENDENT ON OAS PENSION AND SOME SAVINGS OR OTHER INCOME	DEPENDENT ON OAS PENSION AND SUBSTANTIAL SAVINGS OR OTHER INCOME	N
Atlantic Provinces	45 71.4%	17 27.0%	1 1.6%	63 100%
Quebec	31 96.9%	1 3.1%	0 0%	32 100%
Ontario	61 67.0%	27 29.7%	3 3.3%	91 100%
Prairies	23 44.2%	26 50.0%	3 5.8%	52 100%
British Columbia	37 80.4%	7 15.2%	2 4.3%	46 100%
TOTAL	197 69.4%	78 27.5%	9 3.2%	284 100%

CHAPTER 4

FACILITIES

Table 23 indicates the availability of recreation areas. The same data
is broken down for self-contained and hostel and mixed developments in
Tables 24 and 25. If a facility was lacking in a development, the
questionnaire attempted to elicit the manager's appreciation of the
need for the service.

	TABLE 23			
AVAILABILITY OF RECREATION AREAS FOR ALL DEVELOPMENTS				
	AVAILABLE IN DEVELOPMENT	AVAILABLE WITHIN FIVE BLOCKS	NOT AVAILABLE	N
Central Recreation Room	220 77.5%	0 0%	64 22.5%	284 100%
Senior Citizens Centre (or club)	27 9.9%	177 65.1%	68 25.0%	272 100%
Library Room	83 29.6%	84 30.0%	113 40.4%	280 100%
Crafts Room	71 25.4%	34 12.2%	174 62.4%	279 100%
Garden Plots	92 32.9%	13 4.6%	175 62.5%	280 100%
Bowling Alley	3 1.1%	101 36.2%	175 62.7%	279 100%
Card and Table Games Room	88 31.4%	13 4.6%	179 63.9%	280 100%
Auditorium	34 12.1%	57 20.4%	189 67.5%	280 100%
Coffee Room	60 21.4%	27 9.6%	193 68.9%	280 100%
Lawn Games Area	15 5.4%	41 14.6%	224 80.0%	280 100%
Greenhouse	5 1.8%	29 10.4%	246 87.9%	280 100%

TABLE 24

AVAILABILITY OF RECREATION AREAS FOR SELF-CONTAINED DEVELOPMENTS

	AVAILABLE IN DEVELOPMENT	AVAILABLE WITHIN FIVE BLOCKS	NOT AVAILABLE	N
Central Recreation Room	151 71.9%	0 0%	59 28.1%	210 100%
Senior Citizens Centre (or club)	21 10.6%	148 74.7%	29 14.6%	198 100%
Library Room	34 16.5%	74 35.9%	98 47.6%	206 100%
Crafts Room	26 12.7%	31 15.1%	148 72.2%	205 100%
Garden Plots	62 30.1%	9 4.4%	135 65.5%	206 100%
Bowling Alley	2 1.0%	70 34.1%	133 64.9%	205 100%
Card and Table Games Room	39 18.9%	11 5.3%	156 75.7%	206 100%
Auditorium	11 5.3%	47 22.8%	148 71.8%	206 100%
Coffee Room	30 14.4%	24 11.5%	154 74.0%	208 100%
Lawn Games Area	7 3.4%	34 16.5%	165 80.1%	206 100%
Greenhouse	1 .5%	21 10.2%	184 89.3%	206 100%

TABLE 25

AVAILABILITY OF RECREATION AREA FOR HOSTEL AND MIXED DEVELOPMENTS

	AVAILABLE IN DEVELOPMENT	AVAILABLE WITHIN FIVE BLOCKS	NOT AVAILABLE	N
Central Recreation Room	69 93.2%	0 0%	5 6.8%	74 100%
Senior Citizens Centre (or club)	6 8.1%	29 39.2%	39 52.7%	74 100%
Library Room	49 66.2%	10 13.5%	15 20.3%	74 100%
Crafts Room	45 60.8%	3 4.1%	26 35.1%	74 100%
Garden Plots	30 40.5%	4 5.4%	40 54.1%	74 100%
Bowling Alley	1 1.4%	31 41.9%	42 56.8%	74 100%
Card and Table Games Room	49 66.2%	2 2.7%	23 31.1%	74 100%
Auditorium	23 31.1%	10 13.5%	41 55.4%	74 100%
Coffee Room	30 41.7%	3 4.2%	39 54.2%	72 100%
Lawn Games Area	8 10.8%	7 9.5%	59 79.7%	74 100%
Greenhouse	4 5.4%	8 10.8%	62 83.8%	74 100%

Central Recreation Room

A central recreation room was the most common facility. Seventy-eight per cent of all developments had one - 72 per cent of the self-contained developments and 93 per cent of the hostel and mixed developments. Central recreation rooms were equally available in both public housing and non-profit developments as well as in large urban areas and small towns. The facility was more likely to be available in Quebec than in other regions, and least likely to be available in Ontario.

Table 26 illustrates the extent to which central recreation rooms are regularly used in relation to accommodation type. In 39 per cent of developments the room was used regularly by all residents; in 35 per cent of developments it was used by only half or fewer of the residents; in 16 per cent it was used by only a few residents; in 7 per cent it was used mainly on special occasions such as teas and birthday parties; and in 2 per cent it was never used. This facility received slightly heavier use in hostel and mixed developments than in self-contained developments.

When use of these central recreation rooms was analyzed by residents' physical capacity, it was found that in developments with residents having few physical incapacities the room was used slightly more extensively than in developments in which more residents had physical incapacities (which presumably made outside activities less possible).

Over a third of the developments reported that from time to time use was made of the central recreation room by non-residents. In fact, in many cases central room activities were organized by a non-resident group.

TABLE 26

DEVELOPMENTS, PROPORTION OF RESIDENTS REGULARLY USING CENTRAL RECREATION ROOM, BY ACCOMMODATION TYPE

	ALL RESIDENTS USE IT REGULARLY	ONLY ½ OR LESS OF RESIDENTS USE IT REGULARLY	ONLY A FEW RESIDENTS USE IT REGULARLY	MAINLY USED ON SPECIAL OCCASIONS	NOT USED AT ALL	N
Self-Contained	54 / 37.5%	47 / 32.6%	26 / 18.1%	12 / 8.3%	5 / 3.5%	144 / 100%
Hostel	16 / 40.0%	17 / 42.5%	6 / 15.0%	1 / 2.5%	0 / 0%	40 / 100%
Mixed	14 / 48.3%	10 / 34.5%	3 / 10.3%	2 / 6.9%	0 / 0%	29 / 100%
TOTAL	84 / 39.4%	74 / 34.7%	35 / 16.4%	15 / 7.0%	5 / 2.3%	213 / 100%

Table 27 indicates some of the main activities that took place in the central recreation rooms. Table games such as cribbage, cards, checkers, and bingo were the most common (in 56 per cent of developments), followed by television watching (in 37 per cent of developments), religious services (in 29 per cent of developments), and coffee hours (in 22 per cent of developments).

Managers were asked to identify the main areas used by residents to meet together to exchange a few words or sit. The central recreation room seemed to be the most common place, especially in the winter months. Other areas mentioned were lobbies, halls and, in a few developments, laundries or floor lounges. Lawns, sun decks, and parks were also mentioned for summertime.

TABLE 27

DEVELOPMENTS, TYPES OF ACTIVITIES IN CENTRAL RECREATION ROOMS

	TAKES PLACE IN RECREATION ROOM	TAKES PLACE ELSEWHERE IN DEVELOPMENT	NO SUCH ACTIVITY	N
Table Games	151 55.7%	23 8.5%	97 35.8%	271 100%
Television Watching	104 37.4%	15 5.4%	159 57.2%	278 100%
Religious Services	78 28.6%	26 9.5%	169 61.9%	273 100%
Coffee Hour	61 21.5%	32 11.3%	191 67.3%	284 100%

Floor and Wing Lounges

When it comes to planning community space in residential environments for the elderly, there has been some controversy as to whether it is preferable to design a large multi-purpose recreation room or, alternatively, floor or wing lounges, or perhaps both. Twenty-eight per cent of the developments did have lounges on most floors or in most wings; these lounges were in fact used more heavily than the central recreation facilities. In 49 per cent of developments with floor lounges, practically all residents used them regularly; in 28 per cent less than half of the residents used them regularly; in 19 per cent only a few residents used them regularly; and in 4 per cent they were used only on special occasions.

Floor or wing lounges were principally a feature of hostel and mixed accommodation: they existed in 91 per cent of these developments, compared with 12 per cent of self-contained developments. But where they existed there was little variation in the degree of regular use between the different types of developments.

Senior Citizens Centre

In 75 per cent of developments, residents had access to a senior citizens centre or golden age club. In 10 per cent of cases the centre was located on site and in 65 per cent of cases it was within five blocks. A senior citizens centre within the development complex was about equally likely for both accommodation types, but the self-contained developments were much more likely than the hostel and mixed developments to have a centre within five blocks - 75 per cent, compared with 39 per cent. Also, only 15 per cent of self-contained developments had no access to a senior citizens centre, compared with 53 per cent of hostel and mixed developments. This can all be seen in Tables 23 to 25.

Residents of small-town developments had considerably less opportunity to attend a senior citizens centre or club in or near their development than those living in large urban areas: 86 per cent of metropolitan area developments and 96 per cent of major urban area developments had a senior citizens centre in or close to their development, compared with only 64 per cent of developments in small towns and rural areas. Also, there was considerable variation in the availability of the senior citizens centre or club by region: 92 per cent of developments in British Columbia had a senior citizens centre in or near the development, compared with 89 per cent in Ontario, 71 per cent in the Prairies, 55 per cent in Quebec, and only 53 per cent in the Atlantic Provinces.

As far as the use of a senior citizens centre or club was concerned, on-site facilities were used much more than those in the community. This held good for all types of accommodation. Also, use tended to be higher in self-contained developments than in hostel and mixed accommodation. This may have been because the majority of senior citizens centres and golden age clubs tended to be located outside of developments and were therefore less accessible to the older, less mobile residents of hostel and mixed accommodation. Perhaps, too, residents of hostel accommodation - who necessarily have more contact with other residents in dining halls, TV rooms, and the like - felt less need to seek out opportunities to socialize than do residents of self-contained units. In any event, hostel and mixed developments were considerably more likely than self-contained developments to be in small towns, and small-town developments offered less in the way of senior citizens centres.

Library

Sixty per cent of the developments had a library available: 30 per cent had one on site and another 30 per cent had one within five blocks. The facility was less common in or near self-contained developments than in hostel and mixed developments: 52 per cent of self-contained developments had a library available, compared with 80 per cent of hostel and mixed developments. Library facilities were more available in Quebec and British Columbia than in other regions - and least available in Ontario. They were also much more available in metropolitan than in smaller centres.

Managers were asked to indicate if they had no library available but felt such a facility would be useful. Only 23 per cent of managers of self-contained developments that did not have a library noted that such a facility would be useful - compared with 32 per cent of hostel and mixed development managers.

The lack of reading material in the 48 per cent of self-contained and 20 per cent of hostel and mixed developments that had no library facilities was mitigated in some instances by visits from a mobile library. About 19 per cent had such a service available (18 per cent of self-contained and 20 per cent of hostel and mixed). But since some of these developments probably already had a library available, this still leaves a considerable number of developments with no planned provision for reading material.

Crafts Room

There was a crafts room in 25 per cent of developments; in another 12 per cent there was one nearby in the community. Such a room was much less likely to be available in self-contained than in hostel and mixed accommodation: only 13 per cent of self-contained developments had a crafts room, compared with 61 per cent of hostel and mixed. A crafts room was found to be slightly more likely in non-metropolitan areas.

As for the managers recognizing a need for such a facility, 32 per cent of the managers of those self-contained developments that lacked a crafts room felt that this facility would be useful - compared with 52 per cent of the managers of hostel and mixed developments.

Garden Plots

The managers were asked if residents had opportunities to grow flowers or vegetables. Thirty-three per cent of the developments had garden plots for residents - 30 per cent of self-contained developments and 41 per cent of hostel and mixed developments. However, as these proportions seem far higher than is likely, it is possible that many respondents misunderstood the question and replied affirmatively if the development had a garden area, regardless of whether it was maintained by residents or staff.

Bowling Alley

There was a bowling alley in only three developments (1 per cent); however, in 36 per cent of the developments there was a bowling alley within five blocks. Thirty-four per cent of self-contained developments had a bowling alley nearby, compared with 42 per cent of hostel and mixed developments.

The vast majority of managers without a bowling alley did not see the need for one: only 6 per cent of the managers of self-contained developments that lacked one, and 14 per cent of the managers of hostel and mixed developments, considered that such a facility would be useful.

Card Room

There was a room for cards and other table games in 31 per cent of developments and in another 5 per cent there was one within five blocks. A card room was less likely to be found in self-contained developments: only 19 per cent of self-contained developments had a card room, compared with 66 per cent of hostel and mixed developments. These proportions may be too high due to some managers having in mind that the central recreation room was used for table games when they replied "yes".

A fair proportion of the managers who did not have a card room considered that it would be a welcome addition to their developments: 35 per cent of the managers of self-contained developments that lacked a card room indicated that this facility would be useful, compared with 32 per cent of managers of hostel and mixed developments.

Auditorium

There was an auditorium in 12 per cent of developments, and in another 20 per cent there was one within five blocks. Five per cent of self-contained developments had an auditorium, compared with 31 per cent of hostel and mixed developments. Again, it is likely that there were different interpretations by managers as to what was meant by an auditorium.

As for recognizing the need for an auditorium, 15 per cent of the managers of self-contained developments lacking this facility indicated that it would be useful, compared with 22 per cent of the managers of hostel and mixed developments.

Coffee Room

There was a coffee room in 21 per cent of all developments and in another 10 per cent there was a coffee shop nearby in the community. Fourteen per cent of self-contained developments had a coffee room in the development, compared with 42 per cent of hostel and mixed developments.

123

Few managers who lacked a coffee room in their development thought that it would be a useful addition: 15 per cent of the managers of self-contained developments that lacked one thought it would be useful, compared with 20 per cent of the managers of hostel and mixed developments.

Area for Lawn Games

An area for lawn games such as croquet, bowling or putting existed in only 5 per cent of developments; in another 15 per cent there was one within five blocks. Three per cent of self-contained developments had an area for lawn games on site, compared with 11 per cent of hostel and mixed developments.

Twenty per cent of the managers of self-contained developments lacking an area for lawn games considered that such a facility would be useful, compared with 26 per cent of the managers of hostel and mixed developments.

Greenhouse

A greenhouse existed in only 2 per cent of developments. In another 10 per cent of developments, there was one within five blocks. One of the developments with a greenhouse was self-contained, the other four were hostel and mixed.

Fourteen per cent of the managers of self-contained developments lacking a greenhouse considered such would be useful, compared with 24 per cent of managers of hostel or mixed developments.

Personal Care Facilities

The availability of personal care facilities is shown in Table 28. There was a laundry in 91 per cent of developments; in another 3 per cent there was one within five blocks. Only 6 per cent of developments had no laundry in the vicinity; these were presumably hostel developments in which all of the major washing was sent out to a commercial laundry.

TABLE 28

AVAILABILITY OF PERSONAL CARE FACILITIES IN ALL DEVELOPMENTS

	AVAILABLE IN DEVELOPMENT	AVAILABLE WITHIN FIVE BLOCKS	NOT AVAILABLE	N
Laundry	257 91.1%	8 2.8%	17 6.0%	282 100%
Beauty Shop	25 8.9%	174 62.1%	81 28.9%	280 100%
Barber Shop	29 10.4%	165 58.9%	86 30.7%	280 100%

124

A beauty shop was available in 9 per cent of developments; in another 62 per cent there was one within five blocks. However, in 29 per cent of developments residents lacked easy access to a beauty shop - something which must have been distressing for the predominantly female population. There was one on-site in 2 per cent of the self-contained developments and in 34 per cent of hostel and mixed developments. Developments in metropolitan areas were considerably more likely to have a beauty shop on-site than those in major urban areas and small towns. Managers in those developments where there were none appeared to feel little need for a beauty shop: only 8 per cent of the managers of the self-contained developments and 32 per cent of the managers of hostel and mixed developments felt that one would be useful.

A barber shop was slightly more likely to be available on-site than a beauty parlor, despite the predominance of female residents. Ten per cent of all developments had a barber shop on-site and another 59 per cent had one within five blocks.

There was no suggestion that either beauty parlors or barber shops were maintained full-time and in many instances the managers may have responded affirmatively to this question even if a private operator offered the service only periodically.

Infirmary

As Table 29 indicates, 13 per cent of developments had an infirmary or sick room where temporary nursing care of up to one month could be offered.

TABLE 29

DEVELOPMENTS, AVAILABILITY OF INFIRMARY BY ACCOMMODATION TYPE

	INFIRMARY OF 1-2 BEDS	INFIRMARY OF 3 BEDS OR MORE	NO INFIRMARY	N
Self-Contained	3 1.6%	0 0%	185 98.4%	188 100%
Hostel	10 25.0%	5 12.5%	25 62.5%	40 100%
Mixed	9 29.0%	7 22.6%	15 48.4%	31 100%
TOTAL	22 8.5%	12 4.6%	225 86.9%	259 100%

Only 2 per cent of self-contained developments had such a facility, compared with 38 per cent of hostel developments and 52 per cent of mixed self-contained and hostel developments. In 65 per cent of the developments that had infirmaries, they contained one or two beds; in the other 35 per cent of developments with infirmaries, they contained three or more beds. On the whole, infirmaries were more likely to be found in developments that had a high proportion of residents with physical incapacities: 38 per cent of the developments where managers reported that all residents had some incapacities had infirmaries, compared with only 3 per cent of developments where over three-quarters of the residents had no incapacities.

Telephones

Seventy-four per cent of developments had a telephone in each dwelling unit or hostel room. In self-contained developments, 81 per cent of units had telephones, compared with 57 per cent of the units or rooms in hostel and mixed developments. Telephones in each unit were less likely to be found in developments as the proportion of residents with physical incapacities increased. As for the need for a telephone in each unit, 22 per cent of the managers of those developments that did not have telephones in each unit felt that they would be useful.

CHAPTER 5

SERVICES

The questionnaire contained a number of questions designed to find out
to what extent residents in housing developments for the elderly had
access to a variety of personal social services. Respondents were asked
to identify whether or not the service was available, whether it was
provided in the development or as a special development service, as
opposed to being available in or for the general community. They were
also asked to estimate the extent to which the residents used the service
and whether or not a fee was charged.

In Tables 30, 31, and 32, basic data about service availability is
analyzed by accommodation type. In addition, each service will be discussed individually.

Group Leadership

An inquiry was made about the existence of group leadership or group
work in order to ascertain the extent to which residents were being
assisted to organize activities for themselves. It was found that a
group leadership service was available in only 8 per cent of developments;
in another 6 per cent of developments, it was available elsewhere in the
community. Hostel and mixed developments were considerably more likely
to have the services of a group worker on-site than were self-contained
developments: the service was available in only 5 per cent of self-
contained developments, compared with 17 per cent of hostel and mixed
developments. Quebec had a considerably higher proportion of developments
with group leadership services than other regions had - perhaps because
of its predominance of hostel accommodation as well as more widespread
appreciation of social animation techniques in this province.

Social Work Counselling

Social work counselling was available in relation to 51 per cent of the
developments: in 6 per cent of the cases it was available on-site and
in 45 per cent of cases it was provided elsewhere in the community.
Social work counselling was available on-site in only 4 per cent of the
self-contained developments and in 12 per cent of hostel and mixed
developments. The availability of social work counselling did not appear
to be related to community size, but there was variation between regions:
it was most available in Quebec and least available on the Prairies.

127

128

TABLE 30

AVAILABILITY OF SERVICES IN ALL DEVELOPMENTS

	AVAILABLE ON SITE OR AS A SPECIAL DEVELOPMENT SERVICE	AVAILABLE IN OR FOR THE GENERAL COMMUNITY	NOT AVAILABLE	N
Group Leadership	21 7.9%	16 6.0%	229 86.1%	266 100%
Social Work Counselling	16 6.1%	117 44.5%	130 49.4%	263 100%
Legal Aid Counselling	6 2.3%	67 25.6%	189 72.1%	262 100%
Food Shopping	1 .4%	52 19.2%	217 80.4%	270 100%
Homemaker	19 7.4%	85 33.1%	153 59.5%	257 100%
Meal Delivery	15 5.6%	85 31.6%	169 62.8%	269 100%
Home Nursing	23 8.4%	177 64.6%	74 27.0%	274 100%
Medical Checkup	29 11.1%	21 8.0%	212 80.9%	262 100%
Friendly Visiting[1]	88 33.6%	– –	174 66.4%	262 100%
Telephone Contact[1]	45 16.9%	– –	222 83.1%	267 100%
Maid Service[1]	41 15.2%	– –	229 84.9%	270 100%
Volunteer Transportation[1]	66 24.4%	– –	204 75.6%	270 100%

1 Available as a special development service or community service.

TABLE 31

AVAILABILITY OF SERVICES IN SELF-CONTAINED DEVELOPMENTS

	AVAILABLE ON SITE OR AS A SPECIAL DEVELOPMENT SERVICE	AVAILABLE IN OR FOR THE GENERAL COMMUNITY	NOT AVAILABLE	N
Group Leadership	9 4.6%	7 3.6%	181 91.9%	197 100%
Social Work Counselling	8 4.1%	88 45.1%	99 50.8%	195 100%
Legal Aid Counselling	6 3.1%	61 31.4%	127 65.5%	194 100%
Food Shopping	1 .5%	39 19.5%	160 80.0%	200 100%
Homemaker	7 3.7%	74 39.2%	108 57.1%	189 100%
Meal Delivery	11 5.4%	75 36.9%	117 57.6%	203 100%
Home Nursing	13 6.4%	152 74.5%	39 19.1%	204 100%
Medical Checkup	15 7.7%	13 6.7%	167 85.6%	195 100%
Friendly Visiting[1]	50 26.3%	– –	140 73.7%	190 100%
Telephone Contact[1]	31 15.7%	– –	166 84.3%	197 100%
Maid Service[1]	9 4.5%	– –	191 95.5%	200 100%
Volunteer Transportation[1]	42 21.0%	– –	158 79.0%	200 100%

[1] Available as a special development service or community service.

TABLE 32

AVAILABILITY OF SERVICES IN HOSTEL AND MIXED DEVELOPMENTS

	AVAILABLE ON SITE OR AS A SPECIAL DEVELOPMENT SERVICE	AVAILABLE IN OR FOR THE GENERAL COMMUNITY	NOT AVAILABLE	N
Group Leadership	12 17.4%	9 13.0%	48 69.6%	69 100%
Social Work Counselling	8 11.8%	29 42.6%	31 45.6%	68 100%
Legal Aid Counselling	0 0%	6 9.1%	60 90.9%	66 100%
Food Shopping	0 0%	13 18.6%	57 81.4%	70 100%
Homemaker	12 17.6%	11 16.2%	45 66.2%	68 100%
Meal Delivery	4 6.1%	10 15.2%	52 78.8%	66 100%
Home Nursing	10 14.3%	25 35.7%	35 50.0%	70 100%
Medical Checkup	14 20.9%	8 11.9%	45 67.2%	67 100%
Friendly Visiting[1]	38 52.8%	– –	34 47.2%	72 100%
Telephone Contact[1]	14 20.0%	– –	56 80.0%	70 100%
Maid Service[1]	32 45.7%	– –	38 54.3%	70 100%
Volunteer Transportation[1]	24 34.3%	– –	56 65.7%	70 100%

1 Available as a special development service or community service.

131

Legal Counselling

Legal counselling was available on-site in only 2 per cent of developments, although in 26 per cent of developments it was available elsewhere in the local community. It was available in or near the development in 34 per cent of self-contained developments, but in only 9 per cent of hostel and mixed developments. There were considerable regional differences: in 49 per cent of Ontario developments it was available on-site or in the community, compared with 27 per cent of British Columbia developments, 15 per cent of Prairie developments, 8 per cent of Atlantic Provinces developments, and no Quebec developments. Some of this regional variation can be accounted for by the fact that Ontario is the only province to have a comprehensive publicly funded legal aid scheme.

Food Shopping

We were interested in whether the residents of self-contained developments received help with food shopping when they lived some distance from a supermarket, or in the winter months. But only 20 per cent of all developments had food delivery services available, and in all but one development this was a community service, not one specially attached to the development. Both self-contained and hostel and mixed developments had about equal access to this service; however, since the hostel residents take their meals in a dining room or cafeteria the service would be used mainly by residents of self-contained accommodation. A food shopping service was less likely to be available in the Atlantic Provinces and Ontario than in other regions. Also, it was more likely to be available in developments whose residents had a high rate of physical incapacities. In a third of the developments that had a food shopping service available there was a fee, indicating that the service was probably a supermarket or grocery store delivery service and not a specially organized voluntary one.

Homemaker Service

A homemaker service (defined as "general home management") was available as a special development service in 7 per cent of the developments and as a community service in another 33 per cent. In 4 per cent of the self-contained developments, compared with 18 per cent of the hostel and mixed developments, a homemaker service was available in the development. In 39 per cent of the self-contained developments, compared with 16 per cent of the hostel and mixed developments, it was available in the community. Such a service was most likely to be available in Ontario and least likely in the Atlantic Provinces. Where a homemaker service was available, approximately 62 per cent of the managers said it was used by most residents and 38 per cent said it was used by a few. In 30 per cent of the cases where a homemaker service was available, no fee was charged; where a fee was charged it was geared to income in approximately three-quarters of cases. The availability of a homemaker service did not appear to be related to the physical capacity of residents.

Meal Delivery

A prepared meal delivery or meals-on-wheels service was available as a special on-site development service in 6 per cent of developments; in another 32 per cent it was available as a general community service. For some reason, this service was slightly less likely to be attached to the development itself in self-contained accommodation than in hostel and mixed developments, despite the fact that many residents of the latter were eating in a central cafeteria or dining room. Possibly some hostel managers considered room service to be a meal delivery service.

A meal service was considerably more likely to be available in metro-politan and major urban areas than in small towns. It was somewhat more available in Ontario than in other provinces; but availability did not appear to be related to the physical capacity of the majority of residents.

In 93 per cent of cases where there was a prepared meal delivery service a fee was charged, and where a fee was charged it was geared to income, in approximately one-third of the cases. In developments that had a meal service available only a few rather than most of the residents used it; this might be expected since such a service is usually designed for a minority of the elderly population.

Home Nursing

A home nursing service supplied by public health nurses or the Victorian Order of Nurses was available as a special development service in only 8 per cent of developments; in another 65 per cent it was available as a general community service. Six per cent of the self-contained developments had a special home nursing service and another 75 per cent had one available for the general community. Fourteen per cent of hostel and mixed develop-ments had a special home nursing service and 36 per cent relied on a community service. In 43 per cent of the cases where a home nursing service was available there was a fee, and where there was one it was geared to the residents' income in 86 per cent of the developments.

Home nursing was more likely to be available in metropolitan and major urban areas than in small towns. It was most available in Ontario develop-ments and least available in Quebec. Most Quebec developments had nurses on their own staff, although not necessarily providing "home nursing" to particular residents.

Home nursing was more likely to be available in developments where residents had a low physical incapacity rate than for those where a high proportion of residents were seriously incapacitated. Seventy-five per cent of develop-ments where over three-quarters of residents had no incapacity had a home nursing service - compared with 71 per cent of developments where one-half to three-quarters had no incapacity, 73 per cent of developments where one-quarter to one-half had no incapacity, 34 per cent of developments where

one-quarter or fewer had no incapacity, and 29 per cent of developments
where all residents had some physical incapacity. It is known that
developments with a high proportion of residents in poor health were
likely to have special nursing wings or at least some nursing assistance
on staff; nevertheless, the inverse availability of a service to probable
need is surprising.

Medical Checkup

Only 19 per cent of developments provided a regular medical checkup for
residents: in 11 per cent of developments it was provided on-site and
in another 8 per cent in the community. A regular checkup was available
to 14 per cent of self-contained developments and 33 per cent of hostel
and mixed developments. It tended to be more available in metropolitan
developments than in major urban and small town areas.

Friendly Visiting

A service in which volunteers visited residents to provide companionship
was provided for 34 per cent of developments - 26 per cent of self-
contained developments and 53 per cent of hostel and mixed developments.
Friendly visiting was considerably more available in metropolitan than in
smaller areas. It was most available on the Prairies, followed by Quebec,
British Columbia, Ontario, and the Atlantic Provinces. Availability did
not appear to be related to residents' health.

Telephone Contact

In some communities a telephone contact service has been established to
check up on the health and well-being of elderly residents. However, such
a service only operated in 17 per cent of our developments - 16 per cent
of self-contained developments and 20 per cent of hostel and mixed
developments. It was most likely to be found in British Columbia, followed
by Quebec, the Prairies, Ontario, and the Atlantic Provinces.

Maid Service

There was a maid service in 15 per cent of all developments - 5 per cent
of self-contained developments and 46 per cent of hostel and mixed
developments. The service was not much more available in developments
with a large proportion rather than a small proportion of incapacitated
residents. Where the service was available, 69 per cent of managers
reported that most residents used it and 31 per cent reported that only
a few did. In 64 per cent of the cases in which a maid service was
available, there was no fee charged; but if a fee was charged it was
not geared to income in 94 per cent of cases.

134

Volunteer Transportation

A volunteer transportation service was provided in relation to 24 per cent of all developments: 21 per cent of self-contained and 34 per cent of hostel and mixed developments. Thirty per cent of non-profit developments reported that a volunteer transportation service was available, compared with 14 per cent of public housing developments. The availability of this service was fairly even; it did not vary much in relation to residents' health in various developments.

Availability of Physician

As Table 33 indicates, a full-time physician was on staff in only two developments (less than 1 per cent of the sample). In 3 per cent of developments a physician made regular daily or weekly visits. In another 29 per cent a doctor was available on call. The remainder of developments either lacked regular liaison with a physician or did not reply to the question. A physician was more likely to make daily or weekly visits and to be on call in developments that had a high proportion of residents with physical incapacities - and much more likely in Quebec than in any other region. One was more likely to be on call for small town developments than for metropolitan and urban developments.

TABLE 33

DEVELOPMENTS, AVAILABILITY OF PHYSICIAN BY PROPORTION OF RESIDENTS
WITH NO PHYSICAL INCAPACITY

	FULL-TIME PHYSICIAN ON STAFF	DAILY OR WEEKLY VISITS BY PHYSICIAN	PHYSICIAN ON CALL	NONE OR NO ANSWER[1]	N
All residents with some physical incapacity	1 6.7%	2 13.3%	8 53.3%	4 26.7%	15 100%
¼ of residents or less with no physical incapacity	0 0%	6 13.7%	21 47.7%	17 38.6%	44 100%
¼ to ½ of residents with no physical incapacity	0 0%	1 5.3%	6 31.6%	12 63.2%	19 100%
½ to ¾ of residents with no physical incapacity	0 0%	0 0%	13 39.4%	20 60.6%	33 100%
¾ or over of residents with no physical incapacity	1 .6%	0 0%	36 21.1%	134 78.4%	171 100%
TOTAL	2 .7%	9 3.2%	84 29.8%	187 66.3%	282 100%

1 This column is believed to largely represent none rather than no answers.

CHAPTER 6

STAFFING

The most startling finding to emerge from this part of the questionnaire
is that 32 per cent of all developments had no paid staff working on-site
more than 10 hours per week. As Table 34 indicates, 36 per cent of
developments had only one or two paid staff, 7 per cent had three to five
staff members, 9 per cent had a staff of six to 14, and 18 per cent had
15 or more staff.

TABLE 34

DEVELOPMENTS, NUMBER OF PAID AND VOLUNTARY STAFF[1]
WORKING ON-SITE MORE THAN 10 HOURS A WEEK

	NONE	1-2 STAFF	3-5 STAFF	6-14 STAFF	15 STAFF	N
Paid	89	99	18	24	49	279
	31.9%	35.5%	6.5%	8.6%	17.6%	100%
Voluntary	260	12	4	3	0	279
	93.2%	4.3%	1.4%	1.1%	0%	100%

1 Full and part-time.

The size of developments' staff appeared to be related to accommodation
type and the number of residents. Self-contained developments had
considerably fewer staff than hostel and mixed developments. And on the
whole, developments with a large number of residents tended to have more
staff, although even small hostel developments always had a larger staff
than large self-contained ones. In fact, only six self-contained
developments had over five staff members and only two hostel developments
had fewer than six.

There was not much difference between the proportions of public and
non-profit developments that had no staff; but non-profit developments
were much more likely to have more than five staff members (because many
of the non-profit developments were hostels). There were also more staff
in developments which had a fairly high proportion of residents with
disabilities. Nevertheless, a disturbingly high proportion of developments in which over half of the residents were incapacitated had either
no staff at all or only one or two persons.

Quebec had more intensive staffing than any other province; all Quebec
developments reported having at least some staff working on-site over
10 hours a week and two-thirds of Quebec developments had 15 or more
staff persons. Of course, developments in Quebec were predominantly
of the hostel type.

Volunteers

Most non-profit developments, except where they were sponsored by a
province or municipality, used some type of volunteer help. This ranged
from simply serving on a board of directors to many hours of work in
management, bookkeeping or tenant relations. However, as Table 34
shows, only 7 per cent of all developments had volunteers putting in
over 10 hours per week. Use of volunteer staff tended to be most likely
in British Columbia and least likely in Ontario. This can be accounted
for by the high proportion of non-profit housing in British Columbia
and of public housing in Ontario. In no public housing developments
were there volunteers serving more than 10 hours a week.

Types of Staff

Tables 35, 36, and 37 show the types and size of development staff, by
accommodation type. Developments were more likely to have maintenance
staff for over 10 hours a week than any other types of staff. Maintenance
staff were followed by administrative staff (including the managers),
kitchen staff, housekeeping staff, nurses, office staff, auxiliary
medical staff, chaplains, occupational therapists, and physicians. Both
self-contained and hostel and mixed developments were most likely to have
a maintenance man on staff and least likely to have a physician.

Maintenance Staff

Maintenance staff were found in 76 per cent of all developments - in 68
per cent of self-contained developments and 97 per cent of hostel and
mixed developments. In 38 per cent of all developments maintenance
staff worked on a part-time basis only; and 55 per cent of the self-
contained developments that had maintenance staff had them part-time
only. In many - especially smaller - developments, many of the maintenance
staff were very likely to be resident caretakers (paid about $60 a month
in addition to rent); they were frequently the only staff intimately
connected with the site.

Of the small developments (20 units and under) that had maintenance
staff, 79 per cent had them on a part-time basis only; of the developments with 21 to 40 units that had maintenance staff, 38 per cent had
them part-time only; of developments with 41 to 80 units, 29 per cent
had them part-time only; of developments with 81 to 149 units, 28 per
cent had them part-time only; and of developments with 150 units or
over, 10 per cent had them only part-time. Small town developments
were less likely than developments in larger communities to have maintenance men on staff. There was not much variation between non-profit
and public housing.

137

TABLE 35

ALL DEVELOPMENTS, SIZE OF STAFF BY TYPE OF STAFF[1]

	NONE	ONE[2]	TWO[3]	THREE-FOUR[3]	FIVE[3]	N
Administrative Staff	187 67.0%	58 20.8%	23 8.2%	8 2.9%	3 1.1%	279 100%
Maintenance Staff	68 24.4%	141 50.5%	34 12.2%	28 10.0%	8 2.9%	279 100%
Office Staff	228 81.7%	42 15.1%	6 2.2%	2 .7%	1 .4%	279 100%
Chaplains	263 94.3%	12 4.3%	0 0%	4 1.4%	0 0%	279 100%
Kitchen Staff	205 73.5%	5 1.8%	7 2.5%	34 12.2%	28 10.0%	279 100%
Housekeeping Staff	207 74.2%	9 3.2%	6 2.2%	28 10.0%	29 10.4%	279 100%
Physicians	277 99.3%	2 .7%	0 0%	0 0%	0 0%	279 100%
Nurses	225 80.6%	27 9.7%	6 2.2%	10 3.6%	11 3.9%	279 100%
Auxiliary Medical Staff	239 85.7%	11 3.9%	0 0%	8 2.9%	21 7.5%	279 100%
Occupational Therapists	271 97.1%	8 2.9%	0 0%	0 0%	0 0%	279 100%

1 More than 10 hours a week.

2 Full-time or part-time (less than 35 hours weekly).

3 At least one full-time.

Administrative Staff

Managers and assistant managers, public housing area supervisors, non-profit housing secretary-treasurers, directors and superintendents of homes for the elderly, were classified as administrative staff if they worked over 10 hours a week for a specific development. Only 33 per cent of all developments had administrative staff working in the development for more than 10 hours a week: 11 per cent of self-contained developments and all hostel and mixed developments. Of all the developments that had administrative staff, 11 per cent employed them on a part-time basis only; of the self-contained developments that had administrative staff, 41 per cent employed them part-time only. In all hostel developments there was at least one full-time administrator.

Public housing developments were considerably less likely than non-
profit developments to have administrative staff attached to them.
This can be partly accounted for by the fact that there was no hostel
accommodation in public housing; but in addition it looks as if non-
profit developments tended to be more heavily staffed. Indeed, some
of the administrators of non-profit housing developments reported working
as much as 56 and 72 hours a week. Small town developments were somewhat
more likely to have administrative staff than those in larger centres:
this may be because management staff in larger centres sometimes divided
their time between a number of developments, thus being unable to spend
more than 10 hours per week on each one.

TABLE 36

SELF-CONTAINED DEVELOPMENTS, SIZE OF STAFF BY TYPE OF STAFF

	NONE	ONE[2]	TWO[3]	THREE-FOUR[3]	FIVE+[3]	N
Administrative Staff	187 / 89.5%	20 / 9.6%	2 / 1.0%	0 / 0%	0 / 0%	209 / 100%
Maintenance Staff	66 / 31.6%	115 / 55.0%	16 / 7.7%	10 / 4.8%	2 / 1.0%	209 / 100%
Office Staff	194 / 92.8%	15 / 7.2%	0 / 0%	0 / 0%	0 / 0%	209 / 100%
Chaplains	205 / 98.1%	2 / 1.0%	0 / 0%	2 / 1.0%	0 / 0%	209 / 100%
Kitchen Staff	205 / 98.1%	1 / .5%	0 / 0%	3 / 1.4%	0 / 0%	209 / 100%
Housekeeping Staff	204 / 97.6%	1 / .5%	0 / 0%	3 / 1.4%	1 / .5%	209 / 100%
Physicians	209 / 100%	0 / 0%	0 / 0%	0 / 0%	0 / 0%	209 / 100%
Nurses	207 / 99.0%	2 / 1.0%	0 / 0%	0 / 0%	0 / 0%	209 / 100%
Auxiliary Medical Staff	207 / 99.0%	2 / 1.0%	0 / 0%	0 / 0%	0 / 0%	209 / 100%
Occupational Therapists	207 / 99.0%	2 / 1.0%	0 / 0%	0 / 0%	0 / 0%	209 / 100%

1 More than 10 hours a week.

2 Full-time or part-time (less than 35 hours weekly).

3 At least one full-time.

Small developments were much less likely than large ones to have administrative staff: only 6 per cent of developments with 20 residents or
under had administrative staff, compared with 33 per cent of developments
with 21 to 40 residents, 45 per cent of developments with 41 to 80
residents, 53 per cent of developments with 81 to 149 residents, and 43
per cent of developments with 150 residents or more.

Developments in Quebec were most likely to have administrative staff,
and those in Ontario least likely: 94 per cent of Quebec developments
had administrative staff, compared with 36 per cent of Prairie developments, 30 per cent of Atlantic Provinces developments, 27 per cent of
British Columbia developments, and only 11 per cent of Ontario developments.

Kitchen Staff

Twenty-seven per cent of all developments had kitchen staff working in
excess of 10 hours a week (2 per cent of self-contained developments
and all the hostel and mixed developments). Presumably the four self-
contained developments with kitchen staff provided some sort of coffee
or meal service to residents. Practically all kitchen staff worked on
a full-time basis.

Housekeeping Staff

Twenty-six per cent of all developments had a housekeeping staff working
more than 10 hours a week - 2 per cent of self-contained developments
and 96 per cent of hostel and mixed developments. Like kitchen workers,
nearly all housekeeping staff were employed on a full-time basis.

Nurses

Nineteen per cent of all developments had nurses on staff - 1 per cent
of self-contained developments and 74 per cent of hostel developments.
Of the developments that had nurses on staff, 11 per cent had them on
a part-time basis only. As one might expect, nurses tended to be
concentrated in developments where there was a relatively high incidence
of disability: 60 per cent of developments in which all residents had
some physical incapacity had nurses on staff, compared with 59 per cent
of developments in which three-quarters or over of the residents had
incapacities, 16 per cent of developments in which half to three-quarters
of residents had physical incapacities, 18 per cent of developments in
which one-quarter to one-half of residents had physical incapacities,
and 4 per cent of developments in which less than one-quarter of residents
had physical incapacities. Eighty-eight per cent of Quebec developments
had at least one nurse on staff, compared with 25 per cent of Atlantic
Provinces developments, 8 per cent of Prairie developments, 4 per cent
of Ontario developments, and 4 per cent of British Columbia developments.

140

TABLE 37

HOSTEL AND MIXED DEVELOPMENTS, SIZE OF STAFF BY TYPE OF STAFF[1]

	NONE	ONE[2]	TWO[3]	THREE-FOUR[3]	FIVE+[3]	N
Administrative Staff	0 0%	38 54.3%	21 30.0%	8 11.4%	3 4.3%	70 100%
Maintenance Staff	2 2.9%	26 37.1%	18 25.7%	18 25.7%	6 8.6%	70 100%
Office Staff	34 48.6%	27 38.6%	6 8.6%	2 2.8%	1 1.4%	70 100%
Chaplains	58 82.9%	10 14.3%	0 0%	2 2.9%	0 0%	70 100%
Kitchen Staff	0 0%	4 5.7%	7 10.0%	31 44.3%	28 40.0%	70 100%
Housekeeping Staff	3 4.3%	8 11.4%	6 8.6%	25 35.7%	28 40.0%	70 100%
Physicians	68 97.1%	2 2.9%	0 0%	0 0%	0 0%	70 100%
Nurses	18 25.7%	25 35.7%	6 8.6%	10 14.3%	11 15.7%	70 100%
Auxiliary Medical Staff	32 45.7%	9 12.9%	0 0%	8 11.4%	21 30.0%	70 100%
Occupational Therapists	64 91.4%	6 8.6%	0 0%	0 0%	0 0%	70 100%

1 More than 10 hours a week.

2 Full-time or part-time (less than 35 hours a week).

3 At least one full-time.

Office Staff

Eighteen per cent of all developments had office staff working more than 10 hours a week - 7 per cent of self-contained developments and 51 per cent of hostel and mixed developments. Of those developments that had office staff, 26 per cent had them part-time only.

Auxiliary Medical Staff

Auxiliary medical staff, such as orderlies and nurses aids, were found in 14 per cent of developments - 1 per cent of self-contained developments and 54 per cent of hostel and mixed developments. Fifteen per cent of the developments that had auxiliary medical staff had them part-time only.

Chaplains

Only 6 per cent of all developments had chaplains on staff - 2 per cent of self-contained developments and 17 per cent of hostel and mixed developments. Thirteen per cent of the developments that had chaplains had them on a part-time basis only.

Occupational Therapists

Three per cent of all developments - 1 per cent of self-contained developments and 9 per cent of hostel and mixed developments - had an occupational therapist on staff. In seven of the eight developments occupational therapists worked only on a part-time basis.

Physicians

Only two hostel developments had a physician on staff. In both cases they were employed on a part-time basis.

CHAPTER 7

SOCIAL PARTICIPATION

This chapter deals with formal arrangements for resident participation
in development life, as well as location factors that affect involvement in community affairs and access to social and commercial facilities.

Residents' Associations

As Table 38 indicates, 29 per cent of all developments had some type of
residents' association, and these associations were fairly evenly distributed throughout the different accommodation types. However, a
greater proportion of residents tended to participate in self-contained
developments than in hostel and mixed ones. In three developments the
managers reported that no residents participated at all, which means,
presumably, that the associations were defunct. In 11 per cent of
developments less than half of the residents participated in the association.

TABLE 38

DEVELOPMENTS, PARTICIPATION IN RESIDENTS' ASSOCIATION BY ACCOMMODATION TYPE

	LESS THAN ½ RESIDENTS PARTICIPATE	½ OR MORE RESIDENTS PARTICIPATE	NO RESIDENTS PARTICIPATE	NO RESIDENTS ASSOCIATION	N
Self-Contained	21 9.7%	40 18.4%	3 1.4%	153 70.5%	217 100%
Hostel	7 16.3%	5 11.6%	0 0%	31 72.1%	43 100%
Mixed	4 13.3%	4 13.3%	0 0%	22 73.3%	30 100%
TOTAL	32 11.0%	49 16.9%	3 1.0%	206 71.0%	290 100%

Table 39 indicates that there was no appreciable difference between the
likelihood of non-profit and public housing developments having residents'
associations; but where they did exist, public housing tenants tended to
participate more than non-profit ones.

144

TABLE 39

DEVELOPMENTS, PARTICIPATION IN RESIDENTS' ASSOCIATION BY SPONSOR TYPE

	LESS THAN ½ RESIDENTS PARTICIPATE	½ OR MORE RESIDENTS PARTICIPATE	NO RESIDENTS PARTICIPATE	NO RESIDENTS ASSOCIATION	N
Non-Profit	27 13.0%	32 15.5%	0 0%	148 71.5%	207 100%
Public Housing	5 6.0%	17 20.5%	3 3.6%	58 69.9%	83 100%
TOTAL	32 11.0%	49 16.9%	3 1.0%	206 71.0%	290 100%

Table 40 shows that metropolitan area developments were much more likely to have residents' associations than developments in other communities: 48 per cent of metropolitan area developments had a residents' association, compared with 15 per cent of developments in major urban areas and 19 per cent of those in small towns.

TABLE 40

DEVELOPMENTS, PARTICIPATION IN RESIDENTS' ASSOCIATION BY COMMUNITY SIZE[1]

	LESS THAN ½ RESIDENTS PARTICIPATE	½ OR MORE RESIDENTS PARTICIPATE	NO RESIDENTS PARTICIPATE	NO RESIDENTS ASSOCIATION	N
Metropolitan Areas	18 17.5%	28 27.2%	3 2.9%	54 52.4%	103 100%
Major Urban Areas	2 7.7%	2 7.7%	0 0%	22 84.6%	26 100%
Small Towns	12 7.5%	19 11.8%	0 0%	130 80.7%	161 100%
TOTAL	32 11.0%	49 16.9%	3 1.0%	206 71.0%	290 100%

1 Census classification.

Resident Participation on Management Boards

Only 5 per cent of all developments had a resident on their management
board: all were non-profit developments. Quebec had the highest rate
of tenant participation in management: 13 per cent of developments had
at least one resident on their board. This was followed by British
Columbia with 10 per cent, the Prairies with 4 per cent, the Atlantic
Provinces with 3 per cent, and Ontario with 1 per cent. Of the developments reporting tenant participation on the management board, 72 per cent
had only one tenant.

Resident Assistance with Chores

Table 41 shows that in a surprisingly high 51 per cent of developments
residents took on duties such as cleaning halls, gardening, or helping
out in the kitchen. However, only 23 per cent of the developments in
which residents helped out had more than half the residents involved.
British Columbia had the highest incidence of resident assistance: in
63 per cent of developments residents were involved. This was followed
by the Prairies with 59 per cent, Quebec with 56 per cent, the Atlantic
Provinces with 55 per cent, and Ontario with 36 per cent. The regional
differences can be largely accounted for by variations in the distribution
of public and non-profit housing: public housing developments made very
little use of resident help. The need for residents to assume chores
probably stems from the difficult financial position of many non-profit
housing developments - but it also can spring from an interest in providing
purposeful roles for old people.

TABLE 41

DEVELOPMENTS, RESIDENT ASSISTANCE WITH CHORES BY REGION

	LESS THAN $\frac{1}{2}$ RESIDENTS ASSIST	$\frac{1}{2}$ OR MORE RESIDENTS ASSIST	NO RESIDENTS ASSIST	N
Atlantic Provinces	19 30.6%	15 24.2%	28 45.2%	62 100%
Quebec	15 46.9%	3 9.4%	14 43.7%	32 100%
Ontario	32 34.8%	1 1.1%	59 64.1%	92 100%
Prairies	22 43.1%	8 15.7%	21 41.2%	51 100%
British Columbia	24 50.0%	6 12.5%	18 37.5%	48 100%
TOTAL	112 39.3%	33 11.6%	140 49.1%	285 100%

Buddy Systems

A common form of preventing isolation in housing developments is a buddy system that involves pairing up residents so that one checks regularly on the other, in order to ascertain health condition and other needs. Thirty-eight per cent of the sampled developments had a buddy system operating: 36 per cent of non-profit developments and 43 per cent of public housing ones. A slightly higher proportion of self-contained developments had buddy systems than hostel and mixed ones: 41 per cent, compared with 28 per cent.

The prevelance of buddy systems did not appear to be related to the physical capacity of residents. Buddy systems were more available in developments located in large communities (48 per cent of metropolitan developments had one, compared with 40 per cent of major urban and 32 per cent of small-town developments). Regionally, buddy systems were most available in Ontario: 56 per cent of Ontario developments had a buddy system, compared with 47 per cent of Prairie developments, 40 per cent of Quebec developments, 27 per cent of British Columbia developments, and 12 per cent of Atlantic Provinces developments.

Relationship with Community Groups

Managers were asked to indicate the degree to which churches, service clubs and social clubs had contact with their residents. Churches were the organizations most frequently mentioned as having "major contact" with residents, followed by service clubs and social clubs.

Churches were reported as having "major contact" with residents in 22 per cent of developments, a "fair amount" of contact in 53 per cent of developments, and "little contact" in 26 per cent of developments. Small-town developments were considerably more likely than developments in larger communities to report that churches had major contact with their residents. The extent to which churches had major contact with developments did not appear to vary with the physical capacity of residents. On a regional basis, Quebec developments were the most likely to have major contact with churches - 45 per cent, compared with 28 per cent of Prairie developments, 19 per cent of British Columbia developments, 19 per cent of Atlantic Provinces developments, and 14 per cent of Ontario developments. Churches were more likely to have a major contact with non-profit developments (25 per cent) than with public housing ones (16 per cent).

Eleven per cent of developments had major contact with service clubs, 38 per cent had a fair amount, and 51 per cent had little contact. Developments in British Columbia were the most likely to have a major amount of contact - 27 per cent, compared with 14 per cent of Quebec developments, 11 per cent of Prairie developments, 7 per cent of Ontario developments, and 4 per cent of Atlantic Provinces developments. As far as different sized communities were concerned, developments in metropolitan

areas were more likely to have major contact with service clubs than
those in smaller communities. Service clubs were more likely to have
major contact with non-profit developments (14 per cent) than with
public housing developments (4 per cent).

Only 5 per cent of all developments reported having major contact with
social clubs; 32 per cent had a fair amount of contact; and 63 per cent
had little contact. Prairie developments were most likely to have major
contact with social clubs - 9 per cent, compared with 7 per cent of
Quebec developments, 5 per cent of Ontario developments, 4 per cent of
Atlantic Provinces developments, and 2 per cent of British Columbia
developments. Again, developments in metropolitan areas were slightly
more likely to have major contact with social clubs than those in
smaller communities. Social clubs were more likely to have major or a
fair amount of contact with residents of non-profit developments than
with residents of public housing developments.

Isolation

We wanted to explore the extent to which developments for the elderly
were socially isolated from surrounding residential areas. Development
managers may not be the most unbiased persons on this question: nevertheless, 12 per cent of the managers said that their developments were
considered "largely isolated", 47 per cent said their developments were
considered "slightly isolated", and 41 per cent considered their development to be "just another residence on the street." This can be seen in
Table 42. Self-contained developments appeared to be more integrated
into the community than hostel and mixed developments: they were more
likely to be considered "just another residence" and less likely to be
considered "slightly isolated." Both accommodation types were about
equally likely to be considered "largely isolated."

TABLE 42

DEVELOPMENTS, DEGREE OF ISOLATION BY ACCOMMODATION TYPE

	JUST ANOTHER RESIDENCE ON THE STREET	SLIGHTLY ISOLATED	LARGELY ISOLATED	N
Self-Contained	94 / 43.7%	95 / 44.2%	26 / 12.1%	215 / 100%
Hostel and Mixed	25 / 34.2%	40 / 54.8%	8 / 11.0%	73 / 100%
TOTAL	119 / 41.3%	135 / 46.9%	34 / 11.8%	288 / 100%

Public housing developments were considered somewhat less isolated than non-profit housing developments (probably because they comprised self-contained accommodation only). Fifty-one per cent of public housing developments were considered "just another residence on the street", compared with 38 per cent of non-profit developments; 51 per cent of non-profit developments were considered "slightly isolated", compared with 36 per cent of public developments. The same proportion of public and non-profit housing managers considered their developments "largely isolated."

Table 43 indicates the degree of isolation by neighborhood type. The closer the development was to the downtown core, the more likely it was to be considered as just another residence on the street, and the less likely it was to be considered slightly isolated. However, when it came to the "largely isolated" category, the opposite relationship was found: downtown developments were considerably more likely than rural developments to be considered largely isolated.

TABLE 43

DEVELOPMENTS, DEGREE OF ISOLATION BY NEIGHBORHOOD TYPE

	JUST ANOTHER RESIDENCE ON THE STREET	SLIGHTLY ISOLATED FROM OTHER RESIDENCES	LARGELY ISOLATED FROM OTHER RESIDENCES	N
Downtown	30 46.2%	25 38.5%	10 15.4%	65 100%
Older Residential	46 44.7%	45 43.7%	12 11.7%	103 100%
Suburban	34 38.6%	43 48.9%	11 12.5%	88 100%
Rural	5 33.3%	9 60.0%	1 6.7%	15 100%
TOTAL	115 42.4%	122 45.0%	34 12.5%	271 100%

Access to Community Facilities

The participation of residents in the social life of any community is bound to be largely determined by the degree of access that they have to the main social and commercial facilities. These places not only provide various services but also important opportunities for socializing -

indeed, shopping can be an opportunity to observe and meet others just as much as to purchase goods. For old people in particular, it is important to know what community facilities are within close and easy walking distance. Table 44 indicates the ease of access, by walking and public transport, to a number of important community facilities, which are dealt with in greater detail in the following paragraphs. In the case of each of these facilities, public housing developments were somewhat more likely than non-profit ones to be located in out-of-the-way places where access to facilities was difficult either by a walk or public transport. However, compared with non-profit developments, public housing ones were more likely to be within easy walking distance of all but the libraries and churches - while being less likely to be within easy reach by public transport of all facilities. Such differences could be related more to accommodation type than to sponsor type.

TABLE 44

DEVELOPMENTS, ACCESS TO COMMUNITY FACILITIES

	EASY WALK FOR MOST RESIDENTS	EASY ACCESS BY PUBLIC TRANSPORT	DIFFICULT BY PUBLIC TRANSPORT OR WALKING (OR NO SUCH FACILITY AVAILABLE)	N
Shopping Centre	155 56.0%	89 32.1%	33 11.9%	277 100%
Grocery Store	239 83.3%	43 15.0%	5 1.7%	287 100%
Medical Office/Clinic	126 44.7%	131 46.5%	25 8.9%	282 100%
Major Churches	169 58.3%	95 32.8%	26 9.0%	290 100%
Hospital	55 20.8%	166 62.6%	44 16.6%	265 100%
Library	117 44.8%	113 43.3%	31 11.9%	261 100%
Park	134 51.0%	97 36.9%	32 12.2%	263 100%
Senior Citizens Centre[1]	71 32.8%	102 47.2%	43 19.9%	216 100%

1 It is believed that many of the managers who did not answer this question did so because there was no such centre in this community.

150

Fifty-six per cent of developments were within an easy walk of a shopping centre, 32 per cent were within easy reach by public transport,
and in 12 per cent there was difficulty either way (or no shopping
centre at all). Hostel and mixed developments were more likely than
self-contained developments to be within easy walking distance of a
shopping centre. Also, downtown developments were about twice as likely
as residential and suburban developments to be within an easy walk of
a shopping centre (85 per cent, compared with 47 per cent and 45 per
cent); 66 per cent of the developments in rural areas were within easy
walking distance of shopping.

Eighty-three per cent of developments were within an easy walk of a
grocery shop; 15 per cent were within easy reach by public transport;
in 2 per cent there was difficulty either way (or no grocery store at
all). Hostel and mixed developments and self-contained ones were about
equally likely to be within an easy walk of a grocery shop. Downtown
developments and rural developments were equally likely to be within an
easy walk of a grocery shop; suburban developments were the least likely.

Forty-five per cent of developments were within easy walking distance
of a medical office or clinic, 47 per cent were within easy public
transport ride, and in 9 per cent there was difficulty either way (or
no such facility). Hostel and mixed developments were less likely than
self-contained developments to be within an easy walk of medical offices.
In terms of neighborhood type, downtown developments were the most
likely to be within easy walking distance and suburban developments the
least.

Fifty-eight per cent of developments were within easy walking distance
of a church, 33 per cent were within easy reach by public transport,
and in 9 per cent there was difficulty either way (or none at all nearby).

Twenty-one per cent of developments were within easy walking distance
of a hospital, 63 per cent were within easy reach by public transport,
and in 17 per cent there was difficulty either way (or no hospital at
all in the area).

Forty-five per cent of developments were within easy walking distance
of a library, 43 per cent were within easy reach by public transport,
and in 12 per cent there was difficulty either way (or no library at all).

Fifty-one per cent of developments were within easy walking distance of
a park, 37 per cent were within easy reach by public transport, and in
12 per cent access was difficult either way (or there was no park around).

Thirty-three per cent of developments were within easy walking distance
of a senior citizens centre, 47 per cent were within easy reach by public
transport, and in 20 per cent there was difficulty either way (or no such
centre at all). Hostel and mixed developments were slightly less likely

than self-contained developments to be within an easy walk of a senior
citizens centre. Also, downtown and rural developments were the most
likely to be within easy walking distance of a senior citizens centre
and suburban developments were the least likely.

Table 45 indicates the number of community facilities difficult to
reach (by walking or public transport); the eight facilities referred
to are the ones in Table 44. Sixty-eight per cent of developments
reported that none of the eight facilities were difficult to reach (if
they existed in the community), 19 per cent reported that two or less
were difficult to reach, 6 per cent reported that three to four were
difficult to reach, and 7 per cent reported that five or more were
difficult to reach. A slightly higher proportion of hostel and mixed
developments than self-contained developments reported that none of
the eight facilities were difficult to reach, and a higher proportion
of self-contained developments than hostel and mixed ones reported that
up to four of the facilities were difficult to reach.

TABLE 45

DEVELOPMENTS, NUMBER OF COMMUNITY FACILITIES DIFFICULT TO REACH[1],
BY ACCOMMODATION TYPE

	5 OUT OF 8 DIFFICULT TO REACH	3-4 OUT OF 8 DIFFICULT TO REACH	2 OR LESS DIFFICULT TO REACH	NONE DIFFICULT TO REACH	N
Self-Contained	11 6.3%	12 6.9%	36 20.7%	115 66.1%	174 100%
Hostel and Mixed	4 6.9%	2 3.4%	9 15.5%	43 74.1%	58 100%
TOTAL	15 6.5%	14 6.0%	45 19.4%	158 68.1%	232 100%

1 Not within easy walk or easy reach by public transport.

In terms of sponsor type, 70 per cent of non-profit developments
reported that none of the eight facilities were difficult to reach,
compared with 63 per cent of public housing developments. Also, a
higher proportion of public housing developments than non-profit
developments reported that up to four of the services were difficult
to reach.

In terms of community size, all eight facilities appeared to be easier to reach in metropolitan areas than in smaller centres, perhaps because of better public transport. Seventy-six per cent of metropolitan area developments reported that all eight facilities were easy to reach, compared with 52 per cent of major urban areas and 65 per cent of small town developments. At the other end of the scale, only 3 per cent of metropolitan area developments reported that five or more out of the eight facilities were difficult to reach, compared with 4 per cent of major urban and 9 per cent of small town developments. Forty-three per cent of major urban developments reported difficulty in reaching up to four facilities, compared with 25 per cent of rural developments and 21 per cent of metropolitan developments.

Table 46 shows the relationship between neighborhood type and access to community facilities. Eighty per cent of downtown developments reported that none of the eight facilities were difficult to reach, compared with 69 per cent of developments in older residential areas, 67 per cent of developments in suburban areas, and 55 per cent of developments in rural areas.

TABLE 46

DEVELOPMENTS, NUMBER OF COMMUNITY FACILITIES DIFFICULT TO REACH[1],
BY NEIGHBORHOOD TYPE

	5 OUT OF 8 DIFFICULT TO REACH	3-4 OUT OF 8 DIFFICULT TO REACH	2 OR LESS DIFFICULT TO REACH	NONE DIFFICULT TO REACH	N
Downtown	0 0%	2 3.7%	9 16.7%	43 79.6%	54 100%
Older Residential	8 10.0%	4 5.0%	13 16.3%	55 68.8%	80 100%
Suburban	3 4.2%	7 9.7%	14 19.4%	48 66.7%	72 100%
Rural	1 9.1%	0 0%	4 36.4%	6 54.5%	11 100%
TOTAL	12 5.5%	13 6.0%	40 18.4%	152 70.0%	217 100%

1 Not within easy walk or easy to reach by public transport.

There did not appear to be much regional variation in access to the eight facilities, except for the Atlantic Provinces. There, a higher than average proportion of developments reported that four and five facilities were difficult to reach and a considerably lower than average proportion reported that none of the eight facilities were difficult to reach.

CHAPTER 8

MANAGEMENT

The important role of management in housing programs for the elderly has
come to the fore time and time again in this study. This chapter provides
some information about the characteristics of the people who run housing
developments for the elderly, their perceptions about the relative importance of their various tasks, the problems they encounter, and specific
aspects of their administrative policies.

It should be noted that the questionnaire was not always completed by a
professional manager or administrator. Sometimes there was no such
official (as in the case of many non-profit developments); in other
instances another employee completed the questionnaire. Nevertheless,
because it was requested that the questionnaire be filled out by "the
management person who has the most direct contact with the residents
and is closest to supervising the overall operation of this particular
housing development," it is likely that the respondents were usually
performing management functions - even if they lacked the official title
of manager. The respondent was asked to indicate his or her title and
position. Approximately three-quarters of all respondents were either
managers or other professional staff; in approximately one-quarter of
cases the questionnaire was completed by a member of the sponsoring non-
profit corporation, most frequently the secretary-treasurer or president.

Characteristics of Managers

Twenty per cent of the respondents were female and 80 per cent were male.
Compared with public housing, non-profit housing had a slightly higher
proportion of female managers and a slightly lower proportion of males.

Two per cent of the respondents had less than high school education,
22 per cent had some high school education, another 22 per cent had
graduated from high school, 27 per cent had up to two years of post
secondary education, 19 per cent had three to four years of college, and
7 per cent had some postgraduate education. There was not a great deal
of difference between the educational level of public and non-profit
housing managers, except that the non-profit ones tended to be rather
more widely distributed throughout the top and bottom educational levels,
whereas the public housing managers were more homogeneous in educational
level - being clustered more in the intermediate levels (grade 12, 13,
and one or two years of college). This presumably reflects more standard-
ized hiring practices in the public housing sector.

The respondents were predominantly middle-aged. Only 4 per cent were under 30, 25 per cent were 30 to 44 years, 28 per cent were 45 to 54 years, 28 per cent were 55 to 64 years, 13 per cent were 65 to 74 years, and 2 per cent were 75 years and over. As in the case of educational level, the public and non-profit sectors did not differ greatly, except that the non-profit sector encompassed a wider age range.

The respondents' experience in working with the elderly varied widely. Fifty-six per cent of respondents had worked for the elderly for five or more years, 28 per cent for two to four years, and 15 per cent for less than two years. The non-profit sector had managers with the longest experience: 60 per cent had worked with the elderly for five or more years, compared with 49 per cent of public housing managers. Twelve per cent of the non-profit managers had worked with the elderly for less than two years, compared with 23 per cent of the public housing managers.

The managers of metropolitan area developments were much more likely to have worked over five years with the elderly than other urban and small-town managers (74 per cent, compared with 48 per cent and 46 per cent). Given the age range of the sample, it is clear that approximately half the managers had taken on their present job fairly late in life.

Managers' Attitudes about their Tasks

A particular interest was taken in respondents' attitudes toward the various tasks involved in operating their development and, in particular, how the attitudes of hostel and self-contained managers varied, if any.

Table 47 shows that 78 per cent of the managers either kept the accounts and managed finances or felt it should be "very much" their responsibility; 11 per cent did not, but felt that it should be their responsibility. Another 11 per cent of managers reported that they did not keep accounts and look after finances and felt that it should not be their responsibility. Managers of non-profit developments were more likely than those of public housing developments to be either doing the job already or be very favorably predisposed toward doing it. If they did not already manage development finances, public housing managers were more likely than the non-profit ones to want the added responsibility; however, the public housing managers themselves were evenly split between those who felt that the extra responsibility should be part of their job and those who did not.

155

TABLE 47

DEVELOPMENT MANAGERS, ATTITUDES CONCERNING KEEPING ACCOUNTS
AND MANAGING FINANCES, BY SPONSOR TYPE

	PRESENTLY MY JOB AND/OR FEEL SHOULD BE "VERY MUCH" MY RESPONSIBILITY	NOT MY JOB BUT SHOULD BE MY RESPONSIBILITY	NOT MY JOB AND SHOULD NOT BE MY RESPONSIBILITY	N
Non-Profit	130 82.3%	15 9.5%	13 8.2%	158 100%
Public Housing	49 69.0%	11 15.5%	11 15.5%	71 100%
ALL MANAGERS	179 78.2%	26 11.4%	24 10.5%	229 100%

Table 48 shows managers' attitudes toward running social service programs. Only 26 per cent were either doing this already or were very favorably inclined toward doing it. If it was not their responsibility, only 14 per cent felt that it should be - and 60 per cent felt that it should not be. Managers of non-profit housing developments appeared more involved in and sensitive to meeting social needs of residents than public housing managers did; 31 per cent of non-profit managers, compared with 10 per cent of public housing managers reported that they were presently responsible for running social service programs (or felt that it should be very much their responsibility). If it was not their responsibility, a higher proportion of non-profit than public housing managers felt that it should be - and, conversely, a lower proportion felt that it should not be. These differences, of course, had much to do with the fact that public housing was entirely self-contained.

The fact remains, however, that 53 per cent of non-profit managers and 73 per cent of public housing managers did not have responsibility for running social service programs and did not think this should be their responsibility. This might be easier to understand if most developments had other staff on whom the responsibility fell. But since they tended not to, and since the respondents were the persons who had closest contact with residents, these findings suggest that social needs are a low priority for many managers - perhaps because of the competing demands of financial and maintenance matters, perhaps because of their own conceptions about the role of a housing manager.

TABLE 48

MANAGERS, ATTITUDES CONCERNING RUNNING SOCIAL SERVICE PROGRAMS
BY SPONSOR TYPE

	PRESENTLY MY JOB AND/OR FEEL SHOULD BE "VERY MUCH" MY RESPONSIBILITY	NOT MY JOB BUT SHOULD BE MY RESPONSIBILITY	NOT MY JOB AND SHOULD NOT BE MY RESPONSIBILITY	N
Non-Profit	38 31.4%	19 15.7%	64 52.9%	121 100%
Public Housing	10 16.1%	7 11.3%	45 72.6%	62 100%
ALL MANAGERS	48 26.2%	26 14.2%	109 59.6%	183 100%

Table 49 shows that 55 per cent of managers were in contact with and
helped residents on an individual basis, or were very favorably inclined
toward seeing this as part of their job. Twenty-six per cent were not
already doing this, but felt that it should be part of their job. There
was not much difference between the two sponsor types here, except that
if helping residents individually was not part of their present job, a
higher proportion of public housing than non-profit housing managers
felt that it should be - and, conversely, fewer felt that it should not
be. This might be partially accounted for by the larger staff complements
that non-profit managers were responsible for supervising.

TABLE 49

DEVELOPMENT MANAGERS, ATTITUDES CONCERNING HELPING RESIDENTS WITH NEEDS ON
INDIVIDUAL BASIS, BY SPONSOR TYPE

	PRESENTLY MY JOB AND/OR FEEL SHOULD BE "VERY MUCH" MY RESPONSIBILITY	NOT MY JOB BUT SHOULD BE MY RESPONSIBILITY	NOT MY JOB AND SHOULD NOT BE MY RESPONSIBILITY	N
Non-Profit	77 55.0%	31 22.1%	32 22.9%	140 100%
Public Housing	38 55.9%	24 35.3%	6 8.8%	68 100%
ALL MANAGERS	115 55.3%	55 26.4%	38 18.3%	208 100%

Table 50 shows that 43 per cent of managers were presently obtaining community services for residents as a part of their job, or felt that they should be very much responsible for doing this. Twenty-five per cent were not doing this but felt it should be their responsibility, and 33 per cent were not and did not think it should be their responsibility. The non-profit managers were considerably more likely to be involved in or inclined toward this role as a part of their job.

TABLE 50

DEVELOPMENT MANAGERS, ATTITUDES CONCERNING OBTAINING COMMUNITY SERVICES, BY SPONSOR TYPE

	PRESENTLY MY JOB AND/OR FEEL SHOULD BE "VERY MUCH" MY RESPONSIBILITY	NOT MY JOB BUT SHOULD BE MY RESPONSIBILITY	NOT MY JOB AND SHOULD NOT BE MY RESPONSIBILITY	N
Non-Profit	61 46.2%	36 27.3%	35 26.5%	132 100%
Public Housing	21 35.0%	11 18.3%	28 46.7%	60 100%
ALL MANAGERS	82 42.7%	47 24.5%	63 32.8%	192 100%

Table 51 reveals that 78 per cent of managers collected rents or felt this to be very much a part of their responsibility; 12 per cent did not, but felt that this should be a part of their responsibility; 11 per cent did not, and felt it should not be their responsibility. There was not much difference in the responses of non-profit and public housing managers; however, the public housing managers were slightly more likely to be already collecting rents or to be in favor of doing so.

TABLE 51

MANAGERS, ATTITUDES CONCERNING RESPONSIBILITY FOR RENT COLLECTION, BY SPONSOR TYPE

	PRESENTLY MY JOB AND/OR FEEL SHOULD BE "VERY MUCH" MY RESPONSIBILITY	NOT MY JOB BUT SHOULD BE MY RESPONSIBILITY	NOT MY JOB AND SHOULD NOT BE MY RESPONSIBILITY	N
Non-Profit	124 77.5%	17 10.6%	19 11.9%	160 100%
Public Housing	60 76.9%	11 14.1%	7 9.0%	78 100%
ALL MANAGERS	184 77.3%	28 11.8%	26 10.9%	238 100%

158

Table 52 indicates managers' attitudes toward being responsible for
building maintenance. Sixty-four per cent were either already
responsible or felt strongly that they should be, 15 per cent were
not but felt that they should be, and 21 per cent were not and felt
that they should not be. Public housing managers were considerably
more likely to be looking after maintenance or be favorably inclined
toward doing so - and, conversely, they were less inclined to reject
the responsibility of building maintenance.

This section suggests that, compared with the non-profit managers,
public housing managers tend to see their role more in terms of rent
collecting and building maintenance and less in terms of running social
service programs and obtaining community services.

TABLE 52

MANAGERS, ATTITUDES CONCERNING RESPONSIBILITY FOR MAINTENANCE, BY SPONSOR TYPE

	PRESENTLY MY JOB AND/OR FEEL SHOULD BE "VERY MUCH" MY RESPONSIBILITY	NOT MY JOB BUT SHOULD BE MY RESPONSIBILITY	NOT MY JOB AND SHOULD NOT BE MY RESPONSIBILITY	N
Non-Profit	87 57.2%	30 19.7%	35 23.0%	152 100%
Public Housing	58 77.3%	4 5.3%	13 17.3%	75 100%
ALL MANAGERS	145 63.9%	34 15.0%	48 21.1%	227 100%

Management Problems

We asked managers to identify their two greatest problems in running
their developments. Thirty-three per cent of those who answered said
they had no problems. As Table 53 indicates, of those who responded
to the question, financial problems were by far the most frequently
mentioned. The next most frequently mentioned problem area was
administration and tenant relations. These were followed by residents'
medical and dietary problems, staffing problems, design problems,
maintenance problems, lack of social and recreation services, a high
demand for accommodation and difficulty with expansion, location factors,
and security matters.

TABLE 53

MANAGEMENT PROBLEMS*

Finances (including budgets and rent collection)	105
Administration (including relationships with board and government)	33
Tenant Relations	30
Residents' Medical and Dietary Problems	22
Staffing	20
Design (including machanical system and poor construction)	20
Maintenance	19
Lack of Social and Recreation Services	18
Demand for Accommodation and Difficulty with Expansion	18
Location	15
Security	8
None	75

* N = 229

Demand for Accommodation

Managers were asked about the extent to which there was a shortage of decent and reasonably priced accommodation for senior citizens in their community. Table 54 indicates that 33 per cent of the managers reported a severe shortage of self-contained accommodation, 30 per cent reported a moderate shortage, 24 per cent reported some shortage, and only 14 per cent indicated that there was no shortage. The shortage of self-contained accommodation was most pronounced in major urban areas where 62 per cent of managers reported a severe shortage, compared with 26 per cent of small-town managers and 36 per cent of metropolitan managers. At the other end of the scale, none of the respondents in major urban areas reported that there was no shortage of self-contained accommodation, compared with only 2 per cent of metropolitan area respondents and 24 per cent of small-town respondents.

TABLE 54

DEVELOPMENTS, REPORTED DEMAND FOR SENIOR CITIZENS SELF-CONTAINED ACCOMMODATION, BY COMMUNITY SIZE

	SEVERE SHORTAGE	MODERATE SHORTAGE	SOME SHORTAGE	NO SHORTAGE	N
Metropolitan Areas	33 35.9%	32 34.8%	25 27.2%	2 2.2%	92 100%
Major Urban Areas	16 61.5%	7 26.9%	3 11.5%	0 0%	26 100%
Small Towns	34 25.6%	36 27.1%	31 23.3%	32 24.1%	133 100%
TOTAL	83 33.1%	75 29.9%	59 23.5%	34 13.5%	251 100%

Table 55 shows that 31 per cent of managers reported a severe shortage of hostel accommodation, 30 per cent reported a moderate shortage, 29 per cent reported some shortage, and 11 per cent reported no shortage. Generally speaking, there was a greater perceived shortage of self-contained than of hostel accommodation. However, more small-town managers reported a severe shortage of hostel than a severe shortage of self-contained accommodation.

TABLE 55

DEVELOPMENTS, REPORTED DEMAND FOR SENIOR CITIZENS HOSTEL ACCOMMODATION, BY COMMUNITY SIZE

	SEVERE SHORTAGE	MODERATE SHORTAGE	SOME SHORTAGE	NO SHORTAGE	N
Metropolitan Areas	17 23.3%	26 35.6%	24 32.9%	6 8.2%	73 100%
Major Urban Areas	10 52.6%	4 21.1%	4 21.1%	1 5.3%	19 100%
Small Towns	30 31.6%	25 26.3%	27 28.4%	13 13.7%	95 100%
TOTAL	57 30.5%	55 29.4%	55 29.4%	20 10.7%	187 100%

Tenant Selection Preferences

Managers of non-profit developments were asked whether, because of their organizational affiliation, preference was given to any particular ethnic, language, religious, or service club group. Of the 209 managers of non-profit developments, only 71 answered the question - a significant response in itself. Of those 71, 79 per cent reported that there were no admission preferences of the sort mentioned and 21 per cent admitted that there were such preferences. Of the 15 managers who admitted exercizing preferences, three reported that one-quarter or fewer of their residents were from the preferred group, three reported that about one-quarter to one-half of their residents were, two reported that about one-half to three-quarters of their residents were, six reported that all of their residents were, and one gave no answer.

Admission and Exit Policies Concerning Health

As far as health requirements are concerned, the admission policies of developments varied widely. As Table 56 indicates, 12 per cent of developments would not admit residents having any physical incapacities, 44 per cent would admit people with slightly limited abilities, 38 per cent would admit those with moderately limited abilities, and only 6 per cent would admit those with seriously limited abilities. Hostel developments, in which more special care is usually offered, were more likely than self-contained developments to admit residents with serious disabilities. Many hostel developments had nursing wings into which feeble residents can be moved. It is surprising that 3 per cent of the self-contained developments would admit those with seriously limited abilities. However, these residents would probably have active spouses to look after them.

TABLE 56

DEVELOPMENTS, MAXIMUM DEGREE OF PHYSICAL INCAPACITY PERMITTED
FOR ADMISSION BY ACCOMMODATION TYPE

	NO INCAPACITY	SLIGHTLY LIMITED ABILITY	MODERATELY LIMITED ABILITY	SERIOUSLY LIMITED ABILITY	N
Self-Contained	31	96	77	7	211
	14.7%	45.5%	36.5%	3.3%	100%
Hostel	1	17	15	8	41
	2.4%	41.5%	36.6%	19.5%	100%
Mixed	2	11	13	2	28
	7.1%	39.3%	46.4%	7.1%	100%
TOTAL	34	124	105	17	280
	12.1%	44.3%	37.5%	6.1%	100%

We inquired about when residents were asked to move to another level of care due to health deterioration. Table 57 shows that the majority of developments (77 per cent) appeared to draw the line at what we defined as seriously limited ability. However, in 11 per cent of the hostel developments, many of which had nursing facilities, residents were asked to move only when they required active treatment or hospitalization. In 6 per cent of the hostels, residents were never asked to move. It is strange that in 19 per cent of the self-contained developments and 11 per cent of the hostels residents with moderately limited abilities were asked to move. This may be due to lack of supportive services in these developments.

TABLE 57

DEVELOPMENTS, MAXIMUM DEGREE OF PHYSICAL INCAPACITY PERMITTED
FOR CONTINUED RESIDENCE, BY ACCOMMODATION TYPE

	SLIGHTLY LIMITED ABILITY	MODERATELY LIMITED ABILITY	SERIOUSLY LIMITED ABILITY	NEVER ASKED TO MOVE	WHEN HOSPITALIZATION OR ACTIVE TREATMENT REQUIRED	N
Self-Contained	4 / 2.1%	36 / 19.3%	142 / 75.9%	2 / 1.1%	3 / 1.6%	187 / 100%
Hostel	0 / 0%	4 / 11.1%	26 / 72.2%	2 / 5.6%	4 / 11.1%	36 / 100%
Mixed	0 / 0%	1 / 3.8%	24 / 92.3%	1 / 3.8%	0 / 0%	26 / 100%
TOTAL	4 / 1.6%	41 / 16.5%	192 / 77.1%	5 / 2.0%	7 / 2.8%	249 / 100%

Looking at when residents would be asked to leave a development in relation to sponsor type, we found that the public housing officials were more likely than the non-profit managers to ask residents to leave when they were seriously disabled: 88 per cent of the public housing developments, compared with 73 per cent of the non-profit ones. Four of the non-profit developments never asked residents to move for health reasons, compared with only one public housing development. This can be largely accounted for by the fact that the non-profit housing consisted of 35 per cent hostel or mixed accommodation whereas the public housing consisted of self-contained units only.

The managers were asked if residents were requested to move to single accommodation should they become widowed. Thirty-five per cent of developments followed this practice; 25 per cent followed it "sometimes"; 39 per cent did not follow it.

CHAPTER 9

FINANCES

The financial arrangements for building and operating public housing
are fairly standard across the country. Therefore, questions dealing
with finances were directed only at the non-profit sector (and the
percentages presented in this chapter therefore refer only to the non-
profit developments that responded to particular questions).

Mortgage Financing

As pointed out in Part II, since 1946, non-profit sponsors have been
able to obtain 90 per cent (and lately 95 per cent) CMHC mortgage loans,
repayable at an interest rate of usually $1\frac{1}{2}$ per cent below the current
NHA rate for home buyers. Table 58 indicates that only 19 per cent of
developments received mortgage financing from sources other than CMHC
or the Quebec Housing Corporation (QHC): 7 per cent received loans
covering 10 per cent or less of building and land costs, 8 per cent
received loans covering 11 to 30 per cent of costs, and 4 per cent
received loans covering more than 30 per cent of costs.

TABLE 58

NON-PROFIT DEVELOPMENTS WITH MORTGAGE LOANS OTHER THAN FROM CMHC OR QUEBEC
HOUSING CORPORATION, BY REGION

	LOANS COVERING 10% OR LESS OF BUILDING AND LAND COSTS	LOANS COVERING 11-30% OF BUILD-ING AND LAND COSTS	LOANS COVERING OVER 30% OF BUILDING AND LAND COSTS	NO NON-CMHC OR NON-QHC LOANS	N
Atlantic Provinces	6	3	0	31	40
	15.0%	7.5%	0%	77.5%	100%
Quebec	0	2	1	29	32
	0%	6.3%	3.1%	90.6%	100%
Ontario	3	7	0	15	25
	12.0%	28.0%	0%	60.0%	100%
Prairies	1	2	4	44	51
	2.0%	3.9%	7.8%	86.3%	100%
British Columbia	4	1	3	39	47
	8.5%	2.1%	6.4%	83.0%	100%
TOTAL	14	15	8	158	195
	7.2%	7.7%	4.1%	81.0%	100%

On a regional basis, 40 per cent of Ontario developments received non-CMHC mortgage financing, compared with 23 per cent of Atlantic Provinces developments, 17 per cent of British Columbia developments, 14 per cent of Prairie developments, and 9 per cent of Quebec developments (the Quebec figures exclude Quebec Housing Corporation loans as well as CMHC loans). Non-CMHC mortgage financing tended to account for a greater proportion of total costs in the Prairies and British Columbia than in other regions. Whether developments received non-CMHC or QHC mortgage financing did not appear to depend on whether they were hostel or self-contained. Mixed developments, however, were for some reason less likely to receive such assistance - 22 per cent of hostel developments were supported with non-CMHC and non-QHC mortgages, compared with 20 per cent of self-contained developments and only 10 per cent of mixed developments.

Operating Subsidies

Table 59 indicates that 30 per cent of non-profit developments received operating subsidies of some type: 8 per cent received help from municipalities, 16 per cent from provincial governments (these were mainly Quebec developments), and 7 per cent from unspecified private organizations. Self-contained developments were slightly more likely to receive subsidies - 34 per cent, compared with 29 per cent of hostel and 18 per cent of mixed developments. For all types of accommodation, the provincial government was the main source of operating subsidies.

TABLE 59

NON-PROFIT DEVELOPMENTS RECEIVING OPERATION SUBSIDIES, BY ACCOMMODATION TYPE

	SUBSIDIES FROM MUNICIPALITY	SUBSIDIES FROM PROVINCE	SUBSIDIES FROM UN-SPECIFIED PRIVATE GROUPS	NO SUBSIDIES	N
Self-Contained	12 10.5%	19 16.7%	8 7.0%	75 65.8%	114 100%
Hostel	2 4.8%	8 19.0%	2 4.8%	30 71.4%	42 100%
Mixed	0 0%	3 10.7%	2 7.1%	23 82.1%	28 100%
TOTAL	14 7.6%	30 16.3%	12 6.5%	128 69.6%	184 100%

165

Rent Subsidies

Table 60 shows that, according to managers, 18 per cent of developments
had some residents receiving rent subsidies: 6 per cent had tenants
receiving subsidies from municipal agencies, 11 per cent from provincial government agencies, and 2 per cent from federal agencies. Rent
subsidies were more common in hostel developments: 29 per cent of
hostels had residents receiving rent subsidies, compared with 25 per
cent of mixed developments and 12 per cent of self-contained ones.
Most of the rent subsidies mentioned must have been supplements to the
old age security pension and guaranteed income supplement, and administered by provincial or municipal welfare administrators, because other
rent supplement programs were not known to be operating in Canada at
the time the study was conducted.

TABLE 60

NON-PROFIT DEVELOPMENTS IN WHICH SOME RESIDENTS' RENTS
WERE DIRECTLY SUBSIDIZED, BY ACCOMMODATION TYPE

	MUNICIPAL RENT SUBSIDIES	PROVINCIAL RENT SUBSIDIES	FEDERAL (NON-CMHC) RENT SUBSIDIES	NO RENT SUBSIDIES	N
Self-Contained	5 5.6%	6 6.7%	0 0%	78 87.6%	89 100%
Hostel	2 5.7%	7 20.0%	1 2.9%	25 71.4%	35 100%
Mixed	2 7.1%	3 10.7%	2 7.1%	21 75.0%	28 100%
TOTAL	9 5.9%	16 10.5%	3 2.0%	124 81.6%	152 100%

Municipal Taxes

Table 61 shows that in addition to various types of capital and
operating subsidies, 82 per cent of non-profit developments were getting municipal tax relief: 48 per cent paid no taxes, 35 per cent
paid reduced taxes, and only 18 per cent paid full taxes. Ontario
developments were less likely to obtain tax relief than those in
other regions: 38 per cent of Ontario developments paid full municipal
taxes, compared with 25 per cent of Atlantic Provinces developments,

20 per cent of Quebec developments, 15 per cent of Prairie developments, and 2 per cent of British Columbia developments. Developments in Quebec were the most likely to pay no municipal taxes - 80 per cent, compared with 65 per cent of Atlantic Provinces developments, 48 per cent of British Columbia developments, 38 per cent of Prairie developments, and no Ontario developments.

TABLE 61

NON-PROFIT DEVELOPMENTS, MUNICIPAL TAXES BY REGION

	PAY NO MUNICIPAL TAXES	PAY REDUCED MUNICIPAL TAXES	PAY FULL MUNICIPAL TAXES	N
Atlantic Provinces	26 65.0%	4 10.0%	10 25.0%	40 100%
Quebec	24 80.0%	0 0%	6 20.0%	30 100%
Ontario	0 0%	15 62.5%	9 37.5%	24 100%
Prairies	18 37.5%	23 47.9%	7 14.6%	48 100%
British Columbia	22 47.8%	23 50.0%	1 2.2%	46 100%
TOTAL	90 47.9%	65 34.6%	33 17.6%	188 100%

Rents

Table 62 shows the monthly rents charged for one-bedroom self-contained units. Fifteen per cent of the rents were under $50, 49 per cent were $50 to $69, 24 per cent were $70 to $89, and 12 per cent were $90 and over. At the time of the study the federal old age pension and guaranteed income supplement amounted to $133 for a single person; thus such high rents must have been very difficult for residents without other means. As the table indicates, rents for non-profit developments tended to be higher in downtown areas than in other neighborhoods.

The rents for dwelling units in non-profit developments were considerably higher than public housing rents. Comparable public housing rents for a single person without means other than the old age security pension and guaranteed income supplement would have amounted to $32 a month in Newfoundland, New Brunswick, Ontario, and Alberta. In British Columbia, public housing rents went from $34 to $58 for single occupancy (median $48) and from $45 to $70 for double occupancy (median $60). In Saskatchewan, minimum public housing rents were equated with rents charged in non-profit projects in the community.

TABLE 62

NON-PROFIT DEVELOPMENTS, MONTHLY RENTS FOR ONE-BEDROOM UNITS, BY NEIGHBORHOOD TYPE

	UNDER $50	$50-$69	$70-$89	$90 AND OVER	N
Downtown	2 6.1%	10 30.3%	12 36.4%	9 27.3%	33 100%
Older Residential Area	9 17.3%	31 59.6%	9 17.3%	3 5.8%	52 100%
Suburb	9 18.4%	25 51.0%	11 22.4%	4 8.2%	49 100%
Rural Area	1 12.5%	4 50.0%	2 25.0%	1 12.5%	8 100%
TOTAL	21 14.8%	70 49.3%	34 23.9%	17 12.0%	142 100%

One hundred and twenty-eight developments reported the rents charged for bachelor units. Thirteen per cent charged under $40, 27 per cent charged $40 to $49, 31 per cent charged $50 to $59, 17 per cent charged $60 to $69, 8 per cent charged $70 to $79, 2 per cent charged $80 to $99, and 2 per cent charged $100 and over.

Table 63 shows the monthly rents charged for single hostel rooms (meals inclusive). Eight per cent of developments charged less than $100, 36 per cent charged $100 to $120, 16 per cent charged $130 to $159, and 41 per cent charged $160 and over. Given this rent range, one sees that about half of the developments charged a rent for hostel accommodation that was higher than the entire old age security pension and guaranteed income supplement - although it will be recalled that 29 per cent of hostel developments had some tenants receiving direct rent subsidies. Nevertheless,

168

the high rents in this type of accommodation clearly priced it beyond the means of many pensioners. Rent patterns did not appear to be related to neighborhood type, as in the case of rents for self-contained accommodation.

TABLE 63

NON-PROFIT DEVELOPMENTS, MONTHLY RENTS FOR SINGLE HOSTEL ROOMS,
BY NEIGHBORHOOD TYPE

	Under $100	$100-$129	$130-$159	$160 AND OVER	N
Downtown	2	12	0	7	21
	9.5%	57.1%	0%	33.3%	100%
Older Residential Area	2	5	2	9	18
	11.1%	27.8%	11.1%	50.0%	100%
Suburb	0	5	7	5	17
	0%	29.4%	41.2%	29.4%	100%
Rural Area	1	1	1	5	8
	12.5%	12.5%	12.5%	62.5%	100%
TOTAL	5	23	10	6	64
	7.8%	35.9%	15.6%	40.6%	100%

When the rent structure of both self-contained and hostel accommodation was analyzed by the over-all level of physical capacity reported for developments, it was found that rent levels increased with the proportion of disabled residents in a development; and they increased very sharply when over 75 per cent of residents had some form of physical incapacity. Presumably, these rent increases reflected the cost of providing more staff.

Income Ceilings and Floors

Table 64 shows that 49 per cent of non-profit developments had no income ceiling for admission - which suggests that there was no policy of restricting accommodation to low or moderate income residents. On the other hand, 14 per cent of developments required that their residents have monthly incomes of under $200, 22 per cent had a ceiling of $200 to $249, 11 per cent had a ceiling of $250 to $349, and 4 per cent had a ceiling of $350 or more. Self-contained developments tended to restrict accommodation to low and moderate income persons more than hostel and

mixed developments: only 32 per cent of self-contained developments
had no income ceiling, compared with 78 per cent of hostel developments
and 73 per cent of mixed developments.

TABLE 64

NON-PROFIT DEVELOPMENTS, MAXIMUM MONTHLY INCOME PERMITTED FOR ADMISSION OF
SINGLE APPLICANTS, BY ACCOMMODATION TYPE

	UNDER $200	$200-$249	$250-$349	$350 AND OVER	NO INCOME CEILING	N
Self-Contained	19 17.8%	35 32.7%	18 16.8%	1 .9%	34 31.8%	107 100%
Hostel	3 7.5%	2 5.0%	1 2.5%	3 7.5%	31 77.5%	40 100%
Mixed	2 6.7%	2 6.7%	1 3.3%	3 10.0%	22 73.3%	30 100%
TOTAL	24 13.6%	39 22.0%	20 11.3%	7 4.0%	87 49.2%	177 100%

Table 65 indicates that far more emphasis was placed by non-profit
sponsors in British Columbia than in other regions to serve low and
moderate income persons. Ninety-five per cent of British Columbia
developments had an income ceiling for admission, compared with 72 per
cent of Ontario developments, 49 per cent of Prairie developments, 34
per cent of Quebec developments, and 9 per cent of Atlantic Provinces
developments.

As Table 66 shows, in addition to income ceilings, 20 per cent of
developments maintained minimum monthly income floors below which they
would not admit an applicant: 4 per cent required than an applicant
have a monthly income of at least $80, 6 per cent required a minimum
income of $81 to $100, and 11 per cent required a minimum income of
$101 to $150. In addition, 21 per cent of developments indicated that
they used means other than an income floor to assess an applicant's
ability to pay rent. However, as the incomes of a large proportion of
elderly Canadians were restricted to the old age security pension and
guaranteed income supplement of $133 (at the time of the study), it
is obvious that income floors must have been less of a deterrent to
admitting the low income elderly than such persons' sheer inability to
afford high rents. An income floor was more common in British Columbia
developments than in other regions: 31 per cent of British Columbia
developments had some form of income floor, compared with 26 per cent
of Ontario developments, 20 per cent of Prairie developments, 16 per
cent of Quebec developments, and 6 per cent of Atlantic Provinces
developments.

170

TABLE 65

NON-PROFIT DEVELOPMENTS, MAXIMUM MONTHLY INCOME PERMITTED FOR ADMISSION OF SINGLE APPLICANTS, BY REGION

	UNDER $200	$200-$249	$250-$349	$350 AND OVER	NO INCOME CEILING	N
Atlantic Provinces	1 2.9%	0 0%	0 0%	2 5.7%	32 91.4%	35 100%
Quebec	3 9.7%	1 3.2%	0 0%	3 9.7%	24 77.4%	31 100%
Ontario	1 4.0%	7 28.0%	10 40.0%	0 0%	7 28.0%	25 100%
Prairies	6 14.0%	6 14.0%	9 20.9%	0 0%	22 51.2%	43 100%
British Columbia	13 30.2%	25 58.1%	1 2.3%	2 4.7%	2 4.7%	43 100%
TOTAL	24 13.6%	39 22.0%	20 11.3%	7 4.0%	87 49.2%	177 100%

TABLE 66

NON-PROFIT DEVELOPMENTS, MINIMUM MONTHLY INCOMES PERMITTED FOR ADMISSION OF SINGLE APPLICANTS, BY REGION

	$80 OR LESS	$81-$100	$101-$150	OTHER MEANS TO ASSESS ABILITY TO PAY	NO INCOME FLOOR	N
Atlantic Provinces	1 2.9%	0 0%	1 2.9%	21 60.0%	12 34.3%	35 100%
Quebec	0 0%	1 3.2%	4 12.9%	10 32.3%	16 51.6%	31 100%
Ontario	2 8.7%	1 4.3%	3 13.0%	2 8.7%	15 65.2%	23 100%
Prairies	3 6.7%	3 6.7%	3 6.7%	2 4.4%	34 75.6%	45 100%
British Columbia	1 2.2%	5 10.9%	8 17.4%	3 6.5%	29 63.0%	46 100%
TOTAL	7 3.9%	10 5.6%	19 10.6%	38 21.1%	106 58.9%	180 100%

171

Interest in Building Additional Housing for the Elderly

In order to investigate the extent to which financial assistance programs encouraged or deterred non-profit sponsors from developing additional accommodation for the elderly, managers were asked whether their organizations were interested in building or managing other housing developments for the elderly. As Table 67 indicates, 62 per cent were interested: 65 per cent of self-contained managers, 55 per cent of hostel managers, and 61 per cent of mixed development managers replied in the affirmative.

Twenty-seven per cent of managers who were interested in developing additional accommodation saw no particular problems in doing this. However, the remaining 73 per cent of respondents identified a series of problems. By far the most frequently mentioned were financial ones (mentioned by 28 managers). This was followed by difficulty in obtaining provincial government assistance (mentioned by 12), land scarcity (10), staffing problems (7), CMHC red tape (4), lack of municipal co-operation (2), and construction problems (1).

TABLE 67

NON-PROFIT DEVELOPMENTS, INTEREST IN BUILDING
ADDITIONAL HOUSING FOR ELDERLY, BY ACCOMMODATION TYPE

	INTERESTED	NOT INTERESTED	N
Self-Contained	41	75	116
	35.3%	64.7%	100%
Hostel	18	22	40
	45.0%	55.0%	100%
Mixed	11	17	28
	39.3%	60.7%	100%
TOTAL	70	114	184
	38.0%	62.0%	100%

PART IV

CASE STUDIES

CONTENTS

CHAPTER 1

PURPOSE AND METHODOLOGY

From the beginning of this study it was recognized that an adequate understanding of the environment produced by NHA financed housing for the elderly
across Canada could not be gained simply by employing the usual type of
social survey research. Surveys are necessary (and they have been used) to
collect and process a great volume of data from a population large enough to
be statistically valid. But they cannot substitute for on-the-spot observation.

By undertaking a series of case studies, it was intended to explore the
environmental dynamics pertaining to senior citizens housing developments and
obtain a better understanding of the factors that determine satisfaction,
social interaction and community integration. While focusing especially on
the use of facilities and social services, the study staff also wanted to use
the case studies to portray a range of living situations in accommodation
designated especially for old people and, to the extent possible, present
examples of sound design and administration.

Selection

The study team considered a variety of ways of completing the case studies.
Initially it seemed wise to limit the number of developments to be examined
to less than 10 in order to subject them to a fairly in-depth examination,
more along the lines of studies carried out by the Ministry of Housing and
Local Government in the United Kingdom.[1]

Certainly, rigorous investigation, preferably of a longitudinal nature, can
serve to develop insights that are not apparent in a short-term review.
However, a larger number of case studies would be necessary (36 was one figure
considered) in order to sufficiently represent the great variety of housing
developments that exist in different regions of the country. On reflection
this was rejected as it was thought that it would result in too superficial
an approach, considering constraints in the research budget. It was also
thought that such a very large number of case study reports would greatly
complicate the analysis.

It was eventually agreed that the study team would aim at visiting 20 housing
developments across the country. However, in the end, 19 case studies were
actually initiated and completed, this number appearing to adequately satisfy
the selection criteria as well as staff arrangements.

---

1 Ministry of Housing and Local Government. For example, Grouped Flatlets
   for Old People, A Sociological Study, HMSO, 1962.

In consultation with the study's Advisory Committee, it was decided that
the target developments for the case studies should provide for an adequate
recognition of the following criteria:

1) Regions of the country.
2) Location (metropolitan versus small town and downtown
   versus suburban).
3) Size.
4) Accommodation type (self-contained, hostel, and mixed).
5) Sponsorship (public housing versus non-profit).
6) Management type (full-time, volunteer, etc.).
7) User dependency.
8) Scope of facilities and services.
9) Provision of facilities and services (sponsor versus
   community agency).
10) Tenant participation.
11) Building type (high-rise, bungalow, etc.).
12) Degree of institutionalization.

Housing developments were then selected for inclusion in the case studies,
bearing in mind the above criteria. This was difficult because of the lack
of a sufficient knowledge base about housing developments across the country
that could satisfy some of the more subjective criteria (e.g. tenant
participation, institutionalization). It was originally intended that the
returned questionnaires from the manager survey would be used in the selection
process. However, because of a time overlap, the questionnaires had not been
fully returned, let alone analyzed, by the time the case studies were selected.
However, with the help of the study's Advisory Committee, CMHC officials in
Ottawa, and staff of provincial housing corporations, the developments were
selected. They satisfied some of the main criteria as follows:

. Region of the country: Atlantic Provinces 3; Quebec 3; Ontario 6;
  the Prairies 4; British Columbia 3.

. Location: metropolitan areas 12; small towns 7; downtown 8; suburban
  residential 11.

. Size: the developments selected ranged in size from 10 to 400 dwelling
  units. In terms of dwelling units and/or hostel beds, they fell into
  the following categories:

    1-20 units and/or beds   - one development
    21-40 units and/or beds   - one development
    41-80 units and/or beds   - eight developments
    81-149 units and/or beds   - one development
    150 units and/or beds and over   - eight developments

. Accommodation type: self-contained 9; hostel 3; mixed 7.

. Sponsorship: public housing 6; non-profit 13 (church or religious order 4, ethnic 1, service club 4, municipalities 3, housing foundation 2).

. Building type: one storey 5; two and three storeys 4; four to 10 storeys 4; 11 storeys and over 6.

In terms of the actual nature of NHA financed housing for the elderly in Canada,[2] the case study selection was biased in favor of large developments situated in major metropolitan areas. This bias was intentional as the trend of building accommodation for the elderly seems to be in this direction and because it was considered that interesting facilities and services were both more likely to be required and found in such developments. Another bias is that the developments selected for the case studies probably are somewhat atypical in terms of their range of facilities and services. A more accurate picture of actual service and facility provision can be obtained by referring to the report of our manager survey.[3]

Methodological Approach

The aim of the case studies was to gain an understanding of the nature of the residential environment in the target developments. To obtain the necessary data, our field workers engaged in:

1) An examination of the mail questionnaire as completed by the sponsor/manager;

2) An in-depth interview with the senior administrative people of the development;

3) Interviews with a random sample of residents;

4) Interviews with staff of local social and recreational agencies;

5) General on-site observation.

The length of time it took to complete the case studies varied from two to eight working days, with an average of five.

An interview guide was used to assist the field workers in ordering and reporting their work. The guide mainly contained open-ended questions that required a response from the development management. A service profile sheet and a facility profile sheet were also included, however, and one of these had to be completed for each significant internal or external service and facility. Although field workers were requested to complete the case study interview guide in as much detail as possible, they were also reminded that

---

2 See Part II.

3 See Part III.

the purpose of the instrument was mainly to indicate the range of data required for the study; they were encouraged to rephrase or expand on questions as they considered appropriate. In most cases, the data collected in the guide was supplemented by photographs, residents' handbooks and other documents provided both by development managers and community agencies.

A good deal of the field workers' on-site time was occupied in administering the user study. The methodology and responses for this survey are indicated elsewhere in the study.[4] However, field workers were asked to integrate data elicited by the user study in their case study report for each development. In this way, the user survey was considered an integral part of the case study approach and indeed it is difficult to appreciate how a residential environment can be studied without providing for the collection of data from the residents themselves concerning their characteristics, lifestyles, and attitudes. It was decided to opt for individual interviews with residents rather than group meetings, primarily because of the difficulty with data analysis inherent in the latter methodology; however, in many cases, our field workers did have opportunities to talk with residents on a group basis. This happened most frequently in hostels or mixed developments where in many cases our field workers ate in the dining room. Where residents' associations existed, our field workers also sought out their leadership.

After completing a case study, the field worker was asked to write a summary report organized under the following headings: development description, residents' characteristics, sponsorship and management, services, facilities, community relations, social interaction, finances, weak and strong features. This report was later discussed in depth in Ottawa with the dialogue being tape-recorded. At this time a specific theme was selected for the final case study report. Then, using all the documents (case study interview guide, service and facility profile sheet, mailed questionnaire, user interview schedules, miscellaneous papers, as well as the tape-recorded conversation about the development), the senior research assistant prepared a draft of the final case study report along the theme selected. After more discussion, this was again edited and in some cases largely rewritten.

Relevance

For reasons of economy and focus, it was necessary to exclude a great deal of data from the case study reports. Rather than attempt to present a very comprehensive description of the nature of the residential environment occupied by the elderly in each development, we thought it preferable to focus instead on those factors in the development that have particularly unique or interesting characteristics. An appreciation of the fundamental elements of the development and its residents can be gained by glancing at the fact sheet that accompanies each report.

---

4 See Part V.

Persons familiar with our target developments may point out that in the intervening period since our field work (conducted in the summer of 1971, except for work in the Province of Quebec in December of that year), the situations that we write about may have changed considerably. We appreciate this, but it was our intention to record the nature of the residential environment at a particular point in time. Studying the process by which an environment develops and transforms must be the job of other researchers.

In presenting these reports, we naturally attempted to be as objective as possible. Nevertheless, the reader may, from time to time, discern passages in which the study staff indicate a specific reaction to factors present in housing developments. We do not apologize for at times praising or condemning; after all, the task of the social researcher surely becomes a bankrupt one if unravelling social dynamics becomes the supreme objective, rather than the application of insights obtained to human welfare.

CHAPTER 2

THE SMALL DEVELOPMENT'S GOOD NEIGHBOR

Many self-contained senior citizens housing developments in Canada are
located on the outskirts of small towns. These developments are character-
istically small, often providing little in the way of common facilities and
services. As a rule, the small communities in which these developments are
situated are not large enough to support public transportation systems or
visiting nurse, homemaker and food delivery services. While family and
friends can often support the elderly residents, just as often they cannot.
Their relatively isolated location, coupled with the lack of social services,
presents a great potential threat. But, as this case study illustrates,
the problem can be met with a workable solution.

Summerset Court

Summerset Court is located a mile from downtown Summerside, just off
Granville Street, a secondary entrance road to the town. The surrounding
area has been built up over the last 10 years and consists of Canadian Armed
Forces and privately owned family houses, as well as government institutions.
Summerset Court's immediate neighbor is Summerset Manor, a special care home
operated by the P.E.I. Department of Welfare. At the time of the case study,
P.E.I.'s public health offices, a new high school, a public hospital, a small
medical clinic, and a bowling alley were located within a quarter of a mile
of the Court. There was a small supermarket within five blocks of Summerset
Court, although Court tenants did not seem to use it. A quarter of a mile
beyond the Court, the town gave way to pastures and vegetable farms.

The Court contains 42 self-contained dwelling units. Twenty of these were
built in 1966-1967 in the form of five four-unit common-wall bungalows. In
1967-1968, a further 22 units were built in a single one-storey building which
also incorporated a recreation room. Each building has laundry facilities.
Twenty-five of the units are one-bedroom apartments, 17 are bachelors.

Altogether, when the study was done, 53 people lived in the Court, most of
whom were single women. Of the 16 individuals in the 13 households contacted
in our user study sample, 13 were women. The majority of persons interviewed
were between 75 and 79 years of age. Three were between 70 and 74 and two
were 80 or more. Generally, the health of residents was good; over two-thirds
of those interviewed showed no physical disability and no individual interviewed
had more than a slight physical disability. There were, however, some units
in the development temporarily sitting empty because residents were sick in
the hospital or convalescing with a relative. One such household fell in our
sample and had to be substituted. Two-thirds of the residents had some income
over and above the federal old age pension and guaranteed income supplement.
In most of these cases, this was made up of savings or payments on the sale
of family farms. Over half those interviewed were the widowed wives of farmers.

SUMMERSET COURT, SUMMERSIDE, P.E.I.

Fact Sheet

THE BUILDINGS

. Location

On the outskirts of Summerside, Prince Edward Island - a community of 11,000 people.

. Type and Size

Forty-two self-contained units, 20 of which (all one-bedroom) were built in five bungalow rows of four units. Twenty-two of the units (17 bachelors and five one-bedrooms) were built in a one-storey, U-shaped building allowing each unit a direct out of doors exit and an exit to an interior corridor.

. Facilities

A recreation room was attached to the U-shaped building and a washer and dryer facility was located in each building.

. Date of Construction - 1966/1967.

. Rents

Bachelor - $50 a month; one-bedroom - $60 a month.

THE MANAGEMENT

. National Housing Act Provision

Section 16A, limited dividend, and 16, non-profit housing.

. Sponsor

The Prince Edward Island Housing Authority, presently responsible to the Minister of Education for Prince Edward Island.

. Management Staff

The buildings were managed by the Prince Edward Island Housing Authority supervisor of housing with offices in Charlottetown. Maintenance was done by crews from the main offices.

THE RESIDENTS

. Number - 53.

. Sex and Marital Status

Eight were men, 45 were women. A sample of 13 households was composed of: eight widows, one widower, one spinster, one married woman whose husband was in a chronic care hospital, and two married couples.

. Health Condition

Generally, it was good. Over two-thirds admitted to no physical disability. No one interviewed appeared to have more than a slight disability.

. Age

The majority interviewed were between 75-79 years of age. Three were from 70-74, two were over 80.

185

Potential Problems at Summerset Court

Prince Edward Island is not a wealthy province. In 1961, only 55 per cent
of the households in the province had flush toilets although the figure for
Canada was 80 per cent. This was not just a result of the island's rural
nature; 54 per cent of Canada's rural households had flush toilets, but
only 24 per cent of Prince Edward Island's did. The average household
income in Prince Edward Island was $3,335 compared to the national average
of $4,906. One-quarter of Prince Edward Island households had annual incomes
below $2,000 and nearly one-half had below $3,000. While these figures have
no doubt changed in the last 10 years, the 1971 old age security pension and
guaranteed income supplement incomes of $1,620 for a single person or $3,060
for a married couple, along with the relatively low rent of $50 for a bachelor
and $60 for a one-bedroom apartment, made Summerset Court a good place to
live.

As the supervisor of housing for the Prince Edward Island Housing Authority
pointed out, the Court probably provided the best housing many of the
residents had ever experienced. The housing authority saw its role as
providing good accommodation on a scale suitable to the island's public and
private economy; and as far as the Court was concerned, they had done it.

But the Court's elderly residents, though generally in good health, still
had social needs and health care requirements that had to be met if good
morale and health were to be maintained – these included better access to
shopping, films, churches, clubs, medical services and friends. The Court,
however, because of its isolated situation on the outskirts of town, did
not afford easy access to these amenities. Few of the tenants had any
means of transportation of their own. Few could walk downtown to shops and
services and back again on the same day. Few had a family that was at their
beck and call to provide transportation. And the island, because of its low
population density and lack of money, had few services to compensate for this.
There was no public bus; no Victorian Order of Nurses; no meals-on-wheels
service; and no homemaker service.

None of the tenants interviewed made use of the neighboring medical clinic.
The proximity of the hospital may have been comforting but generally, on a
day-to-day basis, this facility was not used. In addition, the grocery store
located close to the development simply did not provide the range of shopping
opportunities that the residents considered necessary. And, although rent
took a relatively small amount of their pensions, there was still not enough
money left for over extravagant use of taxis. The potential problem in
Summerset Court, then, was the distance from local services or facilities in
combination with the absence of home visiting services.

Summerset Court's Good Neighbor

The potential problem of isolation, however, had not been allowed to present
an insuperable problem because of the relationship that Summerset Manor –
the Department of Welfare special care home next to the development – had

developed with the Court's residents. The Manor provided 43 hostel beds and 82 long-term nursing beds for the aged or physically infirm and was built about the same time as the first units in Summerset Court, in a period when the self-contained housing program for the island's elderly was also administered by the Department of Welfare.

Because both the Court and the Manor were originally offshoots of the same department, the Manor's administrator was responsible for rent collection and seeing to any needs that tenants might have in the self-contained units. This relationship had fortunately continued, even though the Court was administered by the Prince Edward Island Housing Authority which was responsible to the Minister of Education. As a sort of low level inter-departmental favor, the Manor's administrator continued to collect the rents the Court residents brought to his office at the start of every month. This process gave the administrator an opportunity to keep informed on the health condition of Court residents, as well as a chance to provide a little assistance or advice when required. He made sure that Court residents were aware that the entertainment programs and dining room in the Manor were available to them. While the residents seldom responded to this invitation, they made good use of one Manor service - the Volkswagen bus.

The Manor bus sat eight to 10 people, and from 9 a.m. to 5 p.m. five days a week, it made about seven trips to downtown Summerside. Nearly all the Court residents used this service which went a long way toward making the Court socially and psychologically a very reasonable place for older people to live in. It allowed them to do their shopping where they wanted, have their hair cut, visit their doctors and dentists and see to their legal matters. Furthermore, residents were not charged for this service because it was a charge on the budget of the special care home. The cost of the service, including the vehicle's depreciation and the driver's salary, was around $6,700 a year.

Some Court tenants reported that the only drawback to the Manor bus service was that it did not run on weekends or in the evenings. Outside of a few churches that would provide transportation for Sunday services, there was no way to get out at these times other than by taxi or a relative's car. A few tenants suggested that they would like to be able to get downtown to a movie or club meeting in the evening. The majority of tenants, however, agreed that the bus service was sufficient to make the place very liveable. In explaining what they liked about the buildings and location, nearly all those interviewed mentioned the bus as a real qualifying factor in making the environment work.

Conclusions

Potential problems in Summerset Court arose from Prince Edward Island's size, its lack of financial resources, and the resulting lack of services. But these problems were prevented by the form of institutional flexibility frequently associated with small-scale jurisdictions, and the less structured

personal relationships that develop between government officials and
citizens in small communities.

The availability of the Manor bus was the essential component in making
the Court a socially successful housing development for elderly persons
in good health. But the informal way in which this service was provided
would probably only be possible with small developments. Certainly, if
there were 500 tenants instead of 53 in Summerset Court, it is unlikely
that the bus service would have been provided because limits would have
to be set on its use. In addition, the flexibility of institutional lines
that allowed the two Prince Edward Island government departments to
co-operate in serving the elderly would have been less likely to develop
in provinces where government is more bureaucratic.

However, this type of co-operation between neighboring government institutions
might perhaps be fostered elsewhere through the development of formulas that
recognize the cost implications of shared service provision and facilities.
Particularly in small towns, it makes little sense for each institution to
develop a complete range of services and facilities for the elderly. Unless
joint planning and cost sharing are possible, it is unlikely that potential
problems will be prevented.

CHAPTER 3

TENANT PARTICIPATION MAKES A HIGH-RISE APARTMENT WORK

There is a popular myth that high-rise apartment buildings mitigate against neighborliness and social interaction. The rationale of the myth runs like this: the apartment unit is a cell which presents a closed door to the remainder of the building and which looks out over the street, away from any physically accessible neighbors. As arrival and departure from the building is through a closed elevator shaft and impersonal hallways, any chance of friendly contact with neighbors is prevented. However, our case study of Northwood Towers found little substance to this view.

Northwood Towers

Northwood Towers is located on the northern fringe of the oldest residential suburb of Halifax. One might even consider it downtown, since it is about 10 minutes by bus from the city centre. The immediate area of the Towers was originally built as wooden two-storey row housing. When the case study was done, many of these dwellings had deteriorated beyond rehabilitation. To the north and east of the Towers, extensive redevelopment had taken place over the last 50 years. Much of the resultant housing was still in good repair and more rebuilding was taking place. The Towers itself really formed a part of the redevelopment process in the neighborhood.

The Towers shares the middle section of a city block with a new building called Northwood Manor. The Towers and the Manor, both projects of the Halifax Senior Citizens' Housing Corporation Limited, are physically and administratively connected. At the time of the case study, the Manor was just beginning to be occupied. Consequently, interviews were restricted to residents of the Towers. The Towers faces Northwood Terrace, the northernmost end of Creighton Street, known as one of Halifax's tougher districts. The Manor faces Gottingen Street, a major arterial route. The military base HMCS Stadaconna, on the other side of the street, was then quite inward looking and presented a barrier to the neighborhood.

The Towers, about five years old when the case study was done, is a seven-storey apartment building containing 73 dwelling units (27 bachelor units and 46 one-bedroom units). The Manor, built during 1970 and 1971, contains 160 dwelling units and 199 hostel rooms (119 of the latter being singles and 80, doubles).

Altogether, there were 117 persons living in Northwood Towers' 73 units. Slightly more than half of these were women. In the random sample of 15 households in the building, 11 were married couples with both spouses living at home, one was composed of two maiden sisters, one of a man whose wife was in a nursing home, and two of widows. The sample of 15 households

189

NORTHWOOD TOWERS, HALIFAX, NOVA SCOTIA
Fact Sheet

THE BUILDING

. Location

In a redevelopment area of Halifax, about 10 minutes from downtown by regular public bus.

. Type and Size

Twenty-seven bachelor and 46 one-bedroom dwelling units in a seven-storey concrete tower. In the summer of 1971, an adjacent building (Northwood Manor) was constructed by the same sponsor providing 150 bachelor and 10 one-bedroom dwelling units and 279 hostel beds in 119 single and 160 double rooms. The two buildings were physically connected.

. Facilities

A recreation room and laundry room on the main floor. The new building was to add to these a meeting and recreation hall, a cafeteria, a tuck shop, beauty and barber shops, greenhouse and playing area, outside game facilities and assorted lounge areas.

. Date of Construction - 1967 (second building - 1971).

. Rents

Bachelor - $94.50 a month; one-bedroom - $112.50 a month. Dwelling units cost the same in the new building. Hostel accommodation was $185.95 for a single; $175.93 for a double room, including meals, housekeeping services and laundry.

THE MANAGEMENT

. National Housing Act Provision - Section 16, non-profit housing.

. Sponsor

Halifax Senior Citizens Housing Corporation Limited - a non-profit corporation composed of representatives of professional, religious, fraternal, service, business and labor organizations in Halifax. Northwood Towers and Northwood Manor were then their only buildings.

. Management Staff

The Towers' staff consisted of the executive administrator (with offices away from the building), a part-time cleaner (28 hours a week), and a tenant social coordinator (who was compensated with reduced rent). With the addition of the Manor, staff was to increase to 64 persons (about 50 of these providing food, housekeeping, and laundry services).

THE RESIDENTS (Towers only)

. Number - 117.

. Sex and Marital Status

Somewhat more than half were women. A random sample of 15 households produced 11 married couples, two widows, one married man whose wife was in a nursing home, and two maiden sisters living together.

. Health Condition

Generally, it was good. Seven of the 15 people interviewed admitted and appeared to have no physical incapacity. Six of the 15 admitted and appeared to have only slight incapacity. Two women were moderately incapacitated.

. Age

Nine of the 15 residents interviewed were 75 years of age or over. Only one person was under 65.

included 12 men and 15 women. Nine of the 15 residents interviewed in
Northwood Towers were 75 years of age or over and only one person (a
married woman whose husband was absent) was under 65 years of age. Seven
of the 15 individuals interviewed admitted no (and appeared to have no)
physical incapacity: four of these were men, three were women. Five of
the 15 persons interviewed either admitted they had or appeared to have
slight physical incapacity: four of these were men, two were women. Two
women residents showed moderate physical incapacities. Generally, the
residents in the building were healthy and active.

An Enthusiastic Administrator and a Talented Tenant Leader

Northwood Towers was the first project of the Halifax Senior Citizens'
Housing Corporation Limited. The corporation was formed in 1962 of members
from various service clubs, local churches, labor and commercial associations.
At the time of our visit, it had a membership of about 100 persons. The
general membership elected 18 directors who serve without remuneration.
While the board of directors was constitutionally vested with complete control
of the corporation, the program had always been carried on by the executive
director. Before Northwood Manor was built, the executive director was the
only paid employee outside of a part-time cleaner. Administrative assistance
was provided on a voluntary basis.

The executive director (and former president of the corporation) involved
himself in senior citizens housing after listening to a local radio phone-in
program about the dilemma of older persons regarding housing. His original
interest was a purely humanitarian one and he had carried this with him in
his organizational style.

Before he became involved in housing the elderly, the executive director
made the acquaintance of an older man who had spent his life operating
small circuses and working in promotion and sales. When the Towers was
about to open in 1967, this man offered to help move in the tenants who
needed assistance. The circus man himself was in good health and owned a
home of his own outside Halifax, but his wife's health was failing. The
Towers was a logical place for the couple to live - close to services, yet
still providing a large degree of independence. The executive director,
sensing the talents this man could bring to the Towers, suggested that he
should not simply help people move in, or simply become a tenant, but
instead (for a rent reduction on the one-bedroom apartment closest the front
door of the Towers) become a sort of social convenor and an "eyes and ears"
for the sponsors. He was to introduce new tenants as they moved in as well
as note complaints and requests concerning the building. Since all the
tenants were aware of his position, he was never considered subversive.
Because of this arrangement, there was never a period in the history of
Northwood Towers when residents did not know one another. The ice was broken
before it had formed.

Maintaining Neighborliness

These events established a feeling of neighborliness and community in
Northwood Towers. The interesting social phenomenon, however, is that
these feelings continued. Popular wisdom might say the high-rise structure
would work against this.

It would seem that the physical design of Northwood Towers could prevent
social interaction if any high-rise could. (The executive director was the
first to point out that it was the sponsoring group's first housing
project). The building, while designed specifically with the elderly in
mind (there were reassuring grab bars, a sprinkler system, individual heat
controls, and mail delivery to each floor) was in no way extravagant. Common
areas consisted only of a small entrance lobby, a recreation room and a
laundry room; nothing more than most ordinary apartment buildings provide.

The limited physical facilities did not, however, prevent the continuing
development of social interaction. Hallway doors were left ajar as an
invitation by the occupant for company. Seldom in the daytime could one
enter the building without hearing the conversations of visiting residents
through partially opened doors. Fortunately, the recreation room, laundry
room, elevator doorways and entrance lobby all were within a few steps of
each other. It was difficult for a person using one facility to be unaware
of persons in another. While doing their laundry, the residents sat in the
recreation room or in the few chairs around the entrance lobby. With 117
persons (most of whom seemed physically active) living in the building's
73 units, traffic through this key area was constant during the day. The
tenants met one another and chatted here, and relayed any news to tenants
on other floors. News spread in this fashion very rapidly. It would be
wrong, however, to assume that the building's structure was the impetus
for this community network; many similar apartment buildings have no such
social activity.

Informal concern and curiosity, encouraged by the administrator and tenant
leaders, made the Towers' sense of community a day-to-day reality. The
tenants talked a great deal about people and events at the Towers. For
example, everyone (including the administrator who was quite preoccupied
with the problem) knew about the old sisters who should long ago have gone
to a nursing home. One of them was thought to be a senile chain smoker
who sooner or later would set her bedclothes on fire. The account of the
situation remained consistent throughout the Towers' seven storeys.

There were many examples of the speed at which information travelled
throughout the building. One evening, a single woman living in the Towers
broke her ankle while she was out. She phoned the doctor, was treated, and
came home. At 11 o'clock the next morning, one of the other residents by
chance dropped in and discovered her condition. By noon, five individuals
had dropped in to inquire about the leg. The story of the accident in most
cases had been passed three or four times before reaching these visitors.

Northwood Senior Citizens Tenants Society

The informal relationships that arose in the Towers were strengthened
through the formal (then actually incorporated) Northwood Senior Citizens
Tenants Society. The society had existed almost since the Towers opened
and the retired circus man had been elected its first president. The key
feature of the society's structure was the floor captain. Each floor
elected a captain who was a resident in the building, though not necessarily
of that floor. The captain sat on the society's council which made
decisions on social programs and outings. He also acted as a "den mother"
for his particular floor. In an extended fashion, the floor captains
carried on what the circus man did when the building first opened: new
tenants were introduced to others on the floor and if anyone had problems
with health, shopping or personal matters, they could request help. If
the floor captain knew someone was in difficulty, he checked up on them.
This was not merely a paper body, for through the personality of the
original president and through the executive director's encouragement, the
residents' group provided a very active service.

Floor captains approached their job very seriously and the residents appeared
to have confidence in them. The residents told the field workers that it was
hard to find people willing to be floor captains (the reason why captains
were taken from any floor). The residents knew it was not just an honorary
position. As well, more than half the tenants interviewed said that in an
emergency they would contact the floor captain. Many indicated that, next
to their families, he would be their choice.

The floor captain system really provided many services one could not get in
any other way in Halifax, or at least in the Towers. Meals could be brought
to convalescents by other residents organized by the floor captain. Besides
informal visiting and daily checks, the floor captains could bring word of
illness and calamities to the council which had a visiting committee to
maintain a contact even if a resident was removed to hospital.

The senior citizens council had one voting member on the board of directors
of the housing corporation. Besides being a regular voting board member,
he acted as a watchdog for the tenants, seeing that their interests or
demands were not misrepresented. The executive director sat in on the
senior citizens society meetings as a resource person and made the occasional
suggestion but he tried not to participate heavily in the discussion.
Indeed, in exercizing responsibility for many of the development's social
aspects, he took into account the council's views. For instance, he allowed
the council to block religious services by specific churches in the building
Sunday mornings, though he personally favored the idea. The council wanted
to avoid any potential source of Catholic-Protestant friction.

Changes in the Northwood Complex

In 1971, the retired circus man's wife became ill enough to require care
in a nursing home. Upset by this and other changes in his life, he retired
as president and gave up his job of introducing new tenants and watching
out for social problems. At this time, the Manor neared completion and
changed Northwood Towers from a modest senior citizens apartment to part
of a major complex offering hostel as well as self-contained accommodation
and a host of services and staff aimed at providing for the needs of the
elderly.

Northwood Towers had always been in a relatively good position for
transportation to downtown areas. A regular bus service ran along Gottingen
Street. However, there were not many home visiting services, although
public health nurses and the Victorian Order of Nurses had always been
present (about six households in the Towers at any one time were making
use of the VON).

With the completion of the Manor, social work and health counselling would
be available on demand within the new complex. There would be a host of
services for hostel residents in the Manor: meals-in-rooms, medical checkups
and so on. These services will also be available to apartment residents
who may also eat in the Manor cafeteria when they wish. All of the new
building's recreational and social facilities (structurally connected to
the Towers) would be available to Towers residents. The Towers and Manor
at full occupancy will have a total population of 568 residents.

Although it would be interesting to find out if the community feeling
exhibited in the Towers extended into the Manor or died in the face of a
greater population with more services on site, the case study was completed
before this could be assessed.

In spite of the circus man's retirement from formal positions on the senior
citizens council, he was already working to encourage Manor residents to
join the tenants society, which had voted to include the new building in
the same systems as the old.

The Future of the Northwood Complex

After launching Northwood Towers with its self-contained accommodation,
the executive director became aware of other needs of Halifax's elderly.
He managed to travel to other successful senior citizens developments in
Canada and held courses on caring for the aged. The extension of activity
by the Halifax Senior Citizens' Housing Corporation into hostel type care
(and now a third level of intermediary care between hostel and nursing
home placements) was an example of how he had matched his growing professional
knowledge with concrete action. As the Manor was being completed, he
gathered around himself a staff of young and professionally oriented assistants.

He had also undertaken a pilot project with the Victorian Order of Nurses to provide a service focusing on rehabilitation and sickness prevention, with a registered nurse located in the Manor complex.

The next stage he envisioned was a special care residence as part of a comprehensive program to meet the shelter needs of the elderly. He hoped to be able to provide this on a non-profit basis at lower charges than usual for nursing care.

Conclusion

Northwood Towers was memorable for at least two factors. First, it was a high-rise development for senior citizens in which a great deal of inter-action was apparent. Second, it illustrated the importance of correct staffing and sensitive administration. Given a different attitude on the executive director's part, Northwood Towers could easily have exhibited the problems that many people associate with high-rise living. However, the Towers was a satisfying place for senior citizens and residents voiced no major complaints.

It is true that some residents chose not to join in the social network. They made their lives outside the development or were simply not gregarious people. But opportunities for warm social relationships, the basis of community spirit, existed and contributed to the quality of the residential environment.

CHAPTER 4

PROVINCIAL PLANNERS USE SOCIAL CRITERIA
TO PLAN A SMALL TOWN DEVELOPMENT

Canada's small rural towns repeatedly present special problems in creating
satisfying housing for the elderly because in a rural or semi-rural area
the population base is usually considered too small to afford many public
facilities and services. To complicate this, the local economy often
operates at a fairly low level. This means that the elderly in such areas
have little more than their federal pensions to count on for retirement.
Furthermore, a lack of local opportunities obliges most young people to
move to urban centres. The result is an older population in a relatively
poor community.

The New Brunswick government has attempted to deal with this situation by
using central planning to a far greater degree than it is used in most of
Canada. The government provides no financial support for non-profit senior
citizens apartment developments, leaving the New Brunswick Housing Corporation
with the sole mandate to develop public housing for the province's elderly.
The corporation, through research and planning, attempts to allocate the
available funds in the most economical way. At the time of this study, it
was thought economical to build senior citizens public housing in communities
already containing certain facilities and services.

The Goulding Street Project

The Goulding Street project is located about 200 yards away from the main
intersection of Sussex - Main and Broad streets. The town had grown in such
a way that vacant land still existed very close to what was then the town
centre. The provincial government bought an abandoned apple orchard that
constituted a large part of this vacant land, and parts of the orchard were
then developed into public family housing, a school, and the Goulding Street
senior citizens project.

The project occupied the developed portion of the site closest to Main Street
but 50 to 100 yards of orchard remained as a buffer to the traffic. The
project was well screened from the public school by a row of bushes. The
public housing development for families, which consisted of some 20 units in
duplex and quadraplexes, was separated from the senior citizens housing by
a stretch of road lined with private housing. This housing was screened
from the project by a tall hedge of evergreens. The project, therefore,
provided some privacy while at the same time being within a short walk of
the town's busiest area.

197

GOULDING STREET PROJECT, SUSSEX, NEW BRUNSWICK

Fact Sheet

THE BUILDING

. Location

About 200 yards from the main intersection of Sussex - a town of about 4,000
people located in the southeastern portion of New Brunswick, 60 miles south-
west of Moncton, 45 miles northeast of St. John and 60 miles east of
Fredericton.

. Type and Size

It was composed of 10 one-bedroom units in one building. Each unit had an
outside exit and one into an interior corridor.

. Facilities

A small lounge/recreation room bisected the building. Washer and dryer
facilities adjoined it.

. Date of Construction - 1970.

. Rents

Geared to income according to CMHC public housing scale. Minimum of $32 for
a single person on old age security (OAS) and guaranteed income supplement (GIS);
$52 for a couple on OAS and GIS.

THE MANAGEMENT

. National Housing Act Provision - Section 35D.

. Sponsor

The New Brunswick Housing Corporation (the housing agency of the government of
New Brunswick).

. Management Staff

Provincial government district municipal service officer acting part-time for
the New Brunswick Housing Corporation; tenant custodian, Sussex Housing
Authority to deal with tenant selection and evictions.

THE RESIDENTS

. Number - 13.

. Sex and Marital Status

Two were men, 11 were women. The following households made up the project: two
married couples, seven widows living alone, one widow living with a maiden sister.

. Health Condition

Generally good. At the time of the study, one tenant was away recovering from a
heart attack. This illness was the first that had brought a doctor to the
project in its year of operation. All persons interviewed said they had no
physical incapacities, although all showed some signs of aging such as failing
eyesight or inability to walk long distances.

. Age

Two of the four tenants interviewed were 70-74 years of age. One was 75,
another was 68.

The project was small by Canadian standards, consisting of 10 dwelling units arranged in a single one-storey building so that each unit had an entrance from the outside and from an inside corridor. The building had a recreation lounge and a laundry room. Outside, as many apple trees as possible were left standing when the building was constructed in 1970 and there was grass extending into the orchard around the building. It was a pleasant setting with which the tenants were very satisfied. The corporation planned within the very near future to add a further 10 units to the site but some of the tenants were not happy about this. They feared they would lose a good part of their cherished lawn to the new building. The corporation architects knew this and were trying to increase the size of the project with the minimum disturbance to the site.

The Plan Behind the Project

The Goulding Street project was not built on that site by mere chance. The housing corporation staff said it was located there because of the corporation's planning criteria. The corporation sets major social requirements for a potential development site. The first requirement is that the community have an auxiliary (hostel and nursing care) home or be affiliated with a region that has such a home. Second, the community must have essential services such as water, sewer, adequate fire protection, a high school (for its auditorium) and churches. Third, there must be a medical doctor and preferably a hospital close at hand. If there is no hospital in the community, the project should be close to the nearest acute care general hospital. Fourth, the community must demonstrate a need for senior citizens housing. This need is ascertained from examining the number of persons over 65 years of age within a 25-mile radius of the proposed site. The province at the time of the study aimed to provide public housing for 5 per cent of this number. The corporation also insists that the future of the community be fairly sound. The corporation's buildings are expected to last 50 years, so the corporation insists that projects be built in viable communities.

The Town of Sussex

Sussex was never a county seat but because of its size did have a public hospital, train station, race track, public schools, many churches, fraternal halls and a wide assortment of shops and stores.

The town met all the criteria the provincial corporation set, except for an auxiliary home. There was a home, however, in the adjacent Queen's county, about 30 miles away. Main Street could be reached from the project by a path that skirted the edge of the school ground and was passable throughout the year. It was used not only by senior citizens but also by residents who were coming from the newly developed area across the street and up the hill from the development. Goulding Street residents were also within a block of at least three churches, and within six blocks of three more. Nearly all important shops, stores and available services were within a quarter mile of the development (none more than a half mile away), except for the public hospital which was nearly two miles away. In other words, the development was so centrally situated that nearly all available services were accessible to the residents by foot. The proximity of shopping services removed the necessity for a public transportation system within the city and within six blocks' walk of the development there was a bus station where tenants could catch buses to nearby towns.

How the Town Meets the Plan

The Goulding Street project came as close to meeting the criteria laid down by the housing corporation as any project could. It was therefore interesting to see what the environment lacked rather than simply what it provided.

The building had only been occupied for a year. This was reflected in the age of the residents - the average age of those interviewed was under 72 years. While a few tenants had heart conditions and had difficulty hearing or seeing, none had physical problems serious enough to limit daily activities. This factor is important to keep in mind in evaluating the success of the project.

Even though Sussex is an older town, not poor by New Brunswick standards, it still does not have highly developed community services. While the list of services set as criteria by the corporation had been filled, the list itself was not very thorough. There were no health services in Sussex other than those provided by residents' private doctors; there was no Victorian Order of Nurses (although the order did operate in New Brunswick). The relative youth of the development's population had not made this lack apparent at the time of the case study, but might do so later. Religious interests were well met, both by the many churches in the vicinity and by visiting teams from the Salvation Army and Baptist Bible College. The latter two groups provided musical programs a few times a year in the project itself. Generally, the tenants found both recreation and social life in the community - as members of the Red Cross, church groups, the Legion, or the community's senior citizens club. This was an important result of the project's central location.

Approximately half of the residents in the sample had daily contact with their families and another quarter had weekly contact. Those with no families, as well as many with families, had daily contact with other residents in the building. No one appeared isolated from either the other residents or from the community, both sources of special aid when necessary. A couple of the more spry residents (one of them the janitor's wife) were known to be willing to help when the need arose. For example, they would bring in a meal to a sick person.

As previously mentioned, the housing corporation planned to expand the project by another 10 units. As the project grew and the residents got older, the need for extensive services, such as the Victorian Order of Nurses, would be felt. One resident who suffered a heart attack would have had the option of being at home rather than with her daughter if such a service had existed.

Conclusion

The situation is basically this: the development's site provided for the maximum use of everything the community had to offer. In this way it was excellent. There could have been very few improvements made in the development, given the small size of the town and New Brunswick's economy. Since the community could not provide formal services such as meals-on-wheels and home nursing, these had to be provided informally by neighbors and residents' children.

The New Brunswick Housing Corporation realized that some services were lacking, but they hoped that as the size of their developments increased, such services would become more feasible. The planned addition of another 10 units and the increasing age of the residents will further test the validity of the planners' social development criteria.

CHAPTER 5

THE HOUSING DEVELOPMENT AS A RELIGIOUS COMMUNITY

In these case studies, the residential environment of the elderly is
generally examined in terms of three components: shelter, families and
services. An attempt is usually made to see how these components have been
linked together to produce a situation of physical and mental wellbeing.
However, a component that is sometimes overlooked is the religious element
in the life of the elderly. The era has no doubt passed when all aged
persons were expected to turn inward to contemplation. Many people, however,
still find relevance in the spiritual aspect of life. In the Foyer St-
Joseph de Lévis, across the river from Quebec City, we found a community
of nuns providing a development suited to such needs.

In St-Joseph de Lévis, the core that bound the development and its residents
together was religion. While present trends suggest the devout generations
are rapidly passing, many elderly people will continue to centre their
lives around the Church - particularly in the Province of Quebec.

Foyer St-Joseph de Lévis

In 1964, a fire destroyed the central portion of a complex for needy children
and old people, operated by the Sisters of Charity. The old building had
been U-shaped, accommodating approximately 1,000 persons in all, with the
elderly living in the central portion. After the fire, the damaged portion
of the building was demolished, although the children's wing continued to
operate as a separate entity. (In July 1972, however, this wing was once
again used by the sisters since the school board no longer needed class-
rooms for children). A retirement home for priests and nuns also continued
to operate in the damaged wing.

In 1968, a new building was built on the site of the old demolished portion.
It accommodated 125 residents in hostel rooms - 77 residents had rooms of
their own, while 48 residents shared 24 double rooms. There were no self-
contained apartments and no nursing facilities (although the sisters tried
to take care of the residents just as long as they possibly could).

Life at the Foyer St-Joseph de Lévis

Breakfast was served from 7:45 to 8:30 a.m. although residents could stay
in the cafeteria as long as they wished to talk. Whereas the younger,
more agile residents encountered no problems with cafeteria serving, the
older and weaker ones found it quite a task to carry their trays from the
counter to the tables. Trays were taken by the sisters to residents confined
to their beds because of illness.

Residents sat where they pleased in the cafeteria. However, cliques existed
in that the same residents usually shared the same table at every meal.
At mealtimes residents seemed pleased to meet others and exchange comments
about the weather or their illnesses and worries. Mealtimes, in fact,
presented an excellent opportunity for social contact.

FOYER ST-JOSEPH DE LÉVIS, LÉVIS, QUEBEC

Fact Sheet

THE BUILDING

. Location

Along the southern bank of the St. Lawrence in Lévis, a town of 15,000 people. To the north, across the river, is Quebec City.

. Type and Size

Seventy-seven single and 24 double rooms in a five-storey concrete building.

. Facilities

These included a cafeteria, a room used by the visiting barber and hairdresser, a lounge on each floor with television and room for playing cards as well as sitting and chatting, a kitchenette, a major recreation room on the main floor, a chapel, washing facilities (there was also a laundry service), a small information counter which sold stamps, cards and so on, a library, a billiard room, and an area with benches for sitting outside in the summer.

. Date of Construction - 1968.

. Rents

In accord with the Department of Social Affairs rent scale that is applied in all developments for the elderly that are financed by the Quebec Housing Corporation. This scale is adjusted so that every resident may have, after paying his rent, at least $31 per month for personal expenses. If a person was living on the old age security pension and guaranteed income supplement alone, his rent would have been $104, i.e., $135 minus $31. On incomes above $135, the resident paid half in rent, up to the actual cost of maintenance. In Lévis, this figure was $180 a month.

THE MANAGEMENT

. National Housing Act Provision

Built under Quebec Housing Corporation loan with NHA funds directed through the Quebec corporation.

. Sponsor

The Sisters of Charity.

. Management Staff

On-site director with a staff of 35, mainly Sisters of Charity.

THE RESIDENTS

. Number - 125.

. Sex and Marital Status

Eighty-five were women; 40 were men. In a sample of 15 households, the following people were met: four spinsters, four widows, five widowers, one married couple, one married woman separated from her spouse due to health.

. Health Condition

In the sample of 15 households, four residents said they had, or appeared to have, no serious incapacity. One was moderately incapacitated, five were slightly incapacitated, and five had no physical disability.

. Age

The average age of residents interviewed was 76 years. None were under 66; none were over 85.

At 10 o'clock every morning, the rosary was recited over the public address system. Residents walked along the halls with their rosary in their hands and joined aloud in prayer. At 10:20, one of the retired priests celebrated mass in the Foyer's chapel for the sisters and residents.

From 11 a.m. to noon, lunch was served, after which many residents returned to their rooms for a short rest period. Following lunch, some people might go down to the recreation room to play billiards or take a book from the library. Others might go for a short walk, watch television, or play cards in the floor lounge. During the afternoon and again in the evening, the residents were served a snack; they were encouraged to gather in the floor lounges for this.

At 4 p.m., a second mass was celebrated for the residents by the Foyer chaplain (who lived in the retirement home next door). The majority of residents usually attended this service. Two other masses each day (at 6:45 a.m. and at 10:45 a.m.) were attended mostly by the nuns and priests, although a number of the more devout residents also went.

Supper was served from 5 to 6 p.m. In general, the residents appeared satisfied with the food, although some residents, especially retired loggers and farmers, found it too bland. They tired of white sauces and spoke fondly of how they used to eat when living at home: bacon and eggs in the morning and the "petits plats" at other times. Most of the residents admitted, however, that in cooking for a crowd the kitchen could not possibly meet individual tastes, so the residents were reluctant to complain. The sisters felt that the residents would be unable to digest the foods they enjoyed years ago and that as they got older their diet had to be more and more carefully balanced - spices had to be eliminated in a lot of cases and a heavy meal at night would prevent them from having a good sleep.

After supper, the residents usually retired to their rooms. At 7 o'clock, they turned on the radio to listen to and recite the rosary (this custom has been a part of French-Canadian Catholics' lifestyle for many years). Later in the evening, the residents watched television, played cards in the floor lounges, visited friends in the development, or took part in the occasional planned activity such as holy day celebrations, films, visiting choirs or theatre groups, or bingo games. The administrator told us that she planned to post a weekly list of residents celebrating their birthdays just outside the cafeteria entrance to provide a further reason for parties and visiting. On some days, trips or pilgrimages were planned for the residents. However, these were not on a scheduled basis.

The Care of the Elderly as a Vocation

The lifestyle at St-Joseph de Lévis could not have existed without the ample staff of nuns. They regarded caring for the aged as part of their holy calling and this dedication provided the residents with a degree of

security unattainable elsewhere. All of the residents interviewed said the
nuns gave themselves totally to their work. Some of the sisters' devotion
rubbed off on the residents. A number of elderly women, especially those
who began life in convent schools, felt very much at home in this religious
atmosphere. They even displayed the attitudes of cloistered nuns - referring
to life in the outside community as "le monde".

Two of the sisters had taken a course in gerontology, two were registered
nurses, and the rest were auxiliary nurses. The administrator herself had
previously been a hospital director. The sisters' training, however, seemed
to have been more in the area of acute care than in providing a lively
environment for the physically well. It was interesting that, while interviews with 15 residents produced four with serious physical incapacities and
only one with moderate incapacity, the administrator felt that three-quarters
of the residents were seriously handicapped. Perhaps this attitude helped
explain the major failings of the Foyer in looking after the secular needs
of residents. In particular, there were two negative factors: failure to
provide transportation to services and facilities in the community in the
face of a poor municipal bus service, and the lack of active recreation
programs within the development.

The lack of transportation to Lévis' commercial area or to Quebec City
vexed numerous residents. A petition was even sent by 100 residents to the
municipal government asking for bus service closer to the development. At
the time of this study, residents had to walk four blocks down a fairly
steep hill to the nearest bus stop and coming back uphill to the Foyer
proved an even harder feat. While persons interested only in pursuing a
private or religious life had little need to leave the Foyer, those with
friends or interests in the community felt quite trapped - taxis were
expensive and friends and relatives not always free to take them. Residents
who had to visit a doctor outside the Foyer found the lack of public
transportation especially annoying. The difficulty of travelling from the
Foyer to downtown Lévis or Quebec meant that anyone too ill or weak to
undertake quite a lot of physical exertion was virtually trapped in the
Foyer. Of course, this transportation problem hardly presented itself as
a conscious neglect on the sisters' part. They were aware of the problem
and regretted it but so far they had not found a way to solve it.

The second shortcoming concerned the lack of secular recreation activity
in the development. As Lévis' only housing development for the ambulatory
elderly that was supported by public funds, opportunities for enjoyment and
learning of interest to all types of people should have existed. It is
difficult to believe that everyone in Lévis needing hostel care would be
in total accord with the lifestyle this residence dictates, even though it
is a lifestyle that came naturally to the majority of residents when this
study was done.

Double Hostel Rooms

There was another problem experienced by residents quite unrelated to the focus on religion. The administrator pointed to the existence of double rooms as the cause of much discomfort. Except for those occupied by married couples, double rooms had proven to be nothing but a problem to residents and consequently to the administration. Residents had different ideas about the room temperature, they wanted privacy, and roommates differed in their habits and preferences (such as watching late movies on television). Not one resident or staff member would have double rooms built again.

Conclusion

The drawbacks described at St-Joseph de Lévis should be weighed against the benefits that stemmed from this religiously oriented milieu. For many people, especially women, the Foyer was not a break with their past but a continuation of their traditional lifestyle. But for a minority who were also interested in carrying on an active secular life, the Foyer presented the problems of distance from transportation systems and lack of a highly developed on-site social program.

Nevertheless, with today's drift away from religious symbols, the type of atmosphere offered in Lévis may come to satisfy fewer and fewer elderly persons. No matter how strong the devotion of the sisters is, the success of the Foyer will be limited without more awareness of the varied needs of healthy old people.

On the other hand, this case study indicates the need of some elderly persons for a residential environment that takes into account their spiritual needs. Therefore, it is important for groups like the Sisters of Charity in St-Joseph de Lévis to continue offering accommodation that relates to the culture of a significant proportion of the population they serve. It is also important that pluralistic housing policies make this possible.

CHAPTER 6

RESPONSE TO CHANGE IN RURAL QUEBEC

As the small family farm becomes less viable in rural Quebec and as small town society grows increasingly secular in nature, community leaders increasingly inherit social duties that once belonged to the family and Church.

The village of Notre-Dame du Bon Conseil is situated 18 miles east of Drummondville on the south bank of the St. Lawrence River. Definitely a village and not a regional centre, Bon Conseil draws its character from the surrounding farms that date back to the founding of New France's seigneurial regime. But profound technological changes occurred in the area in the 1960s. Farms were consolidated and the displaced families moved to larger towns such as Drummondville and Montreal.

In many cases, the youngsters left before their parents on the farm grew too feeble to carry on. In other cases, the move to the city could not, for financial reasons, include aging parents.

In response to this social upheaval, councils of the Village and the Rural Municipality of Notre-Dame du Bon Conseil got together in the late 1960s to build a housing development for the area's elderly. They formed a corporation composed of seven local residents: the school principal, two farmers, a carpenter and two industrial managers. With the assistance of a 90 per cent mortgage loan from the Quebec Housing Corporation and 10 per cent equity put up by the sponsoring municipalities, a squat two-storey building containing four self-contained apartments, 32 single and nine double hostel rooms was erected. After the Accueil opened its doors in May, 1970, it was quickly occupied and by late 1971 contained 58 residents.

The Residents

The average age of residents in our sample was 75 years. Of the 15 individuals interviewed, two were married couples, eight were widows, one was a spinster, and four were single men. There was, therefore, a majority of women - as high a proportion as usually encountered in such developments.

Few residents left the Accueil often. The director cashed their pension cheques, giving back the balance after deducting rent. Residents relied on their families to drive them to town for shopping, as there was no public transportation within Notre-Dame du Bon Conseil. The residents showed no discontent with this situation. They had never used public transportation and the money left after their rent was paid seemed not too adequate. Since they had spent their lives on isolated farms with little surplus cash, shopping never became an important pastime. Also, since many of the residents in the Accueil had known one another in their younger days, they seemed to find enough company in the development.

ACCUEIL DE NOTRE-DAME DU BON CONSEIL, NOTRE-DAME DU BON CONSEIL, QUEBEC

Fact Sheet

THE BUILDING

. Location

On a quiet, dead-end street in the small village of Notre-Dame du Bon Conseil (1,900 people), about 18 miles from Drummondville.

. Type and Size

A two-storey building providing hostel accommodation in nine double rooms and 32 single rooms as well as self-contained housing in four one-bedroom apartments.

. Facilities

A small living room was located on the second floor; on the first floor there was a large living room for general meetings, such as a daily mass, social activities, and sitting. There was a laundry room and a cafeteria.

. Date of Construction - 1970.

. Rents

In accord with the Department of Social Affairs rent scale that is applied in all developments for the elderly financed by the Quebec Housing Corporation. This scale is adjusted so that every resident may have, after paying his rent, at least $31 per month for personal expenses. If a person is living on the old age security pension and guaranteed income supplement alone, his rent would be $104, i.e. $135 minus $31. Ninety per cent of the residents lived on the old age security pension and guaranteed income supplement. The four apartment units rented for $110 a month.

THE MANAGEMENT

. National Housing Act Provision

Built under Quebec Housing Corporation loan with Section 16 funds directed through the Quebec corporation.

. Sponsor

A non-profit corporation sponsored by the village of Notre-Dame du Bon Conseil and the rural municipality of Notre-Dame du Bon Conseil.

. Management Staff

There were 18 on-site staff members. A staff member was present around the clock.

THE RESIDENTS

. Number - 58.

. Sex and Marital Status

Twenty-four were men; 34 were women. The following households were encountered in a random sample of 15: two married couples, eight widows, one spinster, and four single men.

. Health Condition

In a random sample of 15, five residents appeared seriously physically incapacitated, one appeared moderately incapacitated, six had some slight incapacity, and two had no apparent physical disability.

. Age

The average age of residents was 75 years. Six residents were over 80 and two were under 65.

The Accueil had maintained aspects of rural life. Tourtière and baked beans were often on the menu, the men dressed in heavy trousers with suspenders and the women wore traditional "robes d'indienne" and aprons. This gave the place the feeling of a farm kitchen just before the day's chores were begun. The problem was that there were no chores to be done. While the residents often said how glad they were to be free of hard work and the farm's isolation, they did not know how to fill comfortably the seemingless endless idle days.

When the Accueil opened in May, 1970, many residents reportedly came to the development believing they were entering an asylum or poor house. This fear proved false as they had freedom to come and go as they wished and received respectful treatment from the staff. The availability of company was particularly satisfying. One man, who had been living with his daughter before entering the Accueil, was especially pleased with the abundance of companions. His daughter and son-in-law had been so busy with their own family that they had little time for him.

The Executive Director

From the opening of the Accueil, the corporation had employed a full-time executive director to administer the development; he had a staff of 16. This official appeared to be aware of the Accueil's importance in providing accommodation for Bon Conseil's old people. He also realized that he faced a considerable challenge.

The director tried to develop a recreation program. In the summer of 1971, some students organized a game of croquet on the lawn of the Accueil, involving a number of residents (mostly the men). Adding to the participants' enjoyment, strict scores were kept and awards made at the end of the season. Card games were organized in a similar manner, since cards are a traditional pastime on the farm. Residents were very much involved in competing for yearly championships. In the near future, the director hoped to both establish an ongoing croquet tournament and set up a games room in the basement for permanent recreational activities - mostly games.

The concentration on games and social programs at the Accueil was somewhat of a reaction to the traditional religious community refuge concept of care for the elderly in Quebec. The director wanted to provide a balance of religious and secular activity; he strongly believed that developments for the elderly should not be solely administered by nuns. He felt this led to an imbalance in favor of the religious. He did not deny the basic religious feelings of his residents but as farmers they had had little time for formal daily religious exercises. Mass on Sundays and prayers every day were the only religious exercises most farmers could practice. Now, with their daily mass at 9:30 a.m. celebrated in the development by the village priest, and with the option of listening to the 7 o'clock rosary over the radio, the director felt that the residents' religious needs were sufficiently met.

The residents were free to devote much or little time to religious activities without fear of loosing the administration's respect.

The attempt to encourage secular activities had not been the easiest of paths for the director to follow. This stemmed both from the nature of the residents and from his limited resources to provide such activities.

Problems in Keeping Active

Without physical and mental activity, the aging processes are hastened. But the residents of the Accueil seemed to show little interest in group pursuits. The administrator wanted to offer the residents meaningful leisure but little progress seemed to have been made beyond organizing the odd game or party. It almost seemed as if the Accueil residents believed that placid contemplation, interspersed by daily mass said on the premises, was the correct role for the aged. They did enjoy having fun occasionally – for example, when a soirée was held, even residents who were physically incapacitated or could not stand noise made a point of attending.

The residents themselves showed no interest in organizing activities. All the plans were presented to them by the administrator or by the village's Golden Age Club which occasionally visited for a sing-song. It was true that the administrator had appointed a doyen and a doyenne from among the residents but these were really honorary titles that served to designate the senior residents. The doyenne was a cigarette smoking 95-year-old. She could walk around a little but her awareness and memory were failing so that conversation with her was difficult.

Conclusions

In the Accueil, an attempt had been made to provide a modern solution to the housing needs of the locality's elderly. In many ways the scheme had been successful. The residents appeared contented with the environment (e.g. many consciously chose to spend Christmas in the Accueil). On the other hand, because their earlier mode of life had not prepared them for such a prolonged period of leisure, they seemed left without relevant roles and unable to create new ones. The administrator, while conscious of the need to foster activities that would contribute to the social life of the development, was finding it difficult not to be paternalistic. Life in this development appeared comfortable, but perhaps it should have been more meaningful.

CHAPTER 7

A LARGE URBAN DEVELOPMENT CAN HAVE ITS ADVANTAGES

In an attempt to keep up with the soaring housing demand of senior citizens in Canada's major urban centres, an increasing number of very large developments have been built in the last few years. Such developments bring 300 to 500 or more elderly persons together in one complex, making it possible to provide many on-site facilities and services that smaller, more scattered developments cannot sustain.

Résidence Angelica

Résidence Angelica is located in a residential district of Montréal-Nord. Immediately across the street from the development are several low-rise private apartments and mixed in with these are well kept private houses. The development is nothing less than grand in conception.

Constructed in 1968-1969 by the Sisters of Charity of St. Mary as a place for elderly people in good health to live, Résidence Angelica provided a variety of living arrangements ranging from ordinary apartments to nursing care.

At the time of our field work, the Résidence housed 531 individuals in 42 one-bedroom apartments (84 individuals), 53 bachelor suites, 28 single hostel rooms, 134 double hostel rooms (268 individuals), and 44 nursing rooms (88 individuals).

The building provided numerous facilities: a cafeteria (for hostel residents only), coffee shop, barber shop, beauty salon, physiotherapy room, swimming pool, crafts room, carpentry workshop, and library, as well as meeting halls, main recreation rooms and floor lounges. Besides this, a tuck shop, a bank branch and a card and gift boutique were located in the building.

A large complement of services had also been established, including a minibus service to the nearest métro station, a health surveillance and nursing program, physiotherapy, a drug and medication program, and daily mass.

A second tower, which would increase the population of the development to over 800, was being completed. The new building would provide only apartment accommodation and space for a grocery store.

The development was staffed with 135 full-time and 69 part-time personnel. Fourteen of the full-time staff were involved in administrative and clerical work, 16 were employed as nurses and 43 as licenced aids; 26 worked in the kitchen and cafeteria; and 29 did maintenance and security work. Three people were involved in the dispensary and three in the laundry. There was one full-time chaplain and one full-time occupational therapist. The part-time personnel worked in all areas.

RÉSIDENCE ANGELICA, MONTRÉAL-NORD, PROVINCE OF QUEBEC

Fact Sheet

THE BUILDING

. Location

Situated at 3435 Gouin Boulevard East in a residential area of Montréal-Nord, immediately bordering the Rivière des Prairies (the northern branch of the St. Lawrence River); downtown Montreal is 10-12 miles south.

. Type and Size

It was composed of 41 one-bedroom apartments, 62 bachelor apartments, 28 single hostel rooms, 134 double hostel rooms and 44 double nursing rooms. These were arranged in an 18-storey tower over a three-storey podium or base. Hostel and self-contained units were mixed on each floor.

. Facilities

A lounge room on each floor, two large television rooms, a large meeting hall, chapel, library, carpentry shop, crafts room, physiotherapy room, laundry room, swimming pool, cafeteria, coffee shop, barber shop and beauty salon, small tuck shop, as well as a resident-run gift shop.

. Date of Construction - 1970.

. Rents

The rents for the hostel accommodation were in accord wtih the Department of Social Affairs' rent scale (see Foyer St-Joseph de Lévis fact sheet). In Résidence Angelica, the actual cost of maintenance was $90-$100 for a bachelor apartment, $120-$125 for a one-bedroom apartment, $250 for a single hostel room with food, and $225 for a double hostel room with food. Residents in self-contained dwelling units were not subsidized.

THE MANAGEMENT

. National Housing Act Provision

Built under Quebec Housing Corporation loan with section 16 funds directed through the Quebec corporation.

. Sponsor - The Sisters of Charity of St. Mary.

. Management Staff

There were 135 full-time and 69 part-time staff members employed in the development, under the direction of an on-site administrator.

THE RESIDENTS

. Number - 531.

. Sex and Marital Status

Forty were men, 490 were women. In a sample of 25 individuals, the following persons were encountered: 11 widows, two widowers, one man separated from his wife, four spinsters, one single man, and four married couples.

. Health Condition

The health of the residents appeared generally good. In the random sample of 25 interviews, four appeared severely physically incapacitated, three appeared moderately incapacitated, six appeared slightly incapacitated, and 12 either said they had no physical incapacity or appeared not to have any.

. Age

The average age in the development was 74 years. Seven of those interviewed were 80 years of age or over. A third of the tenants interviewed were between 70 and 74 years old. Half of the tenants interviewed were between 65 and 74 years old. Only one was less than 65 years old.

A Feeling of Security

The residents of Résidence Angelica could be split into two distinct types: apartment dwellers and hostel residents. Generally, the former were not intensively involved in day-to-day life within the Résidence; the hostel residents derived the most from the on-site facilities and services. However, both groups, if asked to identify the most important benefit of life at the Résidence, tended to reply "security."

Apartment dwellers were provided with a valuable type of security because they were assured of residence in the complex for as long as they desired. When a spouse died, the survivor could continue living in an apartment or move to hostel accommodation. Nursing accommodation was also available in the residence.

Residents understood and appreciated the progression from one-bedroom to bachelor apartment, and from bachelor apartment to hostel room with meals. Awareness of the nursing beds within the development completed the security plan. The feeling of security was further enhanced by the knowledge that the Sisters of Charity of St. Mary, the order that ran the Résidence Angelica, also administered Marie Clarac Hospital, a general hospital located a block away.

Hostel residents were also reassured in other ways. Every resident was given a weekly medical examination and drugs required were professionally dispensed in return for a lump sum payment included in the rent. Through an intercom in each room, nurses could be notified around the clock and a doctor was always on call.

Spiritual support was also readily obtainable - not only by presence of the sisters but also through the full-time chaplain who celebrated mass daily for about 150 persons. On Sunday, the great majority of residents attended mass.

Social Interaction

Residents came to Angelica from all parts of the Island of Montreal but there was nothing to stop others from other parts of Quebec coming as well. Because of this, residents did not usually know others in the building when they arrived (a contrast with many small town developments). In fact apartment residents, who were often married and more active in the local community, usually did not become very involved in Résidence life. Hostel residents, since they ate together, were more socially integrated.

The size of the development appeared to have had a dampening effect on developing friendships quickly. Most residents said they had not made many new friends since their arrival. Most had made acquaintances with whom they might eat their meals or chat cordially, but they had seldom found friends in the most meaningful sense. The men were usually more lonely than the women. Outnumbered 490 to 40 by women, they did not appear to participate much in casual social exchange in the public areas.

Services and Facilities

The reported difficulty in establishing friendships within the Résidence was somewhat surprising in view of the opportunities for group activities that were available. The recreation rooms allowed ample space for chatting, playing cards and family visiting. Residents were also able to casually drop in and watch television programs in two rooms designated for this purpose, although practically all residents appeared to have television sets of their own. The library was well equipped with books and magazines and seemed to be used regularly. A number of the men kept busy in the carpentry shop (some producing wooden articles what were sold in the gift shop), while the ladies met in the crafts room to do their knitting and needlework and socialize.

The indoor swimming pool was an asset that many other developments must envy. A startling number of old people enjoyed its use under the direction of the full-time physiotherapist. One lady in her late sixties said she had learned to swim the previous winter.

The large hall in the development had a stage and was often used by visiting choirs and drama groups as well as for monthly bingos. It was also used for a monthly dance with orchestra. A parochial Golden Age Club arranged monthly outings and one energetic woman had planned 29 excursions for fellow residents in the two-year period from September, 1969, to September, 1971. These included trips to industrial plants, the Place Des Arts, the circus, shrines, Ottawa, and Man and His World. Unfortunately most subsidized hostel residents, restricted to an allowance of $31 after paying their rent, found the cost of such outings too much.

Except for the woman who took the initiative to plan outside excursions, practically all the social activities were organized by the staff or volunteers. The chaplain spent a good deal of his time in this work and one of his favorite tasks was to help tenants to produce an in-house bulletin. A group of 15 volunteer women from the local parish appeared to carry the rest of the load in planning activities for residents (e.g. they set up the gift shop to sell handiwork although it was looked after by a resident). The residents did not seem to be involved in the planning process and seemed to lack information about the variety of activities. Even though notices were posted in the elevators, residents were often unaware of planned events.

The staff seemed aware of the risks of an impersonal atmosphere that were inherent in a large development. They therefore went out of their way to encourage a good deal of personal contact. For example, the women volunteers saw that everyone received a small birthday gift. Everyone in the development received a Christmas gift and when people were ill they got flowers. However, the emphasis was on doing and planning things for the residents, rather than on encouraging them to plan services and events themselves. For example, despite the development's size, no move had been made to form an over-all residents' association.

Design and Location Drawbacks

The residents considered the provision of two-bed rather than single-bed hostel rooms a serious design flaw. Almost half Angelica's residents shared rooms. Although the administration attempted to match the occupants of such rooms through a questionnaire, success was quite rare. Perhaps newcomers were too shy and agreeable when they first entered the development but later became more willing to voice their personal preferences. No residents sharing rooms with other than spouses, relatives or life-long friends were happy with this situation. They said that the hours they kept and their interests and habits had become fixed long before they moved in, and therefore it was difficult for them to constantly compromise in sharing their new home. They wanted some space to call their own. As well, if a spouse or close friend died, his roommate had to make the rather hard adjustment of seeing a former spouse's or friend's bed occupied by a stranger. When roommates varied greatly in age or health, the lack of privacy became a problem of abnormal proportions.

Another design shortcoming often mentioned by residents had to do with the elevators. Because the elevators were too small and there were not enough of them, they were crowded and there were long queues at mealtimes.

The location of the development made it difficult in terms of time and distance to reach other parts of Montreal. To overcome this, the Résidence operated a minibus that ran twice a day to the nearest subway station (about three miles away). There was a 10 cent charge for this service. The same bus took residents free of charge to a clinic or hospital outside Angelica on the specific recommendation of the development's doctor.

However, the minibus operated neither at night nor on weekends, and this troubled residents as they were then compelled to wait for a public bus across the street from the Résidence. With strong winds blowing in from the river, a busy street that is icy in winter, and long waiting periods, many residents were reluctant to venture forth and consequently felt isolated. Some suggested that Angelica generated enough fares to warrant the bus swinging around the Résidence's driveway and picking up residents at the door.

Conclusion

Résidence Angelica successfully provided 530 residents with a convenient and comfortable place in which to live. The high density of elderly persons, combined with substantial subsidies from the Quebec Department of Social Affairs, had enabled the sponsoring group to develop an impressive range of accommodation and care, plus extensive facilities and services. The resulting physical and social environment supplied a high degree of security to residents.

The large size of the complex, however, magnified design deficiencies and made social interaction formal and lacking in spontaneity. Professional help to encourage residents to do more of their own planning for social and recreation programs would be useful.

On the whole, though, the Résidence Angelica was undoubtedly a good place for senior citizens to live. The staff were not blind to its shortcomings and were working to ameliorate them.

CHAPTER 8

AN ISLAND OF OLD PEOPLE IN THE INNER CITY

In urban areas with extensive community services, there is some debate
concerning who should supply services to people living in senior citizens
housing. In some cases, development administrations prefer to avoid any
involvement with the health and social service needs of their residents
and simply provide shelter. Generally, this situation exists where
developments have only self-contained dwelling units. The opposite of
this situation is the development that ignores existing community services,
preferring to provide complete care with its own staff. This situation is
more likely to exist in hostel developments such as St. Anne's Tower.

The Building

St. Anne's Tower is located in an old residential area of Toronto. The
neighborhood had undergone demographic changes typical of many North American
cities. It was first largely inhabited by persons of British extraction and
then by a Jewish population. As these groups in turn migrated to Toronto's
suburbs, a large number of Italians settled in the area and continued to be
the neighborhood's prime ethnic group, although Portuguese immigrants were
also arriving. Housing in the area consisted mainly of two-storey single
family dwellings and small numbers of row dwellings. Most of this housing
suffered from age, with the buildings crowding the sidewalk and each other,
leaving little space for lawns or gardens.

In such a neighborhood, St. Anne's Tower stood out conspicuously. It was
a modern, 13-storey high-rise building faced with white brick, surrounded
by spacious lawns and a black iron railed fence. This lack of physical
continuity was matched on a social level by the little or no contact between
the Tower's residents and their neighbors - a situation that was hardly
surprising in view of the mainly British background of the senior citizen
development's population. The Tower was constructed on Anglican Church
property, right next to the church hall and the church itself, on a site
previously occupied by the parish manse. The church hall had numerous
facilities which were rented to the St. Anne's Tower Corporation as required.
However, as Tower residents were not enthusiastic about going outside to
get to the hall for activities, the development's dining room was the scene
of most social events.

An electric buzzer system controlled the entrance to the spacious lobby.
Two elevators and the administrative offices were located on the main floor,
while the basement level contained a tuck shop, laundry room, beauty shop,
small recreation area, and a comfortable sitting room.

ST. ANNE'S TOWER, TORONTO, ONTARIO

Fact Sheet

THE BUILDING

. Location

On Dufferin Street, in an inner residential area of Toronto.

. Type and Size

It was composed of 86 single and 46 double hostel rooms with bathrooms, arranged in a 13-storey tower.

. Facilities

Ten lounges and a dining room with a sundeck on the roof; beauty shop, crafts rooms and laundry rooms in the basement; auditorium and gymnasium in an adjacent hall.

. Date of Construction - 1967.

. Rents

$150-$170 for one person in a one-bedroom hostel unit; $175-$195 for one person in a two-bedroom hostel unit; $270 and up for two people in a double hostel room.

THE MANAGEMENT

. National Housing Act Provision

Section 16, non-profit.

. Sponsor

The St. Anne's Tower Corporation.

. Management Staff

There was a full-time administrator in charge of 21 staff members.

THE RESIDENTS

. Number - 138.

. Sex and Marital Status

Management estimated that approximately one-quarter of the residents were men and three-quarters women. In a sample of 13 residents, 60 per cent were women. Of the 13 persons interviewed, three of the five men were separated from wives who lived in nursing homes; two were widowed; five of the eight women were widowed and three were single.

. Health Condition

Health was generally good considering the average age. In the random sample, about half appeared not to be physically incapacitated, and half had a slight incapacity.

. Age

The average age of the sample was 81.4 years.

Space for socializing was plentiful in the building, for besides sitting areas in the basement and the main lobby, TV lounges were available on alternate floors of the Tower. A large cafeteria and a small lounge area occupied the top floor of the building. Use of the cafeteria as the scene of many activities compensated for the lack of a main recreation room.

St. Anne's Tower contained only hostel units - 36 single and 46 double rooms. As the double rooms had not proven to be popular and there was little demand for them, only six rooms were occupied by two persons at the time of this study. Each hostel room was equipped with a private bathroom and a balcony, both of which were sources of satisfaction to residents. Over half of the residents interviewed said that having private bathrooms contributed to their satisfaction with the building. One woman even suggested that having her own bathroom was worth half the rent she was paying.

Sponsorship and Management

The idea of constructing the development originally came from the rector of St. Anne's parish. The rector, through his dealings with parishioners and with the general community, had become aware that many senior citizens were enduring poor living conditions and loneliness. His idea was to provide a community-based home for senior citizens where they would be given not only superior housing conditions but also sufficient interaction with their contemporaries to relieve loneliness.

The rector and nine of his parishioners formed a non-profit corporation to be responsible for developing and managing such a home. At the time of our study, the rector was still involved in the project as vice-president of the corporation.

The development administrator felt that many housing developments for the aged were depressing. He had, therefore, made a considerable effort to keep Tower residents active, while at the same time preserving their human dignity. He particularly believed that residents should be kept "trim and looking good." To this end. he believed that the hairdressing salon and the development's social activities were both necessary and effective. While from time to time there had been disagreement among board members about the amount of social activities and the way they should be stimulated, there had been no disagreement about merit of the administrator's intentions.

To operate the Tower, the administrator had a staff of 21 persons: 11 were kitchen workers, four were nurses, two were housemaids, and four were maintenance men. All the residents interviewed felt that there was an adequate staff, although some said residents tried to help out as much as possible, particularly at mealtimes when several residents required special assistance.

The Residents

The Tower housed 138 residents. The majority were over 75 years old and the administrator estimated that the average age was about 80. In our sample, the average age was 81 years. Considering their age, most residents enjoyed reasonably good health although we considered that almost one-third of the sample had serious or moderate incapacities. The residents' incomes tended to be somewhat higher than in most of the other case study developments: 31 per cent of the sample said they had substantial savings in addition to their old age pensions.

Applicants were admitted if their physical ability was slightly limited and were requested to move if their ability seriously declined. The majority of persons who had left the development in the last year had moved to nursing homes or hospitals. The administrator suggested that there were approximately six residents in the building who should have been in nursing homes. However, if the number of incapacitated people did not grow very much greater, he felt they could be adequately cared for.

Social Services and Facilities

The residents of the Tower relied almost totally on services that were provided within the development. This situation might have been partly a reflection of the scarcity of community resources, but it also had to do with the administrator's perception of the proper role of the sponsoring corporation. For example, even though public health nurses had asked to visit the development on a regular basis, the administrator suggested to them that this would be unnecessary since the building had its own nursing staff.

Nevertheless, despite the lack of community-based services, one could hardly say that the residents' needs had been neglected. A maid service and meals were available in the building, four staff nurses cared for health problems, and a beauty parlor and tuck shop were in the basement. The residents' council organized bus trips to places such as the Ontario Science Council and the Stratford Theatre. Weekly activities included bingo, shuffleboard, sing-songs, and hymn sings. In addition, a birthday party was held every three months. A newsletter produced by the residents kept everyone informed of events.

Some of the residents interviewed made a few suggestions about extra services they thought were required. For example, one person felt that a transportation service, particularly to medical clinics and doctors' offices, was needed. Another resident would have liked a delicatessen in the building. For the most part, however, residents that were interviewed felt there was little more the development could provide. One elderly man indicated that although it might be nice to have more services in the building, it would not be very practical. He said that a barber shop was removed from the building because the demand had not been high enough.

Only one of the services in the building appeared to rely on assistance from other than management staff or residents: this was the tuck shop run by the corporation's ladies' auxiliary. These women had financial and administrative control over the shop and staffed it on a voluntary basis. Milk and food were donated by the Tower's dining room and for sale to residents at a very reasonable price. The shop also provided a market-place for residents interested in selling their handicrafts.

The most serious gap in the Tower's facilities was the absence of a major recreation room. The room was not included in the building for financial reasons; instead, an arrangement was made whereby the corporation rented space in the parish hall next door. The hall was well equipped with a large auditorium, meeting rooms, a kitchen and lounges - but very little use was being made of it by Tower residents. The administrator suggested that there were two reasons for this. First, in order to use the parish hall, the old people had to go outside and this was a problem, particularly in the winter months. Second, he believed that the residents did not feel at home in the hall because it was not part of the Tower. Whatever the reason, the dining room was used for most social and recreational events even though it was not as appropriately designed for them as the parish hall.

Friendships

Most residents that were interviewed continued to maintain some contact with relatives and friends outside the development, but few participated in outside clubs and organizations. Most residents relied on the Tower for social contact. This occurred to some extent at mealtimes. As one resident said, however, chances to meet a variety of people in the dining room were hindered in that 80 per cent of the residents sat at the same tables with the same people for three meals every day, although no planned seating arrangements existed.

There were cliques in the building, but the manager suggested that organized activities helped to break them down and provided an opportunity for residents to relate with others. Floor lounges were used to a certain extent for informal gatherings. However, the main areas of social contact continued to be the main lobby and the dining room. Some residents visited in each other's rooms but this was not too common.

A residents' council was responsible for several activities. Special interest groups had been formed, including the knitting group, the ladies' choir, the sick committee, and the newsletter committee. These groups met ostensibly to carry out various tasks, but companionship was an important by-product. Activities were available for those interested, but there appeared to be little attempt to involve other individuals.

Tenant participation in management had not been neglected. One tenant was a member of the board of directors but he was not elected as a representative of the residents. The administrator also appeared to relate to the tenants more on an individual basis than through the residents' council.

Only 38 per cent of the sample claimed to be very satisfied with the development, compared to 61 per cent of all the users interviewed across the country. One man in good health expressed disappointment and said that he wanted to keep house for himself again and found the health services annoying. Another man, who also claimed not to need the health services, complained of loneliness. Other complaints had to do with the run-down nature of the neighborhood and the sometimes difficult public transportation. Also, almost 9 per cent of the residents interviewed indicated that they might have to move to obtain more intensive nursing care. The somewhat lower satisfaction level in this development could have had to do with the high financial assets of its population, wealthier people perhaps being more prone to expect higher standards.

Conclusion

Despite the insular nature of St. Anne's Tower within the city, it had nevertheless achieved a fair resident satisfaction. This came about neither through paternalism on the part of the staff nor over-dependence on the part of the residents. The high level of physical and emotional health was the product of the full range of the development's medical, social, and recreational services.

The lack of integration with community services did not seem to have greatly affected the level of care offered the residents; nevertheless, such insularity for a younger population might well have had a very different effect.

CHAPTER 9

WHERE THE ACTION IS

The fact that many senior citizens developments were located on the outskirts of towns and cities often presented itself as a source of incon-
venience for both tenants and management. Lack of shopping, recreation,
social services, and transportation close at hand tends to create a feeling
of isolation. It is, therefore, often advocated that senior citizens
developments should be built in the downtown core - where the action is.
This sentiment was behind the construction of College View Apartments.

The Location

The College View Apartments constitute a 340-unit senior citizens project
located at Yonge and McGill Streets in downtown Toronto. To its west,
across Yonge Street, is Eaton's College Street store; one block north and
one block east is Maple Leaf Gardens; across McGill Street is Ryerson
Technological Institute; and three blocks to the east is Allan Gardens,
the major downtown green area.

Scattered along Yonge Street to the north and south of the project are
dime stores interspersed with restaurants, pornographic book shops, burlesque
houses and movie theatres. Banks, grocery stores and a variety of professional
offices are located within blocks of the development. There are six hospitals
within a very short distance of College View, and an office of the Family
Service Association, which runs a senior citizen program, is located
about four blocks away. The Second Mile Club, the largest community senior
citizens centre in Toronto, is located six blocks away.

Streetcars and the subway stop within a few feet of College View's front
door. The Municipality of Metropolitan Toronto provides its senior citizens
with a reduced fare of eight rides for $1 or one for 15 cents on these
modes of transportation.

Thus, one could hardly find a more central location or one better endowed
with services of all kinds in the whole of Metropolitan Toronto.

The Building

The apartment building itself is 20 storeys high and 17 of these storeys are
given over to housing. The street level provided commercial space, including
a finance company office, a wholesale beauty supply shop, and a greeting
card shop. The building's front door, also on this level, is controlled by
the intercom security system from the tenants' apartments. Residents have
access to floors above street level by three elevators.

225

COLLEGE VIEW APARTMENTS, TORONTO, ONTARIO

Fact Sheet

THE BUILDING

. Location

In the central shopping and entertainment district of downtown Toronto.

. Type and Size

A 20-storey building providing 198 bachelor units, 68 one-bedroom units, and 74 hostel rooms.

. Facilities

A large recreation room, laundry room, a cafeteria for the hostel residents, and two recreation lounges. There was also two large sundecks - one off the second floor, the other on the 20th floor.

. Date of Construction - 1969.

. Rents

In accord with the CMHC public housing rent geared-to-income scale.

THE MANAGEMENT

. National Housing Act Provision

Section 35D.

. Sponsor

The Metropolitan Toronto Housing Company Limited.

. Management Staff

A superintendent who was in attendance eight hours a day, five days a week, and several cleaners. One of the latter worked a shift ending at midnight. A dietitian supervised the cafeteria services.

THE RESIDENTS

. Number - 408.

. Sex and Marital Status

In the 23 interviews successfully completed in the building, the following households were encountered: six married couples, 10 widows living alone, three single men, one man separated from his wife, one widower, and two spinsters.

. Health Condition

Of the 23 persons interviewed, 15 appeared to have no incapacity, seven suffered slight physical incapacities, and one was moderately incapacitated.

. Age

The average age of residents interviewed was 75 years.

The building's second floor is given over to a cafeteria, a kitchen, a lounge, locker rooms, the superintendent's offices, and a large empty room. The third to seventh floors of the building have a mixture of self-contained apartments and "hotel units" (hostel rooms). The eighth to nineteenth floors consist totally of apartments, while the top storey contains a large recreation room, a laundry room, more lockers, public washrooms, and a sundeck.

When the study was made, College View Apartments' 340 units were occupied by 408 residents. Of these, 198 lived in bachelor apartments, 116 in the 68 one-bedroom units and the remaining 74 individuals in single hostel rooms. The hostel rooms, which had no cooking facilities, always included cafeteria meals in their rental. These rooms were identical to bachelor units in size and facilities but lacked a kitchen. However, unlike most hostel rooms in other parts of the country, they were unfurnished. The administration of College View Apartments also differed from that of most buildings providing hostel accommodation in that no special services or facilities other than the cafeteria were provided for the residents.

The Residents

In both apartment and hostel rooms, the rent was geared to income. Individuals tended to choose a hostel room for a number of reasons, the prime one being the convenience of having meals prepared by someone else.

Approximately a quarter of the tenants interviewed had lived in the immediate neighborhood prior to moving into College View. Two-thirds had lived in a hotel or boarding house and the remainder in apartments. The other three-quarters of College View's residents had previously lived in other parts of Metropolitan Toronto, one-fifth of the total sample having previously lived in other projects managed by the Metropolitan Toronto Housing Company (over 50 of the building's residents had moved en masse from another Metro building when College View Apartments were opened).

Seventy per cent of the tenants interviewed said they had no physical disabilities. Many of these, however, suffered mild health problems such as high blood pressure, stomach or heart trouble. But more than a quarter of the tenants interviewed had some degree of physical incapacity, and a few appeared in very poor health. Social service workers active in the building said the health of certain tenants was their agency's major concern. They claimed some of the hostel units housed decrepit people, most of whom required a different level of care.

Social Services

The management provided no on-site social services or facilities other than the cafeteria and the building staff consisted simply of a super-intendent and several assistants who worked five days a week. But because

of its central location, a host of outside community services were
available to the tenants of College View. Some of these activities were
not used as much as they could be since they were unknown to many tenants
requiring them. However, community workers familiar with the building
felt that the residents were already seriously taxing the local social
service system.

Residents' satisfaction with College View depended on their prior residence
as well as on their health conditions. Tenants who had previously lived
downtown and were still healthy and mobile found College View's location
excellent. But for those who had known suburban trees and lawns and those
with some degree of incapacity, the building was a source of discomfort,
especially in the heat of the summer. Because of poor internal communication and fear of the management, many of those residents interviewed had
turned inward. Others raged in frustration; they talked of earning the
mark of "troublemaker."

College View's sponsor, the Metropolitan Toronto Housing Company, indicated
that they were firmly committed to the idea that senior citizens apartments
were for well people. The apartments were not supposed to accommodate
people who had had trouble maintaining themselves because of a health
condition. Therefore, the existence of residents with serious health needs
in College View Apartments became an aberration to the administration,
rather than the normal situation in senior citizens housing. In an effort
to make certain prospective tenants were in reasonable health, the management
insisted that they apply in person at City Hall and that they allow a
Metro Housing worker to visit them at home to evaluate their situation.
The Metro Housing commissioner was quite concerned that many people "dressed
up" to gain entrance and then degenerated.

But even if all residents were in good health on entering the building, as
they got older they became more dependent. A social worker in contact with
most agencies working in College View (as well as in other Metro senior
citizens apartments) reported that the agencies were concerned that "Metro's
senior citizens developments were turning into homes for the aged without
resources." A VON nurse who spent about half her time working in College
View dealt with an average of 12 to 15 patients a week, many of them
receiving more than one visit.

The area's public health nurse worked about eight hours a week in the
building; she had 36 active cases at the time of the study. For two hours
a week she kept office hours in a room provided by the administration at
the City of Toronto Department of Public Health's request. A sign on her
door invited tenants to walk into the office for any help they might need.

Both the Public Health Department and the VON were concerned as early as
College View's opening about the health needs of residents. According to
the nurses, some people had waited for as long as three years for their

years for their apartment. The VON was particularly concerned that there was no reliable staff person in the building to even call an ambulance after midnight and even during the day no one was really charged with this duty. Because the management did not recognize that the tenants had health needs, communication channels had not been established to make the most efficient use of available community services. Because there was no acknowledgement of the special needs of the elderly for social services in the planning of the development, the community agencies suddenly found themselves with a taxing new concentration of clients.

Design Problems

College View also had certain design problems. Being located on a relatively small parcel of land, College View Apartments hugged the side-walk on both Yonge and McGill Streets, and one side of the building butted against an adjoining building on Yonge Street. At the back of the building was a small paved area serving as a loading zone for the apartments and the stores located on the ground floor. This produced a reaction among the residents; many felt trapped in their rooms because the streets outside were so noisy and crowded and had no green space to sit on.

The dwelling units had no balconies but a large sundeck was located on the top floor of the building, adjacent to the recreation room, and an even larger deck was situated off the second floor at the front of the building. However, in the summer, both sundecks were virtually unused. The air outside was noisy and polluted and anyway, from two in the afternoon the decks were generally too hot to sit on. They were both on the west side of the building and thus received direct sunlight from noon until the early evening. Some benches were provided but canopies to provide a little shade would also have been useful.

Satisfaction with Location

For residents who were accustomed to the lifestyle of the downtown area, College View's location represented no hardship. These people knew the streets and could visit their old haunts, and a good quarter of the residents fit into this category. Many of the residents who had moved to College View from elsewhere in Metro Toronto had come from a senior citizens development situated close to an OHC family public housing project and these people indicated that they were glad to be away from the noise of their youthful neighbors. It was true that they were disturbed about the heat and traffic noise on College View's streets but they felt that they had known worse.

However, 42 per cent of the sample were very unhappy with the location. These residents had moved in from the outlying suburbs in the belief that living in College View would put them in the heart of things - close to services, stores, and entertainment. Instead of this, they found themselves on the Yonge Street strip - a street full of hippies and rushing shoppers. Many of the stores in the area, such as Eatons across the street, were beyond the reach of their purse and most of the nearby beauty and barber shops were so expensive that a number of residents ended up returning to the old districts for such services. Noise was also bothersome to this group - not only the traffic roar and honking of cars that continued on Yonge Street until the early morning hours but also the deep rumble of the subway as it passed beneath the front of the building.

As the Metropolitan Toronto Housing Company normally allowed tenants only one transfer between their various developments, if certain College View tenants had moved from other Metro developments and become dissatisfied with their accommodation, they had no chance of remaining in Metro housing if they wished to escape the downtown location.

Some of the problems of College View in some ways seemed inherent in the design and location of the building; but others stemmed from the perceptions of management. One such perception was that the objective of senior citizens apartments, such as College View, was to only house the healthy elderly, thus eliminating the need for specialized facilities and services. As the Metro housing commissioner put it, "Privately owned high-rise apartments don't provide special social services. Why should we?" This view, of course, provided no recognition of the fact that elderly people have special needs related to their accommodation that go beyond the provision of warm, decent shelter.

The housing commissioner for Metropolitan Toronto, under whose administration College View falls, was also responsible for the administration of nursing care accommodation in homes for the aged. Because of this dual responsibility, he was able to rationalize the lack of services in College View by arguing that a transfer to a home for the aged could easily be arranged for residents who became too feeble to look after themselves. Perhaps this type of liaison was effective; however, none of the residents who were interviewed indicated any awareness of the possibility of progressing between accommodation and care levels in the Metro housing system. Thus, they were denied the feeling of security that such knowledge might afford.

Unfortunately, the administration's assertion that Metro housing was only responsible for the physical maintenance of the building tended to label residents needing services or aid as troublemakers and complainers. It was reported that at one point in College View there had been many complaints about food services. Among other things it was claimed that the meal hours made it difficult for residents to attend church and return in time for lunch. Not many residents were involved; nevertheless, apparently College View's superintendent and Metro housing's head office had been reluctant to even listen to the objections. The apparent communication gap was illustrated when one resident told the field worker: "I have enough trouble getting through to that office [the administration's] but how do you think those poor souls who are deaf or blind make out?"

Despite an apparent lack of concern for social service planning, College View's management had made some effort to encourage a tenant club. In fact, it was the College View Senior Citizens Club that facilitated what group activities did take place in the development. The president of Alexandra Park Apartments' senior citizens club was among those who moved into College View when it opened. A Metro housing official suggested that she form a club in the new development and she did. In less than a year, she had managed to furnish the recreation room and set up a club structure that included floor monitors. The job of the floor monitors was, in theory, to look in on the sick and attend funerals.

Practically none of the tenants interviewed, however, participated in the College View Senior Citizens Club nor knew their floor monitors. Some residents claimed that the club was a clique. Others said they were reluctant to get involved; when they moved into College View the management had warned them to be careful making friendships since "all types" lived in the building. Thus, it was almost a rule that residents had friends outside the development. Those without such friends were often very lonely.

Conclusion

It was an imaginative and adventuresome step to build a senior citizens residence in the downtown commercial core - where the action is. For residents with a background in the neighborhood and who were sufficiently physically and mentally alert, College View offered reasonably priced and functional housing in a choice location, with lots of opportunity for independence. But it appeared that to simply locate a development close to services and recreation was insufficient in itself, unless some provision was also made for design features and service arrangements that foster security and help to stimulate a sense of community. In addition, College View illustrated that even the most perfect location cannot be regarded as a substitute for a social orientation by administrators of senior citizens housing.

College View also demonstrated that the provision of hostel accommodation was not regarded by all senior citizens housing sponsors as representing a different level of care from that of self-contained accommodation. In College View, the hostel residents, although more dependent, simply were provided with meals - nothing else.

CHAPTER 10

A HIGH-RISE IN THE SUBURBS

The typical land development pattern in large North American cities is
concentric. That is to say, new housing is generally located in the
urban fringe area because of land costs. This is particularly true for
new low income housing as the high acquisition costs of land in the downtown core are usually difficult to recover - even with a substantial subsidy
program - unless additional land writedowns provided under urban renewal
programs are available.

Senior citizens housing developments are thus frequently located in
the same area as new family housing: in the suburbs. This has led to a
certain amount of concern. It is alleged that housing senior citizens
in the suburbs frequently separates them from their familiar environment,
makes shopping and transportation difficult, restricts recreational
opportunities, and leads to isolation from social services. In order to
examine this theory, the experience of Downsview Acres was reviewed.

The Building and Its Location

Downsview Acres, an apartment building built by the Metropolitan Toronto
Housing Company Limited under NHA section 16A, the non-profit section,
is located at the intersection of Jane Street and Wilson Avenue in the
Toronto borough of North York. North York, with a population of close to
500,000 people, lies to the north of the City of Toronto; thus, the
development was located near the northernmost extremities of the metropolitan area.

The brick building has 11 storeys and an L-like structure. At the time
of the study, it provided housing for 374 residents in 260 bachelor and
79 one-bedroom self-contained apartments. About 20 per cent of the
residents were men, the great majority of whom lived in one-bedroom units
with their spouses. The majority of the female residents were widowed
or single and lived in bachelor apartments. The building was designed so
that all one-bedroom units were in one wing of the "L", while the bachelor
units were in the other.

The development was on a well landscaped site with its entrance facing
away from the busy intersection. Jane Street and Wilson Avenue are both
major traffic arteries. Jane Street, in this district, is lined with
gas stations, drive-in restaurants, and supermarkets. Across Jane from
the development there is a shopping centre. Another shopping centre is
located close to the intersection and Wilson Avenue. But in the summer,
residents are able to sit on benches and visit in front of the development's
entrance, relatively protected from the noise of the traffic.

DOWNSVIEW ACRES, NORTH YORK, ONTARIO

Fact Sheet

THE BUILDING

. Location

At the intersection of Jane and Wilson Streets, major traffic arteries in Metropolitan Toronto's Borough of North York.

. Type and Size

It consisted of an 11-storey L-shaped building made up of 216 bachelor and 79 one-bedroom units.

. Facilities

Facilities consisted of a small recreation room, a laundry room, and benches on the lawn in front of the building.

. Date of Construction - 1966.

. Rents

A bachelor apartment rented for $47.50 a month and a one-bedroom for $69 a month.

THE MANAGEMENT

. National Housing Act Provision

Section 16A, limited dividend.

. Sponsor

The Metropolitan Toronto Housing Company Limited.

. Management Staff

The staff consisted of a building superintendent and three assistants who were in attendance five days a week during the daytime. There was no all-night staff although one resident was designated as "key man," to open tenants' doors when they locked themselves out. The administration of the building was carried on from the Metro Toronto Housing Company's head office in the downtown Toronto City Hall.

THE RESIDENTS

. Number - 364.

. Sex and Marital Status

Of the 24 interviews completed, the following households were encountered; seven married couples and 17 widowed women.

. Health Condition

The health of residents interviewed was generally good. Only one resident appeared to have a more than minor physical incapacity; half the tenants interviewed had no physical incapacity; 11 of the tenants had some minor physical incapacity.

. Age

The average age of those interviewed was 75 years.

The Residents

Downsview Acres opened its doors six years ago, and this was reflected in the relative old age of the building's population for a self-contained development: the average age of persons interviewed was 75 years; nearly 80 per cent of them had lived in the building for more than three years.

Physical health in the building, however, appeared to be very good. Only one person that was interviewed had more than a minor disability - severe arthritis making the use of a cane necessary. Half of those interviewed, nevertheless, appeared to suffer from some minor health problem that limited their ability to travel.

One-third of the residents interviewed had lived in the neighborhod prior to moving into the development. This proportion could be considered quite high since elderly people were more predominant in the city and the older boroughs of Metropolitan Toronto.

Despite a fair degree of community participation, a minority of Downsview Acres residents appeared to have little or no human contact with persons outside the development. Half of those interviewed had daily contact by telephone or in person with a member of their family but a sixth had negligible contact (once a year or less). None of the residents had daily contact with friends outside but a third of those interviewed had weekly visits and nearly as many again monthly contacts. A good third of the residents had little or no contact with friends. This infrequency of external participation (which probably became heightened during the winter months) was probably fairly typical of large urban apartment developments for senior citizens.

Services and Facilities

Other than the benches in front of the building, the only planned space for socializing was a small recreation room on the development's ground floor. This space was used by the residents' club for various activities but because of its limited size, fire regulations restricted its occupancy to 13 card tables (52 people for sit-down affairs). Even when tables were not required - when a variety night or films were planned - few people could be accommodated since large pillars blocked the line of sight in the room. A fifth of the residents interviewed cited the size of the recreation room as a reason for not participating in programs. A number of people reported that they preferred to stay in their apartments as they did not like to jostle for space. This was backed up by a North York recreation worker who claimed that in buildings similar to Downsview, where there were better facilities, twice as many residents participated in activities.

Housing administrators frequently claim that substantial facilities are not built into residences for the elderly so that they will not be discouraged from participating in activities outside the development.

Given an often underdeveloped state of community services for the elderly in suburban areas, this might not make much sense. Fortunately for this development, there was a senior citizens club located in the immediate area.

The Downsview Senior Citizens Club was located in the Downsview Arena, a quarter of a mile west of the development on Wilson Street. A third of the residents that were interviewed reported having attended the club on at least one occasion. The North York Department of Parks and Recreation organized activities in the arena's club, and claimed that approximately 150 members attended from the development. Interestingly, though, the tenants who attended the Downsview Arena Club generally appeared to be those with over-all stronger family and friendship ties in the community. Only one resident who attended the Downsview Arena Club did not have at least a weekly contact with family, and this resident was married. Half the residents that were interviewed and who participated in the Downsview Arena Club did not participate in the development's own club. Nearly all of these gave the size of the recreation room as the reason, although one resident said there was too much gossip.

Residents who did not participate in the Downsview Arena Club cited several reasons: they were afraid of slipping on the icy road to the arena in winter (the time of year when most programs are run); they could not stand the noise and/or did not like the members; a quarter did not know about the club. One thought the club was full and another was too busy playing in a concert band (not attached to any senior citizens club or building).

Social Services

Despite its suburban location, Downsview Acres' residents appeared to be receiving attention from several social service agencies. The Victorian Order of Nurses spent at least two hours daily in the building, much of this time in assisting patients suffering from diseases such as diabetes, ulcers, and cataract surgery or in providing personal care. However, we found that certain residents who appeared in need of this service were unaware of its existence.

The Visiting Homemakers Association, a United Appeal agency, had only two clients in the building at the time of the study. The service, one very much required by residents, provided shopping, housekeeping, and cooking help on a referral basis from another agency. The client paid a fee related to his income but a senior citizen receiving the guaranteed income supplement paid nothing. As his ability to pay increased, so did the cost - up to $2.50 an hour. Agency staff indicated that they were reluctant to make many referrals to the Visiting Homemakers Association because the association did not come close to meeting the need. However, we suspect that the overall problems had more to do with unmet needs in the cases of both the Victorian Order of Nurses and the Visiting Homemakers Association than the development's suburban location.

The Downsview Acres Club

Not a great deal of visiting appeared to take place in Downsview Acres. A quarter of the tenants reported visiting other persons in the development daily, a third weekly, and an eighth monthly, but a full quarter visited within the development on less than a monthly basis. However, Downsview Acres Senior Citizens Club did sponsor programs in the small ground-floor recreation room. The social activities included bingos, card games, a weekly sing-song, and special events. Once a week, a general meeting was held and the room was nearly always filled.

Much of the initiative for the club's activities appeared to be connected with assistance provided by a recreation worker, available on a part-time basis from the North York Department of Parks and Recreation. The Department was available to provide materials and instructors for any activities that the club wishes to engage in. In addition, the recreation worker assisted the club in having bulletins run off, obtaining folding chairs and other equipment when needed. This service was obviously beneficial in stimulating social interaction within the development. However, the worker regretted that insufficient community space appeared to hamper activities. He said that any club meetings that he attended were unbearably "jammed packed."

The Downsview Acres Citizens Club's main activity, other than sponsoring events of a social nature, had been the buddy system that was organized for the bachelor wing of the development. Each floor was supposed to appoint a monitor to check every floor resident each day. Tenants were supposed to place a sign on their door in the morning showing whether they were all right. If no sign was out the monitor was to knock on the door, and if the monitor still believed something was wrong, the superintendent was fetched. A number of residents, however, told us they did not like the system and considered it a nuisance. There had also been a problem in finding reliable monitors. At the time of the study, the system was not operating on most floors.

Resident-Staff Relations

A building superintendent and three assistants looked after the development. Their job was to care for the halls, recreation room, grounds and heating plant. In these tasks, most residents agreed that the staff served them well. However, many residents - especially the women - said they could do with some help in the way of heavy housekeeping and minor repairs. Many residents complained, for example, that their apartments had not been repainted for six years. One said, "The housing company will supply the paint but the maintenance men want $75 to paint an apartment after working hours." Many residents indicated that they could not afford this, nor could they do it themselves.

One lady said that she had given up asking the superintendent for help: "He won't do anything for you. They expect you to move the stove out to clean, but if you break the cable you have to pay." Apparently, the staff

did sometimes help some people, but this was supplied capriciously.
There was no provision for fixing things than an active person could do
on his own - replacing tap washers, or washing venetian blinds. One
lady, after paying $6 to have her blinds washed by one of the maintenance
men, had them wrapped up and put away so they wouldn't get dirty. Tenants
whose apartments had two large blinds paid $15 to have them cleaned.

It was understandable that the superintendent and his crew found it
difficult to meet such needs since they had no explicit instructions
to do more than their normal cleaning and maintenance tasks. It is
obvious that if the residents were living in private apartment houses,
this problem would exist. However, one would think that in a publicly-
sponsored residence containing a wide range of elderly people in various
states of health, there would be provision for special needs. As things
stood, the staff had become insolent and rude in the eyes of many tenants
and failed to respond to their needs. On the other hand, the tenants had
become demanding and troublemakers in the eyes of the staff.

Many tenants felt the staff completely lacked understanding of their needs.
Forty per cent of those interviewed indicated that they disliked the
staff in general. A further 10 per cent said that they disliked all the
staff save one man. Half of the residents had no complaints and many, in
fact, indicated that they were pleased that the staff did such a thorough
job of maintaining the public areas of the building. In examining which
tenants had poor relationships with the staff, the reason for their
hostility became clear.

Eighty per cent of the married men indicated that they liked the staff.
None of these men had health problems that incapacitated them to any great
degree and thus did not require special assistance or services. The only
man who had anything bad to say about the staff related the story of
witnessing a "snappiness" by a staff member toward an old lady. Although
the two married women interviewed had complaints about the staff, neither
were strong in their opinion and their relationship lacked bitterness.
But only 40 per cent of the widowed and single women had no complaint
about the staff. Of the 50 per cent of those interviewed who disliked
the superintendent, three-quarters were women living alone. One such
woman, when interviewed, pulled herself up in her chair, leaned forward,
and said:

> One day I was sitting in the recreation room waiting for the
> Gem Bus [the Gem Bus is a service of a local department store
> which picks up and delivers customers once a month for a 50
> cent fee] to arrive. The superintendent came in - didn't
> even look at me - and opened the windows. It was 5° below zero
> outside! Another tenant came into the room and shut the windows.
> The superintendent came back and accused me of shutting the
> windows. I told him I hadn't. He said I had. Finally, the

lady who had shut the windows told the superintendent he was
wrong, that she had done it. 'Anyway, you shouldn't have
opened that window in the first place', the lady said.
'We're senior citizens, you know, drafts can be bad for us!'

She took a breath:

Well, do you know what the superintendent said back? He
said: 'You're not senior citizens, you're just in this
building because you couldn't afford better!'

It appeared that the greater the needs of the residents for help and
companionship, the more negative were their views concerning the staff
and the more strained their relationship.

Conclusions

This case study started with the hypothesis that suburban living imposed
special difficulties for senior citizens living in self-contained
apartments since community services were inadequate and transportation
was poor. However, this was not conclusively borne out in this development.
While only 31 per cent of the sample said they were very satisfied with
the development's location (as opposed to 56 per cent of the residents
interviewed in all 19 case studies), only 8 per cent of the Downsview
Acres sample indicated that they did not have easy access to most important
services.

It was found that more social interaction and opportunities for recreation
and participation could have been developed with more ample community
space in the development, but that other service deficiencies could largely
be accounted for by the generally underdeveloped state of services in the
whole Metro area. The fact that the area surrounding Downsview Acres,
although suburban, was already well developed commercially accounted for
the lack of shopping problems. Transportation was not a major problem
as a good proportion of residents had previously lived in North York and
the development was near two bus routes.

One important finding had to do with the very narrow perceptions Downsview
Acres management shared about the task of housing senior citizens.
Practically no effort, except on an extremely informal basis, was made to
provide physical assistance with dwelling maintenance - let alone any
support for health, social, and emotional problems. For example, greater
use of services would probably have occurred if some effort had been made
to acquaint residents with what was actually available in the neighborhood.
It is fair to say that many of the residents of Downsview Acres felt
neglected by the development's administration and that this bred hostility
toward the caretaking staff as well as poor relationships within the
development. As the population of Downsview Acres grows older and more
feeble, these problems will be exacerbated in the absence of more purposeful
service programs and a realization by the management that the task of housing
the elderly is far more than simply to provide shelter.

CHAPTER 11

A SERVICE CLUB ADDS A DAY CENTRE

Two results of building a housing development for senior citizens in a
community are: 1) a concentration of elderly persons in a limited
geographic area, and 2) new public sector investment. This population
concentration and funding makes it possible for development sponsors to
provide recreational facilities that the community would otherwise not be
able to build. The step from supplying facilities only for the residents
to supplying new recreational opportunities for the whole community of
senior citizens is a short one - though not often taken.

In the case studies, there were several developments where elderly
persons living elsewhere were encouraged to make use of on-site communal
facilities. Sometimes these situations were quite informal, other times
they were highly institutionalized, with a specialized staff from a
community agency operating the program. The Kiwanis Apartment in Owen
Sound, Ontario, illustrates one way of how attaching a community recreation
facility to a senior citizens housing development worked out.

The Kiwanis Apartment

The Kiwanis Apartment was the first OHC subsidized housing development
built in Owen Sound. Since its construction, two more Ontario Housing
Corporation (OHC) apartment blocks have been built in the same vicinity,
a suburban district on one of the many hills surrounding the city core.
An older apartment complex built by the municipal Owen Sound Housing Company
as a non-profit project is also located in the same district; in fact, all
of Owen Sound's senior citizens housing is concentrated in a four or five
block radius.

The building itself is a two-storey affair, the first being half below
ground. It is composed of 24 bachelor suites and 12 one-bedroom units.
The Kiwanis recreation centre is attached to the building. It consists
of three rooms: a library/sitting room, a lounge, and a kitchen. The
library is furnished with several shelves of books (donated by residents
and outsiders) and comfortable easy chairs. The lounge contains several
chairs and tables for cards, a sitting area somewhat larger than that in
the library room, and a piano. The kitchen is fully equipped with a
refrigerator and stove (as one resident put it, "everything you need for a
turkey dinner"). The residents raffled off two handmade quilts to make
money for the hallway carpets but aside from this, all the furniture and
kitchen equipment was provided by the Kiwanis Club.

KIWANIS APARTMENTS, OWEN SOUND, ONTARIO

Fact Sheet

THE BUILDING

. Location

In a suburban district of Owen Sound, on one of the many hills surrounding the city. Accessible to the downtown area by public bus.

. Type and Size

A two-storey building containing 24 bachelor and 12 one-bedroom units.

. Facilities

A recreational complex was attached, which included a library/sitting room, a lounge and a kitchen. The development also had laundry facilities.

. Date of Construction - 1966.

. Rents

Rents geared to income according to the CMHC scale, with the minimum monthly rent being $32.

THE MANAGEMENT

. National Housing Act Provision

Section 35D.

. Sponsor

The Ontario Housing Corporation, managed by the Owen Sound Housing Authority.

. Management Staff

There was no full-time, on-site staff. Maintenance was carried out by a superintendent from an adjoining building and management services by the Owen Sound Housing Authority manager.

THE RESIDENTS

. Number - 43.

. Sex and Marital Status

The residents were predominantly women, with fewer than 20 per cent men. In a sample of 11 households, there were nine widows, one widower and one married couple.

. Health Condition

Health was generally good. One-quarter of the residents appeared to have slightly limited physical capacity; three-quarters had no incapacity at all.

. Age

The average age of the sample was about 72 years. This corresponded with the management's estimate of the average age for the entire population of the development.

In 1965, when the original plans for the building were still on the drawing board, the Owen Sound Kiwanis Club assessed their community programs and concluded that facilities and services for senior citizens were needed. They approached the Ontario Housing Corporation with a proposal that a recreation centre be included in the new apartment complex. OHC's reaction was extremely favorable and further negotiations resulted in the three-room centre. The Kiwanis Club agreed to pay OHC $1,000 a year for 25 years, interest free, to cover the cost of building the recreation centre and furnishings. The cost of furnishing the kitchen was assumed by the Kiwanis Club over and above their annual payments. The Club also agreed to assume the cost of cleaning and supervising the recreation room. The Kiwanis Club wanted the centre to make a positive contribution to all senior citizens in Owen Sound since, in 1965, only one senior citizens club existed in the district.

As it worked out, however, the centre had been used to a lesser degree than was originally anticipated. Regularly scheduled events planned by the building's tenant organization included only euchre (Tuesday and Friday nights) and bingo (Thursday nights). An executive member of the tenant organization estimated that about 40 people came to euchre on Tuesday nights and 20 on Friday nights; however, only five of these lived outside the building. Bingo was not very popular; only about 10 people came regularly, one of these from outside.

Once a month, the Association for the Mentally Retarded used the facilities and once every three weeks the Anglican Church held a communion service in the library room. Community people had shown slides and home movies in the centre but this was infrequent. The Salvation Army and a barbershop quartet had also provided musical entertainment. On occasion, the centre had been used by women residents for quilting and other needle-work, and by individual tenants for private dinners. Nevertheless, most days and often in the evening, the recreation centre stood silent and empty.

The chairman of the Owen Sound Housing Authority board cited several reasons why the facilities were not used extensively. First, he thought that the centre was not large enough to serve Owen Sound's entire senior citizens population, particularly when one considered the two new developments in the area. Second, he believed that although it was desirable for senior citizens to plan and organize their own activities, there was also a need for some individual or social agency to provide motivation and guidance. The Kiwanis Club did have a committee to oversee the recreation centre but the committee members did not actively participate in its daily operation. They had considered inviting a church or social service group to take on this responsibility. A third reason had to do with the centre's location in a housing development. He said that the residents felt that it was their recreation centre, and thus did not encourage outsiders to use it.

There was also the fact that several other senior citizens centres with
more comprehensive programs had been developed in the city since the
Kiwanis Apartment was constructed. Centres such as Knox Church, the
YMCA, the Salvation Army, and the Lutheran Church provided competition
and an alternative place for local people to visit.

The size of the centre did not appear to be a real major factor in
deterring people from using it. It was never overcrowded. Also residents
denied that they were unenthusiastic about outsiders making use of the
facilities; residents who were interviewed indicated that they were
fully aware of the Kiwanis Club's intention that the centre be made
available for all senior citizens and indicated that they were not at
all resentful of that intention. However, the residents probably did
not completely understand that outsiders must have felt some sense of
intrusion.

Community Relations

One argument for shared communal facilities was that they help to
integrate residents of senior citizens developments into the local neighborhood. However, in this case, the recreation centre did not appear to be
an important factor in involving residents with senior citizens living in
the community. Residents' community relationships were primarily on a
bilateral basis; only one of the residents that were interviewed continued
to be involved in the activities of an outside organization; two others
had been members before moving to the housing development but had dis-
continued their involvement; the remaining residents had not been members
of social clubs or organizations. However, all respondents had families
and saw them at least once a month. Four of these were in daily contact
with at least one family member and four others saw their relatives at
least once a week. In addition, only one respondent indicated that she
had no friends outside the building; the rest saw their friends at least
once a month.

All residents we interviewed expressed satisfaction with the size of the
building. Several indicated that because there were only 36 apartments
they got to know everyone, so that a general atmosphere of neighborliness
prevailed. There appeared to be a good deal of friendliness among
residents; it was reported that many offers of assistance were forthcoming
when needed. There was, for example, a resident who had just returned
from a hospital and was being visited and helped by concerned neighbors.
The main centres for informal gathering, however, appeared to be in the
apartments - not the recreation centre.

There was no full-time staff in the building. The superintendent of the
52-unit OHC apartment building next door looked after the physical
maintenance. There was a general consensus among the tenants that while
maintenance was good, they would prefer to have their own caretaker for
security reasons.

The development appeared to be successful from the housing point of view, with residents expressing a high degree of satisfaction. The local housing authority manager was well known to the tenants and she took a personal interest in them, beyond the normal administrative duties of rent collection and account keeping. She believed that public relations was an important part of her job - getting community acceptance for public housing and treating residents as individuals were her prime considerations. In this regard, the Kiwanis centre somewhat complicated her work.

The housing authority manager knew most of the tenants in the building by name and interacted with them on an individual basis. In developments that lack a recreation centre, the manager tended to devote more time to the social aspects of her work. In the Kiwanis Apartment, she felt obliged to leave some social concerns to the recreation centre's operators. But, as already outlined, the centre had no effective management.

Conclusions

The Kiwanis Apartment arrangement of OHC and a service club cooperating to provide a day care centre has not been repeated in Ontario. While the concept was good in theory, there had not been sufficient follow-through to make it work on a day-to-day basis. The chairman of the Owen Sound Housing Authority board claimed that he had learned three things from the experience. He believed that before any such centre is built onto another public housing development, there should be a thorough investigation so that a building of an appropriate size is constructed. Second, he felt that such a facility should not be provided without first making solid arrangements for staffing it. Finally, he thought that any recreation centre should be built apart from the actual housing development, in order to decrease feelings of possessiveness by residents.

Community facilities should not be undertaken without proper social planning and provision for staffing of an on-going program. In this case, the need for programing obviously had not been fully appreciated. However, the value of the Kiwanis Apartment day centre must not be considered a loss; the space was being used, although at less than capacity. In addition, the building was financed over a 50-year period and certainly arrangements may be developed to one day make it a great asset to the neighborhood.

CHAPTER 12

THE SOCIAL COSTS OF A HUGE HIGH-RISE APARTMENT BUILDING

The issue that recurred most during the case studies of urban housing developments for the elderly concerned the effect of high-rise design on environmental quality. If it appears that these case studies dwell too much on this question, it should be remembered that high-rises are the dominant building type in many large Canadian cities. Given the need for accommodation and the constraints our ideas about building place on the form of high density housing, high-rises are in many cases the only solution. Yet the gathering together of large numbers of elderly persons does create special needs. Some case studies show that these needs have been met and have resulted in excellent living situations. Others have illustrated the difficulties that can arise when proper recognition is not given to the non-housing needs of old people. Ouellette Avenue Apartments in Windsor, Ontario, further demonstrates this aspect.

The Building

Ouellette Avenue Apartments are located on the city's main street, about five blocks from the city centre. Although the building is a massive 24-storey high-rise tower, it was not out of place beside the street's many high-rise structures and the soaring buildings visible across the river in Detroit.

The size of the building was its most striking quality, with 450 residents housed in the development's 400 self-contained units. Each of these units was equipped with a living room, kitchen, bedroom, bathroom and balcony. The design was standard with a few added features for senior citizens. Communal facilities included a laundry room and lounge on every floor, a central recreation room on the main floor and a penthouse lounge 25 storeys above the ground.

Construction of a high-rise complex such as the Ouellette Apartments certainly had some obvious benefits. In Windsor, even after the completion of this 400-unit development, the Windsor Housing Authority reported that there was still a waiting list for 1,300 households for senior citizens accommodation. It was therefore understandable that the Ontario Housing Corporation should feel compelled to build on a large scale. Two more apartment complexes of comparable size were in the planning stage for Windsor; yet even with these additional units, the waiting list would not be completely absorbed.

The location of the Ouellette Avenue Apartments within walking distance of downtown, on a major bus line, and convenient to stores, churches, a hospital, and a senior citizens centre, was very popular with the residents. Only one resident mentioned noise and pollution as disadvantages of a central location. Most residents indicated that they had easy access to all services that were important to them. A large high-rise building thus seemed to afford a favorable location for more senior citizens than would less dense accommodation.

OUELLETTE AVENUE APARTMENTS, WINDSOR, ONTARIO

Fact Sheet

THE BUILDING

. Location

On Windsor's main street, about five blocks from city centre.

. Type and Size

It was a 24-storey tower with 400 one-bedroom apartments.

. Facilities

There was a main recreation room, lounges on each floor and a penthouse at the top of the building. There was a laundry room on each floor and balconies for each suite.

. Date of Construction - 1969.

. Rents

According to the CMHC rent geared-to-income scale.

THE MANAGEMENT

. National Housing Act Provision

Sections 35D and 35E.

. Sponsor

The Ontario Housing Corporation.

. Management Staff

Management was by the Windsor Housing Authority. There were three maintenance men at the development, two of whom lived in the building - one of these was responsible for floors one to 11, while the other was responsible for floors 12 to 24.

THE RESIDENTS

. Number - 450.

. Sex and Marital Status

In a random sample of 25 households, there were four married couples, 15 widows living alone, three spinsters living alone and another spinster living with her sister, and one woman separated from her husband because he was in a special care institution.

. Health Condition

Health was generally good. The manager estimated that most residents had no physical incapacity and one-quarter or less were slightly incapacitated. Of the 24 interviews completed, 13 residents showed no incapacity, eight had slight incapacities, two were moderately disabled and one was seriously incapacitated.

. Age

The residents were quite young. About half were between 65 and 74 with one-quarter under 65 and one-quarter over 75. The average age of the sample was 72 years.

Facilities and Services

The concentration of 450 residents in one building meant that facilities
and services, which in a smaller development would not be viable in
terms of cost and usage, could be built in. Facilities in the Ouellette
Apartments were certainly adequate in size. Each floor was equipped with
a comfortable lounge and a laundry room. There was also a recreation room
on the main floor and a penthouse lounge on the top storey. However,
only limited use was made of the lounge facilities.

The ground floor recreation room was the scene of formally scheduled
events but the penthouse was considered by many residents to be an almost
complete waste of funds and was used only on rare occasions to admire
the view of the city. Probably one reason for this was that the elevator
went only to the 24th floor and there were 17 steps to the penthouse.
This undoubtedly affected persons with some incapacity but for the
remaining residents, both the penthouse and other lounges were not
significant places in their immediate environment. If social and recreational events were planned for these areas, residents might have felt
more comfortable using them and would have begun to consider their
possibilities for informal gatherings, but the Windsor Housing Authority
did not consider it their responsibility to obtain community services
for the building.

Only one agency had developed an affiliation with the development. This
was the Victorian Order of Nurses who, on their own initiative, had
approached the Housing Authority with a proposal that a counselling service
be provided in the building. Although the service was still experimental,
the nurse in charge suggested it appeared to be worthwhile. She felt that
residents in many cases were not equipped to deal with their own problems
and that she could act as a liaison with local agencies, letting residents
know what was available and assisting them in approaching services.
Involvement of an outside agency was required, she suggested, because
residents might feel apprehensive about voicing their problems and complaints
if the service were provided directly by the Windsor Housing Authority.

Social Costs

Staff in the development consisted of three maintenance men, two of whom
lived in the building; they had the added responsibility of collecting rents.
The maintenance men had little to do with the social and personal needs
of the residents, other than to provide for their physical comfort. The
social aspects were dealt with to a certain extent by housing authority
project officers and newly hired community relations officers. The
community relations officers, however, had done little to organize or
stimulate group activities and resident participation but concentrated rather
on interacting with individual residents. As a result, there was no resident
association in the building, few social and recreational activities, and
very little use made of lounge facilities. Indeed, the community relations
officer assigned to this development was formerly on the housing authority's
management staff and lacked training in counselling or community work.

The size of the development inhibited informal social interaction among residents. Generally, relationships were restricted to immediate neighbors or, at the most, residents of one floor. Almost half of the residents interviewed stated that they had made very few friends in the building. The absence of scheduled events provided little opportunity for meeting residents of other floors. Residents met their neighbors only by using the laundry room or riding the same elevator.

Most residents turned to family and friends outside the building for social activities, with the result that their building became simply a place to live rather than the centre of a satisfying social environment. Because of their relatively young age and good health, some residents continued to work as well as be active in clubs and organizations; this contributed to the general lack of involvement with the development and added to the feeling of isolation experienced by some residents. However, several residents, particularly those who had active community interests, expressed satisfaction with the great amount of privacy they enjoyed. The building was obviously meeting the needs of these tenants by providing them with a place to live where nobody bothered them.

An alternative to having the development itself provide social and recreation services was to arrange for outside community agencies to offer them. The Windsor Housing Authority was currently moving in this direction although they had not originally invited community involvement. The VON, besides undertaking the counselling service mentioned previously, continued to provide nursing and homemaking care on an individual basis. They were also planning to assume responsibility for a meals-on-wheels program administered by a local senior citizens centre.

The senior citizens centre was located about one block from the development and conducted a great many activities for old people in the area. However, it could not cope with the increasing demand for meals-on-wheels services or meet the demand for recreational activities for the building's 450 residents. The centre staff were enthusiastic about the VON taking over the meals-on-wheels program and also felt that it would be beneficial if the Ouellette Apartments developed their own recreation program for residents, leaving the centre service open to elderly persons living in private dwellings.

In response to this sentiment, the housing authority indicated that it planned to work in conjunction with the Windsor United Community Services to develop a tenants organization and encourage recreational and social activities. However, at the time of our field work, UCS was unaware of any plans by the housing authority to involve them in the development.

Conclusion

It seemed apparent that the pressing needs of senior citizens justified constructing the large apartment building in Windsor and similar projects in other major urban centres. The housing crisis as experienced by the elderly makes it difficult to argue against building on a large scale. Few residents objected to the high structure _per se_; in fact, 42 per cent of the sample (higher than for any other development) agreed that there were many advantages for senior citizens in high-rises. It was the scale rather than the structure of the building that presented the major problems.

Senior citizens have needs beyond adequate housing, and the greater the concentration of old people in one development, the more obvious these needs become. The social costs that accompany very large developments must be compensated for by investment in social programs that aim to overcome feelings of alienation. It is unrealistic to expect existing neighborhood services to absorb the needs of 450 residents and it is just as unrealistic to expect all elderly persons to care for their own social and personal needs.

Fortunately, the VON involved themselves in the development and were performing several required functions. If the United Community Services and the Windsor Housing Authority's community relations staff initiated the planning, a strong tenants organization could develop to cope with social and recreational activities. But it would be advisable to take these steps before large developments are occupied and a portion of their residents become isolated socially.

CHAPTER 13

A SOCIAL AGENCY ADOPTS A DEVELOPMENT

Many senior citizens developments built under the non-profit section of the National Housing Act are projects of service clubs and other small organizations. While some developments sponsored by service clubs are very large and able to support extensive on-site staff, the majority are small and tightly financed. Providing social services for tenants in such cases is always a problem. While tenants are generally expected to obtain health and social services in the community, they often do not know how to go about this.

In the Aubrey Jones Apartments in Hamilton, the social needs of a small urban apartment building have successfully been met through the virtual adoption of the development by the Hamilton Family Service Agency.

The Parties Involved

In 1962, the downtown branch of the Kiwanis Club of Hamilton decided to build a non-profit apartment development for senior citizens. They had become aware of a need for more senior citizens housing through their program of delivering Christmas packages to needy persons. Incorporating under the name of the Hamilton Senior Citizens Apartments Ltd., they set up a seven-man board of directors to build and manage the development. Board members were elected from the club's membership of 70 business and professional people.

When the eight-storey apartment building was visited in 1971, it housed 94 residents in 48 bachelor and 24 double rooms. In 1964, before the building opened, applications outnumbered the capacity by more than two to one. To evaluate who should be given preference, the Kiwanis invited the Family Service Agency of Hamilton to appraise applicants. Once the Family Service Agency became involved, the Kiwanis realized that their elderly tenants would need more than shelter. Since the size of the building did not allow for much on-site staff, the Kiwanis requested assistance from the agency in working with residents.

The Family Service Agency, mainly funded by the United Appeal of Hamilton and District, initially placed a social worker in the building for a three-month period to explore the needs and service potential. The social worker told us that the residents were at first concerned mainly with their ability to pay the rents, with maintaining their independence and privacy, and with the proximity of shopping. However, as the development matured, the availability of health and welfare services and recreation became important concerns.

AUBREY JONES APARTMENTS, HAMILTON, ONTARIO

Fact Sheet

THE BUILDING

. Location

On Hamilton's main street, a few blocks away from the central downtown area.

. Type and Size

An eight-storey concrete building, with 48 bachelor and 24 one-bedroom units.

. Facilities

A large recreation room, an office for the building's social worker, a laundry room, a mail room, and a few chairs inside the entrance hall.

. Date of Construction - 1965.

. Rents

$53 per month for a bachelor unit, and $65 for a one-bedroom unit.

THE MANAGEMENT

. National Housing Act Provision

Section 16, non-profit.

. Sponsor

The Hamilton Senior Citizens Apartments Limited, sponsored by the downtown Hamilton branch of the Kiwanis Club.

. Management Staff

A half-time maintenance man in the building and a full-time social worker. There was no 24-hour on-site staff.

THE RESIDENTS

. Number - 94.

. Sex and Marital Status

A random sample of 14 households contacted five married couples, one widower, six widows, and two single women.

. Health Condition

Only one respondent in the sample appeared to have moderately limited ability; all the rest had just slight or no physical incapacities. The management believed that most of the residents had no physical incapacities.

. Age

The average age of the sample was 79 years. This was consistent with the management's records.

The Family Service Agency believed that the success of their work in the building would depend on the degree to which the tenants themselves became involved. The tenants had organized a council in 1965, and by the fall of that year the council was strong enough to organize social events. For a period, a recreation group worker was made available by the Family Service Agency and with his assistance the council developed a program of social activities for the first Christmas holiday period they spent together in the builidng. Within months of its opening, therefore, the three main actors in the building - the Kiwanis, the Family Service Agency, and the tenants council - had begun to engage in a purposeful arrangement to ensure that the residents were secure and happy.

The Operation in 1971

Five years had elapsed from the opening of the Aubrey Jones Apartments. The Kiwanis Club continued to be responsible for the financial and administrative aspects of the building and the rents charged allowed the Club to employ a half-time maintenance man. All other staff were financed from community sources and supplied or coordinated through the Family Service Agency, which continued to work closely with the building's sponsor. The tenants council acted as a spokesman for the residents and continued to organize its own social events. The Family Service Agency still paid for a full-time social worker in the building. This worker, in consultation with the tenants council, stimulated activities in the development, helped individual tenants with their personal problems, and coordinated the various health and welfare agencies servicing the building.

Three community service agencies provided their services in the building - the Public Health Department's Nursing Service, the Victorian Order of Nurses, and the Visiting Homemakers. The Public Health Department's Nursing Service had the most specific relationship with the development. One afternoon a week a public health nurse was available in the building to discuss health problems, contact doctors, provide transportation and generally assist with any health needs of the residents. Generally, the nurse dealt with four or five residents a week. She attempted to keep tabs on the severity of residents' disabilities so that proper care could be obtained for them. Her main focus was preventative psychiatric nursing.

The Victorian Order of Nurses provided not only remedial nursing care but also care for persons freshly discharged from hospitals and a meals-on-wheels service. The VON was providing care to two residents of the building and meals-on-wheels to four residents at the time of our visit.

Homemaking service was available in the development from the Visiting Homemakers Association but at the time of the study it was not being used by any residents. The cause of this was twofold, according to the agency staff. First, the cost ($15 a day or $1.90 an hour) was prohibitive to

most residents. The provincial law under which the Visiting Homemakers
Association operates - the Homemaker and Nursing Services Act - precludes
public subsidy as long as old people have savings of $1,000 or more.
As most of the senior citizens in the building had saved this amount
(for funeral expenses if nothing else), they had to pay the full amount.
Secondly, the service was hindered in its availability because of a
lack of trained homemakers.

The health of the residents was generally very good, especially
considering that between half and three-quarters of them were over 75
years of age. Only one of the 14 residents sampled was moderatley
incapacitated, the rest being either slightly incapacitated or completely
fit. There appeared to be no policy on moving tenants out of the apartments as their health declined.

The good health of the Aubrey Jones Apartments residents, especially as
old as they were, suggested both a high selectivity in admission and
good deployment of available services within the building. The Family
Service Agency had provided this service.

The Tenant Association

Of the 14 residents interviewed, 12 were involved actively in the tenant
association's activities. Two did not participate. One was a man living
with his wife, the other was a widowed woman who was so thoroughly
negative in her attitude that all her responses were perhaps questionable.
If the sample is an indication, the tenant association succeeded in
involving over 80 per cent of the residents in its activities.

An example of the degree to which the tenants council participated in
running the development occurred when our field worker was obliged to
appear at a council meeting to explain this study before being granted
access to the building.

As the Family Service Agency services were discussed at tenants council
meetings, the residents knew what was available and even when it was time
for them to seek another level of care. This high degree of integration
had been obtained in a building whose physical design was in no way
elaborate. The communal facilities were limited to a recreation room,
an office (for the social worker and public health nurse), and a laundry
room. Actually, the recreation room and office were not included in the
original building design; space on the top floor was made into a
recreation room after the tenants council had been formed. The tenants
collected money to furnish the lounge with tables and chairs and
accumulated a small library in one corner of the room. The social worker's
office was originally a storage room.

Considering Aubrey Jones Apartments' limited facilities, a great number
of activities were carried on by the tenants. Bingos and cards, films,
shuffleboard, choir practice, sewing and knitting, socials, dinners and

outside entertainment were regular events in the recreation room. It was staffed by individual tenants or the tenants council with some assistance from the Family Service Agency social worker (and previously from the recreation worker).

The full schedule of events allowed many of the tenants to help plan rather than just participate in activities. The tenants council consisted of a president, secretary-treasurer, and one representative from each of the six floors as well as committees on recreation, discussion groups, interest groups and emergencies. Besides the program in the recreation room, the council had coordinated a wide range of development activities including bus tours, a buddy system and, of course, negotiation with the Kiwanis and the Family Service Agency about tenant problems.

A past president of the tenants council summed up her experience with the group this way. When she first came to the apartments, she thought she would be "put on the shelf." Instead, she became active in tenant activities. During her term in office, she had to drop out to care for her ill daughter and grand-daughter, but she was able to carry on. When re-elected to her office, she said she had been anxious about becoming president but the job had brought back her ability to direct meetings.

Besides the participation in the council's organized programs, there was a great deal of friendly visiting and neighborliness between residents. The few chairs in the lobby and the residents' apartments were the scene of frequent informal gatherings and social contact. Generally, the atmosphere was one of warmth and friendliness such as one might find in a boarding house or small community. No one visited informally less than weekly with friends within the building. Five of those interviewed visited daily and seven visited more frequently within rather than outside the building.

Residents only expressed two types of complaints. Nearly all occupants of bachelor units dearly wanted one-bedroom apartments. The public health nurse suggested this was desirable both for physical and emotional health. The other complaint concerned the lack of a full-time, live-in maintenance man. Even the highly developed sense of community appeared to be no substitute for someone who could be always available for emergencies - even if the emergency simply took the form of being locked out one's apartment.

Conclusion

Aubrey Jones Apartments illustrated how a development too small to provide extensive services of its own could obtain social resources. Three factors seemed to determine what happened in this specific case. The sponsoring Kiwanis Club was aware from the beginning that they were dealing with a special type of tenant. They also realized that they could

not manage the building entirely on their own and thus willingly invited
support from community services. The Family Service Agency was prepared
to take on the role of social service coordinator and was able to locate
funds to finance a program. Finally, the tenants themselves were able
to effectively build a sense of community in the building through the
tenants council. Both the Kiwanis Club and the Family Service Agency,
rather than fearing tenant participation, encouraged it.

The tenant community, with the Family Service Agency social worker as a
knowledgeable intermediary, was able to get assistance as quickly as
possible to tenants who required it. This may explain why, despite the
advanced average age of residents, health was so good.

Not only did the Aubrey Jones Apartments' tenants have good housing but
also they had the opportunity to lead an active life. A preference for
one-bedroom apartments and the desire for a live-in maintenance man,
while on the tenants' minds, was not enough to negate the positive aspects
of living here.

CHAPTER 14

BUILDING A COMMUNITY OUT OF BRICKS AND MORTAR

Every year more elderly people are seeking convenient accommodation in
the major cities of Canada. As the housing need is mammoth, developers
of senior citizens housing often believe that they must build on a large
scale to match it. Unfortunately, these living arrangements sometimes
provide shelter but no security - or a degree of security at the expense
of paternalism. It is difficult to achieve the combination of facilities
and services that provides for social integration into the broader
community as well as the broadest possible range of lifestyles. But
Winnipeg's Lions Manor has done the job and illustrates the vital role
that can be played by inspired professional staff in building a community
out of a structure of bricks and mortar.

Location

Lions Manor is situated on one of the busiest corners in downtown Winnipeg.
Many shops and major stores are located within walking distance of the
development. Bus service to all points in the city is available at the
streetcorner. As bus fares in Winnipeg are subsidized for senior citizens,
a single fare costs 10 cents.

Most residents were pleased with the location. One volunteered that the
location allowed residents more independence because they were not forced
to rely on others to take them places. Another resident suggested that
the location was good because the neighborhood of Lions Manor was also
the centre of housing need for many older people. Indeed, more than one-
third of the residents interviewed had lived in the immediate area of the
development just prior to their present accommodation. Thirteen per cent
of Winnipeg's 50,000 people over 65 years of age live within five blocks
of the development. Many Lions Manor residents were thus able to maintain
their contact with former neighbors and friends. This factor, together
with the existence of an on-site day centre, resulted in a high degree of
integration between the development and the surrounding community.

The Day Centre

Originally operated by the Age and Opportunity Bureau - a United Way
agency - the Sherbrook Day Centre utilized Lions Manor's communal
facilities to provide a neighborhood recreation and social program for
the elderly. Subsidized by the City of Winnipeg, the Province of Manitoba
and the Winnipeg Foundation, as well as the United Way, at the time of
our visit the centre had a membership of slightly under 400. A little
over half of these members lived outside the development.

LIONS MANOR, WINNIPEG, MANITOBA
Fact Sheet

THE BUILDINGS

. Location

At one of the busiest corners in downtown Winnipeg in an area that while
primarily commercial was highly populated with senior citizens living in
rooming houses, low-rise apartment blocks and private homes.

. Type and Size

A single complex consisting of two towers connected at the base. The development consisted of 218 bachelor dwelling units, 41 one-bedroom dwelling units,
and 135 single hostel rooms.

. Facilities

Floor lounges in hostel portions with kitchenettes, televisions and telephones.
First two floors consist of general facilities also utilized by Sherbrook Day
Centre: lounge, dining room, auditorium, craftsroom, meeting room, lobby
library, reception desk, games room, hairdressing salon, laundry room, workshop.

. Date of Construction

First tower in 1965, second tower in 1970.

. Rents

Bachelor apartments $59-$61 per month; one-bedroom apartments $79 per month;
hostel unit accommodation is $237 per month.

THE MANAGEMENT

. National Housing Act Provision

Sections 16 and 16A, non-profit.

. Sponsor - The Lions Club of Winnipeg.

. Management Staff

Staff consisted of 55 persons, including an executive director and a recreation
leader. There was always a staff member on duty in the building.

THE RESIDENTS

. Number - 435.

. Sex and Marital Status

In 23 interviews, four widowers were encountered, 13 widows, three single women,
a male and a female divorcee, and one married couple. The majority of
residents were female.

. Health Condition

In a sample of 23 residents interviewed, 40 per cent appeared to have no
physical incapacity, 40 per cent only slight physical incapacity, 17 per cent
moderate physical incapacity, and only 3 per cent serious physical incapacity.

. Age

Most of the residents were over 75 years of age. The average age in the sample
was 77 years.

In 1971, operation of the centre was turned over to the management of
Lions Manor. The Manor's activities coordinator supervised the centre
as well as all activities exclusively for Manor residents. During the
day, programs were under the auspices of the day centre which had its own
elected council, while evening activities were sponsored by the residents
council.

Besides offering a professionally directed program of physical recreation, crafts, special interest classes, and social events, the aim of
the day centre was to break the isolation of the elderly in the neighborhood by providing them with an opportunity for companionship and friendship. Members paid a fee of one dollar per annum.

The Facilities that Come with Size

When the first building in the Lions Manor complex was erected in 1965,
it was the third highest building in Winnipeg: 11 storeys. It was filled
immediately. Six years later, even after the construction of a second
building - this time 14 storeys high - 1,650 people were waiting for self-
contained units and 80 for hostel rooms. In mid-1971, the two towers
housed 218 residents in bachelor units, 41 couples in one-bedroom units,
and 135 people in single hostel rooms.

The hostel rooms were located on the second, third and fourth floors in
one tower, with two lounges on each floor, one of which served as a
connecting link between the old and the new towers. Self-contained dwelling
units occupied the remaining floors in both buildings - these floors,
however, had no connecting link.

The connecting lounges of the hostel floors were equipped with easy chairs,
televisions, telephones and kitchenettes and the main floor of the complex
contained a spacious lounge, a dining room, auditorium, craftsroom, meeting
room, lobby, library, two reception desks and administrative offices. The
basement level had a large games room, a hairdressing salon, a laundry room,
and workshop area. Two elevators in each tower allowed easy access to the
facilities on the first floor and basement, which were both used by the day
centre as well as the Manor residents.

Because of the existence of the hostel rooms, cafeteria facilities were
needed in the development. But rather than being restricted to the hostel
tenants alone, they could be used by any senior citizens living in the development or participating in the day centre, a noon meal costing 45 cents.

The high density of old people in the building and using the day centre
allowed for the library to be supplied by the Winnipeg Public Library,
which stacks its shelves on a rotating basis. The Manor cafeteria was
able to provide sick residents with a meals-on-wheels service. Friendly
visiting service by the Lionnelles, a women's version of the Lions Club,

and social work counselling from the Age and Opportunity Bureau were
also available because of the physical concentration of elderly persons.
Nursing services were supplied by the VON.

Despite the availability of a good many services not often found in
housing for the aged, Lions Manor's administrator was not complacent.
He indicated that he would like to see the following services developed:
full-time social work counselling, legal consultation, a preventative
medical program with a small health clinic, a sheltered workshop, and a
better transportation system to bring neighborhood people in to take
advantage of what Lions Manor has to offer.

Staffing

The administrator's ambitious plans are characteristic of the evolution
that had gone on in management objectives through involvement in the
field. Originally, Lions Manor was meant simply to provide adequate
housing for some of Winnipeg's senior citizens. The project was conceived
and carried out by the Lions Club of Winnipeg. The club, with a membership of 140 business and professional men, elects a nineteen-member board
of directors. Through six subcommittees, these directors have been
responsible for developing the general principles and philosophy behind
the Lions Manor.

Staff consisted of 45 full-time and 10 part-time employees. Most of
these staff members were employed in maintenance, kitchen and dining room
work and in caring for the hostel residents. Generally, the residents did
not have sharply defined views about the staff. Hostel residents who ate
every meal in the cafeteria and met housekeeping staff every day had the
most to say. The most complaints (seven of 23 residents interviewed) had
to do with the shortage of waitresses and the quality of cooking. Nine
persons interviewed, all living in apartments, either had no opinions
or thought the staffing was adequate. The remaining residents indicated
considerable satisfaction. No one complained of intimidation, bad feelings,
poor care, or inattention to their needs. The relationship of the staff
to the tenants was that of professional to client in the most strict
sense - residents felt neither beholden to nor resentful of staff.

The administrator claimed his main concern was training and encouraging
his staff to work constructively with the elderly. He said that he
consciously tried to discourage staff members from approaching residents
with a paternalistic attitude.

According to the administrator, the policy in Lions Manor from the
beginning of the development was to encourage the freedom and independence
of the tenants. When the first residents moved in in 1965, he suggested
they form a council which would not only act as sponsor for tenant
activities but would also serve as a link with management, thereby
encouraging the active participation of residents in providing for their
own needs.

The council was formally constituted of one representative from each floor. It had set up its own operating procedures and accepted the responsibility of representing and speaking for all the residents, besides collaborating with the staff in the operation of recreational and social programs. The residents edited and produced their own monthly newspaper. In addition, they operated a canteen, the library, and some of the activities. There was therefore real responsibility available for those residents who wanted to assume it.

The connecting thread in maintaining this combination of facilities and services was the management. Through a professional administrator, the policy of providing not only home comforts but also social contacts, physical and mental development, community participation and a sense of belonging were developed.

Of the 23 residents interviewed, only three responded to life at Lions Manor negatively. Two were hostel guests who disliked the downtown location and having to eat at set hours. Another resident complained of being lonely; she had lived in the building less than six months. The remaining 20 residents appeared generally happy. They cited their independence of movement, and their ability to involve themselves as much as they wanted to in the life of the building while still having easy access to the outside community, as the predominant reasons for their satisfaction.

Conclusions

It is always more difficult to pinpoint the causes of success rather than the causes of failure. However, we believe that the success of Lions Manor lies in the combination of wise location, extensive facilities and good services, pulled together by the indispensable factor of socially sensitive management. It was not the case here of the good manager being he who manages least or most, so much as he who manages inobstrusively.

Nearly all respondents spoke with a notable lack of passion concerning the staff and facilities. They saw their lives as neither vexed nor enhanced by the building. Yet the residents were of an age (mostly over 75) that made them vulnerable to those disabilities that breed discomfort. By encouraging tenant activity and discouraging staff paternalism, the administrator enabled a variety of lifestyles to flourish. The tenants were free to be themselves rather than residents of an institution. More than the soft carpets and modern lounge furniture, it was this policy that made Lions Manor a warm and interesting place to live.

CHAPTER 15

OLD AND INACTIVE IN A RURAL COMMUNITY

In the case studies across Canada, we repeatedly encountered the situation of the lifestyles of yesteryear affecting the present-day living situations. The old people we met had usually solidified their lifestyles by the time they entered maturity. When these lifestyles relied heavily on certain factors, the manner in which these factors were recognized and dealt with within the residential environment became important. For example, we saw in Quebec that many residents had experienced a rich spiritual life and that this concern had been provided for in the housing development.

In Pilot Mound, we found people for whom farm work had given shape and meaning to their lives. Such individuals had great difficulty adjusting to the physical restraints of old age and the work constraints of hostel living.

The Development

Prairie View Lodge was located a quarter of a mile from the shopping area of Pilot Mound, a town in southernmost Manitoba, about 100 miles from Winnipeg. It appeared more isolated than this, however, because much of the distance between the Lodge and town was taken up by lawn and fields.

Sponsored by the United Church of Canada in Pilot Mound, the development was managed by an 11-member board of directors consisting of five farmers, three housewives, two store keepers and a doctor. Actual administration of the development was in the hands of the matron, while finances were controlled by the secretary-treasurer.

The building was constructed in 1965. It was a one-storey structure with three wings. Thirty single hostel rooms were located in two of these wings; the other wing contained four bachelor and eight one-bedroom dwelling units. When the Lodge was constructed, it was supplied with a wide range of common facilities. Besides a cafeteria, the hub of the three wings contained a large lounge, two recreation and sitting rooms, a small library, and a laundry area.

The communal areas were not widely used, however, except for sitting and visiting. There were regular Sunday evening church services and daily coffee hours. There was, however, neither a physical recreation program nor any arts and crafts, no provision being made for tenants to participate in planning recreation.

PRAIRIE VIEW LODGE, PILOT MOUND, MANITOBA

Fact Sheet

THE BUILDING

. Location

On the edge of Pilot Mound, about a quarter mile from the centre of this town of 800 people.

. Type and Size

A three-winged, one-storey structure. Two wings contained 30 single hostel rooms; one wing was composed of eight one-bedroom and four bachelor self-contained dwelling units.

. Facilities

Facilities included a general lounge, two meeting and recreation rooms, and a library room. An organ, pianos and television sets were available to provide entertainment.

. Date of Construction - 1965.

. Rents

Dwelling units were $50 for a bachelor and $65 for a one-bedroom unit; hostel residents paid a daily rate of $5.75, i.e. about $172 a month.

THE MANAGEMENT

. National Housing Act Provision

Section 16, limited dividend.

. Sponsor

The United Church of Canada.

. Management Staff

Fifteen persons were on staff. There was always someone on duty.

THE RESIDENTS

. Number - 50.

. Sex and Marital Status

Within the hostel section, females outnumbered males one to eight. In the sample of 12 households drawn from the whole development, nine were widows, one was a widower, and two were married couples.

. Health Condition

In our sample of 12 households, one resident interviewed appeared severely incapacitated, another three were moderately incapacitated, four had a slight physical incapacity, and three had no physical incapacity. This approximated the management's report on the whole development population.

. Age

The average age of hostel residents was 86, with several over 90 years of age. The average age of all residents interviewed was 83 years.

The lack of interesting activities for the residents was of some concern
to the chairman of the board of directors, but he did not see an immediate
solution. The management staff concurred that there were few activities
involving the residents. They said that the residents had not been much
involved in recreation in the past and were not likely to gain an interest
of this type at the age of 80. The director maintained that city dwellers
were accustomed to an active social life but people who had spent most
of their lives on the farm were not.

In fact, retired farmers comprised most of the resident population. Eight
of the 12 residents interviewed were retired farmers or farmers' wives.
The remainder had been involved, or were the wives of men involved,
in basic service occupations: two storekeepers, a banker and a doctor.
Anxious to remain on the farm as long as possible, the majority of
residents had been at least 80 years old when they applied for admittance.
Only when it was vitally necessary, the management suggested, had the
elderly residents been willing to "sacrifice their independence" by
entering the Lodge.

The average age of the residents interviewed was 83 years. However, the
average age of those in the hostel accommodation was 86, with several
residents over 90 years of age. Considering their age, their health
capacity was not bad. Only one resident interviewed appeared severely
incapacitated, while another three had moderate incapacities. Two-
thirds of all residents, however, found that they could not comfortably
walk to town, a quarter of a mile away. Therefore, while not afflicted
with specific conditions, the majority of residents were generally too
weak to move much beyond the boundaries of the Lodge. At the same time,
however, the population of the development was quite stable. In the last
year, only four people had left - three of these had gone to a nursing
home, one had died. If anything, the residents were simply inactive,
rather than ill.

Although the management expressed some concern about the lack of
activities in the development, the dormancy of the residents was
well matched with the administration's operating practices.

The staff played an authoritarian role vis-à-vis the hostel residents.
There was a plethora of regulations and restrictions within the Lodge.
Men and women were not allowed to visit in each other's rooms; residents
were required to sign out if they left the building and had to be in
by midnight or they were locked out; no telephones were allowed in the
rooms; the rooms did not have locks on the doors and staff entered
immediately after knocking once; a bell was rung at mealtimes which were
always at precise hours; everyone was awakened at 7.00 a.m.; and there
were strict noise restrictions during the afternoon and at night. Nevertheless, residents indicated that they didn't find the many rules and
regulations onerous "as long as they behaved themselves!"

The care available in the Lodge was appreciated by nearly all the residents. Tenants of the self-contained units had little contact with the staff and thus were reluctant to say much about them. (In fact, they made their lives quite independent of the development and are therefore not included in the discussion that follows). Repeatedly, the hostel residents spoke of the willingness of the staff. A third of the residents thought more staff were needed to cope with certain residents who needed more care than the Lodge was designed to provide. Nearly always, feelings expressed about the staff were positive.

Nevertheless, over half the hostel residents spoke about a lack of things to do. Usually, those residents said they were capable of doing little chores but that the staff discouraged them (not all residents who expressed the wish to do chores appeared to have the physical capacity to do so). A desire for a recreation program was expressed by a very few residents.

While the management had never put on a recreation program in the development, a recreation worker who was serving children in a nearby park during the summer had made an attempt to provide such activities. She had apparently had little effect because she had attempted to introduce activities that were too strenuous for the residents' health (e.g. horseshoes, shuffleboard, and so on). In the words of one staff member, "She didn't do anything because she was an outsider and the guests were all inside." An arts and crafts program was cancelled because only five or six people came out for it. (Five or six people represents 20 per cent of the hostel residents or a tenth of all residents in the building).

Besides the lack of formal organized activities, informal visiting within the development was light. No residents claimed to visit daily with other residents; a half visited weekly; just over a third said they visited more than monthly; the remainder did little or no visiting. Several residents mentioned the lack of people to talk to in the Lodge. They felt that many of their neighbors could not carry out a conversation.

Relationships with families offered little stimulation to most residents interviewed. Only one resident saw or spoke with a relative on a daily basis. This relative was her son who was also a resident in the Lodge. Of the remaining hostel residents, half saw or spoke with a relative weekly, with the exception of one woman without relatives; the rest spoke with or saw a relative monthly. Residents visited as much with friends from outside the development as they did with other residents or family. Three of the hostel residents interviewed had such visits weekly; three at least monthly; and three only once a year. Because of the general weakness of most residents, the walk to town ruled out chatting and mixing in the shops there.

The only regular social event for many tenants was Sunday church for which the United Church congregation sent volunteer drivers to pick up residents. A second service in the evening was also popular with the residents. Some individuals and groups in Pilot Mound attempted to interest themselves in the residents. The United Church women, for example, performed friendly visiting and some activities on an informal basis. An elderly man in the community and his wife had made several outings to a nearby lake with development residents. Generally, however, the spontaneity of those forms of assistance and their lack of coordination have not lead to wide use by the residents.

Conclusion

Prairie View Lodge had to deal with a particularly old population of weak (but not ill) residents who came from a background that had not prepared them for leisure. But weak as they were, many of them would have liked to have been involved in chores related to their care. They seemed to feel more of a need for this sort of activity than social activities.

While the response to recreational programs was apparently low, the management did not see them as essential and therefore did not encourage group activities. Instead, they concentrated on providing a high level of physical care. However, the management's paternalism, combined with the absence of social and psychological stimulation, appeared to have resulted in a good deal of regression.

The happiest residents were those who no longer wished for anything but good personal attention. The least happy were those who wished for things to happen in their minds and in the social life of the Lodge. The sponsors made every effort to build a good development with plenty of facilities, but appeared unable to stimulate social and mental activity. And this, indeed, is a difficult task in dealing with people who have found their life's meaning in plain hard work and the earth.

CHAPTER 16

A NON-PROFIT DEVELOPMENT GROWS IN STAGES

A non-profit corporation that has provided housing for the elderly is
often faced with a double problem as the housing that they built ages.
One problem is that the units are simply not sufficient in number -
the community need for senior citizens housing is usually far greater
than the supply. A second problem is that the population of the development changes over the years in regard to the type of accommodation and
care it requires. The answer to both these problems is usually to build
additional units.

However, it has not always been easy for the non-profit corporations to
raise the 5 per cent of the capital cost required under section 16 of the
National Housing Act for addition building, particularly with soaring
construction and land costs. Nevertheless, some non-profit corporations
have been fortunate in obtaining funds from community groups such as
service clubs. A case in point is Jubilee Residences Limited, a non-
profit corporation that has been continually supported by the Saskatoon
Cosmopolitan Club. Jubilee Residences has thus been able to grow as new
needs have become apparent. The evolution of the sponsor's housing
program is interesting.

The Formation of the Jubilee Residences Corporation

In the mid-1950s, the Government of Saskatchewan passed the Housing Act
which provided for provincial grants to complement the National Housing
Act section 16 in order to encourage municipalities and non-profit
corporations to provide senior citizens accommodation.

At that time, the mayor of Saskatoon, who as a private citizen was
concerned about the lack of housing for the elderly, was instrumental in
forming a limited dividend company, Jubilee Residences Limited. The
company quickly drew up plans for a development of 46 one-bedroom units
and appealed to service clubs to provide the sponsor's share of capital
costs. The request was oversubscribed and, as a result, Mount Royal
Court was completed in 1957. In the meantime, the waiting list for
accommodation had grown so long that the directors of the corporation
immediately sought funds for a further building. An agreement was made
with the Saskatchewan Teachers' Federation to build a development with
48 one-bedroom units - Mount Pleasant Court - for retired teachers. At
the same time, it became apparent that some of the residents in the
corporation's first project required hostel care. Fortunately, an estate
left to the company served as a down payment for Mount Royal Lodge, a
home for 98 residents. Both the teachers' building and the Lodge were
opened in 1959. These three buildings were all located on the same site,
referred to now as Jubilee Heights.

JUBILEE RESIDENCES, SASKATOON, SASKATCHEWAN

Fact Sheet

THE BUILDINGS

. Location

On two separate sites, both in suburban Saskatoon though on opposite sides of town.

. Type and Size

One site consisted of two courts of semi-detached bungalows, one with 46 one-bedroom units and the other with 48 one-bedroom units, as well as a four-storey hostel building accommodating 98 persons. The second site consisted of a single-storey, three-winged building with 50 bachelor and 51 one-bedroom units and a second two-storey building containing 101 bachelor and two one-bedroom units.

. Facilities

The two courts on the first site contained laundry facilities and the larger had a dining room, lounge, recreation room and outside shuffleboard courts. The second site had laundry facilities and a recreation room in each building.

. Date of Construction

The development has been built in five stages; the first building in 1957 and the last in 1969.

. Rents

The bungalows on the first site rented for $38 per month, not including gas, water, electricity and telephone. In the first building on the second site, all units rented for $50, including heat, water and hot water. In the second building, rents were $53, including heat, water, hot water and electricity. Hostel accommodation was $104 for a double room and $119 for a single room.

THE MANAGEMENT

. National Housing Act Provision

Sections 16 and 16A, limited dividend and non-profit.

. Sponsor

Jubilee Residences Limited, formerly comprised of various service and professional groups, and lately supported solely by the Cosmopolitan Club of Saskatoon.

. Management Staff

A staff of 39 persons, most of them connected with the hostel operation. There was no round-the-clock staff at the second site.

THE RESIDENTS

. Number - 512.

. Sex and Marital Status

One-quarter to half of the residents were men; half to three-quarters were women. Forty per cent of those interviewed were widowed women, 20 per cent were widowed men and 40 per cent were married couples.

. Health Condition

Most residents of self-contained units had no or slighy physical incapacities; most residents of the hostel appeared to have moderately limited physical abilities and a few had seriously limited physical abilities.

. Age

The average age at the first site, including the hostel, was 86 years. The average age at the second site was 79 years.

The waiting list for accommodation, however, remained substantial. The directors of Jubilee Residences Limited therefore approached the Cosmopolitan Club for help and the club agreed to provide the sponsor's share of a building consisting of 50 bachelor and 51 one-bedroom dwelling units on a new site across town from the older buildings. The new development, Cosmopolitan Court, was completed in 1965. In 1969, a further contribution from the club enabled financing of an additional structure of 101 bachelor and two one-bedroom dwelling units on the same site.

At the time of the survey, the projects on both sites housed 512 persons. A 32-person nursing wing was being added to Mount Royal Lodge.

The Residents and Alternate Forms of Accommodation

At the time of the field work for this study, there were no vacancies in any of the five Jubilee Residences projects, although there were some one-bedroom units occupied by single persons. Because the development was locally initiated with the elderly of Saskatoon in mind, priority was given to Saskatoon residents and secondly to the residents of the immediate district, although all Saskatchewan residents could qualify.

The Lodge was designed to provide a greater measure of care for residents of the cottages, so that these tenants received priority when hostel vacancies arose. Similarly, when the nursing wing of the Lodge is completed, it will first be open to present hostel and cottage residents requiring this form of care.

Because each of the Jubilee Residences projects have been constructed in five stages, each was not only designed to meet the most pressing needs of the day but to avoid the shortcomings of its predecessors.

The first two projects, Mount Royal and Mount Pleasant Court, consisted of two or four attached cottages for married couples; each unit opened to the street and there were no internal corridors. The purpose behind these was simply to alleviate a housing shortage. The tenants were expected to be mobile people with their own lives in the community. No on-site recreational provisions were provided and even today residents of these courts do not visit extensively with one another. None of those in our sample visited daily; a half visited monthly or less. Sixty per cent visited more frequently outside the development than within it.

The residents of the Lodge, on the other hand, tended to rely heavily on their fellow residents for friendship. Only one of eight residents interviewed visited more often with persons outside the building than within. The Lodge, of course, had communal facilities to encourage this neighborliness: a dining room, lounge and recreation room.

While residents of the Courts were invited to participate in Lodge activities and make use of the communal facilities, few in fact did. Many of the Court residents felt the Lodge residents were too old and depressed. Others simply did not feel at home in the hostel building's recreation facilities. An Opportunities for Youth recreation program carried on in Jubilee Heights complex during the summer of 1971 reported that the development needed a specialist in recreation. The residents, they said, had requested such a worker as feelings between tenants in the cottages and Lodge residents were too strong for them to carry on a program together without outside help.

While the lack of integration between Mount Royal Court, Mount Pleasant Court and Mount Royal Lodge residents may have causes that range beyond the limitations of the design, the lack of easily available common facilities appeared to contribute to the situation. But on the second site that Jubilee Residences developed, this condition was mitigated to a degree. Cosmopolitan Court, built in 1965, consisted of three wings joined by a central recreation room and laundry area. The 1969 addition on this site, Eamer Court, again had a recreation room and communal laundry facilities. The same Opportunities for Youth program which found a need for professional guidance at Jubilee Heights, found co-operativeness and natural leadership occurring at the newer site. While the population of the newer courts was younger (79 years versus 86 at Jubilee Heights), this alone seemed insufficient to account for the differences. The fact was that the hostel residents, who made the average age of the Heights as great as it was, were also the most socially active at that location.

Another possible explanation for the greater social activity in the Cosmopolitan Court site, besides the existence of communal facilities, was the composition of the resident population. When Cosmopolitan and Eamer Courts were built, there was a large demand for single-person dwelling units. Consequently, more than two-thirds of the units were of the bachelor type. The Jubilee Heights courts, on the other hand, were composed of one-bedroom units and designed for married couples, who did not appear to rely so heavily on their neighbors for companionship.

At the time of our visit, Jubilee Residences Limited had a waiting list of 17 couples for one-bedroom units, 122 persons for bachelor units and 24 persons for hostel accommodation. The completion of the nursing wing should reduce the latter list somewhat. The bachelor units were in demand not so much because individuals requested bachelor units but because the corporation, in order to produce as much housing as its resources permitted, had chosen to restrict one-bedroom units to couples only. While such a policy may be open to question, it has at least permitted the management to direct their housing starts at very precise areas in the senior citizens market.

The company has also built in communal facilities as it has housed the type of residents who need them most. In this way, building Jubilee Residences in several stages has proven beneficial.

The Shortcomings of Incremental Growth

In less than 15 years, Jubilee Residences Limited had moved from the management of a rather small development to become one of the country's larger sponsors of senior citizens housing. In the same period of time, a major increase in staff had been necessitated with the building of a hostel which required a matron, housekeepers and kitchen workers. As the buildings and sites spread, additional maintenance staff were taken on. Administrative staff, however, had continually consisted of an executive director and his secretary.

While the management had added recreation rooms to their latest two buildings, the development as a whole, when viewed as the home of 500 persons (or perhaps more correctly, two projects of about 250 persons each) was not terribly rich in communal facilities. The Lodge had sufficient facilities but the tenants of the neighboring dwelling units did not feel sufficiently part of the complex that they used the facilities, nor did other old people living in the neighborhood.

During the initial stage of construction and planning of the Jubilee Residences, several sponsoring agencies were involved as outlined above. However, after 1965, the Cosmopolitan Club came to the fore and assumed full responsibility for funding and policy direction by active participation on the Jubilee Residences Board. (The Cosmopolitan Club also sponsored a senior citizens recreation centre in Saskatoon, although it was located in a part of the city not easily accessible to either of the projects' residents).

The 10 members on the Jubilee Residences board of directors ran the organization through five committees: admissions, finance, personnel, extension, and building. The executive director attended each of these committees and was responsible for administering policy directions from the board and providing the board with sufficient information to make wise decisions. While the executive director felt that the provision for the residents' social needs, i.e. adequate housing, levels of care, meals, and some recreation, should be his primary concerns, administrative duties such as rent collection, keeping accounts, and supervising staff prevented him from establishing as close a relationship with tenants as he would have liked.

In effect, what appears to have happened is that the development has outgrown its administrative staff. The geographic spread between two sites and a heavy administrative load gave the executive director little time to provide the social stimulation that he valued. The development, while providing good accommodation, did not take advantage of the potentiality for social services and recreation that such a size of elderly population might suggest. Our interviews did not reveal that many tenants had social service needs; they did, however, indicate that the residents lacked sufficient opportunities for an active and healthy retirement.

Transportation was also a problem for most residents, especially on
weekends when the public bus did not run. While a shopping centre was
within walking distance of both sites, no senior citizens centres were
easy to attend. In other words, the residents were not completely
isolated; nor were they able to participate fully in the community.

Conclusions

Some shortcomings were apparent to the management who saw a partial
remedy in the acquisition of a full-time activities worker. The
experience of the Opportunities for Youth recreation project suggests
that there was both a need and a willingness on the tenants' part to
use such a service, although the role of this worker would have to be
that of "activator" rather than "entertainer," since the management
felt one reason for tenants failing to develop their own programs might
have been that they were well entertained by visiting service clubs,
church groups, etc. The management had also concluded that the
buildings with internal corridors and recreation rooms encouraged
social relationships between tenants. It was in Eamer Court, one of
these buildings, that the only residents' club had been formed. The
management felt that perhaps high-rise buildings would promote social
contact even more, particularly in winter.

Jubilee Residences had been successful in providing a range of accommodation to meet the changing need of existing and potential residents.
But the sponsor had not gone far enough in complementing accommodation
with social facilities and stimulation. In many ways, the Jubilee
Residences complex seemed to be operating as several small developments
(the way it was built) rather than taking advantage of the benefits of
scale. The management was not unaware of this situation and appeared
to be attempting to correct it.

CHAPTER 17

VOLUNTEERS HELP INTEGRATE LODGE RESIDENTS INTO SMALL TOWN LIFE

A number of the case studies record accounts of how the drawbacks of operating a senior citizens housing development in a small town have been successfully met. In Summerside, P.E.I., we saw how an informal relationship with a neighboring institution made a small development more liveable. In Sussex, N.B., we saw the good benefits of thorough planning for centralized government services. This case study illustrates another type of arrangement: the activities of spirited volunteers.

In Melfort, Saskatchewan, an agricultural centre of about 4,000 people, the Melfort and District Pioneer Lodge provides a home for 86 senior citizens from the town and the five neighboring rural municipalities. The Lodge, situated about one mile from the downtown area of Melfort, had 20 one-bedroom units built in groups of two or four attached cottages and a building that had 10 bachelor suites, in addition to the one-storey main lodge that contained 35 single and four double hostel rooms. At the time of our field work, an additional 21 self-contained units with a central lounge area were being constructed on the site. Although they were to be managed by the Lodge staff, they would be Saskatchewan's first public housing for senior citizens.

Almost all residents had spent their lives farming. As the Lodge served a rural area of about 1,300 square miles around Melfort, the friends and relatives of many residents still lived in the outlying districts and therefore were not available for visiting or offering assistance. Still, the majority of those interviewed had at least weekly contact with relatives. Several residents, when asked about the frequency of visits by friends and relatives, explained that it depended on the season; when it was seeding or harvest time, visits were rare.

Generally, the residents were a fairly old group with corresponding physical incapacities. Approximately two-thirds of the residents we interviewed were over 80 years of age, and substantial numbers of them were moderately or slightly incapacitated. These disabilities tended to restrict residents to the development site, particularly in view of the Lodge's location and a lack of public transportation. Despite these factors, the residents' psychological adjustment to their situation appeared good. This could be related to their former lifestyle: many residents, pioneers who had struggled through the Depression and a rugged farm life, were not accustomed to complain bitterly about hardships. Even residents who had obvious physical incapacities tended to describe their over all health as very good.

MELFORT AND DISTRICT PIONEER LODGE, MELFORT, SASKATCHEWAN

Fact Sheet

THE BUILDING

. Location

About one mile from downtown Melfort, a town of 4,000 people.

. Type and Size

Twenty-one one-bedroom units in rows of two or four attached cottages, a one-storey complex with 10 bachelor suites and a one-storey lodge with 35 single hostel rooms and four double hostel rooms.

. Facilities

Two lounges (one for TV and another for sewing), crafts and general sitting, and a laundry area. For residents of self-contained units, individual garden plots were available. In the bachelor units building, there was also a lounge.

. Date of Construction - 1960.

. Rents

One-bedroom units - $56 per month; bachelor units - $48 per month; hostel units rented from $85 to $95 per month, the low unit being for those rooms which shared a public bathroom and the highest unit being for those which shared a bathroom with only one other room.

THE MANAGEMENT

. National Housing Act Provision

Section 16, limited dividend.

. Sponsor

Melfort and District Pioneer Lodge, a corporation of five rural municipalities plus the town of Melfort.

. Management Staff

There were nine management staff members headed by a manager-caretaker.

THE RESIDENTS

. Number - 86.

. Sex and Marital Status

In a sample of 17 households, 10 widows were encountered, one widower, three single men and three couples. Fifty-five of the development's residents were women.

. Health Condition

No one interviewed in the development was severely incapacitated. Six persons were moderately incapacitated, seven had slight incapacities, and one had no physical incapacities at all.

. Age

The average age for the hostel residents was 84 years and for residents of the self-contained units 75 years.

For the older hostel residents, the Lodge's management practices helped
to minimize physical incapacities. Management of the development appeared
to be divided among three people, each of whom ran their particular area
of responsibility fairly independently. The manager/caretaker was the
chief servant of the board of directors and responsible for maintenance.
The secretary-treasurer dealt with the financial aspects of the development,
kept the account books and collected rents. The matron was responsible
for personal and medical needs of the residents in the hostel section;
she also supervised the cleaning and kitchen staff and provided some advice
and counselling. It was obvious that all three presons placed great
emphasis on the provision of good care to residents in the hostel
accommodation. The management felt that the regular nutritious meals,
physical safety, and reduction of loneliness provided in the Lodge had
lengthened the lives of residents from five to eight years.

Residents living in the dwelling units seemed to be practically independent
of the staff, feeling that they did not require the level of care offered
in the hostel but also recognizing that they could move there if necessary.
For these residents, the town provided most of the services and facilities
they needed. Melfort had a bowling alley, beauty parlor, barber shop,
library, grocery stores, churches, medical offices, geriatric centre, parks,
and a senior citizens centre. However, it was difficult to reach these
facilities. The management maintained that most of the town's services
were within walking distance; however, over half the residents interviewed
said that they found the distance prohibitive and unthinkable during the
prairie winter. They therefore depended on friends or relatives to transport
them. Taxis were available but expensive for the residents' limited
incomes. More than half of those interviewed qualified for the guaranteed
income supplement.

Health care was well provided for in Melfort and was not a problem for the
residents. Just across the street from the development was a provincial
geriatric centre that provided rehabilitation and extended care hospital
services to the northeastern quarter of Saskatchewan. It provided 152
beds for persons requiring varying degrees and types of nursing care.
With Lodge residents having top priority on admittance to the geriatric
centre, it is understandable why supportive medical services did not need
to be extensively provided in the development. The staff of the hostel
section administered medication and provided meal trays and other
attention during temporary illnesses. Private doctors in Melfort also
visited the Lodge.

Volunteer Services

The development location and the lack of a public transportation system,
combined with the residents' physical and social characteristics and the
lack of social orientation on the part of the staff, tended to isolate
the development and place constraints on residents. The town and individual

development residents had attempted to cope with this isolation on a
very informal level. To help overcome the Lodge's isolation from the
town, a number of volunteer groups had been active. They both helped
residents get to town and attempted to stimulate activities in the Lodge
itself. Volunteer drivers and friendly visiting were available from
church and women's groups. These were not coordinated, but rather each
church-affiliated group operated on an independent basis to provide
assistance to residents of the same faith.

In addition to this, four Melfort churches held weekly worship services
at the development. Sing-songs, quilting bees, bingos and monthly birthday parties were also put on in the Lodge by church and service club
groups, with some involvement by Lodge staff. These activities provided
the only formal outside contacts for a number of residents.

A volunteer meals-on-wheels program, this time with central coordination,
was also available. Fifteen service organizations and church groups
administered the service, which was used by three apartment residents.
There apparently was no need for an expanded service because hostel
residents were served three meals a day in the dining room and most
residents in the self-contained accommodation had no difficulty cooking
for themselves.

The residents themselves had reacted to the situation of potential
isolation and loneliness by being neighborly. Visiting, transportation,
and housekeeping were frequently forthcoming in an unsolicited manner.
This was particularly noticeable among the women living in bachelor
apartments.

Conclusions

With the combined efforts of church and service groups, the development
staff and residents themselves, most of the drawbacks stemming from the
development's location were being overcome. However, this was almost a
matter of chance rather than the result of any long-range planning.
The lack of service coordination involved duplication in some areas and
unfilled gaps in others. Services tended to be inconsistent, as seen
for example in the lack of a regular daily or even weekly recreation
program. A further drawback lay in the fact that the informal volunteer
system, although helping to overcome existing problems, did little to
help residents to take on more responsibility for their own social and
recreational needs.

Nevertheless, the pattern of volunteer activity in Melfort's Pioneer
Lodge illustrates how local citizens can become involved in a senior
citizens home and thereby go a long way toward making the residents
really feel part of the community. Volunteer activity may have its
drawbacks but these could be overcome with a coordinated approach as
well as some professional direction.

CHAPTER 18

AN ETHNIC GROUP LOOKS AFTER ITS OWN

One of the first groups in Canada to sponsor non-profit housing for the
elderly were the ethnic communities that settled throughout the country.
Many of the elderly members of these communities were born in the old
country and still feel most comfortable with the language and customs of
their homeland. In building a senior citizens development, an ethnic
group provides not only a retirement place where their older members can
feel at ease but also a geographic focus and specific enterprise for the
entire ethnic community. However, ethnic developments can pose difficulties
for residents not of the dominant group. Vancouver's Finnish-Canadian
Rest Home provides some interesting insights into the advantages and
shortcomings of such developments.

The Physical Structure

The Finnish-Canadian Rest Home is one of three ethnic housing developments
for old people located on Harrison Drive near the City of Vancouver's
southern border. Located in the most distant part from the downtown area,
the development is close to one of the main public bus routes which can
take a rider directly downtown or, with a transfer, to almost any other
part of the city.

The rest home provided accommodation for 160 senior citizens. There were
four separate buildings in the development: a two-floor, two-wing building
with hostel accommodation, and three three-storey buildings containing
self-contained units. The buildings were somewhat sunken over the crest
of a hill so that they appeared isolated from the surrounding residential
area.

The hostel part of the development housed 55 residents in single rooms.
This building served as a headquarters for the development with the
management office located at the entrance. All business transactions
for the development, including rent payment, were handled there. The
hostel building was also the recreation and social centre for the development with its large recreation room which also served as a library and a
sauna downstairs, as well as a spacious lounge and dining area upstairs.
Instead of stairs, or elevators, the two floors were connected with
each other by long, wide ramps with rails on the sides and rubber thread
on the floor; hostel residents thus did not have to climb stairs anywhere
in the building.

The three self-contained buildings housed a total of 105 people in 93
bachelor and 12 one-bedroom units. In these buildings, the three floors
were connected by stairs. Each building had its own mailboxes, lobby
and laundry facilities. The residents mentioned that there was a room
on the basement floor of each building that could be used as a lounge,
but these rooms had become storage space.

FINNISH-CANADIAN REST HOME, VANCOUVER, BRITISH COLUMBIA
Fact Sheet

THE BUILDINGS

. Location

In a residential area in the southeastern corner of the City of Vancouver, close to main traffic arteries connecting the development site with all parts of the city. It is one of three ethnic rest home developments in the immediate area.

. Type and Size

There are four separate buildings in the development: a two-storey, two-winged building containing 40 single hostel rooms and eight double hostel rooms, and three three-storey buildings containing 93 bachelor units and one one-bedroom unit.

. Facilities

Each apartment building has a laundry room, a lobby and space for a lounge in the basement which is not used. The hostel building, whose facilities are meant to serve the whole development, contains a dining room, a large lounge, a downstairs meeting and recreation room, a library, a sauna, and laundry facilities.

. Date of Construction - 1963.

. Rents

$42.50 for a single occupancy unit; $52.50 for double occupancy of a bachelor unit. Hostel rent was $120 per person in a one-bed hostel room and $110 per person in a two-bed hostel room.

THE MANAGEMENT

. National Housing Act Provision - Section 16A, non-profit.

. Sponsor

Finnish-Canadian Rest Home Association, an ethnic group especially organized to provide this housing development for the elderly.

. Management Staff

There was a staff of 10, nine of them being full-time. There was a resident caretaker.

THE RESIDENTS

. Number - 105 in dwelling units and 55 in hostel units. Total 160 persons.

. Sex and Marital Status

The ratio of female to male residents was 5:1. In a sample of 15 households, there were nine widows, one single man, one divorced man and four married couples.

. Health Condition

Of the 15 residents interviewed, only one was seriously incapacitated while six were moderately incapacitated. All but three of these were hostel residents. Three persons interviewed were slightly incapacitated; two of these were apartment residents. Four of those interviewed had no incapacity (three were apartment residents). Management felt that three-quarters of residents had no limiting incapacities.

. Age - The average age of those residents interviewed was 81 years.

Residents of these self-contained apartments were free to use the facilities of the hostel building, including the dining room and the sauna, but they were generally very independent and appeared to go to the hostel building only for special events, if at all.

Building the Development

The development was built and managed by the Finnish-Canadian Rest Home Association. The association was founded in 1958 specifically to raise funds to build a senior citizens home in Vancouver. In late 1971, it had 1,100 members, mostly living in British Columbia, although a few lived across Canada and even in Finland. Membership in the association cost $10 a year or $200 for a lifetime. Members received a monthly newsletter, a vote in the annual meeting, the opportunity to join in social activities, and priority in admission to the development. This was actually the main Finnish-Canadian organization in Vancouver and it conducted many social activities. Thus, the development served as a focus of interest and helped to bind the Finnish-Canadians in Vancouver together.

Many of the social events in the development, such as coffee hour, concerts by touring Finnish groups, and religious services appeared to be directed as much to the larger Finnish community as to residents of the Home. In other words, the Home acted as a physical facility where Finnish-Canadian community activities could be held. Members of the Finnish-Canadian Rest Home Association were encouraged to become involved with the development. A group of women provided coffee parties for residents and men members handled the landscaping around the buildings. Of course, the number of association members who could pitch in was limited. Thus, the actual group closely involved in running the Home was more like 100 than 1,100.

The Finnish sponsorship was reflected throughout the development. A large proportion, about 70 per cent, of the residents were of Finnish origin. Many of these were first generation Finnish-Canadians and although most spoke some English, Finnish was the language usually employed for conversation, social activities and business transactions. The manager and most of the staff of nine shared Finnish descent.

The Ethnic Atmosphere

There was a good deal of social activity in the development. The Finnish-Canadian Association and the Finnish-Canadian Womens' Auxiliary sponsored special events such as picnics, concerts, bingos and coffee parties. Every Sunday afternoon, there was a Finnish church service and singing, followed by afternoon tea. About 40 of the hostel and self-contained residents regularly joined in this event. But the non-Finnish residents complained about the lack of activities in which they could join in.

284

The Finnish nature of the development was very apparent in the library. Two walls of the downstairs recreation room were lined with hundreds of Finnish books donated by individuals and groups in Canada and in Finland. Most residents said that they enjoyed the books but non-Finnish residents remarked that they would have liked to see more English books.

One of the facilities in the development most frequently mentioned by residents was the sauna, situated next to the recreation room. We were told that Finns are very fond of taking saunas, whenever possible, and preferred to have one built into their home. The sauna was open three days a week with staff supervision and 30 to 40 residents used it on each of these days. Finally, meals were prepared in the Finnish manner; these were highly praised by Finns and non-Finns alike.

About the only major shortcoming of the development mentioned by both Finns and other residents was its location - both in regard to the rest of the city and the road. While residents appreciated the almost country atmosphere (an atmosphere that urban development was bringing to a rapid end), most found it somewhat isolated from the rest of the community. For those able to walk the long block down from the development to the bus stop, there were frequent buses to the downtown area or any of the several shopping areas on the way. But because of the slope to the bus stop, the five-hour limit on senior citizens bus passes in Vancouver, and the usually rainy and windy winters, most residents we interviewed felt the development's location somewhat discouraged them from getting out. Consequently, involvement outside the development was not as full as it could have been.

In a total sample of 15, nine had at least weekly visits or talks over the telephone with friends or relatives; two had talks or visits once a month; and four said they had talks or visits only once a year. Tenants in self-contained units were physically more mobile and participated more in activities outside the development than hostel residents - some attended senior citizens activities sponsored by the YWCA. Others, only a few in our sample, participated in Parks Board programs held in the adjacent German-Canadian Rest Home. As these programs were conducted in English, they were mostly attended by non-Finns.

We found that the sense of isolation could be great for non-Finns unable to participate in social activities outside the development. Indeed, the Home had one flaw in that while it made such good use of ethnicity to build a comfortable environment for the dominant group, non-Finns often felt like aliens. We even found one woman who spoke mostly Danish and a gentleman who spoke mostly Russian.

Many non-Finns moved to the Finnish-Canadian Rest Home as it was the only accommodation available; there were waiting lists for all senior citizens developments in Vancouver. The building had a reputation for being spotless, the food excellent, and the rent reasonable. Besides this, the

British Columbia government ruled that, to receive a provincial capital grant, ethnic groups sponsoring senior citizens accommodation had to include in their constitution the principle of residency upon application (not restricting residency to any ethnic group). Indeed, the management of the Finnish-Canadian Rest Home told us that they had been told by the government to ensure that 30 per cent of their residents were not Finns. It is possible that non-Finnish applicants could be given preference over Finns to keep within this ratio. At the time of our field work, there was not a strong enough demand from Finns for hostel accommodation to make the provincial ethnic ratio operative but more Finns could have been accommodated in the dwelling units.

Conclusion

The Finnish-Canadians in Vancouver succeeded in creating a highly satisfying and secure environment for their elderly. In terms of the quality of the building's design, its facilities, the grouping of two care levels, the development might serve as a model for other non-profit groups. The ethnic atmosphere as expressed in language, architecture, facilities, social activities, and food also supplied qualities that responded to the environmental needs of older members of the Finnish community. At the same time, the ethnic factor resulted in a degree of community spirit rarely achieved in the construction and management of housing developments for the elderly. However, the inevitable result of the ethnic focus were feelings of exclusion on the part of residents with non-Finnish descent.

It is understandable that the provincial government and other funding bodies should be concerned about discrimination on the part of voluntary bodies in assigning accommodation to applicants. However, this case study suggests that in those instances where a sufficient demand for housing exists from the constituency of the sponsoring organization, it might be wiser to allow preference to be exercized in a manner that does not result in a minority of residents being ill at ease in a milieu that corresponds little to their cultural background. This particularly applies to hostel accommodation.

On the other hand, where situations already exist of a few tenants feeling excluded by reasons of ethnicity (or religion) from the daily life of a housing development, the sponsors should accept responsibility for ensuring that the interests of the minority are adequately recognized.

CHAPTER 19

A VOLUNTARY GROUP DISCOVERS COMPLEXITIES IN CARING FOR THE ELDERLY

National Housing Act loans have allowed non-profit groups and municipalities to initiate housing developments on their own rather than under
the direction of provincial governments. Generally, a municipality,
service club, church or ethnic organization, after making a case for
senior citizens housing in the community and after raising their 5 or
10 per cent of the capital cost, has been able to procure an NHA loan.
However, many non-profit groups find that coping with the red tape
involved in obtaining a loan, raising their equity funds and even
constructing the building is fairly straightforward compared to the
problems involved in administering the project.

This case study illustrates some of the problems that small non-profit
groups may confront in housing the elderly and the way in which the
changing demand for accommodation and care levels can strain such a
group's resources.

The Community

Powell River is a mill town of about 10,000 persons located a day's drive
north of Vancouver on the west coast of the British Columbia mainland.
Westview, the actual site of the development, is located five miles south
of Powell River but is in effect a part of the community, sharing the
same commercial and social facilities and services.

The area has roughly the same climate as Vancouver. While damp in winter,
it is not overly cold. The summers can be somewhat dryer than further
down the coast. The town is in fact climatically well suited for retirement and as the population of elderly persons has increased the demand
for suitable accommodation has also risen.

The Development

The Olive Devaud Boarding Residence and Centennial Home are two adjoining
senior citizens buildings operated by the Powell River Sunset Homes
Society. In late 1971, the Olive Devaud Boarding Residence provided
hostel accommodation for 41 residents in 40 single and four double rooms
and the Centennial Home housed 11 residents in 10 bachelor and two one-
bedroom units.

The Centennial Home was built in 1958 as a community project to celebrate
British Columbia's centenary. It is a one-storey frame building located
on a hill looking out over the town to the Straits of Georgia. The Olive
Devaud Boarding Residence was built in 1967 on contiguous land immediately
up the hill from the Centennial Home. The area at the bottom of the hill
and on both sides of the property contains single family homes, while the
top of the property is marked by forest. As the buildings share the same
site and as the sponsor now views them as a single development, we followed
the same approach in this study.

OLIVE DEVAUD BOARDING RESIDENCE AND CENTENNIAL HOME, POWELL RIVER, B.C.

Fact Sheet

THE BUILDINGS

. Location

In the residential community of Westview, about five miles south of Powell River, British Columbia, a town of 10,000 persons.

. Type and Size

Two buildings built at different times on the same site. The first provided 10 bachelor and two one-bedroom units in a one-storey row and the second, 40 single and four double hostel rooms on one floor.

. Facilities

In the hostel building: a lounge, a dining room, laundry facilities, and a basement recreation room.

. Date of Construction

The first building was constructed in 1958 and the second in 1967.

. Rents

$55 (plus $2 for television connection) in a self-contained unit; $135 for a hostel room and board.

THE MANAGEMENT

. National Housing Act Provision

Sections 16 and 16A, limited dividend and non-profit.

. Sponsor

Powell River Sunset Homes Society, a non-profit society.

. Management Staff

A staff of 12, mainly concerned with the hostel development.

THE RESIDENTS

. Number - 52.

. Sex and Marital Status

The majority of residents were women, mainly widows. In the 11 interviews conducted, six widows, two widowers, one man separated from his wife and two married couples were encountered.

. Health Condition

Most residents had some physical limitations in the areas of mobility, hearing and sight. According to the matron, 13 of the 41 residents required inter-mediate nursing care. Within our sample of 11 households, three were moderately incapacitated, seven were slightly incapacitated, and one had no physical incapacities.

. Age

The average age in the development was estimated to be 80 years. In our hostel sample, the average age was 81.

The Sunset Homes Society is a voluntary organization in which a membership subscription may be purchased in return for a $1 annual fee. Sixty-five members attended the last annual meeting. The society had received a good deal of community support. In addition to a municipal capital grant, the local service clubs and businesses donated time, money and goods. The Kiwanis, Rotary and Lions clubs landscaped the grounds and individuals as well as firms donated furniture for the lounges.

Management of the development has been carried out over the years by a board of directors elected directly by the membership. Actually, the self-contained units built in 1958 gave little trouble. But with the opening of the Devaud Residence problems began to develop. There was an immediate crisis in that the residence did not fill with tenants. Since the project was tightly financed and bound to a CMHC mortgage, the absence of a full rent revenue quickly developed into an operating deficit. At the time of our visit, the 12 self-contained units of Centennial Home housed 11 people, and the 40 hostel rooms housed 41 people. However, four of the hostel rooms were doubles; thus the development still had an over all vacancy rate of 7 per cent. Not only did these empty beds continue to pose a financial problem but the health condition of many residents complicated it.

The hostel building had been staffed to accommodate persons generally able to care for themselves and needing only minor or temporary help. In fact, however, the health of residents had deteriorated at such a rate and the facilities in the Powell River area for more intense care were so limited that the management had to give care it had neither the staff nor the money to provide. According to the development's matron, 13 of the 41 residents required intermediate nursing care. In the past 12 months, nine residents had died and three had left for chronic care hospital accommodation.

Intermediate nursing care is defined in British Columbia not as bed care but as personal care in which ambulatory people are attended by 24-hour nursing staff able to do considerable remedial work, give baths, and so on. Such a care level, of course, demands a greater number of staff than required for ordinary hostel or boarding accommodation. In Powell River, there are two facilities that provide nursing (not "intermediate") care for the elderly. One is an 18-bed private nursing home; the other is the chronic care unit attached to the local hospital. However, even if these facilities had the space to accept Olive Devaud's more incapacitated residents, it still would have hardly alleviated all the problems of the development. With the 13 residents requiring this nursing care gone, only 28 (or 64 per cent) of the 44 hostel beds would have remained occupied.

We gathered that the Sunset Homes board of directors was unable to fully cope with the development's problems. The community, so active in building the residence also was unable to substantially help, although the municipal government made a grant of $5,000 on top of its original $25,000 capital grant.

As a result, some of the founding members attempted to strengthen the composition of the board. It became composed of what were claimed to be almost all the responsible citizens of the community. In 1971, the members of the board included a retired man (the treasurer), the local hospital administrator, a mill executive, several business men, a bank manager, a medical doctor, an electrician, and, as a non-voting member, the matron of the Olive Devaud home.

Day-to-day administraion was handled by the treasurer, one of the founders of the association, who had supervised the development's planning and construction. As a volunteer he collected rents, kept the books, and visited residents. The matron was also a strong presence in the management. It was she who administered the day-to-day operation of the boarding residence.

The strengthened board was well integrated into the community. Through its membership, it connected the financial and commercial elements of the town and through the matron it was connected with the public health and hospital professionals. In late 1971, changes in plans were afoot to convert one wing of the home into the needed intermediate nursing accommodation. The staff was being increased by one practical nurse, with the intention of hiring two more to provide round-the-clock care.

To meet the increased costs, the board intended to raise the rents and seek further provincial aid. The latter, however, was by no means certain. Unfortunately, these problems were being compounded by a strong personality and attitudinal conflict that existed between some board members. According to some of the residents and board members, the matron, while an efficient and thorough person, tended to be intimidating and overbearing. She repeatedly walked into rooms without sufficient warning, threatened to expel residents if they did not behave and insisted that all grievances be channelled to the board through her.

The matron felt that her main job was to supervise the residence's kitchen, cleaning and nursing staff and attend to the personal care of residents. The treasurer of the board agreed on this point but added that she required "ability to handle the aged."

The importance of an "ability to handle the aged" related to the problems encountered with occupancy rates and health problems. The residents interviewed expressed mixed feelings about the pending change in care levels. One felt that there was little need for new facilities, as only two residents really needed nursing care. But fears that the rent would be increased to pay for the extra staff were more common. Residents also believed that as part of the redevelopment plan, they would be forced to double up in the hostel rooms. At the time of our visit, there was only one doubling-up in a previously single room; however, the plans were, in fact, to move to joint occupancy for new residents.

The residents seemed rather uninformed about the likely impact of changes
in their development and fearful of inquiring too loudly. In fact, rents
had recently been increased from $120 to $135 a month for single hostel
accommodation. In the Centennial Home apartments, which had been spared
nearly all of the controversy, there was also some concern about rents.
One tenant claimed that the rent had climbed from $35 a month in 1969, to
$45 in 1970, and to the then current rate of $55 (plus $2 for a TV connection).
In any event, few tenants expressed complete security about their position
in the uneasy atmosphere.

It is not too easy to understand why the Olive Devaud residence had
experienced under-occupancy. As the only such accommodation in Powell
River, it is puzzling. Staff and local health workers did not have a ready
explanation, nor did the residents have a general opinion. However, several
factors were mentioned.

In two interviews we conducted with dwelling unit tenants, we found that a
widow had been advised to seek accommodation in the Centennial Home by a
social worker in order to take advantage of the rent and to have neighbors
close at hand. A married couple had moved in originally to get away from
the smell of the mill at Powell River and upgrade their accommodation at
the same time.

In the Devaud Boarding Residence, the precipitating reasons for entry
appeared to have been largely medically oriented. Six of the residents
interviewed had been encouraged by a relative or doctor to seek a room.
All but one of these had a medical problem requiring some type of supervision. Most of these residents had, in fact, not entered the building until
a health crisis had occurred. It was not just a general deterioration that
triggered the move but more often a heart attack or stroke. Three other
residents claimed to have made the decision to move to the residence on
their own, citing a need for greater security and an inability to maintain
their own home. It was, however, fairly apparent that the hostel side of
the development was being used by the community as a type of therapeutic
facility rather than simply as a retirement home. It thus perhaps generated
a weaker demand for accommodation than one might have expected for a community
the size of Powell River.

The location of the development in Westview rather than in Powell River
might have also served to reduce the demand for space. A Powell River site
would not have provided a view over the water with fresh sea air, and it is
true that the majority of residents enjoyed being away from the mill's
pollution. The location, however, posed some difficulties for residents
who wished to get to friends and facilities in Powell River. Return cab
fare to Powell River (where the hospital and most doctors were located)
cost $3.50. There was only a very limited bus service.

Building the development at the top of a hill also caused some problems, the closest shopping facilities being in a plaza five blocks down hill. While many residents could make the walk down, few could as easily ascend again. A return taxi fare to the plaza was $2, a cost residents often shared. However, close to half the residents we interviewed thought the development was somewhat isolated.

Unfortunately, over half of the hostel residents perceived the development as an institution and a third felt intruded on by the staff. Others mentioned that they regretted the general lack of interesting activities in the development. Some complaints were made about design deficiencies, e.g. 11 persons shared two toilets and a bath. Also, we were told that the lounge could only be reached by descending a flight of stairs; this made it inaccessible to many tenants.

While the building management wished to have healthier tenants, they did not emphasize a social program to stimulate and keep them that way. As far as physical facilities and design were concerned, they created an institutional atmosphere and worked against a homelike and socially stimulating one.

Conclusion

The Olive Devaud Boarding Residence part of the Sunset Homes Society's housing program experienced a difficult history. The hostel development never experienced full occupancy and, as a result, had suffered a serious budget deficit. The health problems of many residents aggrevated this situation as did tensions between the senior staff and board of directors.

The case study raises a number of questions related to the administration of housing for the elderly. What need determination process should a voluntary group interested in providing accommodation for senior citizens carry out? When it has become apparent that a change needs to be made in care level, what financial and professional resources can a voluntary association recruit? Most important, the case study illustrates the manner in which accommodation built for a specific type of resident (in this case the ambulatory elderly person capable of self-care) will, in the absence of sufficient facilities in the community that can serve a more incapacitated clientèle, gradually become occupied by a population for which the development was neither designed nor staffed.

CHAPTER 20

AN INTEGRATED ELDERLY-FAMILY DEVELOPMENT

The question of integrating old people with, or segregating them from, housing occupied by families has been much debated. The advocates of integration suggest that mixing the elderly with persons of other age groups provides them with a healthier, more normal living situation stimulated by the sight and sound of the children at play and other people carrying out their daily tasks. The detractors claim that most elderly persons, having raised their own families, want quiet surroundings. They say old people like to have short visits with their grandchildren but not be continually exposed to them. This case study illustrates some of the problems that may arise in integrated developments.

The Development

Culloden Court is a federal-provincial public housing development, managed by the British Columbia Housing Management Commission, and located in a residential area of Vancouver. To the east of the development, the houses are small working class bungalows; and to the west, the homes are larger, with three to five bedrooms. The development consists of two-storey row-type buildings containing from four to 44 dwelling units. Attractively shingled with slightly slopping roofs, the buildings blend in with the private homes that typify the area.

Of the 130 dwelling units in Culloden Court, 44 (making up the largest single building) were designated for senior citizens. The remainder (buildings not larger than 14 units) housed low and moderate income families.

The location of the senior citizens building partially isolated it from the rest of the development. However, this isolation was broken by the close proximity of the development's multi-purpose recreation building. The area's elementary school was also located so that children from the development naturally passed by the senior citizens building.

When Culloden Court was built, the residents in the surrounding neighborhood were invited to use the recreation building. The management thought this was desirable for two reasons: the nearest community centre was several blocks away and common use of the recreation building would help to foster integration between the public housing and private residents. This arrangement initially created some resentment and hostility among the senior citizens who saw it as an invasion of their facilities.

The elderly residents complained that children were out late at night. They also complained that people were swearing, throwing rocks, stealing money from milk bottles, playing pool and poker and having loud parties. At the same time, families complained that the senior citizens were dominating the Culloden Court Tenants Association and that the recreation building virtually belonged to them.

CULLODEN COURT, VANCOUVER, BRITISH COLUMBIA
Fact Sheet

THE BUILDINGS

. Location

In a residential area of Vancouver.

. Type and Size

The development is a 130-unit public housing project in which family and senior citizens are integrated. Twenty of the units are bachelor units and 24 are one-bedroom units.

. Facilities

There was a multi-purpose building on site providing recreation and lounge space, as well as laundry facilities. A small lounge on the second floor of the senior citizens building was reserved for their use alone.

. Date of Construction - 1967.

. Rents

Bachelor suites were $53; one-bedroom units were $65.

THE MANAGEMENT

. National Housing Act Provision

Section 35A.

. Sponsor

The British Columbia Housing Management Commission.

. Management Staff

There were no on-site staff. Management was provided from Orchard Park, a public housing project in the same neighborhood.

THE RESIDENTS

. Number - 68.

. Sex and Marital Status

In a random sample of 11 households, there were five married couples, one widower, one divorced man and four widows.

. Health Condition

Of the sample of 11 residents, four appeared to have no physical incapacity, six showed moderate physical incapacity, and one, while confined to a wheelchair, kept house as if without any incapacity.

. Age

The average age of the residents was 70 years.

According to the manager of Culloden Court, the Court was not the worst
experience the British Columbia Housing Management Commission had had in
building integrated developments. The worst developments had been those
in which senior citizens and families shared the same building. Apparently
the British Columbia Housing Management Commission is now avoiding building
developments for a mixture of senior citizens and families. But Culloden
Court had been built and the management, local service agencies, and
tenants were attempting to make the place liveable for all.

The conflict in Culloden Court could be traced to several obvious causes.
Young children needed places to play and play involved noise. They
generally tended to play on the paved area between the centre and the
senior citizens building. This, coupled with the chatter of teenagers
hanging around the entrance of the recreation building no doubt created a
steady din. The community centre director, responsible for a satellite
program run at the development, called it a problem of overexposure. Age
may exacerbate concern about noise, he said. But anyone could be annoyed
by having to listen constantly to children playing. Many elderly tenants
claimed that the children's noisy play (and late-night wandering) impinged
on their rest, and several told stories about children throwing stones
and spitting at them. The families, however, apparently believed that
some of the old residents provoked the children by staring endlessly
from their windows.

Bridging the Gap

The development manager, lacking an on-site office, did not appear to be
especially important in the social life of Culloden Court. The person who
did the most to bridge the gap between the elderly and other residents of
the development was a Vancouver Parks Board recreation worker who also
lived in the Court. Working under the director of the local community centre,
but with considerable autonomy, she ran a 15-hour-a-month recreational
program for senior citizens in the development and acted as a liaison
person between the residents and the manager. Although a resident of the
family side of the development, she had obviously won the trust of the senior
citizens. She helped to involve elderly residents in the programs of the
multi-purpose recreation centre and also attempted to help senior citizens
with individual problems - if only to steer them to the correct resources.

Before the recreational worker made her impact effective, most of the
senior citizens were under the impression that the recreation centre was
theirs. Now, however, they generally had it before 3 p.m. and after that
time other age groups (children, teenagers and their parents) had first
rights - unless a specific program or meeting was scheduled. The senior
citizens no longer seemed to regard other users of the centre as usurpers.

The Culloden Court Tenants Association, while still predominantly composed of senior citizens, has broadened its interests to include the recreation needs of the children and teenage residents. Thanks to the recreational worker, some senior citizens who previously were recluses have been encouraged to participate in the Park Board's program and the tenants association. They have also developed a concern for the well-being of the children, e.g. the amount of toys and sports equipment available. The lack of staff to work with children was, at the time of our visit, a preoccupation of the elderly tenants - an improvement perhaps over what were reported to be earlier feelings of fear and annoyance.

This is not to say that fear and insecurity among the senior citizens had been completely stilled. Many told us that they believed that a round-the-clock watchman was needed in the development. Their desire for a watchman, however, stemmed not only from continuing unease of the children but because of fears about the possibility of health failures.

The majority of residents interviewed also said that they would still prefer their own recreation space to sharing the multi-purpose building. There was a small lounge on the second floor of the senior citizens building; originally it was intended for the development's manager but it was so small that it was seldom used. They resented persons other than Culloden Court residents using the building, even though several of these groups were composed of senior citizens.

Conclusion

In comparison with the residents of many other developments, the senior citizens living in Culloden Court were relatively well-off. The development itself was well integrated into the neighborhood, with good access to transportation, shopping and churches. A good range of services - VON, homemakers, meals-on-wheels, senior citizens clubs - were also available in the community. The residents also had ample indoor recreation space close at hand. Social relationships were good - over half the persons we interviewed visited at least weekly within the building - and a number of residents had even worked out a daily check system among themselves to ensure all was well.

It appeared, however, that having senior citizens accommodation border on fairly high density family housing was a mistake - particularly without adequate provision to contain the exuberant, and at times mischievous activities of young children. This does not imply that housing for the elderly should always be segregated from accommodation for other age groups. However, family public housing with its extremely high child count per household poses special problems of noise and commotion.

Special design solutions might help public housing families and the elderly to become better neighbors - for example, the provision of adventure playgrounds or spacious gathering areas. In this case study the recreation worker's intervention dampened to some extent the makings of an undeclared territorial war between the age groups.

PART V

USER SURVEY

CONTENTS

CHAPTER 1

INTRODUCTION AND METHODOLOGY

This part of the study reports on interviews conducted with a probability
sample of 303 residents living in the 19 housing developments selected for
case studies. There was a dual objective in undertaking this user survey.
For the case studies themselves, it was necessary to talk to residents to
learn more about how each development related to the environmental and
social needs of those who lived there. Since development managers and
local social service agencies staff were interviewed, it was reasonable to
seek residents' views also. Thus, in a sense, the user interviews formed
an integral part of each case study; indeed without them the case study
reports would have been shallow.

In addition, however, to adding some depth to the case studies, the
aggregated user study responses were intended to provide more information
about the general characteristics, lifestyles, and preferences of the
residents of housing developments for the elderly in Canada. That is the
focus for this section.

The value of obtaining information and opinions directly from the recipients
or users of a service has been increasingly recognized in recent years.
Market researchers and sociologists have long employed techniques designed
to elicit consumer response. However, in social programs (such as housing
for the elderly) where there is little or no market competition, it is
especially important to have systematic feedback from users - in order to
judge the appropriateness of the service offered and find ways of improving
it. One writer, Stanley Yolles, believes that seeking the opinions of
elderly people about programs that impinge on their lives helps to preserve
their integrity and gives them opportunities to participate in decisions
about their welfare. He notes that "for too long it has been the practice
of significant individuals, children, physicians, clergymen, social agencies,
to make decisions concerning the lives of older people independent of the
individual's ability to decide (for himself) ... concerning his future."
(Stanley F. Yolles, Prevention of Mental Health Problems in the Elderly"
in Mental Health Care and the Elderly: Shortcomings in Public Policy, U.S.
Senate, Special Committee on Aging, Report, Washington, 1971.)

Throughout the user survey, as in the entire study, special concentration
has been placed on social services and communal facilities. The study team
wanted to explore social services in the broadest sense - recreation, health,
homemaking, and financial assistance - both to determine existing patterns
of service delivery and to get a better idea of the various ways in which
residents of senior citizens housing need help with the problems of growing
old. Once old people's shelter needs are taken care of, are there other
types of community assistance that should be associated with housing programs,
and if so, how?

302

The matter of communal facilities is one that all developers of senior citizens housing have to face. Unfortunately, while good guides are available to provide advice about the importance of design detail such as non-slip floors and grab rails (e.g. Central Mortgage and Housing Corporation, Housing the Elderly, July 1972), there is little information about how senior citizens use community space in housing developments.

Methodology

Interviews were carried out in the 19 developments selected for case studies. The criteria and procedure for the selection of these developments is detailed in Part IV of this report; it is sufficient to say here that the principal criteria included region of the country, community size, accommodation type, sponsorship, and building type. A total of 303 residents were interviewed for the user study. Details of the sample selection and the methodology are given in Appendix 3.

The probability sample selected for the user study appears to correspond well with the total population of NHA financed housing in Canada. There does not appear to be any very significant bias in terms of accommodation type, sponsorship, health status, sex, or financial status. The user sample is somewhat biased in favor of residents living in large developments in metropolitan and major urban areas, and toward the Atlantic Provinces, Quebec, and the Prairies; also, it is representative of a slightly older population. The bias toward large urban developments, however, was intentional, since the trend in the construction of housing for the elderly is definitely in this direction. Consequently, although one cannot claim that the user study strictly represents the characteristics and preferences of all residents of NHA housing for the elderly, the sample is sufficiently representative to warrant inclusion in this study - and serious attention to its findings - particularly since so little has been published about the users of Canadian developments for the elderly.

CHAPTER 2

SOCIO-DEMOGRAPHIC AND HEALTH CHARACTERISTICS

Age

Of the 303 residents sampled in the survey, 21 per cent were under 70
years of age, 19 per cent were 70-74, and 60 per cent were 75 years and
over. Residents of self-contained developments tended to be much younger
than those living in hostel accommodation. Only 10 per cent of the
residents of self-contained apartments were aged 80 years and over,
compared with 48 per cent of residents in hostels.

Sex

Of the sampled residents, 69 per cent were female and 31 per cent male.
As Table 1 indicates, men were slightly more heavily represented in
hostel developments than in self-contained accommodation.

TABLE 1

SEX OF RESIDENTS, BY DEVELOPMENT TYPE

	Female	Male	TOTAL
Self-Contained	84	32	116
	72.4%	27.6%	100%
Hostel and Mixed	125	62	187
	66.8%	33.2%	100%
ALL DEVELOPMENTS	209	94	303
	69.0%	31.0%	100%

Marital Status

Most of the persons in the sample (68 per cent) were living alone. Only
22 per cent were living with a spouse and 10 per cent with other residents.
But nearly half of those residents who were living alone had lived with a
spouse (or someone else) immediately before moving to their present
residence. This may indicate that the move to their present residence
was precipitated by the stress of widowhood or problems encountered in
living with children.

Ethnic Origin

As Table 2 indicates, the predominant ethnic origins of the sample
were English (35 per cent), French (20 per cent), and Irish (12 per
cent). For nearly 19 per cent of the sample, no ethnic origin was
established.

TABLE 2

ETHNIC ORIGIN OF RESIDENTS*

	Number	Per Cent
English	105	34.7
French	59	19.5
Irish	35	11.6
German	12	4.0
Finnish	8	2.6
Dutch	4	1.3
Italian	2	.7
Other	21	6.9
Unknown	57	18.8
TOTAL	303	100.0

* Question 81 (See Interview Schedule,
Appendix 4).

Children

As Table 3 indicates, approximately 44 per cent of the sample had no
children alive or none living in the immediate area. Residents of
self-contained developments were more likely to have children living
nearby than those in hostel developments. This can be accounted for
by the younger age of those living in self-contained dwellings.

TABLE 3

CHILDREN IN AREA*, BY DEVELOPMENT TYPE

	None Living In Area	Some Living In Area	No Answer	TOTAL
Self-Contained Developments	44 37.9%	72 62.1%	0 0%	116 100%
Hostel and Mixed Developments	88 47.1%	98 52.4%	1 .5%	187 100%
ALL DEVELOPMENTS	132 43.6%	170 56.1%	1 .3%	303 100%

* Question 10

Table 4 shows that a significant proportion - 33 per cent - of all persons in the sample had no family member nearby to turn to for assistance or friendship; 75 per cent of those residents with no children nearby had no relatives at all in the area. On the other hand, when both children and other relatives are taken into account, 67 per cent of all residents had at least one relative they could turn to, and 44 per cent had two or more.

TABLE 4

CHILDREN AND RELATIVES IN AREA*, BY DEVELOPMENT TYPE

	None	One In Area	Two In Area	Three Or More	TOTAL
Self-Contained Developments	31 26.7%	27 23.3%	26 22.4%	32 27.6%	116 100%
Hostel and Mixed Developments	68 36.4%	44 23.5%	25 13.4%	50 26.7%	187 100%
ALL DEVELOPMENTS	99 32.7%	71 23.4%	51 16.8%	82 27.1%	303 100%

* Questions 9 and 10.

Looking at proximity of children in relation to residents' health (Table 5), we found a serious situation: 30 per cent of residents with no children alive and 26 per cent of those with no children nearby had seriously or moderately limited physical ability - compared with 18 per cent of residents with children in the area. This is probably because the stress of having a serious disability is excacerbated by having no children at hand to help out; consequently, seriously disabled persons are more likely to enter housing for the elderly than are similar persons with children nearby. Furthermore, of the three groups, the residents with no living children reported seriously or moderately limited abilities most frequently; this presumably reflects the special role that children continue to play in caring for disabled parents.

Residents with no children in the area were slightly younger - not older - than those with children nearby. This may seem surprising at first. It is possible, however, that these persons feel problems associated with old age earlier than do persons with children nearby; and this may lead them to enter housing for the elderly at an earlier age.

TABLE 5

CHILDREN LIVING IN AREA BY RESIDENTS' PHYSICAL CAPACITY*

	No Children Alive	Children Alive But None in Area	Children In Area	No Answer	TOTAL
Seriously Limited Ability	5 6.2%	3 5.9%	7 4.1%	0 0%	15 5.0%
Moderately Limited Ability	19 23.5%	10 19.6%	24 14.1%	0 0%	53 17.3%
Slightly Limited Ability	22 27.2%	21 41.2%	65 38.2%	0 0%	108 35.7%
No Incapacity	35 43.2%	17 33.3%	74 43.6%	1 100%	127 42.0%
TOTAL	81 100%	51 100%	170 100%	1 100%	303 100%

* Question 13.

Social Class

We estimate that between one-quarter to one-third of the sample came from a middle-class background and two-thirds to three-quarters from working-class or blue-collar families. This estimate is based on the previous occupations of male respondents or widowed spouses, as detailed in Table 6, with adjustments for unmarried women.

TABLE 6

PREVIOUS OCCUPATION OF MALE RESIDENTS OR WIDOW'S SPOUSE*

Occupation	Number	Per Cent
Sales Work	28	9.2
Managerial	17	5.6
Professional, Technical Work	13	4.3
Clerical Work	9	3.0
ALL WHITE COLLAR	67	22.1
Farmers and Farm Workers	48	15.8
Transport and Communications	38	12.5
Laborers	38	12.5
Craftsmen	36	11.9
Service and Recreation, Non-Professional	27	8.9
Loggers, Hunters, Fishermen, Miners	6	2.0
ALL BLUE COLLAR	193	63.6
No paid work	1	.3
Women never married[1]	31	10.2
No answer	11	3.6
TOTAL	303	100.0

* Question 64.

1 Of the women who never married, well over half were in non-manual work.

Financial Status

Table 7 shows that 36 per cent of the respondents indicated that they were dependent solely upon the old age security pension and guaranteed income supplement, 53 per cent indicated they had <u>some</u> savings of their own, but only 11 per cent admitted to having <u>substantial</u> savings. Residents in public housing were poorer than those in non-profit housing: 46 per cent were dependent solely on the old age security pension and guaranteed income supplement, compared with 32 per cent of those in non-profit housing; and only 5 per cent admitted to substantial savings, compared with 15 per cent of non-profit residents. There were significant variations between individual developments, however, and the aggregated figures do not suggest that either type of sponsor was serving <u>only</u> the poor or <u>only</u> the rich.

TABLE 7

INCOME SOURCE OF RESIDENTS*, BY SPONSOR TYPE

	Solely Old Age Security and Guaranteed Supplement	Some Savings	Substantial Savings	TOTAL
Public Housing	50 45.5%	55 50.0%	5 4.5%	110 100%
Non-Profit	60 31.1%	104 53.9%	29 15.0%	193 100%
ALL DEVELOPMENTS	110 36.3%	159 52.5%	34 11.2%	303 100%

* Question 65.

Residents who did not have substantial savings were asked if they felt their resources were strained. Of the total sample, 44 per cent said "yes" (see Table 8). A higher proportion of public housing residents said their resources were strained (47 per cent compared with 42 per cent of the non-profit housing residents).

TABLE 8

FINANCIAL STRAIN BY SPONSOR TYPE*

	Financial Strain	No Financial Strain	No Answer	TOTAL
Public Housing	52	14	44	110
	47.3%	12.7%	40.0%	100%
Non-Profit Housing	81	6	106	193
	42.0%	3.1%	54.9%	100%
ALL DEVELOPMENTS	133	20	150	303
	43.9%	6.6%	49.5%	100%

* Question 66.

Table 9 shows that 55 respondents attributed their financial strain to inflation, 37 to rent, 37 to medical expenses, and 37 to food. The concern about medical expenses is perhaps surprising considering the recent introduction of medicare schemes in all provinces; however, it may have reflected worry about the cost of drugs. Not surprisingly (in view of the higher rents in the non-profit sector), 30 respondents living in non-profit housing mentioned the cost of rent as a cause of financial strain, while only 7 public housing residents mentioned it. Only 4 per cent of the entire sample said they believed their future financial situation might cause them to seek cheaper housing, rents in NHA financed developments being lower than those in private housing.

TABLE 9

SOURCE OF RESIDENTS' FINANCIAL STRAIN*[1], BY SPONSOR TYPE

	Inflation	Rent	Medical Expenses	Food	Other
Public Housing	21	7	15	20	5
Non-Profit	34	30	22	17	3
ALL DEVELOPMENTS	55	37	37	37	8

* Question 66.
1 Some residents gave more than one reason for financial strain.

Health

In any research related to the elderly, it is important to consider the health of the population being studied. A fairly sound understanding of their state of health is essential in planning their physical and social environment. Contrary to some popular notions, the relative incidence of illness and disability varies greatly among old people.

In this study we were not, unfortunately, able to undertake the complete medical examination ideally needed to ascertain the state of residents' health. Instead, we relied upon respondents' perceptions of their physical capacity as an index of general health. Residents were asked to place themselves in one of four categories ranging from "no physical incapacity" to "seriously limited ability." Although this method by no means provides a complete and objective statement of residents' health, it does provide a reasonable index of health by focusing on the kinds of behavioral manifestations that the layman uses in judging his own physical condition (such as ability to get around and to lead a normal life). And these are the sorts of health factors that planners and designers should be particularly concerned with. Insofar as respondents were telling the truth about their physical ability (and the impressions of interviewers and housing personnel indicated that they were), the measures of physical capacity used in this study seem appropriate for purposes of planning housing environments for the elderly. In short, when speaking of the "health" of residents, we are dealing with a limited operational definition - but one which we considered adequate for the purpose of this study.

Considering the advanced age of the sample, the residents were in fairly good health. Table 10 indicates that 42 per cent of the residents reported no incapacities at all, and 36 per cent reported only slightly limited physical ability (minor difficulty either in moving about, communicating, or keeping house). Thus, 78 per cent of the residents, or almost eight out of 10, cannot be considered much more physically dependent than people in other age groups.

TABLE 10

RESIDENTS' PHYSICAL CAPACITY*, BY DEVELOPMENT TYPE

	Seriously Limited Ability	Moderately Limited Ability	Slightly Limited Ability	No Incapacity	TOTAL
Self-Contained Developments	2 1.7%	12 10.3%	38 32.8%	64 55.2%	116 100%
Hostel and Mixed Developments	13 7.0%	41 21.9%	70 37.4%	63 33.7%	187 100%
ALL DEVELOPMENTS	15 5.0%	53 17.5%	108 35.6%	127 41.9%	303 100%

* Question 13.

When it came to disabilities, 18 per cent of the respondents reported
moderately limited physical ability (a noticeable handicap in one type
of activity or facility and one which requires limited or continuous
aid), and only 5 per cent of the respondents reported seriously limited
ability (in walking, seeing, hearing, or inability to accomplish many
daily tasks on their own). These figures are not surprising since,
generally speaking, persons with moderately limited physical ability
require a good deal of special care, while those with seriously limited
ability usually need nursing accommodation.

As Table 10 indicates, there was much more physical disability among
hostel residents than among residents of self-contained apartments.
(Furthermore, our figures probably understate the incidence of
disability among hostel dwellers because the "mixed" developments
contained some self-contained units also). Only 34 per cent of hostel
residents reported no disability compared to 55 per cent of those in self-
contained developments. At the other end of the scale, 7 per cent of
hostel residents reported seriously limited ability, compared to only 2
per cent of those in self-contained accommodation. Some of the hostel
developments had an extremely high proportion of residents with seriously
or moderately limited ability; on the other hand, five of the self-
contained developments had no residents with seriously or moderately
limited ability.

It is interesting that 34 per cent of the residents of hostel and mixed
developments reported no physical disability; one might have expected a
disability or health problem as their reason for seeking hostel accommodation (with its superior care). This figure, however, is probably
exaggerated because of the mixed developments, which housed some residents
living in self-contained units.

The fact that 12 per cent of the residents of self-contained accommodation
reported seriously or moderately limited physical abilities seems cause
for concern; it leads one to wonder whether these residents are in the
right type of accommodation.

Only 11 per cent of the residents of public housing developments reported
seriously or moderately limited abilities, compared to 29 per cent of
those in non-profit developments. This is no doubt because public housing
agencies have built hardly any hostel accommodation.

Table 11 analyzes physical capacity by age. There was not much significant
variation between the level of ability of residents aged 70 to 79 years.
However, among residents aged 80 and over, the deterioration in physical
capacity was considerable. Fifty-four per cent of the residents with
seriously limited ability and 57 per cent with moderately limited ability
were aged 80 and over. Furthermore, only 26 per cent of the residents
aged 80 and over, compared with 51 per cent of those under 80, reported
no physical disability. Residents under 70 years old had a higher rate

of seriously limited ability (6 per cent) than those who were 70-74
(4 per cent) or 75-79 (1 per cent); indeed, they had nearly as high a
rate as residents 80 and over (7 per cent). To put it another way,
of the seriously disabled, 27 per cent were under 70, 13 per cent
were 70-74, 7 per cent were 70-79, and 53 per cent were 80 and over.
Indeed, of all four levels of physical capacity, the seriously
disabled residents were the most likely to be under 70; they were also
the only ones more likely to be under 70 years than 70-79.

In short, disability is concentrated in two groups: those 80 and over
and those under 70 (though the absolute numbers of disabled in the
latter group are low). This suggests that many of the residents under
70 entered their present housing because of a serious disability and at
an earlier age than is usual, and that the other residents 80 and over
became disabled with age. If these patterns of disability are representative of the total population in NHA housing for the elderly, they have
relevance for sponsors, designers, and managers.

TABLE 11

RESIDENTS' PHYSICAL CAPACITY*, BY AGE

	Seriously Limited Ability	Moderately Limited Ability	Slightly Limited Ability	No Incapacity	TOTAL
Under 70 years	4 26.7%	9 17.0%	19 17.6%	32 25.2%	64 21.1%
70-74 years	2 13.3%	5 9.4%	19 17.6%	30 23.6%	56 18.5%
75-79 years	1 6.7%	9 17.0%	26 24.1%	37 29.1%	73 24.1%
80 years and over	8 53.3%	30 56.6%	44 40.7%	28 22.0%	110 36.3%
TOTAL	15 100%	53 100%	108 100%	127 100%	303 100%

* Question 13.

313

In addition to the respondents assessing their own degree of disability, there was a health assessment by the interviewer. Table 12 indicates that of the total sample only 6 per cent appeared obviously ill or infirm, 33 per cent appeared somewhat infirm, and the remaining 61 per cent appeared healthy. This was, admittedly, a very crude assessment based on approximately an hour's observation; nevertheless, it tended to confirm residents' own reports about their health. Both sets of figures indicate that only a small group, approximately 5 to 6 per cent, were obviously ill or seriously disabled, 42 to 60 per cent were in good health, and the remainder were somewhere in between. The interviewers confirmed that there were more health problems in hostel accommodation. This is not surprising, of course, since many more hostel dwellers than apartment dwellers were aged 80 and over, and because people tend to seek a setting with built-in services when they can no longer manage on an independent basis.

TABLE 12

INTERVIEWER'S IMPRESSION OF RESIDENT'S PHYSICAL CAPACITY*, BY DEVELOPMENT TYPE

	Obviously Ill or Infirm	Somewhat Infirm	Healthy	Uncertain	TOTAL
Self-Contained Developments	3 2.6%	36 31.0%	77 66.4%	0 0%	116 100%
Hostel and Mixed Developments	14 7.5%	64 34.2%	108 57.8%	1 .5%	187 100%
ALL DEVELOPMENTS	17 5.6%	100 33.0%	185 61.1%	1 .3%	303 100%

*   Interviewer Impression 3.

Another indication of poor health was confinement to bed at home or in hospital during the past year. Table 13 shows that a surprisingly high proportion of the sample - 72 per cent - reported no confinement to bed; this surely indicates a generally healthy population; 18 per cent had been confined to hospital but only 5 per cent had spent a month or more there. A small group - 6 per cent - had been confined to their bed at home, mostly for only a week. Age affected the incidence of hospitalization somewhat. Residents in both the under 70 and the 80 and over groups were considerably more likely to have spent time in hospital than those between 70-79. This is probably because these two age groups have higher rates of serious disability than do the in-between age groups.

TABLE 13

CONFINEMENT TO BED OR HOSPITAL IN PAST YEAR*, BY AGE

	Not Confined To Bed	Confined To Room Less Than One Month	Confined To Room One Month Or More	Confined To Hospital Less Than One Month	Confined To Hospital One Month Or More	No Answer	TOTAL
Under 70 years	47 73.4%	2 3.1%	0 0%	8 12.5%	4 6.3%	3 4.7%	64 100%
70-74 years	43 76.8%	2 3.6%	1 1.8%	7 12.5%	1 1.8%	2 3.6%	56 100%
75-79 years	53 72.6%	5 6.9%	1 1.4%	7 9.6%	3 4.1%	4 5.5%	73 100%
80 years and over	75 68.2%	7 6.4%	0 0%	19 17.3%	6 5.5%	3 2.7%	110 100%
TOTAL	218 71.9%	16 5.3%	2 .7%	41 13.5%	14 4.6%	12 4.0%	303 100%

* Question 14b.

Residents were questioned further about the types of health problems they had. The responses are given in Table 14. They may, however, be biased because some respondents may not have divulged all their health problems, either through ignorance or shyness. Also, 33 per cent of the respondents either said they had no problem or failed to respond. Heart and circulatory disorders were the problems most frequently identified - by 35 per cent of the sample; 16 per cent of the sample had arthritis or rheumatism - the second most frequently identified problem; 12 per cent had eye trouble; 9 per cent had problems with arms or legs; 7 per cent had digestive or intestinal problems. Table 14 gives the other problems, which were reported less frequently.

TABLE 14

TYPES OF HEALTH PROBLEMS*

	Number[1]	Per Cent Of Sample
Heart and circulation problems (including disorder of blood forming organs, disorders of circulatory and respiratory systems)	106	35.0
Arthritis and Rheumatism (joints, back, orthopedic)	49	16.2
Eye trouble not relieved by glasses (cataracts, glaucoma, blindness)	36	11.9
Disabilities involving arms or legs (including amputations, paralysis and disorders of the bones and limbs)	26	8.6
Disorders of digestive system and gastro-intestinal problems	22	7.3
Hearing problems	11	3.6
Foot trouble	3	1.0
Dental problems	1	.3
Skin problems	1	.3
Other	4	1.3
No problem according to respondent	55	18.2

* Question 14.

1 The 254 residents responding to this question identified a total of 259 health problems.

Table 15 indicates the health aids used by residents: 56 per cent of the sample took medication once or more daily; 19 per cent used a cane, crutch, brace or artificial limb; 11 per cent needed a special diet (this certainly should have relevance for food services in homes for the elderly); 10 per cent used a hearing aid; 3 per cent used special shoes; 3 per cent used a wheelchair or walker.

TABLE 15

HEALTH AIDS USED BY RESIDENTS*

	Number[1]	Per Cent of Sample
Medication once or more a day	170	56.1
Cane, crutch, brace, or artificial limb	58	19.1
Special diet	33	10.9
A hearing aid	29	9.6
Special shoes/other foot care	9	3.0
A wheelchair or walker	9	3.0
No aid required	57	18.8

* Question 14.

1 The 260 residents responding to this question said they used a total of 308 health aids.

Summary

This chapter indicates that the social and health characteristics of our sample varied widely. There is obviously no typical resident. Nevertheless, at the risk of over-simplification, one can briefly point to some prevailing trends. Six out of 10 of the residents were aged 75 years or older and seven out of 10 were female. Seven out of 10 lived alone, two out of 10 with a spouse, and one out of 10 with another resident. As far as finances were concerned, more than 5 out of 10 had some savings in addition to their old age pension, although more than four out of 10 said their financial resources were still strained. About two-thirds of the sample had a working-class background. On the whole, the residents enjoyed good health. Less than one-quarter reported moderate or serious physical incapacity and less than three in 10 had been confined to bed in the past year. But, in the event of illness, over four in 10 of the residents lacked children living in the area as potential sources of assistance, and one-third of them had no family members at all living nearby.

CHAPTER 3

PREVIOUS HOUSING EXPERIENCE

People generally evaluate their homes in relation to their previous
residence. Thus, it was necessary to find out something about residents'
previous housing in order to understand both the effects that moving to
a development had on their lives and their attitudes toward their present
accommodation.

Table 16 shows the previous and present household composition. Comparing
the figures, one can see that the proportion of the sample living alone
almost doubled on entry to the development, jumping from 37 per cent to
68 per cent. Correspondingly, the proportion living with spouses,
relatives, or friends sharply declined. Coming to terms with living
alone - a strange combination of privacy and loneliness - must surely
rank as one of the major adjustments that people entering housing for
the elderly have to face.

Of the total sample, 63 per cent were currently living in self-contained
dwelling units (29.4 per cent in bachelor apartments and 33.3 per cent
in one-bedroom ones). The remaining 37 per cent were in hostel accommodation (of this group, 9 per cent shared a double room). Of the sample,
10 per cent lived with someone other than their spouse.

TABLE 16

HOUSEHOLD COMPOSITION IN PREVIOUS AND PRESENT ACCOMMODATION*

	Alone	With Spouse	With Relative	With Friend	With Assigned Roommate	No Answer	TOTAL
In Previous Accommodation	113 37.3%	114 37.6%	50 16.5%	7 2.3%	15 5.0%	4 1.3%	303 100%
In Present Accommodation	206 68.0%	65 21.5%	12 4.0%	2 .7%	18 5.9%	0 0%	303 100%

* Question 3.

317

318

As Table 17 shows, for 23 per cent of the residents, moving into housing for the elderly entailed giving up living in their own homes. The proportion of homeowners was as high as 38 per cent in the Atlantic Provinces and 34 per cent on the Prairies, but only 8 per cent in Ontario. For this group of residents, no longer being master of their own homes must have been a situation requiring considerable personal adjustment. Only an extremely small proportion of residents (4 per cent) previously lived in institutions such as nursing homes.

TABLE 17

PREVIOUS TENURE*, BY REGION

	Tenant	Home Owner	Lodger	Free	TOTAL
Atlantic Provinces	18 56.3%	12 37.5%	2 6.3%	0 0%	32 100%
Quebec	15 27.3%	15 27.3%	25 45.5%	0 0%	55 100%
Ontario	83 76.1%	9 8.3%	14 12.8%	3 2.8%	109 100%
Prairies	34 48.8%	24 34.2%	12 17.0%	0 0%	70 100%
British Columbia	26 70.3%	11 29.7%	0 0%	0 0%	37 100%
CANADA	176 58.1%	71 23.4%	53 17.5%	3 1.0%	303 100%

* Question 3.

Table 18 shows that 79 per cent of the sample had lived in the same city or town immediately before moving to their present housing; 18 per cent had lived in the same neighborhood. Residents of small town developments were much less likely than residents of large city developments to have lived in the same neighborhood or centre before moving. Of the small-town residents, 46 per cent had lived in the same centre and 54 per cent had lived elsewhere; of the city residents, 89 per cent had lived in the same centre and 11 per cent had lived elsewhere. The differences in the two groups can be accounted for by the fact that small-town developments generally draw residents from a large and comparatively sparsely populated rural hinterland. It is likely that for many of these out-of-towners in small-town developments there were special problems to be faced in adjusting to their new environment.

TABLE 18

AREA OF PREVIOUS RESIDENCE*, BY LOCATION OF DEVELOPMENT

	Same Neighborhood	Same City Or Town	Other Than Same City Or Town	No Answer	TOTAL
Small Town Developments	3 4.2%	30 41.7%	39 54.2%	0 0%	72 100%
Large City Developments	51 22.1%	154 66.7%	25 10.8%	1 .4%	231 100%
ALL DEVELOPMENTS	54 17.8%	184 60.7%	64 21.2%	1 .3%	303 100%

* Question 2.

Reasons for Moving to the Development

To understand the social and economic roles that housing developments for the elderly play in today's society, it is important to investigate residents' reasons for entering them. As Table 19 shows, financial reasons were most frequently mentioned - by 35 per cent of the sample. Many of these persons moved to a development because they could not afford suitable housing in the private market. Difficulty in maintaining their previous home (usually on account of size) was mentioned as a reason for moving by 27 per cent of the residents. It is estimated that the attractiveness of the location of the housing was mentioned by approximately one-quarter of residents: 16 per cent said the accommodation itself was more comfortable or modern than what they had previously, and 8 per cent wanted to be closer to relatives, friends, or downtown.

Concern about security and safety was mentioned by 22 per cent of the residents. Many indicated that they or their relatives were concerned about them living on their own - a factor that has special relevance for the design and helping services available in senior citizens housing.

Interestingly, it is estimated that approximately one-fifth of the residents named opportunities for social interaction within the development as attracting them: 14 per cent said they needed company as they had previously been lonely, and 8 per cent said they wanted to be close to other residents who had previously moved to the development. The interest in mixing with people socially seems to be an important feature of homes for old people - and one that is not always given enough consideration.

TABLE 19

REASONS FOR MOVING TO DEVELOPMENT*

	Number[1]	Per Cent Of Sample
Felt financially best housing choice (including reasonable rent) in view of limited income	105	34.7
Unable to keep up maintenance of own home (previous house too roomy)	82	27.1
Security and safety	67	22.1
Needed help in cooking, shopping, homemaking	48	15.8
Wanted more comfortable or modern housing than former accommodation	48	15.8
Needed company (formerly lonely, depressed or isolated)	43	14.2
Relatives, social agency, doctor, friends/neighbors, encouraged entry	40	13.2
Needed nursing/medical services	32	10.6
Planned move as part of retirement	31	10.2
Previously living with family who needed room or made them feel uncomfortable (19 cases) or housing rules made move necessary when spouse died	28	9.2
Preferred location (e.g. close to children, relatives, or downtown)	25	8.3
Loss of previous home (due to expropriation or financial need to sell)	25	8.3
Wanted to be close to other people in development	23	7.6
Too many steps in previous accommodation	12	4.0

* Question 6.
1 Some residents gave more than one response.

The assistance that many developments offered – particularly the dining rooms – was mentioned by 16 per cent of the residents, notably those who had difficulty cooking and shopping on their own. The nursing and medical services offered by some developments was mentioned as a reason for moving by 11 per cent of the residents.

Other reasons given were: encouragement of a relative, social agency or doctors; moving as part of a retirement plan; other family members requiring the room at home; losing a home by expropriation or selling it because of financial need; and too many steps in the previous residence.

The residents were also asked if some person had helped them make the choice to move to the development (it was suspected that in many cases the decision had been influenced by others). However, 70 per cent of the residents indicated that they had decided to move on their own (it is possible, of course, that pride kept them from saying otherwise). For those who did say others helped them make the decision, assistance most often came from relatives (14 per cent of the sample), followed by social agencies and doctors (7 per cent) and friends (5 per cent). A higher proportion of persons living in hostel than in self-contained accommodation had received help in deciding to move. This can be accounted for by both the age and health of hostel residents and possibly also because of the more drastic changes in living arrangements that moving to hostel accommodation entailed.

Table 20 indicates the length of time residents had been in the development, by age group. Of the sample, 40 per cent had lived in their present development over three years, 37 per cent between one and three years, and 23 per cent for less than one year. Not surprisingly, the older groups had been in the development much longer than the younger. Indeed, of those residents who had been in the development for over three years, 74 per cent were 75 years of age or older; to put it another way, residents 75 and over were nearly twice as likely as the 70-74 group to have been in the development more than three years.

TABLE 20

LENGTH OF RESIDENCE IN DEVELOPMENT*, BY AGE

	Less Than One Year	1 - 3 Years	Over 3 Years	TOTAL
Under 70 years	21 32.8%	27 42.2%	16 25.0%	64 100%
70-74 years	16 28.6%	24 42.9%	16 28.6%	56 100%
75-79 years	21 28.8%	19 26.0%	33 45.2%	73 100%
80 years and over	11 10.0%	43 39.1%	56 50.9%	110 100%
ALL RESPONDENTS	69 22.8%	113 37.3%	121 39.9%	303 100%

* Question 1.

Summary

It was found that entry to a development for the elderly imposed a
number of stresses on residents. Many had to begin living alone,
perhaps for the first time in their lives (the proportion living alone
almost doubled on entry). For almost a quarter of the residents, entry
meant having to give up their own homes. Many residents were obliged
not only to start life in a new residential setting but also in a strange
neighborhood or town: eight out of 10 residents formerly lived in a
different neighborhood. Particularly in small-town developments, many
residents had to adapt to a new community.

Reasons for moving to the development were explored and it was found
that while there was considerable mention of negative influences –
in particular, financial need and difficulty looking after a previous
dwelling – a great many residents mentioned various positive attractions
of the accommodation, such as its comfortableness, security, services,
location, and the availability of companionship. The majority of
residents made the decision to move to their development on their own,
although some said they received help from relatives, friends, or
professionals.

CHAPTER 4

ACCESS TO SERVICES AND LOCATION

Residential location is important for most people. Among other things, it determines the journey to work, the availability of recreational opportunities, the style of life that surrounds one's home, and - to a significant extent - patterns of social interaction. The distribution and types of social services tend to vary considerably within urban areas; research has shown that the quality and variety of social services that are available to persons are often determined by where they live. Furthermore, standards of commercial services also vary from district to district, and significant variations in the prices charged by a single supermarket chain are not uncommon.

If residential location is important to all of us, it is vital to the well-being of the aged. The reason is self-evident: old people find it less easy to get about. This occurs partly because of physical infirmities that make it more difficult to stand up to sun, cold, and wind; but perhaps the prime reason has to do with loss of authority to drive a car. More than one observer has remarked that in the automobile age, loss of the right to drive is one of the greatest possible forms of deprivation. Yet this indignity must be faced by most old people. With their mobility limited in this way, it becomes the community's responsibility to ensure that the elderly are not prevented from visiting friends and relatives, and attending meetings, church services, medical clinics, the cinema or the library. Because of the importance of residential location, the interview schedule included questions designed to elicit how residents felt about the location of their development, especially in relation to their mobility needs.

Access to Important Social and Commercial Services

Residents were asked if they had easy access to the type of social and commercial services they considered important; for example, grocery stores, shopping centres, churches, and medical offices. Easy access meant that the services in question could be reached either by an easy walk or bus ride.

As Table 21 indicates, only 54 per cent of the residents said that the principal social and commercial services were easily accessible; 21 per cent said access to services was not easy; 19 per cent had mixed feelings or easy access to only some services; and 7 per cent said they simply did not go out. Among those residents who found access to services easy, 6 per cent (19 residents) drove cars.

TABLE 21

EASE OF ACCESS TO IMPORTANT SERVICES*, BY PHYSICAL CAPACITY

	Access[1] Easy	Access Easy To Some But Not All	Access Some- what Easy	Access Not Easy	Don't Go Out	No Answer	TOTAL
Seriously Limited Ability	2 13.3%	0 0%	0 0%	2 13.3%	11 73.3%	0 0%	15 100%
Moderately Limited Ability	9 17.0%	8 15.1%	6 11.3%	26 49.1%	4 7.5%	0 0%	53 100%
Slightly Limited Ability	54 50.0%	12 11.1%	14 13.0%	22 20.4%	6 5.6%	0 0%	108 100%
No Incapacity	97 76.4%	8 6.3%	9 7.1%	12 9.4%	0 0%	1 .8%	127 100%
TOTAL	162 53.5%	28 9.2%	29 9.6%	62 20.5%	21 6.9%	1 .3%	303 100%

* Question 44.

1 Includes 19 persons who said they drive to services.

As expected, health affected ease of access to services. Table 21 shows that only 13 per cent of residents with seriously limited ability found access to services easy, compared with 76 per cent of those with no incapacity. Of course, the majority (73 per cent) of the residents with seriously limited ability simply did not go out.

Between residents of small-town and urban developments there were - somewhat surprisingly - no clear-cut differences in feelings about access to services. Between different age groups, however, there were definitely differences: not surprisingly, access became more difficult with age. Of those residents under 70 years of age, 20 per cent said access to services was difficult - or they simply did not go out at all - compared with 42 per cent of those aged 80 or over.

In order to verify the findings of the question about ease of access and to consider the need for transportation services, the residents were asked another similar question: whether they had trouble getting to the places they wanted to go most (again grocery stores, shopping centres, and churches were mentioned as examples).

Table 22 indicates that 30 per cent of the residents said that they had difficulty - an even higher proportion than the 21 per cent who said access to most social and commercial services was not easy. Residents of self-contained accommodation reported less difficulty getting around in the community than did those in hostel accommodation: 74 per cent of the residents of self-contained developments, compared with 55 per cent of the residents in hostel and mixed developments, said that they had no difficulty. This is probably related to the fact that hostel residents tend to be older and more disabled; also because hostels had more built-in services, residents presumably had less need for close access.

TABLE 22

DIFFICULTY IN GETTING PLACES*, BY DEVELOPMENT TYPE

	Difficulty	Not Difficult	Don't Go Out	No Answer	TOTAL
Self-Contained Developments	28 24.1%	86 74.1%	2 1.7%	0 0%	116 100%
Hostel or Mixed Developments	62 . 33.2%	104 55.6%	19 10.2%	2 1.1%	187 100%
ALL DEVELOPMENTS	90 29.7%	190 62.7%	21 6.9%	2 .7%	303 100%

* Question 19.

It is clear that access to important facilities and services must be taken more seriously in planning housing developments for old people.

Volunteer Transportation Services

Volunteer transportation systems have sometimes been used to overcome a development's lack of access to services. Unfortunately, our survey indicated that public transit systems were nonexistent or ineffective in most developments: only 15 per cent of the sample actually used such a service (mostly to attend church). In large urban developments,

public transportation was often used, although residents complained about
poor scheduling, bus stops too far away, and unsheltered waiting areas.
Most residents said they relied on friends and relatives to take them
to necessary services; 7 per cent mentioned pooling together with other
residents to employ taxis.

General Satisfaction with Location

Satisfaction with the location of their development was found to depend
on a number of things - each of which was not equally important to all
residents. The main reasons given for satisfaction were easy access to
services, family, and friends (this included both their closeness and
the quality of available transportation services), the general pleasant-
ness of the surroundings, and residents' familiarity with the neighborhood.
The main reasons given for dissatisfaction were distance from shopping,
noise, and generally unpleasant surroundings.

Table 23 indicates that 56 per cent of the residents were very satisfied
with the location of their development and 30 per cent were somewhat
satisfied; 14 per cent were dissatisfied. When satisfaction was looked
at in terms of residents' physical capacity, those with various degrees
of disability expressed more dissatisfaction than did those with no
incapacity. Indeed, residents with seriously limited ability were the
ones most likely to be "not at all satisfied" (13 per cent), followed by
those with moderately limited ability (16 per cent), slightly limited
ability (4 per cent), and no incapacity (none). On the other hand, those
with seriously limited ability were also the ones most likely to be "very
satisfied" - 73 per cent (compared with 61 per cent of the residents with
no incapacity, 53 per cent with moderately limited ability, and 48 per
cent with slightly limited ability). This may be because many residents
with seriously limited ability tend not to go out, limit their social
activities to within the development, and therefore have fewer expectations
involving the community in which the development is located. In contrast,
persons with less limited ability may have far greater expectations about
getting around as usual - and, because their physical condition makes it
somewhat difficult, they may feel more dissatisfied with location than
persons who expect less. Of course, with more help and encouragement,
seriously disabled persons might also expect to get around more.

Younger residents were more likely than older residents to be satisfied
with the location of their development.

TABLE 23

SATISFACTION WITH LOCATION*, BY PHYSICAL CAPACITY

	Very Satisfied	Somewhat Satisfied	Not Very Satisfied	Not At All Satisfied	No Answer	TOTAL
Seriously Limited Ability	11 73.3%	1 6.7%	1 6.7%	2 13.3%	0 0%	15 100%
Moderately Limited Ability	28 52.8%	18 34.0%	4 7.5%	3 5.7%	0 0%	53 100%
Slightly Limited Ability	52 48.1%	35 32.4%	16 14.8%	4 3.7%	1 .9%	108 100%
No Incapacity	78 61.4%	35 27.6%	12 9.4%	0 0%	2 1.6%	127 100%
TOTAL	169 55.8%	89 29.4%	33 10.9%	9 3.0%	3 1.0%	303 100%

* Question 45.

Downtown Versus Residential Area Location

Because satisfaction with location involves a number of tradeoffs, it is difficult to say which were most satisfied - downtown residents or suburban residents. In fact, satisfaction tended to vary greatly from one development to another. In three-quarters of the downtown developments, a high proportion of residents were satisfied with accessibility; but in three developments few were satisfied. Many of the residents in downtown developments were pleased about the access to services, shopping, and transportation but unhappy with the commercial surroundings and the hustle and bustle. In residential areas, feelings were also mixed. Usually the residents appreciated the pleasant surroundings but were bothered by the lack of access to services and transportation. The analysis does not reveal any clear preferences on the part of elderly people for either downtown or suburban locations. It does reveal, however, that both access to services and neighborhood surroundings are very important to residents - and expectations about them must be met regardless of where in the urban area the development is located.

Attitude to Age Mix

It is frequently said that our modern society is forcing the elderly
into an environment in which they have very little opportunity to mix
with persons outside of their own age group - and that this process
constitutes an unnatural form of segregation. We therefore asked
residents about the sort of age composition they would prefer in the
neighborhood of their development, and also within their own building.

When asked if they would prefer to have persons of different ages and
families with children living in the immediate neighborhood, the majority
of residents who expressed an opinion were in favor of a homogeneous
neighborhood. Of the sample, 43 per cent said they preferred not to
live in a mixed area, but only 18 per cent said they would somewhat
prefer an age mix, and only 7 per cent said they would definitely prefer
an age mix (23 per cent said they did not care and 9 per cent gave no
answer). Residents were also generally opposed to sharing their
building with persons of other ages and children. Seventy per cent of
the sample indicated that they would somewhat prefer to live in a
building occupied mainly by people of their own age, and 17 per cent
indicated that they definitely preferred to live with their own age
group. Only 8 per cent somewhat preferred an age mix, and only 2 per
cent definitely preferred an age mix.

Proximity to Children

From the point of view of family relationships, it was interesting that
so small a proportion of the sample placed top priority on having the
development located in the same neighborhood or city as their children.
Only 40 per cent of those residents with children said that it was "very
important"; on the other hand, 36 per cent said it was "somewhat important"
(23 per cent said it was "not very important"). As Table 24 indicates -
rather surprisingly - old people living alone were not any more eager
than those living with spouses to have their children close at hand.
Table 25 shows, however, that residents with seriously limited ability
were more likely than those in better health to feel it was of some
importance to live near their children - and indeed none of them felt
it was "not very important." Sex also made a slight difference in the
importance placed on having children nearby: more women than men agreed
that it was of some importance to live near their children.

TABLE 24

IMPORTANCE PLACED ON PROXIMITY TO CHILDREN*, BY HOUSEHOLD TYPE

	Very Important	Somewhat Important	Not Very Important	No Answer	TOTAL
Living Alone	59	54	36	2	151
	39.1%	35.8%	23.8%	1.3%	100%
With Spouse, Relative or Friend	24	22	13	2	61
	39.3%	36.1%	21.3%	3.3%	100%
With Assigned Roommate	6	3	1	0	10
	60.0%	30.0%	10.0%	0%	100%
TOTAL	89	79	50	4	222[1]
	40.1%	35.6%	22.5%	1.8%	100%

* Question 12.

1 These responses do not include those of 81 persons (26.7 per cent of the total sample) who said they had no children.

TABLE 25

IMPORTANCE PLACED ON PROXIMITY TO CHILDREN*, BY PHYSICAL CAPACITY[1]

	Very Important	Somewhat Important	Not Very Important	No Answer	TOTAL
Seriously Limited Ability	4	5	0	1	10
	40.0%	50.0%	0%	10.0%	100%
Moderately Limited Ability	11	15	7	1	34
	32.4%	44.1%	20.6%	2.9%	100%
Slightly Limited Ability	36	27	22	1	86
	41.9%	31.4%	25.6%	1.2%	100%
No Incapacity	38	32	21	1	92
	41.3%	34.8%	22.8%	1.1%	100%
TOTAL	89	79	50	4	222
	40.1%	35.6%	22.5%	1.8%	100%

* Question 12.

1 These responses do not include the 81 persons (26.7 per cent of the sample) who said they had no children.

Summary

The survey revealed that only about half of the residents had easy
access to essential social and commercial services. Residents with
physical incapacities, older residents, and those living in hostels
encountered more difficulty in getting to these services than other
users. The very few residents who had access to a volunteer transportation service usually found that it operated only on Sundays –
to church.

Only 56 per cent of the residents reported that they were very satisfied
with the location of the development, with older and more incapacitated
residents expressing a high rate of dissatisfaction. Reasons for
satisfaction with location included easy access to services, family,
and friends, pleasant surroundings, and familiarity with the neighborhood. The most frequently mentioned reasons for dissatisfaction were
distance from shopping, noise, and general unpleasantness of the
neighborhood. The findings indicate that satisfaction with both access
to services and the surroundings are necessary for overall satisfaction
with location, but no clear preference for downtown or suburban areas
emerged.

Few residents were enthusiastic about having a wide age range living
near the development or in their building. Only 7 per cent of the users
said that they would definitely prefer to live in a mixed neighborhood
and there was a widely shared feeling against housing families and
people of different age groups in the same building as senior citizens.

Surprisingly, the majority of residents did not place top priority on
living in a development which was close to their children. Only 40 per
cent of the sample said that this was very important.

CHAPTER 5

SOCIAL PARTICIPATION

The possible effects of a development on the extent of residents' social
participation was an interesting aspect of our study. For many of the
residents, the opportunity to mix socially was a main reason for entering
their development. We were interested in exploring the extent to which
residents still participated in the broader community as well - the
extent to which the social sub-system within the development had become a
substitute for social relationships outside.

Outdoor Activity

Perhaps the simplest indicator of participation in community life outside
is the frequency with which residents leave the development, even if
simply for fresh air or a short journey. As Table 26 indicates, a
surprisingly low proportion of the residents - only 46 per cent - went
out for more than an hour each day (except sometimes in winter); 23 per
cent went out daily for less than an hour; 32 per cent did not go out on
a daily basis. Considering that in many cases outdoor activity took place
in the immediate area of the development (for example, sitting on a patio
bench or a walk around the garden), one has to conclude that living in a
senior citizens development is generally accompanied by a low level of
regular social participation in the community.

Table 26 also indicates that a slightly higher proportion of residents in
self-contained developments got out for an hour or more each day (53 per
cent) than did those living in hostel and mixed developments (40 per cent).
Furthermore, of the two accommodation types, the residents of downtown
developments were more likely than those in the suburbs to leave the
development for an hour or more each day; conversely, suburban residents
were much more likely not to go out on a daily basis. In short, location
appears to have a considerable bearing on the frequency of outdoor activity.

As Table 27 shows, there is a strong relationship between physical capacity
and outdoor activity. Of those residents with no incapacity, 69 per cent
got out for an hour or more daily - compared with 30 per cent of those
with slightly or moderately limited ability, and none with seriously
limited ability.

There appeared to be no significant relationship between children living
in the area and outdoor activity; in fact, a larger proportion of residents
with no children in the area than residents with children in the area got
out for an hour or more daily.

TABLE 26

OUTDOOR ACTIVITY*, BY DEVELOPMENT TYPE AND LOCATION

	Less Than Daily	Less Than One Hour Daily	One Hour Or More Daily	No Answer	TOTAL
ALL SELF-CONTAINED DEVELOPMENTS	40 34.5%	15 12.9%	61 52.6%	0 0%	116 100%
Downtown Location	18 31.6%	8 14.1%	31 54.4%	0 0%	57 100%
Suburban Location	22 37.3%	7 11.9%	30 50.8%	0 0%	59 100%
ALL HOSTEL OR MIXED DEVELOPMENTS	57 30.5%	55 29.4%	74 39.5%	1 .7%	187 100%
Downtown Location	11 18.6%	17 28.8%	31 52.5%	0 0%	59 100%
Suburban Location	46 35.9%	38 29.7%	43 33.6%	1 .8%	128 100%
ALL DEVELOPMENTS	97 32.0%	70 23.1%	135 44.6%	1 .3%	303 100%

* Question 80.

TABLE 27

OUTDOOR ACTIVITY*, BY PHYSICAL CAPACITY

	Less Than Daily	Less Than One Hour Daily	One Hour Or More Daily	No Answer	TOTAL
Seriously Limited Ability	11 73.3%	4 26.7%	0 0%	0 0%	15 100%
Moderately Limited Ability	27 50.9%	10 18.9%	15 28.3%	1 1.9	53 100%
Slightly Limited Ability	44 40.7%	31 28.7%	33 30.6%	0 0%	108 100%
No Incapacity	15 11.8%	25 19.7%	87 68.5%	0 0%	127 100%
TOTAL	97 32.0%	70 23.1%	135 44.6%	1 .3%	303 100%

* Question 80.

Participation in Community Activities

The main activities of residents who did get out of the development often appear to have involved shopping, informal visiting, going for drives, or simply walking. Table 28 shows that 65 per cent of the residents said they never participated in outside clubs or organized activities. Participation in community activities appears to have declined considerably with entry to the development; indeed, the proportion of respondents who never participated in community activities was 50 per cent before entry and 65 per cent at the time residents were interviewed.

Residents of self-contained developments, although healthier, younger, and more centrally located than hostel residents, were only slightly more likely to participate in community activities.

TABLE 28

PARTICIPATION IN OUTSIDE COMMUNITY ACTIVITIES*

	Weekly	Monthly	Yearly Or Less	Never	No Answer	TOTAL
Prior to Entering	60	79	12	151	1	303
	19.8%	26.1%	4.0%	49.8%	.3%	100%
Currently	47	38	18	197	3	303
	15.5%	12.5%	6.0%	65.0%	1.0%	100%

* Questions 72 and 73.

Church Attendance

The elderly are often thought to attend church more than other age groups. Table 29 shows, however, that only 44 per cent of the residents attended church at least once weekly. In self-contained developments 31 per cent attended at least weekly, while in hostel and mixed developments 51 per cent attended at least weekly. The figure for the hostel and mixed developments is probably distorted by the very high rate of church-going in the three Quebec developments (two of which were operated by religious orders). Nevertheless, it is still probably correct to say that going to church was the most popular activity outside or inside the developments.

TABLE 29

CHURCH ATTENDANCE*, BY DEVELOPMENT TYPE

	Daily	Weekly	Monthly	Yearly Or Less	Never	No Answer	TOTAL
Self-Contained Developments	1 .9%	35 30.2%	26 22.4%	18 15.5%	35 30.2%	1 .9%	116 100%
Hostel and Mixed Developments	33 17.6%	63 33.7%	23 12.3%	25 13.4%	41 21.9%	2 1.1%	187 100%
ALL DEVELOPMENTS	34 11.2%	98 32.3%	49 16.2%	43 14.2%	76 25.1%	3 1.0%	303 100%

* Question 74.

Visiting with Friends

Respondents liked having contact with friends outside the development. Of the sample, 73 per cent had at least monthly contact with a friend outside the development, and 41 per cent had at least a weekly contact. But for 26 per cent of the residents such contacts were extremely rare.

Visiting with Relatives or Family

Canadians have the reputation of being habitual telephone users. There-fore, to find out about contact with family members, visiting and telephone calls were combined in the same question. As Table 30 shows, 26 per cent reported daily contact, 35 per cent reported weekly contact, and 13 per cent reported monthly contact. But as many as 25 per cent of the residents had virtually no contact with any family members (15 per cent had contact only yearly or less and 10 per cent reported no family). It should be noted that residents may have exaggerated the frequency of visiting or phoning because of pride. In short, a considerable propor-tion of residents had very little contact with relatives.

The frequency of contact with family largely depended, of course, on whether residents had children living in the area. Of those with children in the area, 87 per cent had daily or weekly contact - compared with 37 per cent of residents with no children in the area and only 22 per cent of those with no children (it should be recalled from chapter 2 that 75 per cent of this latter group had no other relatives in the area).

Age seemed to make little difference as far as the frequency of family visiting and telephoning was concerned. Residents aged 80 years and over had as much contact with their family as the younger ones did.

TABLE 30

FAMILY VISITING OR TELEPHONING*, BY CHILDREN'S RESIDENCE

	Daily	Weekly	Monthly	Yearly Or Less	No Family	No Answer	TOTAL
No Children Alive	8 9.9%	10 12.3%	13 16.0%	19 23.5%	29 35.8%	2 2.5%	81 100%
Children Alive But None In Area	6 11.8%	13 25.5%	10 19.6%	22 43.1%	0 0%	0 0%	51 100%
Children In Area	65 38.2%	83 48.8%	16 9.4%	4 2.4%	0 0%	2 1.2%	170 100%
No Answer	0 0%	1 100%	0 0%	0 0%	0 0%	0 0%	1 100%
TOTAL	79 26.1%	107 35.3%	39 12.9%	45 14.9%	31 10.2%	2 .7%	303 100%

*   Question 11.

Participation in Development Activity

We were especially interested in the extent to which social interaction within the development served as a substitute for community participation. Table 31 clearly shows that there was a great deal of social interaction within developments. Of the residents, 43 per cent said they had made many friends since moving to the development, another 40 per cent said that they had made at least some friends, and only 16 per cent claimed to have made hardly any friends. There were, of course, variations in friendship patterns.

Table 31 also indicates that health limitations did not appear to stop people from making friends. Indeed, a higher proportion of those with seriously and moderately limited ability than those in better health made many friends.

TABLE 31

FRIENDSHIP IN DEVELOPMENT*, BY PHYSICAL CAPACITY

	Made Many Friends	Made Some Friends	Made Hardly Any Friends	No Answer	TOTAL
Seriously Limited Ability	7 46.7%	7 46.7%	0 0%	1 6.7%	15 100%
Moderately Limited Ability	25 47.2%	16 30.2%	11 20.8%	1 1.9%	53 100%
Slightly Limited Ability	44 40.7%	46 42.6%	18 16.7%	0 0%	108 100%
No Incapacity	55 43.3%	52 40.9%	19 15.0%	1 .8%	127 100%
TOTAL	131 43.2%	121 39.9%	48 15.8%	3 1.0%	303 100%

* Question 77.

One might have thought that self-contained developments, with their lack of central dining rooms, would have a lower friendship rate. Table 32 shows that this was so - but the differences were much less marked than expected.

Sex was not a barrier to participation in development activity and almost the same proportion of men as women had made friends in the development.

It might be thought that residents with children in the area would be less likely to have made friends in the development because of time spent with children. Table 33, however, suggests otherwise: 47 per cent of residents with children in the area reported having made many friends in the development, compared with 39 per cent of those with no children nearby.

Age was a handicap to participation in development activity. Residents aged 75 years and over were less likely to have made many friends in the development than younger ones - even though they may have lived in the residence longer.

TABLE 32

FRIENDSHIP IN DEVELOPMENT*, BY DEVELOPMENT TYPE

	Made Many Friends	Made Some Friends	Made Hardly Any Friends	No Answer	TOTAL
Self-Contained Developments	50 43.1%	42 36.2%	24 20.7%	0 0%	116 100%
Hostel and Mixed Developments	81 43.3%	79 42.2%	24 12.8%	3 1.6%	187 100%
ALL DEVELOPMENTS	131 43.2%	121 39.9%	48 15.8%	3 1.0%	303 100%

* Question 77.

TABLE 33

FRIENDSHIP IN DEVELOPMENT*, BY RESIDENCE OF LIVING CHILDREN

	Made Many Friends	Made Some Friends	Made Hardly Any Friends	No Answer	TOTAL
No Children Alive	31 38.3%	32 39.5%	18 22.2%	0 0%	81 100%
Children Alive But None In Area	20 39.2%	25 49.0%	6 11.8%	0 0%	51 100%
Children in Area	79 46.5%	64 37.6%	24 14.1%	3 1.8%	170 100%
No Answer	1 100%	0 0%	0 0%	0 0%	1 100%
TOTAL	131 43.2%	121 39.9%	48 15.8%	3 1.0%	303 100%

* Question 77.

338

Residents were asked how often they visited with neighbors in the development. As Table 34 indicates, 67 per cent of the residents visited each
other at least once a week and 39 per cent visited once a day. When the
figures are analyzed by physical capacity, it is clear that residents with
various degrees of limited ability tended to visit each other slightly more
than did those with no incapacity. The latter presumably interacted more
with persons outside the development. Further analysis revealed that the
occupants of self-contained dwelling units visited each other less often
than hostel residents. Also, there was more visiting in non-profit housing
than in public housing developments.

It is clear that in housing developments for the elderly there were
significant minorities of residents who did not participate in activity
within the development or activity in the outside community: 32 per cent
of residents did not go out on a daily basis; 65 per cent never participated
in community activities; 56 per cent attended church less than once a week;
58 per cent had contact with friends outside the development less than once
a week; 38 per cent were in touch with their families less than once a week;
16 per cent had made hardly any friends in the development; and 31 per cent
visited neighbors in their development less than once a week. In many cases,
the same residents probably fall into all or most of these categories, thus
forming an isolated and lonely group of old people - despite the fact that
living in a senior citizens development was regarded by many persons as an
opportunity to make new friends and join in new activities.

TABLE 34

VISITING IN THE DEVELOPMENT*, BY PHYSICAL CAPACITY

	Daily	Weekly	Monthly	Less Than Monthly	No Answer	TOTAL
Seriously Limited Ability	7 46.7%	3 20.0%	3 20.0%	1 6.7%	1 6.7%	15 100%
Moderately Limited Ability	19 35.8%	17 32.1%	6 11.3%	9 17.0%	2 3.8%	53 100%
Slightly Limited Ability	50 46.3%	29 26.9%	11 10.2%	17 15.7%	1 .9%	108 100%
No Incapacity	43 33.9%	36 28.3%	17 13.4%	29 22.8%	2 1.6%	127 100%
TOTAL	119 39.3%	85 28.1%	37 12.2%	56 18.5%	6 2.0%	303 100%

* Question 76.

Sources of Emergency Assistance

Sources of emergency assistance provided us with another indication of the extent to which residents considered themselves part of a larger outside community of relatives and friends - or the extent to which the walls of the development marked the boundries of their world. Residents were asked whom they would turn to first if they needed help because of an emergency or illness. The responses showed there was a split between those who would turn to persons within the development and those who would turn to persons outside.

Table 35 indicates that 54 per cent of the residents said they would turn to persons in the development: 44 per cent mentioned development staff or the use of an internal buzzer or intercom system and 10 per cent mentioned other residents. Less than half (44 per cent) said they would turn to persons outside for assistance: 24 per cent mentioned relatives; 13 per cent mentioned a family doctor or hospital; 3 per cent mentioned the police or fire department. Only one resident named a community agency as a source of assistance - this is disturbing since housing managers often allude to this source.

TABLE 35

SOURCES OF EMERGENCY ASSISTANCE*, BY HOUSEHOLD TYPE

	Development Staff	Relatives	Family Doctor/ Hospital	Other Residents	Police/ Fire Department	Friends, Neighbors Outside Development	Community Agency	Other	No Answer	TOTAL
Living Alone	91 44.2%	52 25.2%	20 9.7%	24 11.7%	5 2.4%	6 2.9%	0 0%	4 1.9%	4 1.9%	206 100%
With Spouse/ Relative/ Friend	27 34.2%	19 24.1%	19 24.0%	5 6.3%	5 6.3%	2 2.5%	1 1.3%	1 1.3%	0 0%	79 100%
With Assigned Roommate	15 83.3%	2 11.1%	1 5.6%	0 0%	0 0%	0 0%	0 0%	0 0%	0 0%	18 100%
ALL RESIDENTS	133 43.9%	73 24.1%	40 13.2%	29 9.6%	10 3.3%	8 2.6%	1 .3%	5 1.7%	4 1.3%	303 100%

* Question 63.

340

Residents living alone were more likely than those living with a spouse, relative, or friend, to turn to assistance within the development. The 18 hostel residents living with an assigned roommate relied almost totally on the development - except for one person who named a doctor or hospital as a source of assistance.

Age appeared to have little effect on whom residents turned to in an emergency. Those 80 years and over were by far the most likely to turn to development staff but those under 70 were the second most likely. Relatives were turned to less by residents 80 years and over (probably because they had fewer relatives alive).

Table 36 shows that residents with children living nearby were more likely than others to be among the small group (only 24 per cent of the sample) who said they would turn to relatives for assistance. Even so, however, only 35 per cent of those residents with children nearby indicated that they would turn to relatives; 48 per cent of this group said they would turn to development staff or other residents. Only 7 per cent of those residents with no children alive and only 16 per cent of those with children living outside the area said they would rely on relatives.

TABLE 36

LIKELY SOURCES OF EMERGENCY ASSISTANCE*, BY CHILDREN IN AREA

	Development Staff	Relatives	Family Doctor/ Hospital	Other Residents	Police/ Fire Department	Friends Outside Development	Community Agency	Other	No Answer	TOTAL
No Children Alive	47 58.0%	6 7.4%	11 13.6%	8 9.9%	4 4.9%	3 3.7%	0 0%	1 1.2%	1 1.2%	81 100%
Children Alive But None In Area	20 39.2%	8 15.7%	11 21.6%	4 7.8%	2 3.9%	5 9.8%	0 0%	1 2.0%	0 0%	51 100%
Children In Area	65 38.2%	59 34.7%	18 10.6%	17 10.0%	4 2.4%	0 0%	1 .6%	3 1.8%	3 1.8%	170 100%
No Answer	1 100%	0 0%	0 0%	0 0%	0 0%	0 0%	0 0%	0 0%	0 0%	1 100%
ALL RESIDENTS	133 43.9%	73 24.1%	40 13.2%	29 9.6%	10 3.3%	8 2.6%	1 .3%	5 1.7%	4 1.3%	303 100%

* Question 63.

This high reliance on development staff and other residents points to
the need for more staff or alternative ways of ensuring that emergency
assistance is available at all times, including evenings and weekends.
A significant proportion of residents had indicated that they came to
the development for safety and security reasons (see chapter 3). And
their concern about this was further revealed by frequent mention of
other residents falling ill or dying without anyone knowing, often being
undiscovered for many hours or even days.

Summary

The responses indicate that the residents of housing for the elderly are
strongly tied to their developments. Only 46 per cent of the residents
admitted to going outside of their building for an hour or more daily and
32 per cent said that they never went out. Residents with no physical
incapacity got out much more than those in poorer health. Also, the
residents of self-contained developments and those located in downtown
areas tended to get outside more than others. Most outdoor activity was
of an informal nature: shopping, visiting, going for drives, and walks.
Two-thirds of the residents never participated in clubs or organized
community activities away from the development. Forty-four per cent of
the sample attended church services weekly and in many cases these were
held in the development. While many residents remained in close contact
with residents and friends, it was found that a minority of approximately
a quarter of the residents seldom ever visited with relatives or friends.

Within the developments, interaction between residents often tended to
be intense; it was more frequent in hostels than in self-contained
developments. Here again, the survey revealed a minority of residents
who had few friends.

As far as sources of community assistance were concerned, slightly over
half the residents indicated that they would turn to either management
staff or other persons in the development. Of those who said that they
would first turn to persons outside, relatives were most frequently
mentioned, followed by medical personnel. Only one resident mentioned
the possibility of turning to a community social service agency.

CHAPTER 6

SOCIAL SERVICES

A considerable amount of data about social service delivery to residents of NHA financed housing for the elderly was obtained for the manager survey which forms part of this study. In our user survey also, an effort was made to find out how old people value different social services, what services they need, and what difficulties they encounter in making use of services. In weighing the value of this chapter, one should bear in mind that the availability of the various services described varied enormously from development to development; thus the users were generalizing on the basis of very different sets of experience. Another methodological point of view is that in most cases few comments were elicited to explain non-use or shortcomings of services. Despite this, however, the data provides some useful information and indicators, and should therefore be helpful to housing administrators and to social service agencies.

Nursing

Residents were asked if they thought it would be helpful to have a nurse come in regularly. If they were already using a nursing service, they were asked who was providing it. As Table 37 indicates, 72 residents (24 per cent of the sample) felt they needed some form of nursing and, in fact, most (70 per cent) of these were already using nursing assistance. Forty residents (13 per cent of the sample) obtained service from a nurse on the development staff; however, this figure mainly reflects the situation in the three hostel and mixed developments located in Quebec. Fifteen residents (5 per cent) were being visited by the Victorian Order of Nurses. Eight residents (3 per cent) received nursing from the local public health service. Six residents (2 per cent) received the nursing assistance they required from friends or relatives. One resident obtained nursing from a nearby hospital. Two residents felt they needed a nursing service but were not receiving it.

Generally, the amount of service provided by community agencies such as the Victorian Order of Nurses and the local public health services was not extensive when one considers that the VON was used mainly by two or three residents in each of six urban developments; furthermore, the use of a public health nurse was concentrated mainly in three other developments. On the other hand, only 23 per cent of users considered that they had seriously or moderately limited ability (see Table 10).

TABLE 37

USE OF NURSING*, BY PHYSICAL CAPACITY

	Help From Friends and Relatives Used	VON Used	Public Health Nurse Used	Nearby Hospital Used	Devel- opment Nurse Used	Not Avail- able Though Need	No Need	TOTAL
Seriously Limited Ability	1 6.7%	1 6.7%	0 0%	0 0%	9 60.0%	1 6.7%	3 20.0%	15 100%
Moderately Limited Ability	2 3.8%	5 9.4%	4 7.5%	0 0%	8 15.1%	0 0%	34 64.2	53 100%
Slightly Limited Ability	3 2.8%	5 4.6%	4 3.7%	1 .9%	15 13.9%	0 0%	80 74.1%	108 100%
No Incapacity	0 0%	4 3.1%	0 0%	0 0%	8 6.3%	1 .8%	114 89.8%	127 100%
TOTAL	6 2.0%	15 5.0%	8 2.6%	1 .3%	40 13.2%	2 .7%	231 76.2%	303 100%

* Question 15

The likelihood of residents feeling they needed nursing depended on a number of things. First, as Table 37 indicates, the proportion of residents saying they required nursing increased gradually, from those with no incapacity to those with moderately limited ability; it then increased sharply in the case of those with seriously limited ability. Residents seemed realistic about their needs for nursing: the better their health, the more likely they were to say they did not need a nursing service. Thus, only 20 per cent of those with seriously limited ability felt they did not need nursing, compared with 90 per cent of those with no incapacity. At all levels of physical ability, where nursing was required it was provided mainly by the development staff, followed by the VON.

As Table 38 shows, age did not greatly affect the proportion of residents indicating that they did not require nursing. The proportion was somewhat lower among the residents under 70 years (70 per cent) than among the other age groups (it was 77 per cent for those aged 70-74 and 78 per cent for those aged 75 and over). But this is not so surprising when it is recalled that residents under 70 years showed a high concentration of seriously limited ability.

TABLE 38

USE OF NURSING*, BY AGE

	Used	Not Available Though Need	No Need	TOTAL
Under 70 years	18 28.1%	1 1.6%	45 70.3%	64 100%
70-74 years	13 23.2%	0 0%	43 76.8%	56 100%
75-79 years	16 21.9%	0 0%	57 78.1%	73 100%
80 years and over	23 20.9%	1 .9%	86 78.2%	110 100%
TOTAL	70 23.1%	2 .7%	231 76.2%	303 100%

* Question 15.

Sex somewhat affected the proportion of residents who said they needed nursing assistance. A slightly higher proportion of females than males felt they needed nursing. A slightly lower proportion of residents living with a spouse than residents living alone said they needed nursing. If a nursing type of help was required, residents living with a spouse were more likely than those living alone to receive it from relatives or friends. Conversely, a higher proportion of residents living on their own turned to development staff for nursing assistance. Having children living nearby did not, however, mean that the respondents saw them as a source of nursing assistance; those with children nearby used development staff or community nursing services as much as other residents did.

Table 39 indicates that residents of hostel and mixed developments were more likely to say that they required nursing than those in self-contained developments (85 per cent of those in hostel and mixed developments, compared with 71 per cent of those in self-contained developments). All 40 (13 per cent of the sample) who were receiving assistance from development nurses were residents of hostel and mixed developments.

Residents had very few complaints about nursing services. About the only one (offered by less than 5 per cent of the sample) was that the service was not frequent enough.

TABLE 39

USE OF NURSING*, BY DEVELOPMENT TYPE

	Help From Relatives And Friends	VON Used	Public Health Nurse, Used	Hospital Nearby Used	Development Nurse Used	Not Available Though Need	No Need	TOTAL
Self-Contained Developments	4 3.4%	8 6.9%	4 3.4%	0 0%	0 0%	1 .9%	99 85.3%	116 100%
Hostel and Mixed Developments	2 1.1%	7 3.7%	4 2.1%	1 .5%	40 21.4%	1 .5%	132 70.6%	187 100%
ALL DEVELOPMENTS	6 2.0%	15 5.0%	8 2.6%	1 .3%	40 13.2%	2 .7%	231 76.3%	303 100%

* Question 15.

Homemaking

Many residents said they entered their development because of difficulty in cleaning and maintaining their previous home. Therefore, it was important to investigate the extent to which their need for assistance with homemaking had been satisfied. Some form of maid service was provided in most hostel developments - and 37 per cent of the total sample were in hostel accommodation. These residents received some help with housework, although in many cases they were partly responsible for cleaning and tidying up their rooms.

Table 40 shows that 30 per cent of the residents said they still had difficulty with everyday housework - making beds, washing dishes, and cleaning the room. Of the group who still had difficulty, 65 per cent lived in hostel developments (where they received some assistance). Looking at it another way, 58 per cent of all the hostel residents said that they had difficulty doing housework, compared with only 17 per cent of apartment dwellers. Thus the greatest need for homemaking assistance was concentrated in homes where help tended to be most available: hostels. As one might suspect, residents aged 80 and over had the greatest difficulty with housework; nearly 50 per cent said they had difficulty, while in the younger age groups only 20 to 25 per cent had difficulty.

```
                            TABLE 40

         DIFFICULTY WITH HOUSEWORK, COOKING AND SHOPPING*

                        Yes      No      No Answer    TOTAL

Difficulty With         91       199        13         303
Housework             30.0%     65.7%      4.3%        100%

Difficulty With         67       192        44         303
Cooking               22.1%     63.4%     14.5%        100%

Difficulty With        107       179        17         303
Shopping In Winter    35.3%     59.1%      5.6%        100%

   *  Questions 16, 17 and 18.
```

As previously noted, in most hostels assistance was available for heavier cleaning. But of the 32 apartment dwellers who said that they were having problems with housework (11 per cent of the sample), only three got help from a visiting homemaker service. Only 3 per cent of all the residents said that they received regular help with housework from relatives or friends. It is therefore obvious that a serious need existed for help with housework - and this need was not being met by either development staff or the community.

Residents with seriously or moderately limited physical ability were much more likely to use maid or homemaker services than those in better health. Approximately the same proportion of men as women received these services. A third of those residents living alone used these services (mainly maid service). Very few (6 per cent) of those residents living with a spouse used a maid or homemaker service. Of course, residents living with spouses tended to be younger, and more likely to live in self-contained than hostel accommodation.

Of the residents who chose not to use an available homemaking service, few gave reasons; those who did usually said they had family or friends who helped them. A number of shortcomings were mentioned by users of such a service: four residents said it did not leave enough work for them to do; two residents said it was too infrequent; two said it was too expensive; and one complained about having to leave while the room was being cleaned.

Meals

As Table 40 indicates, 22 per cent of the residents said they had difficulty cooking hot meals; but most of these residents were in hostel
developments where a dining room was available. Altogether, 75 per cent
of the residents of hostel and mixed developments said they had difficulty
cooking, compared with 7 per cent of those in self-contained developments.
All of the residents in hostel accommodation (37 per cent of the sample)
said they used an on-site cafeteria or dining room.

As to why the dining room was not used when available, the nine residents
(of self-contained units in mixed accommodation mainly) who commented
gave the following reasons: disliking the atmosphere; needing a special
diet; eating in restaurants; and having friends cook for them. Of the
27 users who mentioned shortcomings of the service, approximately 20 per
cent said they did not like the food. Other complaints were overly
regimented dining-room hours, too small portions of food, insufficient
dining-room staff, lack of provisions for special diets, and over-crowding.

A meals-on-wheels service was used regularly by only 1 per cent (four
residents), although some used it occasionally. Since 6 per cent of the
apartment dwellers said that they had difficulty cooking, this indicates
a possible service need. Many of those who said they had difficulty
cooking said they had not heard about a meals-on-wheels service; so either
there was none available or it needed more publicity. Users' complaints
about meals-on-wheels were that meals were too expensive and the service
was available only on weekdays.

Shopping

As indicated in Table 40, 35 per cent of the residents said they had
difficulty shopping in winter. Of the group who reported difficulty, 54
per cent were hostel residents (who actually had no need to do regular
food shopping). Looking at it another way, 59 per cent of the hostel
residents - compared with 26 per cent of the apartment dwellers - said
they had difficulty shopping in winter. The apartment dwellers were
especially eager for improved shopping services since they had to obtain
food supplies regularly.

When asked about assistance with shopping, the most frequently mentioned
sources of help were friends and relatives, followed by grocery store
delivery services (used intensively in four developments). Only an
extremely small number of residents said they received help from staff
(mainly in one development) and a few were assisted by a specially
designed shopping service (all residents of one Ontario development).
Residents with limited physical ability and those with children in the
area were more likely to receive help with shopping from friends and
relatives, whereas residents living alone were slightly more likely to
use a store delivery service.

Reasons for not using shopping assistance were given by only seven
residents – all of whom complained that it (presumably a store delivery
service or outside homemaker service) was too expensive. Other reasons
were irregular service, poor health, and owning a car. Only a few (seven)
users offered definite complaints about shopping services (usually store
delivery). They felt the service was too expensive, inconvenient, too
infrequent, or did not cover a sufficiently wide variety of goods.

Financial and Legal Affairs

Residents were asked a general question about their personal affairs,
designed to explore difficulty with banking, bill payment, or legal matters.
In response, 32 per cent of the sample reported problems. Many of this
group, however, (14 per cent of the sample) were being helped by family
and friends; 3 per cent were using other sources of assistance, mainly
development staff and local senior citizens organizations. Fifteen per
cent of the residents were encountering problems with financial and
legal affairs but receiving no assistance. Thus, even if the present
sources of assistance are entirely satisfactory – which cannot be taken
for granted – there is still a clear need for more help. Of the sample,
61 per cent reported no difficulty or did not answer.

Social Contact Services

Social contact services tend to vary in concept and method of operation,
but generally their objective is to maintain periodic checks on old
people in order to ascertain whether or not they need some form of help
(because of illness); or they may simply offer friendship to help with
feelings of loneliness and isolation.

Probably the most valuable and appropriate way of keeping up-to-date on
the physiological and psychological condition of residents is for development staff to maintain continual contact. However, in cases where this is
not provided – or only provided as a supplement – other forms of social
contact are used. These include friendly visiting, buddy systems and
telephone contact services.

Friendly visiting was described as "volunteers visiting residents." As
Table 41 indicates, 14 per cent of the residents said they received this
service – although use was mainly concentrated in four developments (in
most developments, residents said they did not know anything about the
service). Only 5 per cent said a friendly visiting service was available
that they did not use.

Altogether, only nine residents gave reasons for not using a friendly
visiting service when such was available, e.g.: they had family to visit
them, the service was restricted to hostel residents, visits were only made
to members of the sponsoring organization, they did not like the people
who ran the service, they did not need it, or they were too busy. Of those
who were being visited, eight of the 10 residents who had complaints simply
indicated that the service was too infrequent.

350

TABLE 41

SOCIAL SERVICES*

	Resident Says Not Available	Available And Used	Available And Not Used	No Answer	TOTAL
Friendly Visiting Service	238 78.5%	42 13.9%	14 4.6%	9 3.0%	303 100%
Buddy System	218 71.9%	44 14.5%	37 12.2%	4 1.3%	303 100%
Telephone Contact Service	288 95.0%	2 .7%	5 1.7%	8 2.6%	303 100%
Volunteer Trans- portation Service	94 31.0%	45 14.9%	28 9.2%	136 44.9%	303 100%

* Questions 26, 27 and 28.

A buddy system simply involves pairing residents so that each can maintain frequent contact and see that assistance is provided to the other. Often, an adviser or monitor is given the responsibility for organizing the system and ensuring that it works. As Table 41 shows, a buddy system was used by 15 per cent of the residents. The practice of having a buddy system was concentrated in five developments, where it was used by 20 to 37 per cent of the residents; in two others, it was used by 15 to 20 per cent of the residents; and in four other developments it was used only slightly. According to the respondents, no development had over half of its residents involved in a buddy system.

The 12 per cent of residents who chose not to participate in buddy systems when they were available usually simply indicated that they kept in touch with their own friends on an informal basis. Others said that the buddy system was only for singles whereas they lived with a spouse or friend, the system did not work well because of lack of cooperation, or the service was only used when a resident was sick.

In some cities there are volunteer programs that provide weekly or daily telephone calls to old people to cheer them up and inquire about their health and needs. However, as Table 41 indicates, only two residents reported participating in such a service; most others said it was not available or that it was used only by sick people.

Summary

In this chapter, service needs were uncovered in relation to housework, cooking, shopping, financial and legal affairs, and social contact. A significant proportion of the residents of self-contained developments who were having problems with housework were not receiving assistance.

Residents of self-contained apartments also needed a meal service; many residents were encountering problems with shopping in the winter months; 15 per cent of the sample needed help with financial and legal affairs but were not receiving it. Social contact services such as friendly visiting and buddy systems appeared to be underdeveloped in practically all developments.

As far as nursing was concerned, 72 per cent of the residents considered that they needed assistance and 70 per cent were receiving it. A large proportion of those receiving nursing obtained it from development staff, followed by the Victorian Order of Nurses and the local public health service.

CHAPTER 7

FACILITIES AND RECREATION

The recreation facilities in or near the developments varied greatly,
ranging from a small lounge to elaborate facilities such as games rooms,
bowling alleys, refreshment bars, swimming pools, saunas and elaborate
outdoor areas. Generally, the larger the development, the more recreation facilities. The type of accommodation also had a bearing on the
provision of such facilities, more being provided for hostel residents.

Central Community or Recreation Room

Every development had some type of central community or recreation room.
In some, it was merely the largest of a number of lounges and club rooms,
while in others it was the only indoor meeting place available in the
development. As Table 42 indicates, a central community room was used
by 62 per cent of the residents. Another 5 per cent were unaware that
such a room was available (despite the fact that each development had
one), and 32 per cent said that they never used it. As the table indicates,
the proportion of residents using a central community room was similar
in both self-contained and hostel developments.

Table 43 shows how residents used their central community rooms. The
most frequently mentioned use of such a room was for special programs
such as sing-songs, birthday parties, concerts, and teas; this was
mentioned by 49 per cent of the sample. It appears that a number of
developments lacked regular programs using their central room. The
second most popular activity - mentioned by 35 per cent of the residents -
appeared to be informal sitting, perhaps to read a newspaper or chat
with friends.

Card games were the most popular of the more specific central room
activities and were mentioned by 28 per cent of the residents. It
should also be noted that in 10 of the 19 developments a separate card
room existed which was often used extensively (for example, in five developments, 67 per cent or more of the residents used the card room). In short,
card playing was a very popular activity with the fairly healthy, and all-
in-all 45 per cent of the persons in the sample played cards either in a
central community room or a card room. Persons with moderate and serious
physical disabilities were less likely to engage in table games of any sort.

Only 8 per cent of the residents watched television in the community room
(although in one development 67 per cent did - probably this indicates
a lack of TV sets in residents' rooms); few residents watched TV in any
special TV room. In eight self-contained developments there was no central
room with television but in the other developments a separate lounge was
often set aside for television.

353

354

TABLE 42

USE OF CENTRAL COMMUNITY/RECREATION ROOM*, BY DEVELOPMENT TYPE

	Available And Use	Available And Do Not Use	Resident Says Not Available	No Answer	TOTAL
Self-Contained Developments	76 65.5%	40 34.5%	0 0%	0 0%	116 100%
Hostel and Mixed Developments	112 59.9%	57 30.5%	14 7.5%	4 2.1%	187 100%
ALL DEVELOPMENTS	188 62.0%	97 32.0%	14 4.6%	4 1.3%	303 100%

* Question 31.

TABLE 43

ACTIVITIES IN CENTRAL COMMUNITY/RECREATION ROOM*

Activities	Number of Residents Participating[1]	Per Cent of Sample
Special Programs	149	49.2
Informal Sitting	105	34.7
Card Games	85	28.1
Games (bingo and darts)	29	9.6
Television Listening	22	7.3
Church Group Activities	18	5.9
Piano and Sing-Songs	10	3.3
Special Teas	7	2.3
Movies	4	1.3
Birthday Parties	3	1.0
Don't Use	97	32.0
Not Available (according to resident)	14	4.6
No Answer	4	1.3

* Question 31.

1 299 residents responded to this question. Of these, 188 said that they had a central community/recreation room available and used it. They mentioned participation in a total of 432 activities.

The main reason residents gave for not watching television together was that they had their own set. Other reasons were: "don't like television", "too noisy", "no time", "poor eyesight", and "don't like the people who watch it." Only two of the users had complaints about the television watching: one said that the room was not homey and the other complained about poor programs.

The ways in which residents used the central community room were: games - especially bingo and darts - (10 per cent), church activities (6 per cent), piano playing and sing-songs (3 per cent), special teas (2 per cent), movies (1 per cent), and birthday parties (1 per cent).

Table 44 shows the reasons given by the 32 per cent who chose not to participate in community or recreation room programs. The most frequent reason given - by 9 per cent of the sample - was that they disliked the other persons involved. Other reasons mentioned included poor health (6 per cent), lack of interest or a preference to be alone (5 per cent), use of own sitting room instead (4 per cent), use of the floor lounge instead (1 per cent), preference for doing things with family (1 per cent). One person claimed to be discouraged by staff from using the facility.

TABLE 44

REASONS FOR NOT USING AVAILABLE CENTRAL COMMUNITY/RECREATION ROOM*

	Number[1]	Per Cent of Sample
Don't like the people	28	9.2
Poor health	18	5.9
Not interested, prefer to be alone	15	5.0
Have own sitting room	12	4.0
Use floor lounge instead	3	1.0
Do other things with family, etc.	3	1.0
Discouraged by staff	1	.3
No reasons given	20	6.6

* Question 31.

1 Some residents gave more than one reason. There were 97 non-users.

Bingo

Bingo is an activity which seems to be popular with a wide cross-section of the elderly. Many of the developments sponsored bingo games once or twice a week. As Table 45 shows, 47 per cent of the sample played bingo in or near the development; 44 per cent said it was available but they did not play. Only 8 per cent said that it was not available. Interest in bingo varied a good deal between developments; in one hostel as many as 93 per cent participated and in four other hostels 75 per cent participated. Residents living alone without children in the area were more likely to play bingo than those with children in the area. Those with no health problems were slightly less likely to play than those with health problems, the more active and mobile residents preferring other activities.

When the 46 per cent who did not play bingo were asked why, most (26 per cent of the sample) simply said they did not like the game, and 7 per cent mentioned poor health. A few residents said: "don't have the time," "don't like the people", or "don't like to go out at night." Very few users had complaints about the bingo games, but those who did said: "too many people", "too long to sit", "should have more often", "not many play", or "no loud noise allowed."

TABLE 45

RECREATION IN OR NEAR THE DEVELOPMENT*

	Available And Use	Available And Do Not Use	Not Available	No Answer	TOTAL
Bingo	142 46.9%	134 44.2%	25 8.3%	2 .7%	303 100%
Card and Other Table Games	135 44.6%	155 51.2%	10 3.3%	3 1.0%	303 100%
Floor Games	38 12.5%	84 27.7%	179 59.1%	2 .7%	303 100%
Movies	135 44.6%	71 23.4%	95 31.4%	2 .7%	303 100%
Library (reading room or book mobile)	130 42.9%	94 31.0%	78 25.7%	1 .3%	303 100%
Lawn Games	11 3.6%	33 10.9%	257 84.8%	2 .7%	303 100%
Gardening	50 16.5%	31 10.2%	220 72.6%	2 .7%	303 100%
Senior Citizens Centre	93 30.7%	140 46.2%	67 22.1%	3 1.0%	303 100%

* Questions 29, 32, 35, 36, 37, 38, 39 and 41.

Floor Games

Recreation specialists claim that floor games can be very beneficial to the aged by providing exercize and keeping them fit and it is claimed that many old people enjoy games such as shuffleboard and carpet bowling. Unfortunately - as Table 45 shows - only 13 per cent of our sample were involved in these types of activities in or near their development. Another 28 per cent said that such activities were available but did not use them. Only at one development - located in Quebec - did residents engage in floor games to a great extent.

The main reason given by the 28 per cent who did not participate in floor games was inability to stand up for lengthy periods (mentioned by 13 per cent of the sample); 8 per cent said they simply did not enjoy floor games. Other reasons were: "usually for men only", "cliques", "too busy", "too difficult to climb stairs", and "never played." Of those who played floor games, only eight residents had complaints such as "only available in the summer", "outdoors only", "difficult to find a player", or "restricted schedule."

Movies

Table 45 indicates that, although 68 per cent said films were shown in or near their development, only 45 per cent attended and the other 23 per cent did not care to. In five hostel developments there was no opportunity to see movies; this largely accounted for the 31 per cent who said films were not available. Attendance appeared to differ little by age or health capacity.

Most of the 23 per cent of residents who did not attend movies, even if available, said they simply did not care for films (9 per cent of the sample). Two other major reasons were "physical handicap", and "other things to do." Less frequently mentioned were "like to be alone", "too long to sit", "saw most of them", "poor selection", "none in the area", and "too expensive." Those who attended movies in their development gave mainly the following complaints when asked: "too infrequent", and "romantic movies" (presumably referring to explicit sex). Other complaints were "poor equipment", and "too long to sit."

Library

As Table 45 indicates, 43 per cent of the sample used a library, reading room or bookmobile; 31 per cent said such facilities were available in or near their development but they did not use them, and 26 per cent said no library facilities were available. Most of the latter group lived in five developments (in three small-town ones, and in a suburban and a downtown metropolitan area). Residents under 75 years tended to use library facilities more than older residents; this is probably because the older residents' sight was poorer. Also, those with only slight health problems used library facilities more than those with moderately or seriously limited abilities.

The 31 per cent who did not use an available library service advanced
two main reasons: "don't read much because of eye problems" (16 per
cent of the sample), and "use other sources" (12 per cent). A few
residents mentioned: "no time for reading", "prefer not to use it",
"can't read", and "read periodicals only." Very few of the users had
complaints but the main ones were "books are poor and old", "need more
periodicals", "too small", and "not available very often."

Lawn Games

The residents were asked if there were any golf, putting, or lawn
bowling facilities in or near their development. In only three developments did a sizeable proportion of residents say this sort of facility
was available, and in two of the three almost no one used it.

Table 45 shows that only 4 per cent of the residents said they engaged
in lawn games, 11 per cent said the facilities were available but they
did not use them, and 85 per cent said there were no lawn games available.

The main reason given by the 11 per cent who did not participate in
lawn games, if available, was "poor health", followed by "don't like
golf." No specific shortcomings were mentioned by the few who participated
in lawn games.

Gardening

Gardens or greenhouses are appreciated by many people, either as places
to watch the impact of changing seasons and the beauty of growing things
or simply as a stimulus to physical activity. But - as Table 45 indicates -
only 17 per cent of the residents said there were special garden plots or
a greenhouse where they could garden. Another 10 per cent said gardening
was available but they did not do it, and 73 per cent said gardening was
not available.

The major reason given by the 10 per cent who did not use garden plots
or greenhouses when available was "poor health" (5 per cent of the sample).
Other reasons mentioned were: "don't like gardening", and "there is a
gardener." Only four persons who gardened mentioned shortcomings and
these included: "too small", "not enough room to plant", and "a problem
if you go away."

Senior Citizens Centres

In recent years there has been a growth in the number of drop-in centres
running daytime and evening programs for senior citizens. Their programs
vary enormously in scope, ranging from part-time efforts run by a voluntary
group or the senior citizens themselves, to large multi-service centres
run by public recreation or social service agencies. They provide a
place where old people can meet, feel at home, participate actively in
programs, or watch entertainment. As Table 45 indicates, 78 per cent of

the sample had some form of senior citizens centre or golden age club
close to their development, but only 31 per cent participated in programs.
Residents living in self-contained accommodation were more than twice as
likely to participate as those in hostel accommodation (48 per cent versus
20 per cent). Residents living alone did not tend to participate more
than those living with a spouse. Participation varied with health: of
those residents who said they had a senior citizens centre available,
only 22 per cent of those with seriously or moderately limited ability
used it - compared with 44 per cent of those with slightly limited
ability or no incapacity.

The 46 per cent who did not use an available senior citizens centre
mentioned mainly that there was a waiting list (22 per cent of the
sample). Other reasons given were: "don't like the people there",
"health too poor", "don't enjoy the activities", "too busy with other
things", "too far to get to", "generally don't like", and "club not
active enough."

Laundry

Some type of laundry facility existed in all developments (despite the
fact that 1 per cent of the residents said none was available). As Table
46 indicates, a laundry was used by an extremely large proportion of
residents (83 per cent). Only 16 per cent chose not to use a laundry
they knew was available. Furthermore, only in two hostel developments
was the laundry used by fewer than 75 per cent of the residents. Reasons
for choosing not to use a laundry facility included: "friends do laundry",
"prefer to wash everything by hand", "send laundry out", "don't like to
do laundry", "laundry in the building is no good." The users' major
complaint - and one mentioned in many developments - was that the machines
were frequently broken. Also mentioned were: "coin operated", "inconvenient
schedule", "no dryer", "don't know how to use it", and "no outside clothes-
line."

Beauty Parlor and Barber Shop

As Table 46 shows, hairdressing was available in the development for 68
per cent of the residents. However, only 39 per cent made use of it. As
one would expect, both the availability and use of a hairdressing service
was much greater in hostel developments than in self-contained ones.

Although one might suppose that handicapped persons would make more use
of such a service, our responses indicated that this group actually used
the service least. Indeed, when a beauty parlor or barber shop was
available, only a small proportion of the people with serious health problems
used it. Reasons mentioned for not using it were: "do own hair", or "go
to another shop", and (in a few cases) "too expensive."

TABLE 46

USE OF DEVELOPMENT FACILITIES*

	Available And Use	Available And Do Not Use	Not Available	No Answer	TOTAL
Laundry	250 82.5%	47 15.5%	4 1.3%	2 .7%	303 100%
Beauty/Barber Shop	119 39.3%	87 28.7%	96 31.7%	1 .3%	303 100%
Tuck Shop/Canteen	164 54.1%	28 9.2%	109 36.0%	2 .7%	303 100%
Coffee Shop	69 22.8%	42 13.9%	188 62.0%	4 1.3%	303 100%
Guest Room	4 1.3%	2 .7%	293 96.7%	4 1.3%	303 100%

*   Questions 30, 34, 40 and 42.

Tuck Shop or Canteen

Table 46 indicates that 63 per cent of the residents said a tuck shop or canteen existed in their development, and most (54 per cent) used it when available.

Reasons for not using the shop or canteen were given by only a few residents. These included: "go downtown", "hard to get to", "use other shops around here", "too expensive", "don't like it", or "family shops for me." Very few users had complaints such as: "more expensive than other stores" (2 per cent of the sample), "limited selection", and "volunteers don't show up."

Coffee Shop

Almost two-thirds of the developments lacked a place where residents could purchase tea, coffee or a snack, although all the hostel developments had dining rooms and many served light refreshments during the day. As Table 46 indicates, 23 per cent of the residents said that a coffee shop was available and they used it, and 14 per cent did not choose to use an available one. There was no clear pattern of use related to age or physical capacity.

361

The most common reason given for not using an available coffee shop was that the resident preferred to get snacks in his own room. Other reasons mentioned were: "only for hostel residents", "too expensive", "don't like the atmosphere", "go to restaurants", "don't eat between meals", and "too busy."

Guest Room

In some developments for old people, a special room is set aside for use by temporary guests or relatives who are nursing a resident over an illness. However, in practically all the developments in our case studies no guest room was apparently available. Only six users (2 per cent) said one was available, and four persons had made use of it. Either there was an information gap or a misunderstanding about the use of this facility - since in the few developments where a guest room did appear to be available most residents knew nothing about it.

Summary

Every development had some type of central community or recreation room and 62 per cent of the residents used this facility; there was slightly more use in self-contained than in hostel and mixed developments. Such a facility was not used much for regular recreation programs; residents mainly used the room for special occasions, followed by other informal activities such as reading, chatting with friends, or playing cards.

Bingo was the most popular of the more specific recreational activities, followed by cards, other table games, and movies. Few residents engaged in floor games or lawn games outside the development, despite the beneficial exercise. Seventy-eight per cent of the sample had a senior citizens or golden age club close to their development but only 31 per cent participated in programs there. Residents in self-contained accommodation were more than twice as likely to participate as those in hostel accommodation. The principal barriers to participation were waiting lists and health problems. Libraries and bookmobiles were used considerably. Laundries and shop canteens received very heavy use, when available. On the other hand, beauty shops, barber shops, and coffee shops, were used only moderately.

CHAPTER 8

SATISFACTION

The central aim of any user study is to determine the adequacy of a
product or service from the point of view of the consumer. Thus, the
essence of this study is the residents' perceptions and feelings about
how the environment they were living in met their own particular needs.

Residents were asked questions about their satisfaction with general
life in the development and with various specific features. Residents'
responses were supplemented by interviewers' impressions and assessments
of respondents' satisfaction.

This chapter will first present residents' general evaluations, followed
by their views on specific features of their housing environment.

General Satisfaction

Table 47 shows that when asked, "In general, are you satisfied with
living here?", 90 per cent of the sample replied that they were (61 per
cent were "very satisfied" and 29 per cent "satisfied"). Only 6 per cent
were not satisfied (17 persons were "not satisfied" and one person was
"very dissatisfied"); 4 per cent (12 persons) were ambiguous or had no
opinion.

TABLE 47

GENERAL SATISFACTION WITH DEVELOPMENT*, BY AGE

	Very Satisfied	Satisfied	Ambiguous/ No Opinion	Not Satisfied	Very Disatisfied	No Answer	TOTAL
Under 70 years	43 67.2%	18 28.1%	0 0%	2 3.1%	1 1.6%	0 0%	64 100%
70-74 years	35 62.5%	18 32.1%	2 3.6%	1 1.8%	0 0%	0 0%	56 100%
75-79 years	43 58.9%	20 27.4%	3 4.1%	7 9.6%	0 0%	0 0%	73 100%
80 years and over	64 58.2%	31 28.2%	7 6.4%	7 6.4%	0 0%	1 .9%	110 100%
TOTAL	185 61.1%	87 28.7%	12 4.0%	17 5.6%	1 .3%	1 .3%	303 100%

* Question 49.

363

Residents' satisfaction varied considerably in individual developments; as few as 8 per cent were very satisfied in one development and as many as 84 per cent in another. Differences in satisfaction did not appear to be related to the type of development (self-contained or hostel and mixed), type of sponsor (public or non-profit), or development size. Nor did general satisfaction appear to be related to satisfaction with particular features. For example, many residents who expressed considerable dissatisfaction with the location of one downtown development gave the same development an above-average rating for general satisfaction; on the contrary, residents of another downtown development in the same city did just the opposite - they approved of the location but were generally dissatisfied with the development.

General satisfaction was, however, related to age and health. As Table 47 indicates, when compared with those under 75 years, residents aged 75 and over were slightly less likely to be very satisfied and more likely to be not satisfied. Furthermore, as Table 48 shows, residents with no physical incapacity were most likely to be satisfied or very satisfied (96 per cent of the sample) - followed by residents with slightly limited ability (89 per cent), moderately limited ability (81 per cent), and seriously limited ability (73 per cent). The one respondent who reported being very dissatisfied was under 70 and seriously disabled.

TABLE 48

GENERAL SATISFACTION WITH DEVELOPMENT*, BY HEALTH CAPACITY

	Very Satisfied	Satisfied	Ambiguous/ No Opinion	Dissatis- fied	Very Dis- satisfied	No Answer	TOTAL
Seriously Limited Ability	10 66.7%	1 6.7%	1 6.7%	1 6.7%	1 6.7%	1 6.7%	15 100%
Moderately Limited Ability	26 49.1%	17 32.1%	6 11.3%	4 7.5%	0 0%	0 0%	53 100%
Slightly Limited Ability	63 58.3%	33 30.6%	4 3.7%	8 7.4%	0 0%	0 0%	108 100%
No Incapacity	86 67.7%	36 28.3%	1 .8%	4 3.1%	0 0%	0 0%	127 100%
TOTAL	185 61.1%	87 28.7%	12 4.0%	17 5.6%	1 .3%	1 .3%	303 100%

* Question 49.

The finding that 90 per cent of the residents of NHA housing for the elderly were generally satisfied with their residential environment (and 61 per cent were very satisfied) might be treated with skepticism - perhaps residents said they were satisfied in order to meet what they felt were interviewers' expectations, or to defend their own wisdom in entering such housing. Such possibilities must be admitted; however, it was made very clear that the interviewers were not involved with the development administration when residents were assured about confidentiality. Furthermore, in some developments a considerable proportion of residents failed to indicate strong satisfaction (only 8 per cent were very satisfied in one development and only 27, 33, and 39 per cent in others); this suggests that not all residents felt that they had to express great enthusiasm about where they lived. In three Quebec developments a very high proportion of residents were very satisfied (80, 84, and 93 per cent); this certainly skewed the aggregated "very satisfied" responses upwards.

As a further check on residents' feelings of general satisfaction, interviewers were asked to assess, at the end of each interview, whether the respondent seemed fairly happy or satisfied with the development, or whether criticism or dissatisfaction was evident. As Table 49 shows, the interviewers' impressions seem to confirm that the majority of residents were generally very satisfied, and that although many had specific complaints, few found the environment intolerable. The interviewers reported that 74 per cent of the residents appeared satisfied, 23 per cent had some criticism, and only 3 per cent appeared dissatisfied.

TABLE 49

INTERVIEWER'S IMPRESSION OF RESIDENT'S GENERAL SATISFACTION*, BY DEVELOPMENT TYPE

	Satisfied	Some Criticism	Dissatisfied	No Answer	TOTAL
Self-Contained Developments	83 71.6%	28 24.1%	4 3.4%	1 .9%	116 100%
Hostel and Mixed Developments	141 75.4%	41 21.9%	4 2.1%	1 .5%	187 100%
ALL DEVELOPMENTS	224 73.9%	69 22.8%	8 2.6%	2 .7%	303 100%

* Interviewer Impression 6.

Table 49 also shows that, according to the interviewers' assessment, residents' satisfaction did not vary greatly with type of development (although residents of hostels appeared slightly more satisfied and less critical than residents of self-contained developments). As Table 50 shows, satisfaction appeared to be related more to sponsor type: a lower proportion (69 per cent) of public housing residents appeared satisfied, compared with those living in non-profit accommodation (77 per cent); conversely, slightly more public housing residents appeared critical or dissatisfied. The variation in these figures is not, however, sufficient to justify any assumptions about public housing being a less appropriate way to meet the needs of old people than developments sponsored by non-profit groups - especially since the residents' own responses on general satisfaction do not suggest that satisfaction is related to either development or sponsor type.

TABLE 50

INTERVIEWER'S IMPRESSION OF RESIDENT'S GENERAL SATISFACTION*, BY PUBLIC AND NON-PROFIT DEVELOPMENTS

	Satisfied	Some Criticism	Dissatisfied	No Answer	TOTAL
Public Housing	76 / 69.1%	28 / 25.5%	5 / 4.5%	1 / .9%	110 / 100%
Non-Profit	148 / 76.7%	41 / 21.2%	3 / 1.6%	1 / .5%	193 / 100%
ALL DEVELOPMENTS	224 / 73.9%	69 / 22.8%	8 / 2.6%	2 / .7%	303 / 100%

* Interviewer Impression 6.

Reasons for Satisfaction

Residents were asked to give reasons for their general satisfaction (or dissatisfaction) with their housing development. As Table 51 indicates, good design features were one of the two most frequent reasons given: 21 per cent of the sample mentioned design. Layout, furnishings, balconies, size, and elevator arrangements were the features most often commented on. Also, 21 per cent of the residents liked the privacy and independence that the building afforded them - privacy in the sense of having their own room, dwelling unit, or bath, and independence in the sense of being their own boss, able to come and go as they pleased. The next most frequently mentioned reason for satisfaction had to do with

social factors: 18 per cent of the residents liked the friendly
atmosphere, ease in meeting others and making friends, or availability
of people of their own age. Convenient location was mentioned by 12
per cent of the residents. Other reasons mentioned, in descending
order, were: adequate security (8 per cent); health care and other
services (7 per cent); good staff (6 per cent); good meals (5 per cent);
maintenance (5 per cent); the available recreation activities (5 per
cent); reasonable rent (3 per cent); the apartment being easy to maintain
(2 per cent); and the accommodation being the only option available (2
per cent).

TABLE 51

REASONS FOR SATISFACTION WITH DEVELOPMENT*

	Number[1]	Per Cent Of Sample[2]
Good design features (layout, balconies, furnishings, elevators, size, etc.)	63	20.8
Privacy (own bath, no one bothers me, etc.) and independence satisfactory in this housing	63	20.8
Friendly atmosphere; easy to make and/or meet friends here; people my own age	54	17.8
Convenient location	35	11.6
Adequate security in building, including buzzer	23	7.6
Health care and other services provided	21	6.9
Good staff	18	5.9
Good meals	16	5.3
Good maintenance	16	5.3
Good selection of recreation, leisure activities, gardening	15	5.0
Reasonable rent (or best value)	10	3.3
Apartment easy to maintain	5	1.7
This housing was the only option open to me	5	1.7
No reasons given	17	5.6

* Question 50.

1 Some residents gave more than one reason. There were 272
satisfied residents.

Reasons for Dissatisfaction

After residents had given reasons for their general satisfaction or
dissatisfaction, they were asked if there were any shortcomings or
problems, and if anything could be done to make the place better for
persons like themselves. This meant that even those residents who were
generally satisfied had a chance to bring up any complaints or suggestions they might have.

Shortcomings or problems encountered were mentioned by a total of 87
per cent of the residents. As Table 52 shows, design features were the
most frequently mentioned problems or possible improvements related to
design. Most criticism concerned general design shortcomings, although
there was some mention of special design details of interest to the elderly
and handicapped. The need for more privacy was also brought up, although
in many cases it is not at all certain that this should be considered a
design issue, as opposed to management policy. It is clear that design
is important to residents. It should be noted, however, that since we
measured the frequency - not the intensity - of dissatisfaction, we cannot
assume that design bothers individual residents more than, say, factors
relating to staff, services and facilities, or social life.

The second most frequently mentioned area of concern was shortcomings
concerning management policies and staffing. This was mentioned by 21
per cent of the residents. The main management problem mentioned
concerned the need for better maintenance of the building or development,
although the need for changes in management policy and for better prepared
staff was also mentioned - which suggests the need for a staff training
program. Shortcomings in the area of services and facilities were mentioned by 17 per cent of the sample; these included a good many comments
about the need for more or better recreation. Other things mentioned -
by a very small proportion of the sample - were the need for cheaper rents
and problems about location.

Size

There has been considerable interest in the implications of large buildings
and developments for elderly residents. Therefore, the interview schedule
included a question designed to elicit the residents' views on this matter.
The question focused on the respondents' building rather than development
size, but in 15 of the 19 developments the two were synonymous.

Eighty per cent of the residents said that they were satisfied with the
size of their building; 9 per cent said it was too large. In large developments (over 150 units and/or beds), approximately 14 per cent of residents
said their building was too large (although in two particular developments
approximately 33 per cent said it was too large). In medium-sized developments (41-150 units), almost nobody said their building was too large but
one or two persons said it was too small. Most residents of small developments (40 units and under) said their building size was satisfactory,
although one or two said it was too small.

TABLE 52

REASONS FOR DISSATISFACTION WITH DEVELOPMENT*

	Number[1]	Per Cent Of Sample
- Poor general design features (bedrooms, balconies, closets, light, noise, etc.)	133	43.9
Require more special design features for handicapped (alarm system, grab rails, etc.)	16	5.3
Need elevator	9	3.0
Prefer more privacy (single rooms and private baths)	23	7.6
TOTAL DESIGN SHORTCOMINGS	181	59.7
- Need more maintenance and security staff and medical services	23	7.6
Need better physical maintenance	18	5.9
Need changes in management policies and better prepared staff to deal with residents' problems	14	4.6
Staff should prevent admission of senile residents	7	2.3
TOTAL MANAGEMENT AND STAFF SHORTCOMINGS	62	20.5
- Need more recreation services and facilities	19	6.3
Need meal services	13	4.3
Need transportation service	11	3.6
Need more facilities (tuck shop, pay phone, hairdresser, drugstore, parking, etc.)	9	3.0
TOTAL SERVICES AND FACILITIES SHORTCOMINGS	52	17.2
- Need cheaper rent	14	4.6
- Prefer another location	12	4.0
- Other	4	1.3
- No answer or no complaints	41	13.5

* Questions 51 and 52.

1 The 262 residents who responded to this question gave a total of 325 reasons for dissatisfaction.

There was a surprising lack of strong negative feelings toward large buildings. Indeed, the residents of large developments appeared to be as satisfied with the size of their building as those in medium-sized developments - and more satisfied than those in small developments. This is further supported by the responses to the question about general satisfaction with living in the development: 65 per cent of the residents in large developments said they were very satisfied, compared with 64 per cent of those in medium-sized developments and only 26 per cent of those in small developments.

Development size did not appear to be related to satisfaction with privacy. Of the residents in large developments, 87 per cent were satisfied with privacy; 90 per cent of those in medium sized developments were satisfied; 85 per cent of those in small developments were satisfied.

The residents of large developments appeared to be more active in outside community life than the residents in medium or small developments. Among the residents of large developments, 53 per cent said they got out daily for an hour or more - compared with 37 per cent in medium developments and 37 per cent in small ones. Furthermore, residents in large developments were more likely to visit friends outside the development weekly - 42 per cent compared with 40 per cent of those in medium-sized developments and 37 per cent of those in small developments. Of the residents in large and medium-sized developments, 20 per cent participated at least weekly in a community activity, compared with 15 per cent in the small developments. One should, however, bear in mind that hostel accommodation was heavily concentrated in medium-sized developments and thus the rate of participation outside the development would tend also to be affected by factors such as advanced age and poorer health (found more among hostel residents).

Although residents of larger developments were more socially active in the outside community, they appeared to be less active in socializing within their own development. Social interaction within a development tended to decrease with greater development size. In small developments, 70 per cent of the residents visited friends in the development at least once a week - compared with 79 per cent of those in medium-sized developments and 55 per cent of those in large developments. Residents of medium-sized developments were more likely to have made many friends in the development than residents in large and small developments. In medium-sized developments, 61 per cent of the residents had made many friends - compared with 28 per cent of those in large developments and 26 per cent of those in small ones. Besides the heavy representation of hostel accommodation in medium-sized developments referred to previously, it should be noted that small developments were considerably under-represented in our sample. Nevertheless, large and medium-sized developments were sufficiently represented to permit one to draw tentative conclusions about the implications of development size for residents.

High-Rise Buildings

Residents were asked a question designed to elicit their feelings about high-rise buildings for the elderly. Table 53 shows the proportion of residents who agreed with four statements about high-rises. Forty-four and 36 per cent of the residents agreed with the two unfavorable statements about high-rises; but at the same time 33 per cent and 36 per cent of the residents agreed with the two favorable statements about high-rises. In short, the sample as a whole was neither very opposed to nor very in favor of high-rises.

TABLE 53

OPINIONS ABOUT HIGH-RISE[1] BUILDINGS*

	Residents in Agreement		
	High-Rise Residents	Low-Rise Residents	TOTAL
High-rise buildings are unsatisfactory places for senior citizens to live	59 30.4%	73 67.0%	132 43.6%
Most senior citizens prefer not to live in high-rise buildings	42 21.6%	68 62.4%	110 36.3%
High-rise buildings have many advantages for senior citizens	87 44.8%	13 12.0%	100 33.0%
High-rise buildings are ideal places for senior citizens to live	105 54.1%	5 4.6%	110 36.3%
TOTAL[2]	194 100%	109 100%	303 100%

* Question 55.

1 Developments in which one building exceeded three floors in height were classed as "high-rise".

2 Total percentages are greater than 100 because some residents agreed with more than one item.

Interestingly, the responses of residents living in high-rise buildings and residents living in low-rise buildings differed considerably. Table 53 shows that high-rise dwellers were much less likely than low-rise dwellers to agree with the two unfavorable statements about high-rises and, conversely, they were much more likely to agree with the two favorable statements. The proportions of high-rise dwellers in agreement with the two unfavorable statements were 30 per cent and 22 per cent - compared with 67 per cent and 62 per cent of the low-rise dwellers. The proportions of high-rise dwellers in agreement with the two favorable statements were 45 per cent and 54 per cent - compared with only 12 per cent and 5 per cent of the low-rise dwellers. This, of course, is a striking illustration of how experience affects perceptions and evaluations of a housing environment.

Residents were asked what they thought were the advantages or disadvantages of high-rise living. Over 33 per cent said there were no advantages or gave no answer. Among the advantages most often mentioned were: "a good view", "more and better maintenance services", "less noise", "fresh air", "more privacy", and "the building can be more centrally located because it uses up less land." Two main disadvantages were mentioned: many old people fear heights and thus do not care to live high off the ground (17 per cent of the sample); poor elevator service in high-rises forces residents to climb stairs (17 per cent). A few mentioned the danger of fire and difficulties for firemen; even fewer said high-rises produce claustrophobic feelings and make access to outdoors difficult.

Development Staff

Satisfaction with staff tended to be high in most developments. Residents were asked specifically whether or not staff treated residents with respect and 94 per cent said "yes." However, many residents complained that their developments had an insufficient number of staff. As Table 54 indicates, only 66 per cent of the residents said they were completely satisfied with the number of staff, 15 per cent were somewhat satisfied, and 13 per cent were dissatisfied. A considerably larger proportion of the residents in self-contained developments than in the hostel and mixed developments were dissatisfied with the number of staff (18 per cent compared with 10 per cent). This is probably because self-contained developments do not always have staff available on a 24-hour basis. In one or two large hostel developments a very high proportion of residents believed the number of staff to be insufficient.

Some residents mentioned the type of staff they felt the development lacked. Nursing staff was the most often mentioned (by 4 per cent of the sample), followed by dining-room and kitchen staff and night-duty staff.

Rules Regarding Pets

Pets are important to many persons; they can provide companionship for the lonely or simply add a little variety to a person's life. Many homes for the elderly have rules against keeping pets. Seventy per cent of the residents interviewed said their development did not permit any pets and

27 per cent said they could keep only birds or fish. These restrictions did not bother 77 per cent of the residents; 4 per cent were bothered "a little", 7 per cent "somewhat", and 3 per cent "very much."

TABLE 54

SATISFACTION WITH NUMBER OF STAFF*, BY DEVELOPMENT TYPE

	Satisfied	Somewhat Satisfied	Dissatisfied	No Answer	TOTAL
Self-Contained Developments	80 69.0%	12 10.3%	21 18.1%	3 2.6%	116 100%
Hostel and Mixed Developments	119 63.6%	32 17.1%	19 10.2%	17 9.1%	187 100%
ALL DEVELOPMENTS	199 65.7%	44 14.5%	40 13.2%	20 6.6%	303 100%

* Question 61.

Furniture

Whether accommodation is formal and institutional or warm and homey can greatly affect a person's satisfaction. Residential atmosphere is largely determined by the extent to which residents can furnish and decorate their homes with their own familiar objects. Actually, 64 per cent of the residents had brought all their furniture to their development (this indicates that a number of hostel residents also brought a lot of furniture along with them), and 4 per cent brought along at least one item of heavy furniture such as a chair, sofa or bed. Another 23 per cent brought only ornaments, curtains, or television. Some of the residents in the latter group may have experienced a somewhat institutional atmosphere.

Nearly all self-contained units were rented unfurnished. Interestingly, of the residents in self-contained apartments, 34 per cent said they would prefer their dwellings furnished and 63 per cent preferred them unfurnished. This suggests that more could be provided in the way of furniture for self-contained accommodation.

Privacy

Privacy is another important facet of a person's residential environment. Insufficient privacy can produce feelings of institutionalization; indeed, privacy tends to be minimal in highly institutionalized environments. Table 55 indicates that residents were generally satisfied with the privacy they had: 88 per cent said it was very satisfactory. However, satisfaction with privacy tended to be slightly lower in hostel and mixed developments than in self-contained ones - 91 per cent compared with 87 per cent; in fact, it is surprising that the difference was not greater than this.

TABLE 55

SATISFACTION WITH PRIVACY*, BY DEVELOPMENT TYPE

	Very Satis-factory	Somewhat Satisfactory	Unsatis-factory	No Answer	TOTAL
Self- Contained Developments	106 91.4%	8 6.9%	1 .9%	1 .9%	116 100%
Hostel and Mixed Developments	162 86.6%	14 7.5%	10 5.3%	1 .5%	187 100%
ALL DEVELOPMENTS	268 88.4%	22 7.3%	11 3.6%	2 .7%	303 100%

* Question 56.

Table 56 indicates that the main source of dissatisfaction about lack of privacy, where this existed, was due to the necessity of sharing accommodation and facilities. Altogether, 25 per cent of the residents had to share a room, toilet or bath - and 8 per cent had to share a room with someone other than a spouse or siblings. Those who were obliged to do so (mainly in hostel developments in the province of Quebec) expressed a great deal of dissatisfaction with this. A larger proportion, 14 per cent, had to share a toilet and bath or shower (in one case a number of female residents shared a bathroom located at the end of a hall). Residents complained about this type of sharing, mentioning that it was very inconvenient for elderly people with health problems.

TABLE 56

SHARING ROOMS, TOILETS AND BATHS WITH OTHER THAN SPOUSE OR SIBLINGS*, BY SEX

	Only Bath/ Shower	Toilet And Bath/ Shower	Room And Toilet And Bath/Shower	None	No Answer	TOTAL
Female	8 3.9%	30 14.6%	17 8.3%	150 72.8%	1 .5%	206 100%
Male	4 4.3%	11 11.7%	6 6.4%	73 77.7%	0 0%	94 100%
No Answer	0 0%	0 0%	0 0%	3 100%	0 0%	3 100%
TOTAL	12 4.0%	41 13.5%	23 7.6%	226 74.6%	1 .3%	303 100%

* Question 57.

Compatibility with Other Residents

Satisfaction with accommodation is often related to whether one feels comfortable and compatible with the persons who live in the building or area. Residents were extremely positive about their neighbors within the development: 92 per cent indicated that neighbors were friendly (as opposed to unfriendly); 92 per cent also said their fellow residents were of their own social type (rather than a different type). The correspondence between these two responses is interesting.

Suitability of the Development

The interviewers were asked to assess how well the development met the needs of each resident and to specify the facilities or services (or lack of them) that led to each assessment of suitability or unsuitability.

In the interviewers' opinion, approximately 67 per cent of the sample were in suitable housing, which appeared to be meeting their needs. Table 57 indicates the reasons interviewers mentioned for stating that housing seemed suitable or unsuitable. Services and facilities appeared to make the housing suitable for 31 per cent of the residents;

23 per cent of the residents appeared active and independent and therefore capable of caring for themselves; 9 per cent of the residents had
a spouse, family, or friends who probably supplied important services.
Other reasons for housing appearing suitable were that, for 4 per cent,
residents' desire for security was being met and, for 1 per cent, outside
agencies were supplementing the development's services. As for the
development appearing unsuitable, 11 per cent of the residents did not
appear to engage in sufficient social interaction with other persons;
9 per cent were not provided with adequate nursing services. Other
reasons why the housing seemed unsuitable had to do with lack of transportation to shopping and other services, the need for help with meals
and housekeeping, difficulty living in a group situation, residents
wanting the privacy of a single room, management problems, too little
physical activity, and the housing being too expensive.

TABLE 57

INTERVIEWER'S ASSESSMENT OF SUITABILITY OR NON-SUITABILITY OF DEVELOPMENT*

Housing Suitable Because:	Number of Residents	Per Cent Of Sample[1]
Resident has sufficient services and facilities supplied in the development	94	31.0
Resident is active, independent, and capable of caring for self	69	22.8
Resident has services from spouse, family or friends	27	8.9
Desire for security met by development	12	4.0
Resident has services that the development cannot meet supplied by outside agencies	3	1.0
Housing Unsuitable Because:		
Resident needs more social interaction	33	10.9
Development lacks nursing services	26	8.6
Resident needs transportation service or closer shopping	24	8.0
Resident needs homemaker or maid service	10	3.3
Resident has difficulty living in group situation	10	3.3
Resident needs meals-on-wheels or other food preparation service	9	3.0
Management problems	8	2.6
The resident would like privacy of a single room	6	2.0
Resident needs more physical activity	5	1.7
Housing is too expensive	1	0.3

* Interviewer Impression 8.

1 In 34 cases, the same resident fell into more than one category.

Possibility of Moving

Another method of assessing both the suitability of the housing and residents' satisfaction with it was to ask them if they thought the lack of services in their present accommodation would force them to move some time in the near future. As Table 58 indicates, only 11 per cent (32) of the residents thought that such a move was likely - 5 per cent (15 persons) because of lack of nursing services, and 2 per cent (seven persons) because of lack of a meal service. Other reasons given were lack of elevators (by three persons) and lack of a housekeeping or maid service (by one person). As the table indicates, residents with seriously or moderately limited ability were more likely to be thinking about moving because of lack of services than residents in better health were.

TABLE 58

REASONS FOR POSSIBLY MOVING IN NEAR FUTURE DUE TO LACK OF SERVICES*,
BY PHYSICAL CAPACITY

	No Plans To Move In Near Future	May Move Due To Lack Of Nursing Service	May Move Due To Lack Of Meal Service	May Move Due To Lack Of House-keeping Service	May Move Due To Lack Of Elevator	May Move For Other Reasons	No Answer	TOTAL
Seriously Limited Ability	11 73.3%	2 13.3%	0 0%	0 0%	1 6.7%	0 0%	1 6.7%	15 100%
Moderately Limited Abiliby	47 88.7%	3 5.7%	1 1.9%	1 1.9%	1 1.9%	1 1.9%	0 0%	53 100%[1]
Slightly Limited Ability	98 90.7%	4 3.7%	4 3.7%	0 0%	1 .9%	1 .9%	1 .9%	108 100%[1]
No Incapacity	114 89.8%	6 4.7%	2 1.6%	0 0%	0 0%	4 3.1%	1 .8%	127 100%
TOTAL	270 89.1%	15 5.0%	7 2.3%	1 .3%	3 1.0%	6 2.0%	3 1.0%	303 100%[1]

* Question 69.

1 Percentage totals more than 100 per cent as two persons indicated that they might move due to lack of both a nursing and meal service.

When residents were asked where they would likely move, the most commonly mentioned place was "another development", followed by "a residence offering hostel accommodation." Only a small proportion said they would move to a development offering nursing care; possibly this indicated that they had fears about this type of housing, even though a number of residents obviously needed such care.

Multi-Care Accommodation

Many residents expressed a need for nursing care. Therefore, residents were asked if they thought it was a good idea for housing complexes for the elderly to provide a mixture of accommodation ranging from self-contained to various types of boarding care and to full nursing care. Some studies have indicated that senior citizens who are well and ambulatory do not like the idea of living with persons who are very - or obviously - unwell. Table 59 shows, however, that the majority of residents favored the idea of multi-care accommodation: 72 per cent were in favor (35 "definitely" and 37 per cent "somewhat"); but only 17 per cent were opposed (11.6 per cent "somewhat" and 5.6 per cent "definitely").

TABLE 59

OPINION CONCERNING MULTI-CARE HOUSING COMPLEXES*, BY PHYSICAL CAPACITY

	Definitely Favor	Somewhat Favor	Don't Know	Somewhat Disfavor	Definitely Disfavor	No Answer	TOTAL
Seriously Limited Ability	13 86.7%	2 13.3%	0 0%	0 0%	0 0%	0 0%	15 100%
Moderately Limited Ability	16 30.2%	18 34.0%	11 20.8%	4 7.5%	4 7.5%	0 0%	53 100%
Slightly Limited Ability	35 32.4%	44 40.7%	11 10.2%	12 11.1%	4 3.7%	2 1.9%	108 100%
No Incapacity	41 32.3%	48 37.8%	10 7.9%	19 15.0%	9 7.1%	0 0%	127 100%
TOTAL	105 34.7%	112 37.0%	32 10.6%	35 11.6%	17 5.6%	2 .7%	303 100%

* Question 48.

Residents of both self-contained and hostel developments generally favored
the concept of multi-care accommodation, although those living in hostel
and mixed developments were slightly more likely to favor the idea and
less likely not to favor it than the residents of self-contained developments.
Sixty-eight per cent of the residents of self-contained developments were in
favor ("definitely" or "somewhat") and 24 per cent not in favor ("definitely"
or "somewhat"), compared with 74 per cent of users in hostel and mixed developments who favored the idea and 13 per cent who were against it.

The physical capacity of the residents appeared to influence their
opinion about the value of multi-care accommodation. As Table 59 shows,
87 per cent of residents with seriously limited ability were definitely
in favor of multi-care accommodation - compared with 30 to 32 per cent
of those in each of the other three health categories. Likewise, none
of the residents with seriously limited ability "somewhat" or "definitely"
disfavored multi-care housing - compared with 17 per cent of the residents
in any of the other three health categories.

Summary

On the whole, we found a high level of general satisfaction: 90 per cent
said they were either very satisfied or satisfied. Satisfaction did not
vary significantly by development type, sponsorship, or size. However,
older residents and those with various physical incapacities were less
likely to be satisfied than the sample as a whole.

The most commonly mentioned reasons for satisfaction were design features,
privacy and independence, followed by the development's friendly atmosphere and the convenience of the location. Design features were also the
most commonly mentioned shortcomings and reasons for dissatisfaction,
followed by concern about management policies and staffing, and problems
regarding services and facilities. It is clear that design is of considerable importance to residents: it was the most frequently mentioned reason
for both satisfaction and dissatisfaction. But although we know that
residents considered design important, we do not know whether they considered
it more important than other features. Indeed, of the total reasons given
for satisfaction, many more were about non-design than design features.

A number of specific matters relating to the design and management of
housing developments for the elderly were examined. Size did not emerge
as a very significant factor. Interestingly, however, compared with
residents of small developments, those living in large developments tended
to socialize more outside the development than inside. As for negative
reactions to high-rise living, these came mainly from residents who had
not lived in a high-rise. There were few complaints about development
staff, and many complaints of insufficient staff. Satisfaction with
privacy was high (88 per cent) but where accommodation and bathroom
facilities had to be shared with other residents, dissatisfaction was
frequent and intense. Most residents were in favor of the idea of multi-
care accommodation for the elderly.

PART VI

FINDINGS

FINDINGS

This part of the study draws together data presented elsewhere in the
volume and consolidates it in the form of brief statements of findings
and conclusions. In preparing the findings, account was taken of the
reliability of data generated by the different research techniques
employed - particularly where there was a duplication of information
on a particular question.

On the whole, the findings are directly related to data in the tables
and body of the text; and in most cases the appropriate page numbers
are footnoted after each statement. However, a few of the findings
represent a synthesis of data that has been subjected to some interpretation.

It should be borne in mind that for reasons of brevity it was not
possible to summarize here more than what were considered to be the
most salient findings. Also, it is hoped that readers interested in
particular questions will want to explore them in more depth by
referring to the appropriate parts of the text.

Distribution of Accommodation

1   By the end of 1970, 23,979 self-contained dwelling units and 7,906
     hostel beds had been built under the National Housing Act[1] for (and
     were occupied by) senior citizens. This accommodation was situated
     in 746 different developments.[2]

2   Five hundred and thirty housing developments had been built under NHA
     non-profit housing provisions (variously known as sections 16, 16A,
     and now section 15), and 216 developments under NHA public housing
     provisions (variously known as sections 35A, 35D, and now sections 40
     and 43).[3]

3   Canada as a whole had 13.7 dwelling units and 4.5 hostel beds (financed
     under the NHA) per thousand population aged 65 at the end of 1970.[4]

4   On a provincial basis, British Columbia had built the highest ratio of
     senior citizens dwelling units under the NHA per thousand aged popula-
     tion, followed by Manitoba, Ontario, Prince Edward Island, Nova Scotia,
     Saskatchewan, New Brunswick, Newfoundland, Quebec, and Alberta.[5] This
     ranking does not in itself necessarily indicate provincial priorities
     on building self-contained accommodation (e.g. Alberta for many years
     operated its own program without NHA assistance).

---

1   Page 39.

2   Page 40.

3   Page 40.

4   Page 39.

5   Pages 38 and 39.

5   On a provincial basis, Manitoba had built the highest ratio of senior citizens hostel beds under the NHA per thousand aged population, followed by New Brunswick, Saskatchewan, British Columbia, Nova Scotia, Prince Edward Island, Newfoundland, Quebec, Ontario, and Alberta.[6] Again this ranking represents the use made of NHA assistance programs, not necessarily provincial production of hostel accommodation.

6   By the end of 1970, Manitoba appeared to have made the most use of all NHA assistance programs for senior citizens housing, followed by British Columbia and Ontario. Alberta, Quebec, and Newfoundland had made the least claims on NHA programs to accommodate senior citizens.

7   There was a wide variation on the emphasis that provinces placed on senior citizens' hostel accommodation as opposed to self-contained dwelling units. New Brunswick had concentrated to a greater extent on hostel accommodation than other provinces, followed by Quebec, Saskatchewan, Newfoundland, Alberta, Manitoba, Nova Scotia, British Columbia, and Prince Edward Island.[7]

8   There was wide variation between provinces as far as emphasis on public housing or non-profit sponsorship was concerned. The provinces that leaned most heavily on the public housing technique were Ontario (with 92 per cent of its senior citizens developments built in the public housing sector), and Nova Scotia (58 per cent). There were an equal number of public housing and non-profit developments in New Brunswick. The provinces in which non-profit arrangements were preferred were Prince Edward Island, Quebec, Alberta (all with 100 per cent non-profit sponsorship), Manitoba (94 per cent), British Columbia (93 per cent), Saskatchewan (88 per cent), and Newfoundland (80 per cent).[8]

9   Sixty-one per cent of all senior citizens developments, a surprisingly high proportion, were located in small towns; 32 per cent were in census metropolitan areas, and 7 per cent in other major urban areas.[9]

10   On a provincial basis, Newfoundland had the highest proportion of its senior citizens developments located in census metropolitan areas (80 per cent), followed by Ontario (61 per cent), British Columbia (59 per cent), Alberta (50 per cent), Manitoba (37 per cent), New Brunswick and Saskatchewan (12 per cent), Nova Scotia (11 per cent), and Quebec (9 per cent).[10] No census metropolitan areas exist in Prince Edward Island. It should, however, be borne in mind that developments in census metropolitan areas were larger than those in other areas. The inequitable distribution of accommodation among communities of different sizes was thus not as severe as would appear.

6   Page 39.

7   Pages 38-40.

8   Pages 40 and 41.

9   Pages 44 and 45.

10   Part II, chapters 3-12.

11   Despite the amount of housing for senior citizens that had already been produced, there still appeared to be a serious shortage. In metropolitan areas, this shortage was perceived to be particularly acute as far as self-contained dwelling units were concerned; these areas also had a shortage of hostel rooms but this was perceived to be more serious in small towns than a shortage of self-contained accommodation.[11]

12   Both at the federal and provincial levels there appears to be lack of a comprehensive planning system for senior citizens accommodation which provides a range of different accommodation types and care levels to meet varying needs and to allow for adequate choice.

Legislation and Assistance Programs

13   National Housing Act provisions have, over the years, consistently favored the development of housing accommodation for the elderly by public housing rather than non-profit sponsors. In the main, it has not been possible for non-profit sponsors to obtain federal subsidies to lower rents of residents of limited means.[12]

14   A lack of federal subsidies for non-profit groups has been to some extent offset by provincial assistance programs for self-contained senior citizens accommodation; these had been enacted in all provinces except Prince Edward Island. The provinces of British Columbia, Saskatchewan, and Manitoba have provided a higher level of grant assistance to non-profit sponsors than other provinces. Alberta, until recently, operated its own program of housing accommodation for the elderly outside of the NHA and Quebec has, in recent years, operated a joint program under which the province provides 100 per cent financing to non-profit sponsors.

15   Over the years, National Housing Act provisions have been broadened to allow funding of a large range of hostel accommodation. This accommodation varies widely in and between provinces, ranging from buildings in which the only service provided other than that found in private apartments is a dining room, to accommodation that is practically identical to that found in nursing homes. This accommodation has been supported at the provincial and local levels by a wide variety of programs, usually administered by social service departments.

16   There has also been a trend recently to extend NHA mortgage assistance to commercial, public and non-profit nursing homes.

17   The level of the old age security pension and guaranteed income supplement has a great bearing on the rent-paying capacity of residents for senior citizens accommodation. As more residents become eligible for Canada Pension Plan payments, the level of these, too, will be important.

---

11   Pages 159 and 160.

12   Pages 35 and 36.

18 Municipal tax relief has been extensively used by non-profit sponsors - 82 per cent of non-profit developments have obtained some degree of municipal tax exemption.[13]

19 Rents in non-profit accommodation were considerably higher than those in public housing, and it would appear that a good deal of non-profit accommodation was priced beyond the reach of senior citizens solely dependent on the old age security pension and guaranteed income supplement.

20 Rents were higher in non-profit developments, whether self-contained or hostel, in which a high proportion of residents had physical incapacities.[14]

21 Two-thirds of non-profit sponsors were interested in building more accommodation for the elderly but most saw serious problems in their way - the main one being financing.[15]

22 Nearly one-fifth of non-profit developments had some residents receiving rent subsidies from welfare departments; these residents were mainly concentrated in hostel accommodation.[16]

23 Non-profit senior citizens housing appeared to be in a serious financial squeeze, resulting from escalation in land, building and labor costs.

Resident Characteristics

24 Senior citizens housing is predominantly occupied by women. In over half of all developments, less than one-quarter of residents were men. Hostel developments generally had a higher proportion of male residents than self-contained ones.[17]

25 In over half of the developments, the majority of residents were aged under 75 years. Residents living in self-contained accommodation tended to be younger than those in hostel and mixed developments.[18]

26 The residents of housing developments for the elderly did not, on the whole, have a high rate of physical incapacity, although there was a wide variation between developments - from some managers who reported that practically all their residents were infirm, to others who asserted that their entire population was a healthy and active one.[19]

---

13 Pages 165 and 166.

14 Page 168.

15 Page 171.

16 Page 165.

17 Page 107.

18 Page 108.

19 Pages 108-111.

27   It is estimated that at least six out of 10 residents had no physical
     disabilities which significantly hampered their activities. Three out
     of 10 had minor or moderate self-assessed incapacities (heart and cir-
     culation problems were the most commonly mentioned, followed by
     arthritis and rheumatism, eye trouble, limb disablement, and digestive
     and gastro-intestinal problems).[20] At the most, one in 10 of the
     residents were so seriously incapacitated that they required considerable
     assistance to manage daily tasks.

28   Residents with physical incapacities were concentrated in hostel develop-
     ments. Seventy-four per cent of the managers of self-contained developments
     reported that over three-quarters of their residents had no physical
     incapacities, compared with 26 per cent of the managers of mixed develop-
     ments and 15 per cent of the hostel managers.[21]

29   Many residents used health aids: 56 per cent took medication once or
     more daily, 19 per cent used a cane, brace, crutch, or artificial limb,
     11 per cent needed a special diet, and 10 per cent used a hearing aid.[22]

30   Approximately two-thirds of residents derived their income solely from the
     old age security pension and guaranteed income supplement.[23] Other resi-
     dents received additional income from savings or private pensions. The
     residents of non-profit developments were financially better off than
     those living in public housing.

31   Seventy per cent of residents were single or widowed people living on
     their own, 20 per cent were living with a spouse, and 10 per cent shared
     accommodation with another resident.[24]

32   Almost one-half of residents had no children living in the same community
     and one-third had no family members of any sort in the area that they could
     turn to for friendship or assistance.[25]

Entering Senior Citizens Housing

33   Financial advantage (especially low rent) and physical inability to main-
     tain a previous residence were the most common motivations for persons
     choosing to enter senior citizens developments. Other frequently mentioned
     reasons were the security and safety afforded by the development, the
     availability of dining room and domiciliary services, the pleasantness of
     the accommodation itself, and a desire for companionship.[26]

---

20   Pages 314 and 315.

21   Page 109.

22   Pages 315 and 316.

23   Page 113.

24   Page 303.

25   Pages 304-306.

26   Pages 319-321.

34   Entering a housing development for the elderly usually involves a number
      of special stresses for senior citizens. It was found that the propor-
      tion of residents living alone doubled on entry to developments, that
      almost one-quarter of residents had to give up homes of their own, that
      almost two-thirds were obliged to adjust to a new neighborhood, and that
      one-fifth had to settle in a new town or city.[27]

Design

35   Seventeen per cent of developments consisted of buildings of three or
      more floors, 46 per cent were apartment buildings with less than three
      floors, 24 per cent consisted of row houses, and 9 per cent were detached
      or semi-detached bungalows.[28]

36   Residents were neither strongly in favor nor very opposed to high-rise
      buildings; but those living in high-rises were less likely than other
      residents to have negative reactions to them.[29]

37   Twenty-eight per cent of developments were small (containing 20 residents
      or less), 51 per cent were medium size (containing 21 to 80 residents),
      and 21 per cent were large (containing 81 residents and over).[30]

38   On a regional basis, 45 per cent of developments in the Atlantic Provinces
      were in the small size category (20 residents or less), compared with 32
      per cent of Prairie developments, 28 per cent of Ontario developments, 19
      per cent of British Columbia developments, and 3 per cent of Quebec
      developments.[31]

39   Twenty-nine per cent of developments in British Columbia were in the large
      size category (81 residents and over), compared with 26 per cent of develop-
      ments in Ontario, 25 per cent of developments on the Prairies, 10 per cent
      of developments in Quebec, and 9 per cent of developments in the Atlantic
      Provinces.[32]

40   Self-contained developments generally tended to be smaller than those
      containing hostel accommodation, and public housing developments tended
      to be smaller than those built by non-profit sponsors.[33]

---

27   Pages 317-319.

28   Pages 99 and 100.

29   Pages 371 and 372.

30   Pages 98 and 99.

31   Page 97.

32   Page 98.

33   Page 98.

41   No direct correlation could be established between resident satisfaction and development size.[34] The residents of large developments appeared to participate more in external community activities than those in smaller ones but were less likely to socialize internally; however, the explanation for this behavior requires further analysis.

42   Residents were obliged to share toilets or baths in 70 per cent of hostel developments (in 42 per cent of developments, they were obliged to share both).[35] While residents were generally satisfied with privacy, this sharing of facilities was a source of strong dissatisfaction.[36]

43   Ninety-one per cent of hostel developments had double rooms and many had more double than single rooms.[37] The sharing of rooms with other than a spouse or close friend was a source of considerable dissatisfaction.[38]

44   Most self-contained developments had both one-bedroom and bachelor units; but 6 per cent had bachelor units only, thereby presumably excluding married residents.[39]

Facilities and Recreation

45   A central recreation or community room of some type was the most common recreation facility; one existed in eight out of 10 developments.[40]

46   There was a lack of regular programs in central recreation rooms. Few developments reported that the facility was used hardly at all for organized recreation activities; but in a large proportion of developments it was apparent that the facility was devoid of other than informal sitting most of the time.[41]

47   Table games, television watching (despite the fact that most residents had television sets in their own accommodation), and religious services were the most common activities found in recreation rooms, although special events such as birthday parties, concerts, and teas also figured prominently in the use of this facility.[42]

---

34   Page 370.

35   Pages 100 and 101.

36   Page 374.

37   Page 160.

38   Page 374.

39   Page 100.

40   Page 115.

41   Pages 118 and 119.

42   Page 119.

48 In one-third of developments the central recreation room was also occa-
    sionally used by non-residents.[43] The facility thus served as an amenity
    in the neighborhood or local community.

49 One-third of developments also had floor or wing lounges. They were mainly
    located in hostel and mixed developments.[44]

50 Central recreation rooms were used by a greater proportion of residents
    in hostel developments than in self-contained ones and in developments
    in which residents had a high rather than low rate of physical incapacity.[45]

51 The residents were well served with bingo, television watching, movies,
    and card games but there was a distinct lack of programs of a cultural
    or educational nature.[46]

52 Recreational activities were also mainly of a physically passive nature.
    Only 13 per cent of residents engaged in floor games and only 5 per cent
    of developments had an area for lawn games.[47]

53 In 10 per cent of developments, there was a senior citizens centre (or
    club d'âge d'or) on-site; in another 65 per cent of developments, one was
    located within five blocks. Residents in self-contained developments were
    considerably more likely to have a centre close to their development than
    those in hostel accommodation; also, developments situated in metropolitan
    areas or large urban centres were much more likely to be close to a senior
    citizens centre than those in small towns.[48]

54 Approximately one-third of residents that had a senior citizens centre (or
    club d'âge d'or) available made use of it. Use was considerably higher
    among residents living in self-contained accommodation than those in hostel
    developments. The most common reason mentioned for non-use was the existence
    of a waiting list.[49] In developments in which a senior citizens centre was
    situated on-site, a much higher proportion of residents used it.

55 As far as personal care facilities are concerned, developments were well
    supplied with laundry facilities. But nearly one-third of developments
    lacked easy access to a beauty shop (9 per cent had one on-site); barber
    shops were somewhat more common.[50]

---

43 Page 118.

44 Pages 119 and 120.

45 Page 118.

46 Pages 118-123.

47 Page 356.

48 Page 120.

49 Pages 358 and 359.

50 Pages 123 and 124.

56   Thirty per cent of developments had some type of library and in another 30 per cent there was one within five blocks. In addition, 19 per cent of developments recieved a mobile library service.[51]

57   A crafts room was available in 25 per cent of developments and another 12 per cent had one close by.[52]

58   Most developments lacked opportunities for residents to garden (only 2 per cent had greenhouses), although residents with gardens seemed to appreciate them.[53]

59   Generally less than one-third of the managers of developments that lacked the above recreation facilities considered that they would make useful additions; although managers of hostel and mixed developments were much more likely to express concern about unavailable facilities.

Health Services

60   Except in hostel and mixed developments (particularly those that contained a high proportion of very old and incapacitated residents), sponsors generally left health services to private physicians and nursing agencies. They did not concern themselves with the prevention of health problems; rather, they restricted their role to ensuring that residents received treatment in emergency situations. For example, only 19 per cent of developments reported that their residents had a regular medical checkup service available (in 11 per cent of developments this service was provided on-site).[54]

61   Only 13 per cent of developments (2 per cent in self-contained developments, 38 per cent of hostel developments, and 5 per cent of mixed developments) had infirmaries offering temporary nursing care.[55]

62   Nineteen per cent of developments had nurses on staff (1 per cent of self-contained and 74 per cent of hostel developments), 14 per cent had auxiliary health staff such as orderlies and nurses aids, 3 per cent had[56] occupational therapists, and only one development had a staff physician. Approximately one-quarter of the residents felt that they could use some nursing assistance regularly.[57]

---

51   Page 121.

52   Page 121.

53   Pages 121 and 123.

54   Page 133.

55   Pages 124 and 125.

56   Page 139.

57   Page 343.

63   Seventy-three per cent of developments were in communities which had a home nursing service of some type (supplied by the Victorian Order of Nurses or, in some cases, the public health department).[58] But considerable under-service was evident.

64   Twenty-nine per cent of developments reported that they had a doctor on call; and 3 per cent of developments reported that a doctor made daily or weekly visits.[59]

65   A lack of nursing care was one of the most frequent reasons mentioned by residents who thought that a lack of services in their development would force them to move at some time in the future.[60]

66   Nearly three-quarters of residents were in favor of the concept of multi-care accommodation (ranging from independent dwelling units through various types of boarding accommodation to full nursing care) on the same site. Residents with seriously limited physical abilities tended to favor the concept much more definitely than other residents.[61]

Social Services

67   Generally, development managers took the attitude that the provision of social services was the responsibility of public and voluntary agencies in the community; there was thus little involvement in service delivery. However, sponsors recognized that they had more obligation to provide social services in developments in which a high proportion of the residents were physically incapacitated.

68   Residents of senior citizens housing suffered from a serious lack of supportive social services:[62]

. 86 per cent of developments reported that a group leadership service was unavailable on-site or in the community.

. 49 per cent of developments reported that social work counselling was unavailable on-site or in the community.

. 80 per cent of developments reported that a food shopping service was unavailable on-site or in the community.

. 72 per cent of developments reported that legal aid counselling was unavailable on-site or in the community.

_____

58   Page 132.

59   Page 134.

60   Page 377.

61   Pages 378 and 379.

62   Table 30, page 128.

. 60 per cent of developments reported that a homemaker service was unavailable on-site or in the community.

. 63 per cent of developments reported that a meal delivery service was unavailable on-site or in the community.

. 66 per cent of developments reported that a friendly visiting service was unavailable on-site or in the community.

69   Despite the fact that residents used on-site social services much more extensively than those located elsewhere in the community, only in a very small proportion of developments were the agencies delivering services situated on-site.[63]

70   There appeared to be an information gap concerning the availability of services, as residents often claimed to be unaware of certain services in developments in which they were known to exist.

71   Despite the fact that nearly one-third of residents reported that they had difficulty with housework,[64] a maid service was only available in 15 per cent of all developments (5 per cent of self-contained developments and 46 per cent of hostel and mixed ones).[65]

72   Seven per cent of the residents of self-contained developments said that they had difficulty in cooking a hot meal but only 1 per cent of residents received hot meals from delivery services.[66] On the other hand, managers reported this service was available in relation to 42 per cent of self-contained developments.[67] In hostel developments, meals are available in a dining room or cafeteria.

73   Twenty-six per cent of apartment dwellers and 59 per cent of hostel residents said that they had difficulty shopping in winter.[68] This was largely a function of the lack of access to community facilities.

74   Approximately one-third of residents reported that they had difficulty dealing with financial and legal matters; but only half of these appeared to be receiving assistance.[69]

---

63   Page 128.

64   Page 320.

65   Page 133.

66   Page 348.

67   Page 129.

68   Page 348.

69   Page 349.

75   Although developments appeared to contain a not inconsiderable minority
      of lonely people, only 14 per cent of residents were receiving a friendly
      visitor service.[70] Managers reported that this service was more available
      in relation to hostel and mixed developments than self-contained develop-
      ments - despite the fact that hostel residents have more opportunities
      for socializing.[71]

76   Fairly extensive social services were available in a few self-contained
      developments but, generally, most managers thought that those living
      in self-contained developments neither required nor were entitled to
      more services than residents of private apartments. This is despite the
      fact that many self-contained developments contained a proportion of
      physically incapacitated residents and that this proportion is likely
      to increase with time and in relation to the availability of alternative
      accommodation in the local community. However, sponsors recognized that
      they had more obligation to provide social services in developments in which
      a high proportion of residents were physically incapacitated.

Location

77   Resident satisfaction with location was a function of access to community
      services and facilities, the general attractiveness of the neighborhood,
      and familiarity with the area.[72]

78   Many developments were not situated within easy walking distance of
      community facilities; 66 per cent of developments were beyond an easy
      walk from a senior citizens centre or club, 55 per cent from a medical
      clinic, 46 per cent from a shopping centre, and 42 per cent from churches.
      In addition, residents of many developments could not easily reach these
      facilities by public transportation.[73]

79   There was better access to community facilities in metropolitan areas
      than in smaller communities, and in downtown areas than in other neigh-
      borhoods.[74]

80   Residents with physical incapacities found access to community facilities
      more difficult than other residents.[75]

---

70   Page 349.

71   Page 133.

72   Part V, chapter 4.

73   Pages 148-152.

74   Page 152.

75   Page 324.

81   Nearly one-third of residents indicated transportation problems. They
      had many complaints about public transit systems, including poor scheduling,
      bus stops being too far away, and unsheltered waiting areas.[76]

82   Volunteer transportation services existed in nearly one-quarter of develop-
      ments, according to the managers,[77] but only 15 per cent of residents re-
      ported using this service. The service was mainly available to assist
      residents to attend church.

83   Only 40 per cent of residents indicated that it was very important to live
      in the same neighborhood or city as their children - and residents living
      alone were not more likely than others to say so, although those with
      serious health problems were more likely to feel that this was important.[78]

84   In relation to general satisfaction with location, 50 per cent of residents
      said that they were very satisfied, 30 per cent somewhat satisfied, and 14
      per cent dissatisfied. Younger residents tended to be more satisfied than
      older ones.[79]

85   The residents living in downtown developments were happy with access to
      services, shopping, and public transit but some expressed dissatisfaction
      about commercial surroundings, noise, and hustle and bustle.[80]

Community Contact

86   Most developments tended to stand out conspicuously in their neighborhoods,
      although 40 per cent of managers claimed that their development was "just
      another residence on the street."[81]

87   With the exception of churches, community organizations appeared to have
      little contact with developments for the elderly. According to the
      managers, 26 per cent of developments had little contact with churches,
      51 per cent had little contact with service clubs, and 63 per cent had
      little contact with social clubs. Community groups were considerably more
      likely to have contact with non-profit than public housing developments.[82]

------

76   Page 325.

77   Page 128.

78   Pages 328 and 329.

79   Page 326.

80   Page 327.

81   Page 147.

82   Pages 146 and 147.

88   Housing developments for the elderly were mainly situated in neighbor-
     hoods occupied by younger family households: only one-fifth were located
     in neighborhoods populated mostly by other elderly people, three-quarters
     were in areas occupied by mainly families with children.[83]

89   Participation in community activities declined on entrance to a housing
     development for the elderly: 50 per cent of residents never participated
     in such activities prior to admission, 65 per cent did not afterwards.
     Also, 45 per cent previously participated weekly or monthly, compared
     with 28 per cent after admission.[84]

90   Church was only attended regularly by a minority of residents: 44 per
     cent attended at least once weekly, 16 per cent monthly, 14 per cent
     annually, and 26 per cent never.[85] If the Quebec residents were excluded,
     regular church attendance would be considerably less.

91   Slightly less than half the residents went outside for an hour or more
     daily (considerably fewer in the winter months). People living in self-
     contained developments in downtown neighborhoods and in developments whose
     residents had a low rate of physical incapacity were more likely to get out
     on a daily basis.[86]

92   Visiting with friends from outside the development was not frequent: 41
     per cent visited (or were visited) at least once weekly and 73 per cent
     at least once monthly. Contact with relatives outside the development
     was considerably more frequent than contact with friends: approximately
     one-quarter of residents spoke on the telephone to or visited (or were visited
     by) relatives at least once daily and another one-third at least once
     weekly.[87]

93   It is estimated that in a typical development at least one-fifth of the
     residents lived a lonely life, having few social contacts either inside
     or outside the development. The data indicated that 25 per cent of
     residents had less than a monthly contact with relatives, 25 per cent
     never attended church, 65 per cent never participated in community
     activities, 26 per cent only rarely had contact with friends outside the
     development, and 16 per cent claimed to have made hardly any friends in
     the development. While it is not suggested that the same residents would
     fit into all these categories, there was definitely a minority of isolated
     people.

---

83   Pages 101 and 102.

84   Page 333.

85   Pages 333 and 334.

86   Pages 331 and 332.

87   Pages 334 and 335.

397

94   Residents indicated that in emergencies they would be more likely to
      look for assistance from people inside the development than in the
      community. Forty-four per cent of residents said that they would seek
      help from development staff, 10 per cent from other residents, and only
      24 per cent from relatives.[88]

95   Residents with children living in the area were more likely than the
      remainder of the population to turn to relatives for emergency help; but
      nearly half of this group said that they would turn first to development
      staff or other residents.[89] This suggests that children are by no means
      always seen as adequate substitutes for on-site assistance.

96   There was a divergence of opinion among residents about the desirability
      of having persons of different ages and families with children living in
      the immediate neighborhood of their development, but considerably more
      residents were opposed to such an age mix than favored it.[90]

97   Residents were strongly against sharing their building with persons of
      other ages and children. Only a small minority indicated that they would
      prefer to live in a building of mixed age and household types.[91]

Social Interaction

98   Developments provided a source of friends for most residents: 43 per cent
      of residents reported that they had made many friends, 40 per cent at
      least some, and only 16 per cent hardly any. Residents with physical
      incapacities were more likely to have made many friends than other residents.[92]

99   Hostel residents were slightly more likely to have made many friends than
      those in self-contained accommodation; and younger residents were more
      likely to have made many friends than older ones. Men residents were as
      likely to have made many friends as women.[93]

100   Having children living in the area did not decrease the likelihood of
      residents having made friends. In fact, residents with children living
      in the area were more likely to have made many friends in the development
      than other residents.[94]

---

88   Page 339.

89   Page 340.

90   Page 328.

91   Page 328.

92   Pages 335-337.

93   Pages 335-337.

94   Page 336.

101   There was a good deal of visiting among residents: 39 per cent of residents said that they visited at least daily, 28 per cent at least weekly, and 12 per cent at least monthly.[95]

102   There was more visiting among hostel residents than those in self-contained accommodation, and there was more visiting in non-profit than in public housing developments. Residents with various degrees of physical incapacity tended to visit one another more than other residents.[96]

103   Four out of 10 developments reported that a buddy system existed in which residents checked on their partner daily.[97] However, in most developments where they existed, buddy systems were used by a minority of residents[98] - although informal arrangements for daily checking-up were frequently worked out between friends.

104   Buddy systems were more prevalent in public housing than in non-profit developments and in self-contained developments than hostels.[99] This suggests that they may serve as compensation for a lack of staff.

105   Less than one-third of developments had any type of residents' association. These associations were more common in public housing than in non-profit developments; but in non-profit developments a greater proportion of residents participated in the association.[100]

106   Only 5 per cent of developments had residents on their board of management or governing bodies; all these were non-profit developments.[101]

107   In just over half the developments residents did duties of a domestic nature such as cleaning halls, gardening, and kitchen work. This practice was mainly concentrated in non-profit developments and usually involved less than half the residents.[102]

Admission and Exit Policies

108   Many non-profit sponsors appeared to be giving preference in admission to persons having a similar ethnic, language, or religious affiliation to that of the sponsoring organization.[103]

---

95   Page 338.

96   Page 338.

97   Page 146.

98   Page 350.

99   Page 146.

100 Pages 143 and 144.

101 Page 145.

102 Page 145.

103 Page 161.

109   Half of the non-profit developments lacked any income ceiling for admission; this suggests that accommodation is not necessarily restricted to low or moderate income people.[104]

110   One-fifth of non-profit developments maintained income floors below which they would not admit applicants and another fifth used other means of assessing an applicant's ability to pay the rent.[105] This implies some effective restriction of very low income people.

111   Approximately 15 per cent of the managers of self-contained developments, 2 per cent of the managers of hostel developments, and 7 per cent of the managers of mixed developments indicated that they would not admit residents having any degree of physical incapacity.[106]

112   Twenty-one per cent of self-contained developments, 11 per cent of hostel developments, and 4 per cent of mixed developments required residents who developed slight or moderate physical incapacities to seek other accommodation.[107]

113   Many development managers reported that residents were required to move from double to single accommodation on the death of their spouse. Thirty-five per cent of developments always followed this practice and 25 per cent followed it sometimes.[108]

Staffing

114   There was a surprising lack of staff in the self-contained developments; 43 per cent lacked any on-site staff person working more than 10 hours a week. Only six self-contained developments had over six staff members (working over 10 hours a week) and only two hostel and mixed developments had fewer than six.[109]

115   Ninety per cent of self-contained developments lacked a manager or administrator working on-site in excess of 10 hours a week; all hostel developments had administration staff.[110] In the self-contained sector, the paucity of administrative staff stems partly from managers having responsibility for several developments and also from the inability of many non-profit developments to afford staff of this type.

---

104   Pages 168 and 169.
105   Pages 169 and 170.
106   Page 161.
107   Page 162.
108   Page 162.
109   Page 135.
110   Page 137.

116   Maintenance staff were the most common personnel; they were found in
        76 per cent of all developments. Thirty-two per cent of self-contained
        developments and 3 per cent of hostel and mixed developments lacked a
        maintenance man working in excess of 10 hours a week.[111] In the self-
        contained sector, maintenance was in many cases carried out by a part-
        time resident caretaker who received a small salary in addition to rent-
        free accommodation. Since they were often the only on-site employee of
        the sponsor, caretakers, building superintendents, and custodians
        frequently performed duties quite beyond their maintenance responsibilities.

117   Most non-profit developments used some form of volunteer assistance.
        This ranged from simply serving on a board of directors to many hours
        of work in management, bookkeeping, or tenant relations. Ten per cent of
        non-profit developments had certain volunteers who were putting in over
        10 hours a week. There was little volunteer assistance in public housing
        developments.[112]

118   Residents tended to be generally satisfied with staff but only 56 per cent
        of residents indicated that they were completely satisfied with the number
        of staff. Many, especially those in self-contained developments, expressed
        concern about an insufficient number of on-site employees - particularly
        at night and on weekends.[113]

Managers' Characteristics

119   The people performing the management function were very predominently
        male and tended to be generally middle-aged.[114]

120   The educational background of managers tended to be mixed: approximately
        one-quarter lacked any high school education and slightly less than half
        lacked any post-secondary education. Approximately 51 per cent had some
        type of post-secondary or university education.[115]

121   Just over half of the managers indicated that they had worked with the
        elderly for over five years; however, it was clear that they must have
        assumed their present responsibilities late in life.[116]

122   On the whole, managers were more involved in and oriented to administrative
        responsibilities than those connected with the psychological and social
        well-being of residents; they were more concerned with keeping accounts,
        managing finances, rent collection, and maintenance matters than with
        obtaining community services, running social programs, and assisting
        residents with individual problems.[117]

---

111   Page 136.

112   Page 136.

113   Page 372.

114   Page 153.

115   Page 153.

116   Page 154.

117   Pages 154-158.

User Satisfaction

123   General user satisfaction with developments appeared fairly high: 61 per cent of residents reported that they were very satisfied, 29 per cent satisfied, and only 6 per cent dissatisfied (4 per cent were ambiguous or had no opinion).[118]

124   There was wide variation between developments as far as satisfaction was concerned but it did not appear to relate to development type, sponsor type, development size, or downtown versus suburban location.[119]

125   There was a correlation between residents' satisfaction and age and health. Older residents and those with physical incapacities were less likely to be satisfied than other residents.[120] This suggests that the inability of developments to meet the needs of residents in declining health was likely a source of dissatisfaction.

126   The most frequent general reasons for satisfaction mentioned by residents were good design features, privacy, followed by ease in making friends.[121]

127   The most frequent general reasons mentioned by residents for dissatisfaction were design problems, followed by management and staff shortcomings, and lack of services and facilities.[122]

128   Developments for the elderly appeared to be meeting the needs of the majority of present residents; but there was a sizeable minority of users who suffered from loneliness, insecurity concerning the possibility of illness, and a lack of access to community services and facilities.

Sponsorship

129   Developments operated by non-profit sponsors generally appeared to respond more to the social and health needs of residents than those in the public housing sector.

130   Non-profit sponsors had built a much wider variety of accommodation; there was only one hostel development built by the public housing sector at the time of this study, whereas non-profit sponsors had in a number of cases built a mix of self-contained, hostel and mixed developments (as well as nursing homes - a type of accommodation which fell beyond the purview of this study).[123]

---

118   Pages 363-365.

119   Page 364.

120   Page 364.

121   Pages 366 and 367.

122   Pages 368 and 369.

123   Page 42.

131 In non-profit developments there was considerably more community involvement in the welfare of residents, e.g. more contact with church, service clubs and social clubs, as well as much more volunteer work.[124]

132 Non-profit developments had a higher staff ratio than public housing developments, often volunteers from the sponsoring body substituting for paid staff.[125]

133 There was little difference between managers in the public housing and non-profit sectors as to sex, education, and age, but the managers of non-profit developments on the whole had more experience in working with the elderly.[126]

134 There did not appear to be an appreciable difference in general user satisfaction between the public and non-profit sectors[127] - despite the more social orientation of non-profit staff and the greater availability of facilities and services in non-profit developments. This can perhaps be accounted for by the fact that non-profit sponsors tended to serve a somewhat older and more physically incapacitated resident population than the public housing sector.

135 Non-profit sponsors served a higher income group than public housing agencies.[128] This can be accounted for by the more generous subsidy programs that were available in public housing.

136 Despite serving a financially better-off population and charging higher rents, a large proportion of non-profit sponsors reported serious financial difficulties, both in operating their present development and in developing additional accommodation.[129]

Small Town Developments

137 Small-town developments, being smaller than those in larger centres, tended to have fewer built-in social services and facilities.

138 Access to community facilities was more difficult from small town developments than those in metropolitan areas.[130] Also, frequently, facilities such as senior citizens centres were non-existent in small towns.

---

124 Pages 136 and 147.

125 Page 135.

126 Pages 153 and 154.

127 Page 364.

128 Page 113.

129 Page 171.

130 Page 152.

139   Health services and facilities were considerably less available to the residents of developments located in small towns than those in larger centres.[131]

140   Developments in small towns tended to have more contact with churches than those in larger centres, but contacts with service and social clubs were less frequent - probably because of a less extensive community organization network.[132]

Concluding Observations

141   In a large proportion of developments offering self-contained accommodation, it is evident that the sponsors and managers regard their task as not differing appreciably from that of private landlords - except for ensuring a lower rent. In other words, they aim to provide elderly people with decent shelter at a reasonable cost without taking major responsibility for the physical, psychological, and social well-being of their residents.

142   It is apparent that the character of a development's management is the most important factor in determining whether or not the quality of the residential environment will meet the needs of residents. Other factors such as design, availability of recreation facilities and social services, and location, are also very important; but developments that have inadequacies in these areas can be pleasant places to live if the management has a strong social orientation.

143   It was clear that for most residents of senior citizens housing, the development and its environs represents their world. Except for occasional forays into the community and periodic contacts with relatives and friends, residents look to their residential environment to provide them with most of the social, physical, mental, emotional, and to some extent spiritual, stimulation that life has to offer.

---

131   Part III, chapters 4 and 5.

132   Pages 146 and 147.

PART VII

RECOMMENDATIONS

These recommendations were formulated by the Study Advisory Committee in light of the statement of findings and the data that is presented in various parts of this volume. Recommendations related to particular findings are indicated by footnotes.

Of course, like any set of proposals, these recommendations are also based on the breadth of knowledge and experience of their framers - all of whom have familiarity with housing for the elderly that goes far beyond their involvement in this study.

The Main Objective: Housing Choice in Old Age

1   The overriding objective of policies affecting the housing of senior citizens in Canada should be to provide as wide a variety and range of choice as possible. This means that the government should provide: the necessary income and community services to enable those who prefer to remain in their own homes or to continue living with their children to do so, purpose designated accommodation of the type we have studied, as well as special care homes for those who have suffered a serious decline in health.

2   Contrary to the popular myth, residents of housing developments for the elderly sampled in this study did not feel that they lived in ghettos because they resided with people of their own age.[1] The elderly have as much right to live with their own age group as do students and young people. What is important is that sufficient alternatives exist in every community so that old people can choose the accommodation that suits them best.

3   It is at the provincial level that responsibility for housing the elderly must be firmly assumed.[2] Therefore all provincial governments should prepare comprehensive plans for the accommodation and care of their senior citizens that embrace a range of housing options and a continuum of supportive services. Planning, implementation, and evaluation should be carried out in consultation with:

. federal government agencies such as the Central Mortgage and Housing Corporation (which should provide most of the capital funds) and the Department of Health and Welfare Canada (who can relate the process to the funding of health services and income security programs);

. all provincial government departments that bear on the process (e.g. health, social services, municipal affairs, labor, citizenship - and, of course, housing corporations);

---

1   Finding 97.

2   Finding 12.

. municipal governments (since they are best equipped to articulate accommodation needs and coordinate public and voluntary activities at the local level);

. public and voluntary health, social services, and recreation agencies (in order to relate accommodation planning to the delivery of services);

. citizens groups of all types (who have essential roles to play - from building and managing housing to providing links between the community and residents of senior citizens developments).

4   As a serious shortage of senior citizens housing exists in all regions of Canada, public agencies and governments at all levels should ensure that a vastly increased amount of accommodation is built.[3] It should be recognized, however, that if the financial status of senior citizens materially improves and/or more extensive community services are available, there might be some reduction in the strong demand for this type of accommodation.

Design Suggestions

5   Different accommodation types and care levels for the elderly (ranging from independent living units, hostel accommodation, to various forms of nursing care) should be developed in association with each other - as desired by a large proportion of the residents interviewed in this study. Where possible, consideration should be given to situating them on the same or a contiguous site.[4]

6   Housing developments for the elderly should be integrated as fully as possible with community facilities; for example, there is no reason why developments cannot be built in association with major community facilities such as community centres or in the air space over shopping centres.[5]

7   All developments should provide a suitable balance of accommodation for both married and single persons.[6] In addition, it is apparent in self-contained developments that one-bedroom dwelling units are preferable to bachelor units.

8   Much more consideration needs to be given to the use of roof space in housing developments for the elderly. With careful design treatment, roofs can provide many opportunities for outdoor recreation.

9   As far as possible, private bath and toilet facilities should be provided for residents in hostel rooms.[7]

---

3 Finding 11.

4 Finding 66.

5 Finding 78.

6 Finding 44.

7 Finding 42.

Health

10   It should be the responsibility of sponsors of housing developments for the elderly to adopt a positive and restorative approach to residents' health.[8] Where possible, each development should have a preventive health program under the auspices of either the development's staff or a community agency. This program should consist of both periodic health appraisals and counselling on matters of general health and nutrition.

11   Residents of housing developments for the elderly should be provided with a medical assessment on admission and thereafter be under continuing surveillance from a health care professional.[9]

12   Each development should have an adequate arrangement with a physician to provide emergency care for residents having no medical practitioner.[10]

13   Instead of sponsors requiring residents who develop slight or moderate physical incapacities to move to other accommodation, it would be more desirable to make sufficient personal services available to enable such residents to remain in their present accommodation for as long as possible.[11] On the other hand, it is understandable that residents whose health has seriously deteriorated should be assisted to move to accommodation offering levels of care more appropriate to their needs.

14   There is a need for better liaison between housing developments of the type studied and other forms of accommodation, such as community foster care programs, intermediate or special care homes, nursing homes, and active treatment hospitals, in order to produce continuity of care for old people.

Social Services

15   Sponsors should accept responsibility for the quality of social services provided residents.[12] This does not mean that they will necessarily provide all the services themselves but that they must serve as the effective contact point between residents and community agencies. In particular, they should see that information is made available to residents about existing services.

16   Social services should, as far as possible, be available on site in housing developments for the elderly.[13] Consequently, agencies should, as far as possible, decentralize their services and housing sponsors should ensure that the necessary space is provided.

---

8   Finding 60.

9   Finding 60.

10   Finding 64.

11   Finding 112.

12   Finding 67.

13   Finding 69.

17   As the location of large housing developments for the elderly frequently has major implications for community social service agencies, these agencies should be involved at the planning stage in designing health, social service, and recreation program plans for developments prior to their occupancy.

18   Because a significant minority of lonely people exist in practically all developments, friendly visiting programs are a vital need.[14]   Such programs should be expanded. Also, sponsors should ensure that someone checks on the well-being of each resident daily.

19   More extensive domiciliary and home help services should be provided for the residents of housing developments for the elderly. Even relatively active residents of self-contained developments occasionally require help with heavy cleaning.[15]

20   It is clear that considerable work remains to be done to upgrade social and health services in small towns in Canada. It is apparent that the residents of small communities or rural areas (including those living in housing developments for the elderly) have services that are vastly inferior to those of their city brethren.[16] Mobile units carrying staff and equipment could be used to service areas too small to support permanently established agencies.

Recreation

21   Activity is vitally necessary for most people's physical and mental health; for the elderly it is essential for their well-being. It is therefore desirable for developments for the elderly to be located as close as possible to community recreation facilities.[17] However, if it is not possible to provide easy access to such facilities, they should be built into the development.

22   Senior citizens centres that are open to the whole community should be located in association with housing developments for the elderly.[18] This would encourage use of the facility and help to keep residents in touch with people outside their development.

23   More recreation programming of all types is required in developments,[19] with an emphasis on assisting residents to plan their own activities. Each sponsor should designate an official or board member to take overall responsibility for recreation.

---

14   Finding 75.

15   Finding 71.

16   Findings 137 and 139.

17   Finding 78.

18   Findings 53 and 54.

19   Finding 46.

24   The range of recreation programs available to the residents of senior citizens housing needs to be improved. As many elderly people enjoy exercise and intellectual stimulation, opportunities for physical activity and learning should be available.[20]

25   Many elderly people are creative and like to make things. Therefore, all developments should have an adequately equipped crafts or hobby room, or managers should at least ensure that an area is available for this purpose.[21]

26   Library services for residents of housing developments for the elderly need to be greatly expanded.[22] More use could be made of mobile libraries and lounges and reading rooms should be stocked with books from local public libraries. A special need exists for books with large print.

Community Contact

27   Before CMHC financial assistance is extended to new housing developments for the elderly, sponsors should be required to demonstrate that residents will have satisfactory access to community facilities. Where the development is in a remote location, sponsors should be required to produce a transportation plan.

28   It should be incumbent on sponsors to ensure that their residents have proper access to community facilities. Where these facilities are located some distance from the development and public transit is inadequate, sponsors should bridge the gap - for example, by supplying a minibus service.[23]

29   Community organizations of all types (churches, service clubs, community colleges, educational institutions, women's organizations, and social agencies), should not assume that community contacts are no longer required simply because an elderly person has been admitted to senior citizens housing.[24] Also, community groups should maintain relationships with residents of housing for the elderly on a regular basis instead of simply putting on special events such as Christmas concerts.

30   More involvement from community groups is required in senior citizens housing and special efforts should be made to encourage more volunteer activity in the public housing sector.[25]

---

20 Findings 51 and 52.

21 Finding 57.

22 Finding 56.

23 Finding 81.

24 Finding 87.

25 Finding 87.

Involving Residents

31   Sponsors need to place more emphasis on obtaining resident participation in all aspects of the residential environment. This can lead to more suitable management policies as well as discourage the paternalism that can too easily become a feature of the manager-resident relationship.

32   Each housing development for the elderly should have a residents' association that plans social and recreation programs and generally takes a hand in managing the accommodation.[26]

33   Sponsors should ensure that at least two representative residents sit on all boards of management of non-profit housing developments for the elderly.[27] Recent moves in the province of Quebec in this direction are to be commended. There should also be an adequate number of elderly tenant representatives on the boards of public housing authorities.

34   There is a pressing need in housing developments for the elderly for more staff with group leadership skills.[28] It is recommended that sponsors assign social animators to each development. They would be responsible for helping new residents adjust, assisting residents to plan their own recreation programs, promoting the development of community services on behalf of residents, and generally encouraging residential involvement and participation.

35   Buddy systems (the pairing of residents so that each can check on the other) can be an important way of promoting mutual aid in housing developments; but they require considerable organizational leadership if they are to be effective and operate over any length of time.[29]

Management Policies

36   Managers should be aware of the stresses that elderly people encounter in moving into a housing development.[30] They should make every effort to assist newcomers to move and adjust to their new environment. One practical way is to provide a handbook indicating the facilities and services at hand.

37   Residents of senior citizens housing are entitled to privacy and should not be expected to share hostel rooms with anyone but a spouse or another person of their choice.[31] Consequently, adjustments may have to be made in financial capital and operating budgets.

------

26   Finding 105.

27   Finding 106.

28   Finding 68.

29   Finding 103.

30   Finding 34.

31   Finding 43.

38   Everything possible should be done to avoid putting residents in the
      position of having to move after the death of a spouse.[32] Ideally,
      sufficient accommodation should be available so that a move is not
      necessary. However, if a move is mandatory, it should be handled with
      great sensitivity and the resident should be relocated as close as
      possible to his or her previous accommodation (if this is the person's
      preference).

Staff

39   The management function in senior citizens housing needs to be greatly
      upgraded and professionalized. Higher salaries and more definite career
      lines are required to attract capable staff. In particular, CMHC should
      take the lead in seeing that training courses with a strong social
      orientation are provided.[33]

40   The basis on which financial assistance is provided to both public
      and non-profit housing for the elderly needs to be reviewed in order to
      permit staffing to be upgraded. It is obvious that more trained staff
      are essential if Canadians are to be proud of their senior citizens
      accommodation.

41   In the selection of administrative staff for housing developments for the
      elderly, attention needs to be given to the employment of a broader age
      group and more women.[34]

42   Sponsors should recognize that competent resident caretakers or super-
      intendents are an essential component of a good housing development.[35]
      As these persons are frequently called upon for assistance that extends
      beyond maintenance duties, it is essential that they are provided with
      good salaries as well as adequate preparatory training and continuing
      support, e.g. through periodic workshops.

43   A paid staff person should be available in all developments on a 24-
      hour basis to look after emergency situations.[36] In small developments
      a resident could take on this duty, with proper compensation.

---

32   Finding 113.

33   Findings 120-122.

34   Finding 119.

35   Finding 116.

36   Finding 118.

Finances

44   The financial crisis in which many non-profit sponsors of housing for the elderly find themselves should be alleviated by equalizing subsidy payments between non-profit and public housing.[37] Non-profit sponsors have been doing a very creditable job in housing senior citizens and their interest in building more accommodation should be encouraged by ensuring that greater financial support and other assistance is available from all levels of government.

45   Public housing agencies appear to be serving a lower income group of senior citizens than non-profit sponsors.[38] This is undesirable and could create class differences between different developments as well as financial hardship for low income people obliged to live in high-rent non-profit housing. It is recommended that qualifications for admission to or continued residence in senior citizens housing should not include fixed minimum or maximum incomes. Instead, an income mix should be encouraged; this could be done by charging all residents an unsubsidized or economic rent and supplementing the incomes of residents to whom this would be a financial burden. Thus, no applicants would be barred from any development because of insufficient income, nor would residents able to pay their own way be subsidized with public funds.

More Study

46   Considerably more research needs to be undertaken in relation to the desirability of different types of residential environments for the elderly. It is apparent from this study that there should be:

. an investigation of the relationship between development size, the quality of the environment, and user satisfaction;

. a study of the accommodation requirements of single elderly men (since it is apparent that the accommodation examined in our study appeals principally to women);

. a comparative study of housing arrangements for the elderly in Canada and those in other countries;

. more research to determine appropriate levels of mental and physical functioning for residents in different settings.

. a review of the cost implications of a range of accommodation types and care levels.

---

37   Finding 23.

38   Finding 30.

47   There has been a plethora of studies on the accommodation needs and lifestyles of low and moderate income senior citizens. To balance this, more research should be done on housing choices made by the affluent elderly. If financial constraints to the freedom of choice of elderly persons needing accommodation were removed, insights into possible alternatives to current arrangements might be explored.

48   The status of elderly homeowners requires study from the point of view of determining what special problems they encounter as a result of soaring municipal taxes and the pressures of urban redevelopment. As part of such a study, the matter of possible under-occupancy of scarce older homes should be examined.

PART VIII

APPENDICES

APPENDIX 1

MANAGER SURVEY METHODOLOGY

Sample Selection

The sampling frame consisted of a list of developments for the elderly
financed by CMHC under NHA sections 16, 16A, 35A, and 35D. The list
was compiled after a complete review of CMHC loan and public housing
files. Nursing homes were as far as possible excluded.

The universe of all NHA developments for the elderly was first stratified
by province. To achieve meaningful national results as well as valid
figures for each region of the country, a 100 per cent sample was
selected in provinces with fewer than 60 developments. This meant that
questionnaires were sent to all developments in Newfoundland, Prince
Edward Island, Nova Scotia, New Brunswick, and Alberta.

For the remaining five provinces, the list of developments in the universe
was then stratified by community size (metropolitan and non-metropolitan,
according to census criteria). In the non-metropolitan areas of each of
these provinces, cluster sampling was used: the developments were first
clustered geographically by census areas into groups of about eight to
12 developments, and then one-third of the clusters were randomly selected.
Within each of the selected clusters all developments were sampled.

In the metropolitan areas of provinces in which the universe was not
sampled, developments were further stratified by sponsor type (public
and non-profit); and the public housing developments were also further
stratified according to whether the site housed old people only or mixed
with families (in different buildings). All metropolitan developments
were further stratified by accommodation type (self-contained, hostel,
and mixed), and development size (1-20 units/beds, 21-40, 41-80, 81-149,
and 150 or over). Then, a uniform sampling fraction of 50 per cent was
used, which meant that one-half of the developments in each of the strata
were randomly sampled.

In order to achieve as high a return rate as possible, two follow-up
letters were sent after the initial mailing to non-profit developments,
followed by a final telegram. Questionnaires for completion by public
housing authorities were channeled through provincial housing corporations - who forwarded them with a covering letter to the various
authorities in each case; the completed questionnaires were returned
directly to the study staff in Ottawa.

Table 1 outlines the sample selection process. The universe from which the sample was drawn was constructed from CMHC loan approval lists and originally consisted of 882 developments. On the basis of further contact with CMHC regional offices and returned questionnaires, it was found that 80 cases in the original sample were inappropriate, i.e. they consisted of duplications, uncompleted and unoccupied developments, family occupied accommodation, and exclusively nursing care accommodation. When these were excluded the original sample was reduced to 746, and the sample to 313. From the final sample of 313, 294 questionnaires or 94 per cent were returned and processed. The response rate was 97 per cent for non-profit developments and 88 per cent for the public housing sector.

TABLE 1

SAMPLING PROCESS

	NON-PROFIT DEVELOPMENTS	PUBLIC HOUSING DEVELOPMENTS	ALL DEVELOPMENTS
ORIGINAL UNIVERSE	585	139	882
ORIGINAL SAMPLE	254	139	393
ADJUSTMENTS			
Duplications in CMHC Loan Records	8	1	9
Developments Uncompleted Or Unoccupied	18	31	49
Occupied by Families	–	3	3
Exclusively Nursing Accommodation	12	7	19
	38	42	80
FINAL UNIVERSE	530	216	746
FINAL SAMPLE	216	97	313
QUESTIONNAIRES RETURNED	209	85	294
RESPONSE RATE	97%	88%	94%
RETURNED QUESTIONNAIRES AS PROPORTION OF FINAL UNIVERSE	39%	40%	39%

The returned questionnaires were coded and key-punched in Ottawa and the data then sent to the Berkeley Survey Research Center for processing.

The results presented were not weighted to compensate for the different sampling fractions used for the metropolitan and non-metropolitan areas of each of the five provinces ($\frac{1}{2}$ and 1/3). Although in terms of community size the over-all national representation is good, it should be remembered in looking at the results that in five provinces metropolitan developments are over-represented and non-metropolitan developments are under-represented.

Sample Validity

Considering the size of the sample, the high response rate and the elaborate sampling procedure, the data would be expected to have a high degree of validity. This was, in fact, confirmed by comparing the basic characteristics of the processed sample with characteristics of the universe of NHA housing presented in Part II - as shown in Table 2.

In terms of sponsor type, the sample was identical to the universe. In terms of accommodation type, self-contained developments were slightly over-represented and hostels slightly under-represented (by 6 per cent). When it came to development size, developments with fewer than 21 units or beds were slightly under-represented (by 5 per cent), and developments with 21-40 were very slightly over-represented (by 3 per cent); the proportion of larger developments was practically identical in the sample and universe.

Regional location was as follows: the Atlantic Provinces were somewhat over-represented in the sample (by 12 per cent); the Prairies were slightly under-represented (by 7 per cent); for Quebec, Ontario, and British Columbia, differences in the sample and universe were negligible. The over-representation in the Atlantic region was due to the high response rate there; this had the effect of slightly deflating the national figures on availability of services and facilities since they were less frequent there than in the rest of Canada.

In terms of community size, metropolitan developments were very slightly over-represented (by 3 per cent) and small towns slightly under-represented (by 6 per cent).

Major Sample Characteristics

This section presents more detailed data on some of the basic characteristics of the processed sample. In itself, this information is not new - it is already available for the universe in Part II; however, it provides a further check on sample validity and may be helpful in interpreting certain findings.

422

TABLE 2

COMPARISON BETWEEN DEVELOPMENTS IN PROCESSED SAMPLE AND UNIVERSE

	PROCESSED SAMPLE	UNIVERSE OF ALL NHA HOUSING FOR ELDERLY UP TO END OF 1970**
Sponsor Type		
Non-Profit	71% (209)	71% (530)
Public Housing	29% (85)	29% (216)
Total	100% (294)	100% (746)
Accommodation Type		
Self-Contained	75% (220)	69% (514)
Hostel and Mixed	25% (74)	31% (232)
Total	100% (294)	100% (746)
Development Size		
20 units/beds or less	28% (81)	33% (244)
21-40 units/beds	23% (67)	20% (153)
41-80 units/beds	27% (78)	27% (199)
81-149 units/beds	12% (36)	13% (95)
150 or more units/beds	8% (23)	7% (55)
Not Known	3% (9)	
Total	100% (294)	100% (746)
Regional Location		
Atlantic Provinces	22% (64)	10% (75)
Quebec	11% (32)	13% (99)
Ontario	32% (94)	34% (256)
Prairies	18% (53)	25% (186)
British Columbia	17% (51)	17% (128)
Total	100% (294)	100% (744)
Community Size		
Metropolitan Area	35% (104)	32% (240)
Major Urban	9% (27)	7% (52)
Small Town	55% (163)	61% (454)
Total	100% (294)	100% (746)

Note: Numbers are in brackets. Percentages are rounded to whole numbers and therefore do not total 100 per cent.

REGION: Most developments were located in Ontario, followed by the
Atlantic Provinces, the Prairies, British Columbia, and Quebec. Table
3 shows that, of the various regions, British Columbia had the highest
proportion of metropolitan developments, Ontario had the highest proportion of major urban area developments, and Quebec had the largest
proportion of small-town developments. After Quebec, the Atlantic
region had the next highest proportion of small-town developments,
followed by the Prairies, Ontario, and British Columbia.

As for accommodation type in relation to region, Ontario had the highest
proportion of self-contained developments (98 per cent), followed by
British Columbia (80 per cent), the Atlantic Provinces (75 per cent),
the Prairies (67 per cent), and Quebec (less than 10 per cent).

TABLE 3.

DEVELOPMENTS, REGION BY COMMUNITY SIZE[1]

	ATLANTIC PROVINCES	QUEBEC	ONTARIO	PRAIRIES	BRITISH COLUMBIA	TOTAL
Metropolitan Areas	8 12.5%	2 6.3%	45 47.9%	15 28.3%	34 66.7%	104 35.4%
Major Urban Areas	7 10.9%	3 9.4%	17 18.1%	0 0%	0 0%	27 9.2%
Small Towns	49 76.6%	27 84.4%	32 34.0%	38 71.7%	17 33.3%	163 55.4%
TOTAL	64 100%	32 100%	94 100%	53 100%	51 100%	294 100%

1 Census classifications.

Table 4 shows the relationship between region and sponsor type. Quebec
had the largest proportion of non-profit developments - indeed, 100 per
cent of its developments were non-profit - followed closely by the
Prairies and British Columbia. As far as public housing was concerned,
Ontario had the largest proportion (61 per cent), followed at a great
distance by the Atlantic Provinces (38 per cent).

SPONSORSHIP: As indicated in Table 4, 71 per cent of the developments
in the sample were operated by non-profit sponsors and 29 per cent were
operated by public housing agencies. The public housing was mainly built
by provincial housing corporations or under joint federal-provincial
arrangements and usually managed by local housing authorities. Although
all the housing in Quebec was managed by non-profit groups, it was mostly
built by the Quebec Housing Corporation. More non-profit developments
were located in the Prairies than in any other region, whereas the public
housing developments were concentrated in Ontario.

TABLE 4

DEVELOPMENTS, REGION BY SPONSOR TYPE

	ATLANTIC PROVINCES	QUEBEC	ONTARIO	PRAIRIES	BRITISH COLUMBIA	TOTAL
Public Housing	24 37.5%	0 0%	57 60.6%	2 3.8%	2 3.9%	85 28.9%
Non-Profit Housing	40 62.5%	32 100%	37 39.4%	51 96.2%	49 96.1%	209 71.1%
TOTAL	64 100%	32 100%	94 100%	53 100%	51 100%	294 100%

Table 5 provides a more detailed breakdown of developments by sponsor
group. Of the slightly under two-thirds of the sampled developments
from whom we were able to obtain the information, 44 per cent were
operated by service clubs, 18 per cent by provincial government agencies,
14 per cent by municipalities, 13 per cent by other types of non-profit
organizations, mainly of a local nature, 8 per cent by churches, and 3
per cent by ethnic groups. Practically all of the provincially operated
developments and many of the municipally run ones would be public housing.

TABLE 5

DEVELOPMENTS, SPONSOR GROUP BY ACCOMMODATION TYPE

	CHURCHES	ETHNIC GROUPS	SERVICE CLUBS	OTHER NON-PROFIT	MUNICIPAL	PROVINCIAL	N
Self-Contained	10 8.4%	3 2.5%	52 43.7%	16 13.4%	17 14.3%	21 17.6%	119 100%
Hostel	9 21.4%	3 7.1%	0 0%	22 52.4%	5 11.9%	3 7.1%	42 100%
Mixed	5 16.7%	0 0%	2 6.7%	17 56.7%	6 20.0%	0 0%	30 100%
TOTAL	24 12.6%	6 3.1%	54 28.3%	55 28.8%	28 14.7%	24 12.6%	191 100%

425

Table 6 shows that all of the public housing developments offered self-contained accommodation only. Of the non-profit developments, 65 per cent offered self-contained accommodation, 21 per cent offered hostel accommodation (some of which contained nursing beds), and 31 per cent offered a mixture of hostel and self-contained accommodation.

TABLE 6

DEVELOPMENTS, SPONSOR TYPE BY ACCOMMODATION TYPE

	NON-PROFIT HOUSING	PUBLIC HOUSING	TOTAL
Self-Contained	135 64.6%	85 100%	220 74.8%
Hostel	43 20.6%	0 0%	43 14.6%
Mixed	31 14.8%	0 0%	31 10.5%
TOTAL	209 100%	85 100%	294 100%

Table 7 indicates the relationship between sponsor type and community size. Non-profit accommodation was concentrated mainly in major small towns and metropolitan areas; this was the case for public housing too, although compared to non-profit housing, more was found in medium-sized cities (21 per cent, compared with 4 per cent). The latter can be accounted for by the operations of the Ontario Housing Corporation, which has not built housing developments for the elderly in Metropolitan Toronto but distributed them throughout numerous other cities in the province.

Table 8 shows the relationship between sponsor type and development size, as measured by the number of dwelling units or hostel beds. Twenty-eight per cent of developments had fewer than 21 units or beds; 23 per cent had 21-40 units or beds; 27 per cent had 41-80 units or beds; 13 per cent had 81-149 units or beds; and 8 per cent had 150 or more units or beds. Both public and non-profit housing tended to be concentrated in developments having 80 or fewer units or beds, but compared with public housing the non-profit sector had a higher proportion of developments with over 40 units or beds.

TABLE 7

DEVELOPMENTS, COMMUNITY SIZE[1] BY SPONSOR TYPE

	NON-PROFIT HOUSING	PUBLIC HOUSING	TOTAL
Metropolitan Areas	77 36.8%	27 31.8%	104 35.4%
Major Urban Areas	9 4.3%	18 21.2%	27 9.2%
Small Towns	123 58.9%	40 47.0%	163 55.4%
TOTAL	209 100%	85 100%	294 100%

1 Census classifications.

TABLE 8

DEVELOPMENTS, SPONSOR TYPE BY SIZE

	NON-PROFIT	PUBLIC	N
20 or under beds/units	48 23.5%	33 40.7%	81 28.4%
21-40 beds/units	48 23.5%	19 23.5%	67 23.5%
41-80 beds/units	61 29.9%	17 21.0%	78 27.4%
81-149 beds/units	30 14.7%	6 7.4%	36 12.6%
150 or over beds/units	17 8.3%	6 7.4%	23 8.1%
TOTAL	204 100%	81 100%	285 100%

427

ACCOMMODATION TYPE: Table 9 shows the distribution of accommodation
types in relation to community size. Metropolitan and major urban
areas had mostly self-contained developments, as did small towns; but
in the latter there was a much better mix, with higher proportions of
hostel and mixed developments than found in larger areas. In fact,
70 per cent of all the hostel developments and 74 per cent of the
mixed hostel and self-contained developments were located in small
towns - compared with 50 per cent of the self-contained developments.

TABLE 9

DEVELOPMENTS, ACCOMMODATION TYPE BY COMMUNITY SIZE[1]

	SELF-CONTAINED	HOSTEL	MIXED	TOTAL
Metropolitan Areas	87 83.6%	11 10.6%	6 5.8%	104 100%
Major Urban Areas	23 85.2%	2 7.4%	2 7.4%	27 100%
Small Towns	110 67.5%	30 18.4%	23 14.1%	163 100%
TOTAL	220 74.8%	43 14.6%	31 10.5%	294 100%

1 Census classifications.

APPENDIX 2

MANAGER SURVEY QUESTIONNAIRE

Please assist us by having this questionnaire filled out by
the management person who has the most direct contact with
the residents and is closest to supervising the overall
operation of this particular housing development. He or she
may want to consult with others involved with the development,
including residents, in deciding on answers to some questions.

We would like to ask you some questions about your housing development, the people
there, and the social services available to them in your community. We would appreciate your answering every question.

A Word on the Terms We Use

As names used for different types of housing vary across Canada, we should explain
some of the terms we use:

Development: This is the general term we use for the senior citizen housing that
we need information about. You might call it "the project", "the home" or just
"the building".

Self-contained units: Are dwellings with living room or bed-sitting room, kitchen
and bath. The units may be built as separate cottages, row houses or apartment
buildings.

Hostel rooms: Offer the resident a bedroom or bed-sitter (either singly or shared)
and meals prepared and served in one or more central areas. The hostel room would
not have a full kitchen facility. We do not consider accommodation offering long-
term medical or nursing care to be hostel accommodation and ask you to exclude such
rooms and their residents in your responses.

A Note on How to Answer

Throughout the questionnaire, multiple choice answers indicated with a box (☐)
should be marked with a check as you think appropriate. Questions with a blank
space for the answer (_____) require a numerical figure, a word, or a sentence.
Please be sure to fill out both sides of each page.

COD

(Car

1 - A SELF-CONTAINED UNITS:

PLEASE RESPOND TO THE QUESTIONS ON THIS PAGE IF YOUR DEVELOPMENT CONTAINS ANY
SELF-CONTAINED UNITS FOR SENIOR CITIZENS. IF YOUR DEVELOPMENT CONTAINS NO SUCH
UNITS, PLEASE GO ON TO THE NEXT PAGE.

1. How many self-contained senior citizens units are there in this develop-
    ment (exclude hostel rooms)?

    1) _____ bachelor-type dwelling units
    2) _____ one-bedroom dwelling units
    3) _____ two or more bedroom dwelling units
    4) _____ none

1.

2. What is the total number of persons living at the present time in self-
    contained senior citizens units in the development (exclude hostel rooms)?

    _____total number of persons

14

3. In what type(s) of building(s) are your self-contained units located?
    Check:

    1) ☐ in apartment building(s) of less than 3 floors
    2) ☐ in high-rise apartment building(s) of 3 or more floors for some part
         of the building
    3) ☐ in row-housing
    4) ☐ in bungalows (semi-detached and detached)

16

4. Do you have an elevator for your self-contained senior citizens units?

    ☐ yes
    ☐ no

1

1 - B HOSTEL ROOMS:

PLEASE RESPOND TO THE QUESTIONS ON THIS PAGE IF YOUR DEVELOPMENT CONTAINS ANY
HOSTEL ROOMS. IF YOUR DEVELOPMENT CONTAINS NO SUCH ROOMS, PLEASE GO TO THE
NEXT PAGE.

1. How many hostel beds are there in the development (exclude self-contained
    units and nursing beds)?

    1) _____ total number of hostel beds in single rooms   6
    2) _____ total number of hostel beds in double rooms   7
    3) _____ total number of hostel beds in rooms with more than two beds   8
    4) _____ none

2. How many hostel rooms do you have?   9

    _____ number of hostel rooms

3. At the present time, what is the total number of hostel residents in the   10
    hostel rooms?

    _____ total number of hostel residents in hostel rooms

4. Are there common kitchenettes for hostel residents' use? Check: 11

    1) ☐ on all floors
    2) ☐ on some floors
    3) ☐ no kitchenettes

5. Concerning baths and toilets - Check:

    1) ☐ residents share baths in most cases
    2) ☐ residents share toilets in most cases
    3) ☐ residents share neither in most cases

6. In what type of building(s) are your hostel units located? Check: 16

    1) ☐ in apartment building of less than 3 floors
    2) ☐ in high-rise apartment building (of 3 or more floors for some part
         of the building)
    3) ☐ in row-housing
    4) ☐ in bungalows (semi-detached and detached)

    5) Do you have an elevator for your hostel rooms?   17

       ☐ yes
       ☐ no

II LONG-TERM NURSING CARE UNITS

7. Do you have any long-term (more than one month) medical or nursing care (not just an infirmary or other short-term facility for a minor sickness)?

18

☐ yes
☐ no

If yes,

_____ number of beds?

III STAFF

8. Could you list the positions of all the staff working in the development (both paid and voluntary staff over 10 hours a week such as maintenance man, nurse, gardener, cook)? Also give the number of people in each category (including nursing staff):

STAFF TITLE	NUMBER OF STAFF		NUMBER OF HOURS A WEEK	
	PAID	VOLUNTEER	PAID	VOLUNTEER
1)				
2)				
3)				
4)				
5)				
6)				
7)				
8)				
9)				
10)				
11)				
12)				

IV FACILITIES

A - Dining Room

(Card 3)

9. Is there a dining room in the development?

5

1) ☐ yes, cafeteria
2) ☐ yes, waitress service
3) ☐ no

10. Check the meals that are available:

    1) ☐ breakfast
    2) ☐ lunch   6
    3) ☐ dinner

11. How are residents charged for meals?   7

    1) ☐ included in rent. Give amount per month $_____$ 8
    2) ☐ by the meal. Give amount for dinner $_____$ 9

12. Is the dining room used by all or just some residents?   10

    1) ☐ all residents on regular basis
    2) ☐ some residents or all residents on an irregular basis

B -- COMMUNITY/RECREATION ROOM(S)

13. Is there one or more <u>central</u> community/recreational room(s) in the development?

    1) ☐ yes, and there is also a lounge on most floors or in most wings
    2) ☐ yes, but no floor or wing lounges
    3) ☐ no central community/recreational room(s) but one on most floors
       or in most wings
    4) ☐ none at all

    IF NO COMMUNITY/RECREATION ROOM(S) AT ALL, SKIP TO PAGE 6, SECTION C.

14. If there is a central community/recreation room or rooms, are they used   12
    only by residents or by residents and outsiders?

    1) ☐ only residents
    2) ☐ residents and other community groups

15. Are particular organizations (e.g., a tenants organization) responsible   13
    for operating and staffing the community/recreation room(s)?

    1) ☐ yes, totally
    2) ☐ yes, give minor or occasional help
    3) ☐ no

    If yes, list organization(s): _____

Activities in Central Community/Recreation Room or Special Room

	NO such activity in community room or special room	YES, in community/recreation room	YES, in special room	What is approximate degree of use?				
				Heavy	Medium	Light		
	1	2	3	1	2	3		
16. Are there table games:	☐	☐	☐	☐	☐	☐	14	15
17. Is there an area for television watching:	☐	☐	☐	☐	☐	☐	16	17
18. Are religious services held:	☐	☐	☐	☐	☐	☐	18	19
19. Is there a coffee hour:	☐	☐	☐	☐	☐	☐	20	21

20. What special events were held in the community/recreation room(s) during the past year? (Please give the name of the group holding the event).

22   23

_____

_____

21. What organized residents group(s), regular outside group(s), or mixed groups meet in these rooms regularly? (Give names)

24

1) Residents groups: _____
2) Outside groups: _____
3) Mixed groups: _____

22. Would you say, as to the use of the central community/recreation room(s), that:

25

1) ☐ all the residents use it regularly
2) ☐ only half or less of the residents use it regularly
3) ☐ only a few residents use it regularly
4) ☐ it is mainly used on special occasions
5) ☐ not used at all

23. If you have floor lounges, do:

26

1) ☐ all residents use them regularly
2) ☐ only a few residents use them regularly
3) ☐ only half or less of residents use them regularly
4) ☐ only used on special occasions
5) ☐ not used at all

24. What are the key areas for residents meeting together and exchanging a few words or sitting together?

    a) In the winter (e.g., hall or elevator): _____

    _____

    b) In the summer: _____

    _____

C - Facilities

AS FAR AS SERVICES AND RECREATION FACILITIES, COULD YOU CHECK WHICH OF THE FOLLOWING EXIST IN THE DEVELOPMENT, WHETHER THEY ARE USED BY NON-RESIDENTS AS WELL AS RESIDENTS, AND, IF NOT IN THE DEVELOPMENT, WHETHER THEY ARE FOUND WITHIN FIVE BLOCKS OF THE DEVELOPMENT - ALSO, WHICH SERVICES NOW LACKING YOU FEEL WOULD BE USEFUL?

Service/Facility	Check if in development	Check if you do not have, but feel would be useful	Check if used by non-residents	Check if not in development but within five blocks	
	1	3	1	1	
25. Crafts or Sewing Room	☐	☐	☐	☐	28 29 30
26. Bowling Alley	☐	☐	☐	☐	31 32 33
27. Laundry Facility	☐	☐	☐	☐	34 35 36
28. Beauty Shop	☐	☐	☐	☐	37 38 39
29. Barber Shop	☐	☐	☐	☐	40 41 42
30. Library Room	☐	☐	☐	☐	43 44 45
31. Greenhouse	☐	☐	☐	☐	46 47 48
32. Special Garden Plots	☐	☐	☐	☐	49 50 51
33. Golf Course, Lawn Bowling or Putting Area	☐	☐	☐	☐	52 53 54
34. Guest Room(s)	☐	☐	☐	☐	55 56 57
35. Separate TV Room	☐	☐	☐	☐	58 59 60
36. Separate Card, Chess, Cribbage, etc. Room	☐	☐	☐	☐	61 62 63
37. Telephone in Each Unit	☐	☐	☐	☐	64 65 66
38. Coffee Room	☐	☐	☐	☐	67 68 69
39. Auditorium	☐	☐	☐	☐	70 71 72

V — Services

WE WOULD LIKE TO ASK ABOUT SPECIAL SERVICES PROVIDED TO SOME OR ALL RESIDENTS OF YOUR DEVELOPMENT, EITHER IN THE DEVELOPMENT OR IN THE COMMUNITY. WE WOULD ALSO LIKE TO KNOW WHO PROVIDES THE SERVICE, WHERE IT IS PROVIDED, THE DEGREE OF USE, AND WHETHER THERE IS A FEE.

CODING

SERVICE	WHETHER AVAILABLE		NAME OF SPONSOR OR ORGANIZATION	LOCATION AT WHICH SERVICE AVAILABLE		DEGREE OF USE BY RESIDENTS		FEE				
	YES	NO		In Development	In Community	Used by Most Residents	Used by a Few Residents	No Fee	Fee Geared to Income	Fee Same For All	Don't Know	(Card 4)
	1	2		1	2	1	2	1	2	3	4	
40. Is there a home-maker service (general home management available?	☐	☐		☐	☐	☐	☐	☐	☐	☐	☐	6 7 8 9 10
41. Is there a maid service? a) for hostel rooms	☐	☐		☐	☐	☐	☐	☐	☐	☐	☐	11 12 13 14 15
b) for apartment units	☐	☐		☐	☐	☐	☐	☐	☐	☐	☐	
42. Is there a prepared meal delivery program? (Meals-on-Wheels)	☐	☐		☐	☐	☐	☐	☐	☐	☐	☐	16 17 18 19 20
43. Is there home nursing assistance (VON or visiting public health nurse)?	☐	☐		☐	☐	☐	☐	☐	☐	☐	☐	21 22 23 24 25

SERVICE	WHETHER AVAILABLE		NAME OF SPONSOR OR ORGANIZATION	LOCATION AT WHICH SERVICE AVAILABLE		DEGREE OF USE BY RESIDENTS		FEE				Coding
	YES 1	NO 2		In Development 1	In Community 2	Used by Most Residents 1	Used by a Few Residents 2	No Fee 1	Fee Geared to Income 2	Fee Same For All 3	Don't Know 4	
44. Is there a telephone contact service? (volunteer checking daily on particular residents)	☐	☐	___	☐	☐	☐	☐	☐	☐	☐	☐	26 27 28 29 30
45. Is there a volunteer friendly visiting service available?	☐	☐	___	☐	☐	☐	☐	☐	☐	☐	☐	31 32 33 34 35
46. Is there a volunteer transportation service?	☐	☐	___	☐	☐	☐	☐	☐	☐	☐	☐	36 37 38 39 40
47. Is there legal aid counselling?	☐	☐	___	☐	☐	☐	☐	☐	☐	☐	☐	41 42 43 44 45
48. Are there social work counselling services?	☐	☐	___	☐	☐	☐	☐	☐	☐	☐	☐	46 47 48 49 50
49. Does a mobile library visit?	☐	☐	___	☐	☐	☐	☐	☐	☐	☐	☐	51 52 53 54 55
50. Is there a food shopping service?	☐	☐	___	☐	☐	☐	☐	☐	☐	☐	☐	56 57 58 59 60

438

SERVICE	WHETHER AVAILABLE		NAME OF SPONSOR OR ORGANIZATION	LOCATION AT WHICH SERVICE AVAILABLE		DEGREE OF USE BY RESIDENTS		FEE				CODING
	YES 1	NO 2		In Development 1	In Community 2	Used by Most Residents 1	Used by a Few Residents 2	No Fee 1	Fee Geared to Income 2	Fee Same For All 3	Don't Know 4	
51. Is there a regular check-up service (free or otherwise)?	☐	☐	|	☐	☐	☐	☐	☐	☐	☐	☐	61 62 63 64 65
52. Is there a buddy system or good neighbour system?	☐	☐	|	☐	☐	☐	☐	☐	☐	☐	☐	66 67 68 69 70
53. Is there a group leadership service or group worker?	☐	☐	|	☐	☐	☐	☐	☐	☐	☐	☐	71 72 73 74 75
54. Are there senior citizens centres or Golden Age Clubs or similar organizations?	☐	☐	|	☐	☐	☐	☐	☐	☐	☐	☐	(Card 5) 6 7 8 9 10

VI MEDICAL FACILITIES/SERVICES

55. Do you have an infirmary or sick room(s) for temporary care (one month or less) in the development? (Exclude long-term care beds)

    ☐ no
    ☐ yes

    If yes,

    _____ number of beds

56. On what basis do you use a doctor in your development?

    a) Is he on your full-time staff?
       ☐ yes
       ☐ no
    b) Does he make daily visits?
       ☐ yes
       ☐ no
    c) Is he on call?
       ☐ yes
       ☐ no
    d) Do your residents almost all have personal doctors?
       ☐ yes
       ☐ no
    e) Is dental care available in the development?
       ☐ yes
       ☐ no

57. Is your development associated with a community medical facility such as a hospital?

    1) ☐ yes, located in or near same facility
    2) ☐ yes, but the development is not located in or near medical facility
    3) ☐ no

VII LOCATION OF DEVELOPMENT

58. Is your development located in a:

    1) ☐ downtown area
    2) ☐ older residential area
    3) ☐ suburban area
    4) ☐ other area. Explain:_____

Coding column values: 11, 12, 13, 14, 15, 17, 18, 19

59. How would you describe the people living in the area around the development? Check one:

    1) ☐ a large proportion are elderly
    2) ☐ they are mostly families with children
    3) ☐ they are mainly childless families or singles
    4) ☐ they are mainly transients

20

60. How close is the development to each of the following?

	Easy Walk for Most Residents	Easy Bus or Public Transportation	Difficult Bus or Public Transportation	
a) Shopping Centre other than grocery store	☐	☐	☐	21
b) Grocery store	☐	☐	☐	22
c) Major denominational churches	☐	☐	☐	23
d) Medical offices or clinic	☐	☐	☐	24
e) Hospital	☐	☐	☐	25
f) Library	☐	☐	☐	26
g) Senior Citizen Centre	☐	☐	☐	27
h) Parks	☐	☐	☐	28

VIII UNIT DEMAND

61. Do you maintain a separate waiting list for this development, make use of a central registry, or do you use no waiting list at all?

    1) ☐ own separate waiting list
    2) ☐ central registry
    3) ☐ no list at all

    If you maintain a separate waiting list for this development, indicate how many applications are currently on file for:

    1) _____ self-contained units
       _____ one-bedroom units
       _____ bachelor units
       _____ two or more bedrooms

35-37

    2) _____ hostel beds
       _____ in one-bed rooms
       _____ in two-bed rooms

38-39

62. If a resident occupying a one-bedroom apartment or a double hostel room with a spouse was to be widowed, would the resident be asked to move to another type of unit or room?

41

    1) ☐ yes
    2) ☐ sometimes
    3) ☐ no

IX RESIDENT PHYSICAL CAPACITY

63. ELDERLY PEOPLE HAVE DIFFERENT DEGREES OF PHYSICAL INCAPACITY; SOME OF
THESE ARE OUTLINED BELOW. COULD YOU GIVE US AN APPROXIMATION OF THE
PROPORTION OF RESIDENTS IN THIS DEVELOPMENT IN EACH CATEGORY? (YOUR
CHECKS MAY COME TO MORE THAN 100%)

Degree of Incapacity	¼ of Residents or Less	About ¼ to ½ of Residents	About ½ to ¾ of Residents	Most of Residents	Don't Know	
a) No incapacity (can move about without difficulty and keep house)	☐	☐	☐	☐	☐	42
b) Slightly limited ability (some minor difficulty either in moving about, communicating and/or keeping house)	☐	☐	☐	☐	☐	43
c) Moderately limited ability (noticeable handicap in one activity or faculty, needing limited or continuous aid)	☐	☐	☐	☐	☐	44
d) Seriously limited ability (residents unable to accomplish many daily tasks such as walking, washing self, keeping house, talking, seeing or hearing)	☐	☐	☐	☐	☐	45

64. What is the maximum degree of incapacity described in question 63 that the
usual applicant is permitted on admission to your development?   46

    1) ☐ no incapacity
    2) ☐ slightly limited ability
    3) ☐ moderately limited ability
    4) ☐ seriously limited ability
    5) ☐ don't know

65. What is the degree of incapacity described in question 63 at which a
person is asked to move to another type of residence?   47

    1) ☐ slightly limited ability
    2) ☐ moderately limited ability
    3) ☐ seriously limited ability
    4) ☐ don't know

66. How many persons have left your development or died in the last 12 months?   48
    (Give number)

    1) _____ died
    2) _____ set up or returned to own home
    3) _____ went to live with relatives
    4) _____ left for nursing home or hospital
    5) _____ went to similar housing development
    6) _____ went to hostel or special care accommodation
    7) _____ other. Explain:_____
    8) ☐ don't know

67. Are residents allowed to keep pets in the development?   49

    1) ☐ birds
    2) ☐ dogs
    3) ☐ cats
    4) ☐ none
    5) ☐ other

X   USER CHARACTERISTICS

68. Regarding the age of your residents in self-contained units, could you   51
    tell us what proportion is in each of the below age groups. (Give
    approximate age breakdown)

	$\frac{1}{4}$ of Residents or Less	About $\frac{1}{4}$ to $\frac{1}{2}$ of Residents	About $\frac{1}{2}$ to $\frac{3}{4}$ of Residents	Most of Residents	Don't Know
1) Under 65	☐	☐	☐	☐	☐
2) 65-74	☐	☐	☐	☐	☐
3) 75 and over	☐	☐	☐	☐	☐
4) No residents in self-contained units ☐					

69. Regarding the age of your residents in hostel rooms, could you tell us   52
    what the approximate proportion is in each of the below age groups?
    (Give approximate age breakdown)

	$\frac{1}{4}$ of Residents or Less	About $\frac{1}{4}$ to $\frac{1}{2}$ of Residents	About $\frac{1}{2}$ to $\frac{3}{4}$ of Residents	Most of Residents	Don't Know
1) Under 65	☐	☐	☐	☐	☐
2) 65-74	☐	☐	☐	☐	☐
3) 75 and over	☐	☐	☐	☐	☐
4) No residents in hostel rooms ☐					

70. Regarding the age of all your residents, could you tell us what approximate proportion is in each of the below age groups? (Give approximate
age breakdown)

	¼ of Residents or Less	About ¼ to ½ of Residents	About ½ to ¾ of Residents	Most of Residents	Don't Know
1) Under 65	☐	☐	☐	☐	☐
2) 65-74	☐	☐	☐	☐	☐
3) 75 and over	☐	☐	☐	☐	☐

71. Could you indicate the approximate proportion of your residents that
depend on each of the income sources given below?

	¼ of Residents or Less	About ¼ to ½ of Residents	About ½ to ¾ of Residents	Most of Residents	Don't Know
1) Dependent solely on government pension and supplement	☐	☐	☐	☐	☐
2) Dependent on above and some savings or private pension	☐	☐	☐	☐	☐
3) Dependent on above and substantial savings or private pension	☐	☐	☐	☐	☐

72. Approximately what proportion of your residents are men, and what
proportion are women?

	¼ of Residents or Less	About ¼ to ½ of Residents	About ½ to ¾ of Residents	Most of Residents	Don't Know
1) Men	☐	☐	☐	☐	☐
2) Women	☐	☐	☐	☐	☐

XI SOCIAL PARTICIPATION

73. Would you say your development is considered just another residence on
the street or is it isolated to a large degree?

1) ☐ just another residence on the street
2) ☐ considered slightly isolated from other residences on the street
3) ☐ considered largely isolated from other residences due to physical
    or social layout or location

444

74. Would you say that the local churches and service organizations or social clubs have a major, a fair amount or little contact with the development?

	Major Contact	Fair Amount of Contact	Little Contact
1) Churches	☐	☐	☐	57
2) Service Clubs	☐	☐	☐	58
3) Social Clubs	☐	☐	☐	59

75. Are any residents on the management board of the development?   60

1) ☐ no
2) ☐ yes
3) _____ how many?

76. Do any residents take on any duties in the development such as cleaning halls, gardening, helping in kitchen, etc.? (If yes, give proportion who do)   61

1) ☐ no
2) ☐ yes, some do and the proportion is: (a) ☐ $\frac{1}{4}$ or less
(b) ☐ $\frac{1}{4}$ to $\frac{1}{2}$ do
(c) ☐ $\frac{1}{2}$ to $\frac{3}{4}$ do
(d) ☐ most do

List duties: _____

77. Is there a residents' association in your development?   62

1) ☐ no
2) ☐ yes

78. If yes, what proportion of residents participate in this organization?

1) ☐ $\frac{1}{4}$ of residents or less
2) ☐ About $\frac{1}{4}$ to $\frac{1}{2}$ of residents
3) ☐ About $\frac{1}{2}$ to $\frac{3}{4}$ of residents
4) ☐ Most of residents

XII INFORMATION ON MANAGERS/SPONSORS

79. What is your name and position? Having your name will give us some one to contact in case follow-up is needed.

Name _____

Position _____

80. Check which of the below are your duties in the development. Give your opinion of how much you feel you should be responsible for each of the duties listed.

Check if Your Job	Very Much Responsible	Should be Responsible	Should Not Be My Job	
1) ☐ Keeping the account books and managing the financial aspects of the development	☐	☐	☐	63 64
2) ☐ Obtaining community services for the development	☐	☐	☐	65 66
3) ☐ Collect rents and rent units	☐	☐	☐	67 68
4) ☐ Maintenance and upkeep of buildings	☐	☐	☐	69 70
5) ☐ Running social service programs in the development	☐	☐	☐	71 72
6) ☐ Making individual contact with residents and helping them with their needs	☐	☐	☐	73 74

81. What are your two greatest problems in running this development?

1) _____

2) _____

82. Could you tell us something about your own background? How many years have you been working with the elderly?

1) ☐ less than two years
2) ☐ two to four years
3) ☐ five or more years
4) ☐ none of these

83. School grade completed (circle last year):

1 2 3 4 5 6 7 8 9 10 11 12 13

College year:

1 2 3 4 5

84. Are you?

1) ☐ female
2) ☐ male

85. In what age group would you fall?   80

    1) ☐ under 30
    2) ☐ 30-44
    3) ☐ 45-54
    4) ☐ 55-64
    5) ☐ 65-74
    6) ☐ 75-79
    7) ☐ 80 or more

(Card

86. In your opinion, is there a shortage of decent and reasonably priced
self-contained and hostel accommodation for senior citizens in your
community?

Self-Contained   6

☐ yes, severe
☐ yes, moderate
☐ yes, some
☐ no shortage
☐ don't know

Hostel   7

☐ yes, severe
☐ yes, moderate
☐ yes, some
☐ no shortage
☐ don't know

XIII SPONSORSHIP

87. What is the name of the organization that built this housing for the   8
elderly?

_____

88. Is it affiliated with another organization, e.g., church, service club   9
or government body or a combination of these?

    1) ☐ yes
    2) ☐ no

89. If so, what is the name of this organization?

_____

90. Because of your organizational affiliation, do you give preference in   10
    housing senior citizens of a particular ethnic, religious, language group
    or service club group?

    1) ☐ no
    2) ☐ yes

    Group: _____

91. What proportion os the residents would you say were from this group?

    1) ☐ ¼ or less
    2) ☐ About ¼ to ½ of residents
    3) ☐ About ½ to ¾ of residents
    4) ☐ Most of residents

92. Some developments want a good mixture of residents of varying incomes and   11
    thus limit the number of residents whose only resource is the federal old
    age security pension and supplements. If you limit the proportion, could
    you give us the approximate proportion you prefer in the pension-only
    group?

    1) ☐ ¼ or less
    2) ☐ About ¼ to ½ of residents
    3) ☐ About ½ to ¾ of residents
    4) ☐ No limit

XIV RENT AND FINANCES

THIS INFORMATION IS VERY IMPORTANT. PLEASE CONSULT OR PASS THE QUESTIONNAIRE
ON TO YOUR TREASURER.

Could you give the monthly rent for different types of units in your development? (If weekly rent, multiply by 4 1/3):

93. Self-Contained

    Apartment rent per month: $ _____ for bachelor apartment (give range)   12
                              $ _____ for one bedroom (give range)   13

94. Hostel

    Rent per month per person: $ _____ in one-bed hostel room   14
                               $ _____ in two-bed hostel room   15
                               $ _____ in three or more bed hostel room   16

95. Have you had other loan(s) to cover building cost besides the CMHC or   17
    Quebec Housing Corporation loan(s)?

    1) ☐ no
    2) ☐ yes

96. If yes, what portion of land and building costs did the other loan(s) cover?

_____ %

97. Were there other loan(s) for any special part of the building (such as community room or medical wing)?

1) ☐ yes
2) ☐ no

18

98. Does any private group or government agency do any of the following?

	No	Yes	What Agency?	Explain:
a) Help defray part of your operating costs?	☐	☐	_____	_____
b) Directly subsidize rents of any residents?	☐	☐	_____	_____
c) Give you (or has in the past given you) a capital grant?	☐	☐	_____	_____

19

20

21

99. Does your development pay:

1) ☐ no municipal taxes?
2) ☐ reduced municipal taxes?
3) ☐ full municipal taxes?

22

100. Do you have an income ceiling for admission and, if so, what is the highest income allowed for singles and for couples?

1) ☐ yes, approximately $_____ for singles
2) ☐ yes, approximately $_____ for couples
3) ☐ no, no income ceiling for admission

16

101. What is the lowest income allowed for admission?

1) $_____ approximately for singles
   $_____ approximately for couples

2) ☐ no income floor. Income residents are expected to assess their own ability to pay

3) ☐ other means used to assess ability to pay rent.

   Explain: _____

17

102. Is your organization interested in building and/or managing other housing developments for the elderly?

1) ☐ no
2) ☐ yes

18

103. If yes, are you having any particular problems in doing this?

1) ☐ no
2) ☐ yes

Explain: _____

THANK YOU VERY MUCH FOR YOUR HELP. PLEASE USE THE ATTACHED
ENVELOPE TO RETURN THE QUESTIONNAIRE TO THE Study of Housing
Developments for the Elderly HEADQUARTERS IN OTTAWA.

APPENDIX 3

USER SURVEY METHODOLOGY

Methodology

The size of the sample selected in each development was proportionate
to the size of the development. In all cases it was sufficiently large
(not under 10 per cent) to satisfy scientific sampling criteria. The
following sampling fractions were used:

TABLE 1	
Number of Dwelling Units and/ or Hostel Beds in Development	Sample Size
15	40%
15-25	35%
26-50	30%
51-70	25%
71-85	20%
86-100	15%
101-125	12%
126-250	10%
Over 250	25%

In each development, residents were selected for interviews by means of
a probability or random* sampling procedure. This was applied to tenant
lists (most were alphabetically ordered) which, in the case of mixed
developments, had been stratified according to accommodation type (hostel
beds and dwelling units). In the one or two developments that lacked a
tenant list, respondents were selected according to the number of their
unit (e.g. every fifth or tenth door, depending on the sampling fraction).
A total of 303 residents were interviewed.

Interviews were arranged through letters, which also introduced the field
worker and explained the purpose of the study. Confidentiality was stressed
and it was made clear that the research staff were not connected with the
development's management. In most developments, a very low rate of refusal

---

* Systematic or "quasi-random" sampling as opposed to simple random sampling.

451

was encountered. Where a refusal or absence occurred, interviewers were instructed to select another respondent. Also, where it was obvious after 10 minutes of interviewing that the respondent was very confused or uncomprehending (the interview was constructed to detect this), the interview was ended and another resident was selected instead; this was necessary in only three cases. The interviewers were four trained staff; three had a background in sociology and psychology, and one was French-speaking.

An interview schedule (see Appendix 4) was used; it contained 81 questions and required the interviewer to record 11 sets of impressions. Some of the questions were open-ended and interviewers were permitted to rephrase questions if they thought it would help the respondent. In the province of Quebec, interviews were conducted in French, using a French interview schedule. The average interview time was 50 minutes, after pretesting.

Residents' responses were coded and punched on IBM cards in Ottawa. The data was then processed at the Survey Research Center of the University of California at Berkeley.

Sample Validity

Although, in a strict sense, our probability sample is representative only of the 19 developments selected for case study, it appears to correspond well in many respects to the total population of NHA financed housing for the elderly in Canada. The national representativeness of our sample is indicated by comparison of some of the user data with the national data reported in Part II, and also with the data that emerged from our national probability sample of housing managers.

In terms of the distribution of NHA financed accommodation for the elderly in the various regions of the country, our sample was fairly representative of the Atlantic Provinces, the Prairies, and British Columbia. Quebec, however, is over-represented in the user survey, and Ontario is under-represented. The regional distribution of the user survey respondents as compared to the distribution of all NHA financed accommodation for the elderly (as indicated in Part II, Table 3) is shown below.

TABLE 2		
Region	Proportion of User Survey Respondents	Proportion of all NHA Units and Beds (end 1970)
Atlantic Provinces	10.6%	7.4%
Quebec	18.1%	5.9%
Ontario	36.0%	50.3%
Prairies	23.1%	17.7%
British Columbia	12.2%	18.7%
CANADA	100.0%	100.0%

The user survey over-represents residents of large urban areas: 73
per cent of the respondents lived in metropolitan and major urban areas
(census terms), whereas by the end of 1970 only 39 per cent of all NHA
financed developments for the elderly were located in metropolitan and
major urban areas (see Part II, Table 6). However, the bias is not as
great as these figures indicate because developments in metropolitan and
major urban centres tend to be much larger than those in small towns
(and consequently the proportion of residents of urban areas would be
higher than the proportion of developments in rural areas).

In terms of sponsor type, the user survey sample is fairly representative
of the population of NHA housing for the elderly. In the user survey
sample, 68 per cent of respondents lived in non-profit developments and
32 per cent in public housing; in the total population, 64 per cent of
all dwelling units and hostel beds were built by non-profit sponsors and
36 per cent by public housing agencies (see Part II, Table 11).

In terms of accommodation type, the user sample was fairly representative
of the national population of NHA financed housing for the elderly built
by the end of 1970. In the user sample, 37 per cent of the respondents
were in hostel accommodation (and 63 per cent in self-contained units).
In the NHA housing, 25 per cent of the residents were in hostel accommodation (see Part II, Table 11).

Some of the demographic characteristics of the user survey sample can be
compared to the national stratified probability sample on which the manager
survey is based, although differences in question wording complicate this
task. Nevertheless, it is clear that, in terms of the age range of
residents, the user sample corresponds fairly closely to the national
sample. In the user study, 60 per cent of respondents were aged 75 and
older. In the manager survey, only 40 per cent of managers said that the
largest group in their development was aged 75 and over (reported by 63
per cent of hostel managers and 22 per cent of the managers of self-contained
developments). However, the apparent discrepancy between respondents' ages
in the user and manager surveys decreases when one takes into account that
hostel developments tend to be much larger than self-contained ones (see
Part II, Table 6). On the basis of further analysis of the statistical
universe and the management study sample, it appears that the user study
respondents were probably slightly older than all residents of NHA financed
housing for the elderly.

When it comes to health status, 78 per cent of the user survey respondents
said that they had no health problems, or only slight disabilities, while
64 per cent of the manager respondents claimed that none of their residents
had serious health limitations. The questions in the two surveys differ
to such an extent that comparisons are difficult; but it would appear
that the prevalence of serious physical incapacities is probably not
significantly different between the two samples.

The sex of over two-thirds (69 per cent) of the user sample was female. This appears to be fairly typical of all housing developments. In the manager survey, only 10 per cent of developments reported one-half or more male residents, 57 per cent reported less than a quarter males, and 32 per cent reported one-fourth to one-half males.

The financial status of residents appears to differ in the user and the management surveys. In the user survey, only 35 per cent of residents said they were dependent solely on the old age security pension and guaranteed income supplement; in the manager survey, however, 69 per cent of developments reported that most of their residents were dependent solely on the pension and supplement. This discrepancy might be explained by managers' lack of awareness of residents' financial resources, or by the reluctance of user survey respondents to admit to having no other income.

APPENDIX 4

USER SURVEY INTERVIEW SCHEDULE

1. How long have you lived here (this development)?   Col. 4

    1) _____ less than six months
    2) _____ 6-11 months
    3) _____ 1-3 years
    4) _____ over 3 years
    5) _____ don't know

2. Where did you live <u>immediately before</u> you moved to this facility or   Col. 5
    development? (IF A TOWN NAMED, PROBE AS TO WHICH BELOW CATEGORY IT
    FITS INTO)

    1) _____ this neighbourhood
    2) _____ in this city/town/village
    3) _____ outside the city

3. (a) Did you live in a?   Col. 6

         1) _____ house
         2) _____ low-rise (garden) apartment
         3) _____ elevator apartment
         4) _____ hostel
         5) _____ nursing home, hospital, other institutional setting
         6) _____ other:_____

    (b) Did you live with someone else?   Col. 7

         1) _____ no
         2) _____ yes

    (c) Who?

         1) _____ spouse
         2) _____ other relative(s)
         3) _____ friend(s)
         4) _____ assigned roommate(s)

    (d) Did you?   Col. 8

         1) _____ rent
         2) _____ own
         3) _____ board

4. Who do you live with now?   Col. 9

    1) _____ alone
    2) _____ with spouse
    3) _____ with other relative
    4) _____ with friend knew before came to this housing
    5) _____ with assigned roommate(s)
    6) _____ don't know

5. Whose choice was it to move here? Who helped you make the choice? Col. 10

   1) _____ entirely own (and spouse's) decision
   2) _____ to a large part choice/decision of a relative
   3) _____ to a large part choice/decision of a friend or neighbour
   4) _____ to a large part choice/decision of social worker/doctor
         or other person from social agency/hospital or other
         medical facility
   5) _____ person working for this development
   6) _____ other _____
   7) _____ don't know

6. Why or what reasons made you decide to move to this housing? Col. 11-12
   (PROBE FOR ALL IMPORTANT REASONS).

   1) _____ needed some nursing/medical services
   2) _____ needed help in cooking, shopping, homemaking - hard to do
         on own any more
   3) _____ unable to keep up maintenance of own home

   4) _____ loss of home (expropriation) or financial need to sell home
   5) _____ felt need of company (lonely, depressed, isolated, etc.)
   6) _____ planned move as part of retirement
   7) _____ knew other people who had moved here (and wanted to be
         close to them)
   8) _____ mainly because relatives, social agency, doctor, friends/
         neighbours, felt it place I should move to
   9) _____ felt financially best choice with limited income to pay for
         housing
  10) _____ felt need for security and safety
  11) _____ felt more comfortable (decent standard) than former housing
         (more modern)
  12) _____ boarding with family and they needed room or made uncomfortable

N.B. (a) INTERVIEWER, IF RENT NOT MENTIONED, ASK IF RENT WAS A MAJOR REASON?

    (b) INTERVIEWER, IF MAINTENANCE OF OWN HOME NOT MENTIONED, ASK IF IT
       A REASON?

PAST HISTORY - Now, could we talk about your own background?

7. In what year were you born? _____ Col. 13

   (CODER, FILL IN CORRECT CATEGORY)

   1) _____ under 65
   2) _____ 65-69
   3) _____ 70-74
   4) _____ 75-79
   5) _____ 80 plus
   6) _____ don't know

457

CODING

8. What is your marital status? (INTERVIEWER, DO NOT ASK UNLESS UNCLEAR)   Col. 14

1) _____ married, living with spouse
2) _____ divorced, separated or married, not living with spouse
3) _____ widowed
4) _____ single
5) _____ don't know

NOTE: IF LOSS OF MEMORY-CONFUSION INDICATED BY LACK OF ANSWERS (DON'T KNOWS) TO QUESTIONS 1-9 WITH AT LEAST FOUR QUESTIONS "DON'T REMEMBER" OR "DON'T KNOW", STOP INTERVIEW HERE.

9. How many living children do you have? (INTERVIEWER, USE AS CHECK FOR BELOW). _____ number of children _____ no children   Col. 15-16

How near do they live? (FOR EACH LIVING CHILD, CHECK AREA):

	In Immediate Area	In or Close to City	Elsewhere
Child 1	_____	_____	_____
Child 2	_____	_____	_____
Child 3	_____	_____	_____
Child 4	_____	_____	_____
Child 5	_____	_____	_____
Child 6	_____	_____	_____
Child 7	_____	_____	_____

10. Do you have other relatives living in the immediate area or city/town?   Col. 17-19

_____ no living brother or sister

LIST EACH LIVING BROTHER OR SISTER	WHERE RELATIVE LIVES		
	In Immediate Area of Facility	In or Near This City/Town	Elsewhere
_____	_____	_____	_____
_____	_____	_____	_____
_____	_____	_____	_____
_____	_____	_____	_____
_____	_____	_____	_____

11. How often do you and your family visit or telephone one another?   Col. 20-21
     Is it daily, weekly, monthly?

     1) _____ no family
     2) _____ daily visit or talk over the phone with at least one
              relative
     3) _____ at least once a week, a visit with or talk over the
              phone with at least one relative
     4) _____ at least once a month, a visit with or talk over the
              phone with at least one relative
     5) _____ at least once a year, a visit with or talk over the
              phone with at least one relative
     6) _____ less than once a year or no visit or phoning

12. ASK ONLY IF CHILDREN

     How important do you think it is for your housing to be located   Col. 22-23
     in the same neighbourhood as your children? Very important,
     somewhat important, not very important? How important is it to
     be in or close to the same city as your children live in?

     _____ no children

                                    Same Neighbourhood   Same City

     1) very important   _____   _____
     2) somewhat important   _____   _____
     3) not very important   _____   _____

HEALTH - Now, we would like to ask about your health. (INTERVIEWER,
         EXPLORE PHYSICAL CAPACITY BY ASKING NECESSARY QUESTIONS).

13. How does your health affect your getting around and doing tasks?   Col. 24
     In general, how would you rate your physical capacity? I'll
     read off different degrees of incapacity. (CHECK ONE):

     1) _____ seriously limited ability in areas of walking, or seeing
              or hearing; unable to accomplish many daily tasks on own

     2) _____ moderately limited physical ability/capacity as noticeable
              handicap in one activity or facility just mentioned so
              that I need limited or continuous aid

     3) _____ slightly limited physical ability as some minor difficulty
              either in moving about, communicating, and/or keeping house

     4) _____ no incapacity (can move about without difficulty, and can
              keep house)

14. (a) (INTERVIEWER, PROBE ON TYPE OF HEALTH PROBLEM AND CHECK   Col. 25
BELOW.   CHECK AS MANY AS APPLY):

    1) _____ a cane or crutch or other brace, artificial limb
            (not a cane for blindness)
    2) _____ a wheelchair or walker
    3) _____ a hearing aid
    4) _____ special shoes/other foot care
    5) _____ medication once or more a day
    6) _____ special diet
    7) _____ blindness
    8) _____ heart problem
    9) _____ other problems - _____

  (b) Have you been confined to your bed at home or in hospital   Col. 26-28
during the last year for more than a week?

    1) _____ at home   Number of days _____
    2) _____ in hospital or nursing convalescent home
        Number of days _____

SERVICES

15. Do you feel that it would be helpful to you to have a nurse come   Col. 30
in regularly? (INTERVIEWER, IF IT IS OBVIOUS THE PERSON NEEDS
NURSING HELP, CHECK NEED EVEN THOUGH THE PERSON ANSWERS "NOT
HELPFUL")

    1) _____ seems helpful to have nurse come in regularly
    2) _____ does not seem to need this help

IF DO NOT NEED, MOVE ON TO QUESTION 16.

  (a) (IF NEED HELP) Is nursing help available and are you getting   Col. 31
it now (from friends or relatives, VON, development nursing
staff, public health department nurse, or adjacent hospital)?

    1) _____ not available though need help
    2) _____ get from friends or relatives
    3) _____ VON
    4) _____ private nursing service
    5) _____ public health nurse
    6) _____ adjacent nearby hospital or nursing home
    7) _____ other. Specify_____

  (b) If do not use though available, why? (PROBE)   Col. 32

    _____

    _____

  (c) If nursing help used (from other than relatives or friends),   Col. 33
any shortcomings or problems?

    _____

16. Do you (or your spouse) have difficulty doing everyday housework (making beds, washing dishes, cleaning)?

Col. 34

1) _____ yes
2) _____ no

IF NO DIFFICULTY, MOVE TO QUESTION 17.

    Is a maid service available and do you use it?

Col. 35

    1) _____ available and use
    2) _____ available but do not use
    3) _____ they say not available

(b) Is a homemaker service available from some source (in community or development) and do you use it?

Col. 36

    1) _____ available and use
    2) _____ available but do not use
    3) _____ they say not available

ASK QUESTION 16 (c) IF ANSWER 2 OR 3 TO BOTH QUESTIONS 16 (a) and 16 (b).

(c) Do relatives or friends regularly help you (or your spouse)?

Col. 37

    1) _____ yes
    2) _____ no

ASK QUESTION 16 (d) IF 16 (a) OR (b) IS ANSWER 2.

(d) If homemaker or maid service is available but you do not use, why?

Col. 38

    1) _____ too expensive
    2) _____ use other service
    3) _____ do not like staff in my room
    4) _____ generally dislike staff
    5) _____ do not think staff does a good job
    6) _____ staff does irregularly so of little use
    7) _____ other. PROBE_____

ASK QUESTION 16 (e) IF 16 (a) OR 16 (b) ANSWER IS 1.

    If use either, are there any things you don't like about the service?

Col. 39

_____

_____

_____

ONLY SELF-CONTAINED ANSWER QUESTION 17 THROUGH 18 (b).

17. (a) Do you (or your spouse) have difficulty doing the shopping   Col. 40
in the winter?

     1) _____ yes
     2) _____ no

IF NO DIFFICULTY, MOVE TO QUESTION 18.

     (b) Does a friend or relative regularly help you?   Col. 41

     1) _____ yes
     2) _____ no

     (c) ASK ONLY IF FRIEND NOT USED FOR ASSISTANCE.
Are any of the following organized sources available for
shopping assistance and do you use them?

     1) Grocery store delivery service?   Col. 42

         1. _____ available and use
         2. _____ available but do not use
         3. _____ they say not available

     2) Development staff help with shopping?   Col. 43

         1. _____ available and use
         2. _____ available but do not use
         3. _____ they say not available

     3) Outside food shopping or homemaker service?   Col. 44

         1. _____ available and use
         2. _____ available but do not use
         3. _____ they say not available

     4) Church or voluntary group (not regular shopping service)?   Col. 45

         1. _____ available and use
         2. _____ available and do not use
         3. _____ they say not available

ASK IF ANSWER 2 TO ANY OF ABOVE:

     (d) If a service is available and you do not use, why not?   Col. 46

     _____

     _____

ASK IF ANSWER 1 TO ANY OF THE ABOVE:

     (e) If do use, any shortcomings or problems?   Col. 47-48

     Service used: _____

     _____

CODING

18. (a) Do you (or your spouse) have trouble COOKING a hot meal?   Col. 49

     1) _____ yes
     2) _____ no

IF NO DIFFICULTY, GO ON TO QUESTION 19.

     (b) Does a friend or relative do major cooking regularly for you?   Col. 50

     1) _____ yes
     2) _____ no

     (c) ASK ONLY IF FRIEND DOES NOT DO MAJOR COOKING.
          Do you have available and use MEALS-ON-WHEELS or another   Col. 51
          hot meal delivery service?

     1) _____ available and use
     2) _____ available but do not use
     3) _____ the resident says not available

          ASK ONLY IF FRIEND DOES NOT DO MAJOR COOKING. ASK ONLY IF
          DINING ROOM (CAFETERIA) AVAILABLE IN THE DEVELOPMENT
          (OR NEARBY).
          Do you use the DINING ROOM or CAFETERIA available in this   Col. 52
          housing/complex (or nearby)?

     1) _____ available and use. ___1 meal ___2 meals ___3 meals
     2) _____ available but do not use, cook for self or friend
              cooks for me
     3) _____ available and do not use, use other food preparation
              services
     4) _____ they say not available

     (e) ASK IF ANSWER IS 2 TO EITHER 18 (c) OR (d).

          If either dining room or hot meal delivery available and you   Col. 53
          do not use, why?

     1) _____ use other type of meal service. Explain_____

          _____

     2) _____ eat in restaurants
     3) _____ don't like food
     4) _____ can't carry trays
     5) _____ need special diet
     6) _____ don't like atmosphere of service

          ASK IF ANSWER IS 1 TO EITHER 18 (c) OR 18 (d).
          If use either, are there any shortcomings, anything you find   Col. 54-55
          unsatisfactory about the service?

          _____

          _____

19. Do you have trouble getting to places you want to go most?
(PROBE FOR TROUBLE GETTING TO GROCERY STORE, SHOPPING CENTRE
OTHER THAN GROCERY STORE, CHURCHES).

Col. 56

1) _____ yes
2) _____ no

20. Do you have regular help from a friend or a relative in getting
to any of the places you want most to get to?

Col. 57

1) _____ yes
2) _____ no

21. Do you have available and use a volunteer transportation system
(or professionally staffed one) - driver, special bus, etc., to
places you especially want to go to?

Col. 58-59

1) _____ available and use. What places?_____

_____

2) _____ available and do not use
3) _____ they say not available for any places I especially
want to go to

(a) If available and do not use, why?

Col. 60-61

1) _____ use other service (taxi, etc.)
2) _____ has fee, charge - too expensive
3) _____ too immobile to use even this help
4) _____ don't like volunteers or staff's attitude
5) _____ doesn't go to the places I want
6) _____ other: _____

22. Could you tell us if there are any problems in using public
transportation?

Col. 62

_____

23. Do you have trouble arranging your banking, bill payment or dealing
with family or legal matters?

Col. 63

1) _____ yes
2) _____ no

24. If yes, do you have regular help in these problems from a member of
your family or a friend?

Col. 64

1) _____ yes
2) _____ no

25. Do you have available and use an organized source of help?

Col. 65

1) _____ available and use
2) _____ available and do not use
3) _____ they say not available

(a) If available, what source?   (INTERVIEWER, CHECK ALL THAT
     APPLY)

    1) _____ general development staff   Col. 66
    2) _____ legal staff in the community   Col. 67
    3) _____ legal assistance in the development   Col. 68
    4) _____ counselling staff in the development   Col. 69
    5) _____ counselling staff in the community   Col. 70
    6) _____ other. Specify_____

CONTINUED ON NEXT PAGE...

SERVICE	NOT AVAILABLE (according to resident)	AVAILABLE NOW AND USE	AVAILABLE NOW AND DO NOT USE	IF AVAILABLE AND DO NOT USE, WHY?	IF AVAILABLE AND USE, NOTE ANY PROBLEMS, SHORTCOMINGS
26. Telephone contact service (volunteer daily checking on particular residents)		Col. 71		1) ___ don't want strangers to contact 2) ___ don't like people who run it 3) ___ don't need 4) ___ other: Col. 72	Col. 73 – Deck 1
27. Friendly visiting service (volunteer visiting residents)	Col. 6 – Deck 2			1) ___ don't want strangers to contact 2) ___ don't like people who run it 3) ___ don't need 4) ___ other: Col. 7	Col. 8 – Deck 2
28. Buddy system or good neighbour system		Col. 9		1) ___ use informal friends Col. 10	Col. 11
29. Senior Citizens Centre		Col. 12		1) ___ don't like people who run it 2) ___ don't like people who come 3) ___ too far to get to 4) ___ don't enjoy the activities 5) ___ other. PROBE Col. 13	Col. 14

SERVICE	NOT AVAIL-ABLE (according to resident)	AVAILABLE NOW AND USE	AVAILABLE NOW AND DO NOT USE	IF AVAILABLE AND DO NOT USE, WHY?	IF AVAILABLE AND USE, NOTE ANY PROBLEMS, SHORTCOMINGS
30. Laundry facility or laundry service	Col. 18	Col. 15		Col. 16	Col. 17
31. Central community/ recreation room(s)		If check, how do you use? (CHECK ALL THAT APPLY)		1) ___ used by special groups from using	1) ___ so formal, unhomelike
		___ Cards Col. 19		2) ___ have own sitting room	2) ___ too many others there
		___ TV watching Col. 20		3) ___ use floor/wing lounge instead	3) ___ don't like cliques there
		___ General sitting Col. 21		4) ___ discouraged by staff	4) ___ used by special groups
		___ Special programs events Col. 22		5) ___ too formal – feels unfamiliar, unhomelike	5) ___ other. Explain: ___
		___ Other Col. 23		6) ___ too many other cliques there using it	
		___ Other Col. 24		7) ___ other; ___	
	Col. 18		Col. 25	Col. 26	Col. 27

DIFFERENT DEVELOPMENTS HAVE DIFFERENT TYPE FACILITIES. LET ME MENTION A FEW AND ASK YOU IF YOU USE THEM IF THEY EXIST IN YOUR DEVELOPMENT. (INTERVIEWER, ONLY ASK USE IF FACILITY EXISTS) AND IF YOU HAVE SOME REASON FOR NOT USING THEM. IF THEY DO NOT EXIST IN YOUR DEVELOPMENT, WOULD YOU LIKE TO HAVE AND USE THIS PARTICULAR FACILITY? LAST, DO YOU FIND AND USE THIS TYPE OF FACILITY IN THE COMUNITY?

FACILITY	AVAILABILITY	IF HAVE AND DO NOT USE, WNY NOT?	IF HAVE AND USE, ANY PROBLEMS, SHORTCOMINGS?
32. Place to play table games?	1) ___ the residents say not available 2) ___ available in or very near this housing Col. 28	Col. 29	Col. 30
33. Place to watch TV (outside own room)?	1) ___ the residents say not available 2) ___ available in or very near this housing Col. 31	Col. 32	Col. 33
34. Coffee shop/room?	1) ___ the residents say not available 2) ___ available in or very near this housing Col. 34	Col. 35	Col. 36
35. Special garden plots/green-house	1) ___ the residents say not available 2) ___ available in or very near this housing Col. 37	Col. 38	Col. 39
36. Bingo?	1) ___ the residents say not available 2) ___ available in or very near this housing Col. 40	Col. 41	Col. 42

Item	Options		SHORTCOMINGS?
37. Library reading room or book mobile?	1) ___ the residents say not available	2) ___ available in or very near this housing	
	Col. 43	Col. 44	Col. 45
38. Movies?	1) ___ the residents say not available	2) ___ available in or very near this housing	
	Col. 46	Col. 47	Col. 48
39. Golf course/ putting green/ lawn bowling?	1) ___ the residents say not available	2) ___ available in or very near this housing	
	Col. 49	Col. 50	Col. 51
40. Shop or stores, canteen?	1) ___ the residents say not available	2) ___ available in or very near this housing	
	Col. 52	Col. 53	Col. 54
41. Floor games (shuffleboard, etc.)	1) ___ the residents say not available	2) ___ available in or very near this housing	
	Col. 55	Col. 56	Col. 57
42. Beauty shop/ barber shop?	1) ___ the residents say not available	2) ___ available in or very near this housing	
	Col. 58	Col. 59	Col. 60
43. Guest room?	1) ___ the residents say not available	2) ___ available in or very near this housing	
	Col. 61	N/A	Col. 62

CODING

LOCATION OF DEVELOPMENT

44. Is there easy access (either easy walk or easy bus ride) to the above services that are important to you (especially the grocery store, shopping centre, churches and medical offices)?   Col. 63

1) _____ easy access to most services that are important to me
2) _____ easy access to some but not all of the services that are important to me
3) _____ somewhat easy access to most or some of services
4) _____ not very easy access to any or most services

(a) Do you own and drive a car?   Col. 64

1) _____ yes
2) _____ no

45. (a) In general, are you satisfied with the location of the development?   Col. 65

1) _____ very satisfied
2) _____ somewhat satisfied
3) _____ not very satisfied
4) _____ not satisfied at all

(b) If not very satisfied, why not?   Col. 66

_____

(c) If satisfied, what are the main reasons for satisfaction with the location?   Col. 67

_____

_____

HOUSING AREA COMPOSITION PREFERENCE

46. In the area around this housing, would you prefer to have people of different ages and families with children?   Col. 68

1) _____ definitely prefer
2) _____ somewhat prefer
3) _____ don't care
4) _____ rather not live in such an area

47. Would you prefer to live in a building where there are also families and people of different ages (or would you prefer living with people mainly your own age)?   Col. 69

1) _____ definitely prefer mix of age groups
2) _____ somewhat prefer mix
3) _____ somewhat rather have mainly people my own age
4) _____ definitely rather have mainly people my own age

48. Do you think it is a good idea for housing complexes for the
elderly to include a mix of self-contained, boarding and nursing
care accommodations?

Col. 70

1) _____ definitely yes
2) _____ somewhat yes
3) _____ don't know
4) _____ somewhat no
5) _____ definitely no

49. In general, are you satisfied with living here?

80/2
Deck 3
Col. 1-3
Col. 5

1) _____ very definitely
2) _____ satisfied
3) _____ ambiguous or no opinion
4) _____ dissatisfied
5) _____ very definitely dissatisfied

50. What are the reasons for your giving this answer? Are there some
things you would especially recommend or feel are good about the
development? PROBE.

Col. 6-7

_____

_____

_____

51. Any shortcomings or problems?

Col. 8-9

_____

_____

52. What do you think could be done to make this place better and more
satisfying for someone like you? (For example, other services
needed). PROBE.

Col. 10-11/3

_____

_____

53. If you were to describe this housing to others, which would you use
of the contrasting statements. I'll read off two contrasting ones
on different aspects and you name the one that is most appropriate.
(INTERVIEWER, CHECK BOX CLOSEST TO WORD THAT BEST REFLECTS THEIR
OPINION)

(a) 1. _____ residents generally active
    2. _____ residents inactive
    3. _____ don't know

Col. 11

(b) 1. _____ residents my own social type
    2. _____ somewhat different social type
    3. _____ don't know

Col. 12

(c) 1. _____ residents friendly
    2. _____ residents somewhat unfriendly
    3. _____ don't know

Col. 13

53. CONTINUED

    (d) 1. _____ building too large or   Col. 14
          2. _____ building too small
          3. _____ size all right
          4. _____ don't know

    (e) 1. _____ building in good condition   Col. 15
          2. _____ needs repairs/upkeep
          3. _____ don't know

    (f) 1. _____ building noisy   Col. 16
          2. _____ not too noisy
          3. _____ don't know

    (g) 1. _____ building atmosphere warm, homelike   Col. 17
          2. _____ atmosphere formal, reserved,
          3. _____ don't know

    (h) 1. _____ administration allows freedom of action   Col. 18
          2. _____ has many rules, regulations
          3. _____ don't know

    (i) 1. _____ this place is homelike   Col. 19

          2. _____ seems like an institution
          3. _____ don't know

    (j) 1. _____ the staff here treats residents with respect   Col. 20
          2. _____ staff disrespectful
          3. _____ don't know

54. What do you think are the advantages or disadvantages that high-rise buildings have for the senior citizens?

    (a) Advantages: _____ Col. 25

    _____

    (b) Disadvantages: _____ Col. 26

    _____

55. Do you disagree or agree with the following statements? I'll read them off one at a time.

	Agree	Disagree	Don't Know
1) High-rise buildings are an un-satisfactory place for senior citizens to live in	—	—	—	Col. 27
2) High-rise buildings for senior citizens have many advantages	—	—	—	Col. 28

55. CONTINUED

	Agree	Disagree	Don't Know	
3) High-rise buildings for senior citizens seem the trend	—	—	—	Col. 29
4) Most senior citizens prefer not to live in high-rise buildings	—	—	—	Col. 30
5) High-rise buildings are an ideal place for senior citizens to live in	—	—	—	Col. 31

56. Do you feel the degree of privary you have in your present housing is: Col. 32

1) _____very satisfactory
2) _____somewhat satisfactory
3) _____not very or not at all satisfactory

(a) If answer is 3, why isn't the degree of privary satisfactory?   Col. 33-34

_____

_____

57. (INTERVIEWER, ONLY ASK IF THEY SHARE FACILITY IF YOU DON'T KNOW)

Do you share?

(a) the toilet   Col. 35

1) _____yes
2) _____no

(b) a bath/shower   Col. 36

1) _____yes
2) _____no

(c) a room   Col. 37

1) _____yes
2) _____no

58. If yes to any of the above, does this bother you?   Col. 38-39

1) _____not at all
2) _____a little
3) _____somewhat
4) _____very much
5) _____don't share any

Comments: _____

59. Are the residents allowed to keep pets in this building?   Col. 40

    1) _____ birds
    2) _____ dogs
    3) _____ cats
    4) _____ none
    5) _____ other

  (a) If you can't keep pets, does this bother you? If so, indicate   Col. 41
     type of animal _____

    1) _____ not at all
    2) _____ a little
    3) _____ somewhat
    4) _____ very much

  (b) If residents can keep pets, does this bother you? If yes, for   Col. 42
     what type of pet? _____

    1) _____ not at all
    2) _____ a little
    3) _____ somewhat
    4) _____ very much

60. IF SELF-CONTAINED UNIT.

Would you prefer to rent this place furnished or unfurnished?   Col. 43

    1) _____ furnished
    2) _____ unfurnished

61. Do you consider the number of staff here to be adequate for your   Col. 44
needs?

    1) _____ yes
    2) _____ somewhat
    3) _____ no
    4) _____ don't know

  (a) PROBE FOR COMMENTS: _____   Col. 45

  _____

62. Is there anything about the staff you think could be changed or   Col. 46-47
improved? MENTION BOTH PAID AND VOLUNTEER WORKERS. PROBE.

_____

_____

_____

63. If you suddenly needed assistance over some emergency or some illness,   Col. 48-49
who would you turn to first for help? (INTERVIEWER, TAKE SOURCE
NAMED FIRST).

For both illness and other emergencies:

1) _____ development staff
2) _____ relative
3) _____ other resident of development
4) _____ friend or neighbour outside development
5) _____ community agency
6) _____ clergyman
7) _____ police
8) _____ family doctor/hospital/clinic
9) _____ other. Specify _____

(a)   (INTERVIEWER, INDICATE HOW MUCH THEY SAY THEY RELY ON THE   Col. 50
     CHILDREN).   Deck 3

_____

_____

MORE PRESENT AND PAST HISTORY

64. Returning to your own background, could you tell me what type of paid   Col. 51
work you or your spouse (for widow, get spouse's) did most of your
life? (INTERVIEWER, IF IN DOUBT AS TO CATEGORY, WRITE OCCUPATION
HERE _____).

_____ answer is for respondent
_____ answer is for spouse

                             (a) Most of Life   Col. 52-54

1) No paid work   _____
2) Managerial work   _____
3) Professional, technical work   _____
4) Clerical work   _____
5) Sales work   _____
6) Service and Recreation, non-professional   _____
7) Transport and communications   _____
8) Farmer and farm workers   _____
9) Craftsmen   _____
10) Labourer   _____
11) Loggers, hunters, fishermen   _____
12) Miners, quarrymen   _____
13) Don't know   _____

65. Regarding your present income sources, are you? (READ CATEGORIES).   Col. 55

  1) _____ dependent <u>solely</u> on government pension and supplement

  2) _____ dependent on above and <u>some</u> savings or private pension
        (or some wages, rents, interest from stocks, mortgages, etc.)

  3) _____ dependent on above and <u>substantial</u> savings or private pension
        (or substantial amount of rent, interest, wages)

  4) _____ don't know

  5) _____ decline to answer

66. (INTERVIEWER, DON'T ASK IF RESPONDENT INDICATES VERY ADEQUATE INCOME)

  If your resources are strained, is it mainly because of the <u>expense</u> of: Col. 56

  1) _____ inflation
  2) _____ cost of rent
  3) _____ present medical expenses including medication
  4) _____ expense of meals/food
  5) _____ other. Specify_____

67. Do you think your future financial situation might cause you to move   Col. 57
    from this housing to cheaper accommodation?

  1) _____ yes
  2) _____ maybe
  3) _____ no

68. Is this due to?   Col. 58

  1) _____ rent
  2) _____ meal costs
  3) _____ other: _____

69. Do you think the lack of some services in this housing will force you   Col. 59
    to move some time in the near future?

  1) _____ yes
  2) _____ maybe
  3) _____ no

70. Lack of what service(s)?   Col. 60

  _____

71. If move, to what type of facility would you move to?   Col. 61

  1) _____ hostel bed type
  2) _____ nursing supervision
  3) _____ chronic care hospital
  4) _____ active care hospital
  5) _____ other: _____

SOCIAL PARTICIPATION IN THE COMMUNITY

Before ending, I'd like to ask you some questions about community activities.

72. Altogether, how often do you go to club or organizational activities   Col. 62
    outside this housing?

    1) _____ attend three times a week (at least for one organization)
    2) _____ attend at least once a week
    3) _____ attend at least once a month
    4) _____ attend at least once a year
    5) _____ attend less than once a year
    6) _____ never go to meetings

73. How often did you go to community club or organization activities   Col. 63
    before you came to this housing?

    1) _____ went three times a week (at least for one organization)
    2) _____ went at least once a week
    3) _____ went at least once a month
    4) _____ went at least once a year
    5) _____ went less than once a year
    6) _____ never went to meetings

74. Do you attend church services?   Col. 64

    1) _____ do not attend
    2) _____ daily
    3) _____ at least weekly
    4) _____ at least monthly
    5) _____ at least once a year
    6) _____ less than once a year

75. How often do you visit friends outside this housing or do friends   Col. 65
    from outside visit you?

    1) _____ daily
    2) _____ at least weekly
    3) _____ at least monthly
    4) _____ at least once a year
    5) _____ less than once a year

76. How often do you visit friends inside the development or they visit   Col. 66
    you in your apartment or room?

    1) _____ daily
    2) _____ at least weekly
    3) _____ at least monthly
    4) _____ at least once a year
    5) _____ less than once a year

77. Since you have come to live here, have you made many friends in   Col. 67
     this housing?

     1) _____ made many friends
     2) _____ made some friends
     3) _____ made hardly any friends

78. Do you have regular visits or get help from your minister, priest,   Col. 68
     rabbi or some church members or group?

     1) _____ very much
     2) _____ some visits/help
     3) _____ little to none

     PROBE FOR DETAILS: _____

     _____

79. Is attendance at development activities such as special events,   Col. 69
     weekly events, etc., usually compulsory?

     1) _____ usually compulsory
     2) _____ somewhat compulsory
     3) _____ entirely voluntary

80. Do you usually get out of the house some time every day throughout   Col. 70
     the year? If so, how many hours on average?

     1) _____ don't go out daily on usual days
     2) _____ out daily less than 1 hour, including winter
     3) _____ out daily less than 1 hour, except winter
     4) _____ out daily 1 hour or more including winter
     5) _____ out daily 1 hour or more except winter
     6) _____ hard to answer, irregular

81. What was the ethnic origin of your father?   Col. 71

     1) _____ English   7) _____ Native Indian
     2) _____ French   8) _____ Netherlands
     3) _____ German   9) _____ Norwegian
     4) _____ Irish   10) _____ Polish
     5) _____ Italian   11) _____ Scottish
     6) _____ Jewish   12) _____ Ukrainian
                               13) _____ Other: _____

INTERVIEWER IMPRESSIONS/ASSESSMENT OF RESPONDENT

Deck 4
Col. 1-3 ID

1. Regarding the respondent's interest in the interview, would you
    say she or he showed: Col. 5

    1) ____ marked interest
    2) ____ mild interest
    3) ____ no interest
    4) ____ don't know

    (a) Was his/her attitude: Col. 6

        1) ____ friendly
        2) ____ somewhat suspicious
        3) ____ hostile

2. Would you say the respondent gave you frank answers or answers to   Col. 7
    please you?

    1) ____ frank answers, how he/she really feels
    2) ____ somewhat answers to please me
    3) ____ definitely answers to please me and not criticize development

3. Was the respondent's physical appearance: Col. 8

    1) ____ healthy
    2) ____ infirm somewhat
    3) ____ obviously ill
    4) ____ couldn't tell

4. Comprehension of the interview was: Col. 9

    1) ____ quick and correct
    2) ____ slow but correct
    3) ____ slow and sometimes confused
    4) ____ quick but not often correct
    5) ____ barely able to follow
    6) ____ don't know

5. Did the respondent have any trouble hearing?   Col. 10

    1) ____ very definitely
    2) ____ somewhat
    3) ____ no

6. Would you say the respondent seemed in general: Col. 11

    1) ____ fairly happy/satisfied with the development
    2) ____ had some criticism
    3) ____ was quite dissatisfied with the development

7. Do you think the respondent seemed to consider his/her residence: Col. 12-13

    1) _____ a homelike, warm setting
    2) _____ an institutional setting, quite different from home, with
           less freedom, etc.

EXPLAIN IF 2: _____

8. How well do you think this housing meets the needs of this respondent?   Col. 14
Were there some services/facilities it looked like he/she could use
that weren't available, such as nursing help, food preparation,
homemaker assistance?

_____

_____

_____

9. Would you say the respondent was in general a person: Col. 15

    1) _____ optimistic and in general satisfied with life
    2) _____ somewhat bitter/complaining/dissatisfied with life in general
    3) _____ very definitely bitter/complaining/dissatisfied with life

10. What type of unit does the respondent live in?   Col. 16

    1) _____ apartment - bachelor
    2) _____ apartment - one bedroom
    3) _____ apartment - two bedrooms

    4) _____ hostel room - single
    5) _____ hostel room - double
    6) _____ hostel room - 3 plus rooms

    7) _____ nursing care unit

11. What furnishings did the resident bring to this development?   Col. 17

    1) _____ all the furnishings
    2) _____ chair/bed/or sofa
    3) _____ only pictures and ornaments, curtains
    4) _____ only TV and radio

Date completed _____

Time _____

Photo credits:

The elderly lady and the budgie is by Chris Lund, Information Canada

Photothèque.

The high-rise is by Michael Audain.